SMALL STORE SURVIVAL

National Retail Federation Series

The National Retail Federation Series comprises books on retail-store management for stores of all sizes and for all management responsibilities. The National Retail Federation is the world's largest retail trade association, with membership that includes the leading department, specialty, discount, mass merchandise, and independent stores, as well as 30 national and 50 state associations. NRF members represent an industry that encompasses more than 1.4 million U.S. retail establishments and employs nearly 20 million people—1 in 5 American workers. The NRF's international members operate stores in more than 50 nations.

The National Retail Federation Series includes the following books:

Competing with the Retail Giants: How to Survive in the New Retail Landscape, Kenneth E. Stone

Credit Card Marketing, Bill Grady

Dictionary of Retailing and Merchandising, Jerry M. Rosenberg

FOR 1996: Financial & Operating Results of Retail Stores in 1995, National Retail Federation

Loss Prevention Guide for Retail Businesses, Rudolf C. Kimiecik

Management of Retail Buying, 3rd edition, R. Patrick Cash, John W. Wingate, Joseph S. Friedlander

MOR 1996: Merchandising & Operating Results of Retail Stores in 1995, National Retail Federation

MasterMinding the Store: Advertising, Sales Promotion, and the New Marketing Reality, Donald Ziccardi with David Moin

Practical Merchandising Math, Leo Gafney

Retail Store Planning & Design Manual, 2nd edition, Michael Lopez

Small Store Survival: Success Strategies for Retailers, Arthur Andersen LLP

The Software Directory for Retailers, 5th edition, Coopers & Lybrand

Specialty Shop Retailing: A Guide to Starting Your Own Shop, Carol Schroeder

The Electronic Retailing Market: TV Home Shopping, Infomercials, and Interactive Retailing, Packaged Facts, Inc.

Value Retailing in the 1990s: Off-Pricers, Factory Outlets, and Closeout Stores, Packaged Facts, Inc.

SMALL STORE SURVIVAL

Success Strategies for Retailers

ARTHUR ANDERSEN LLP

John Wiley & Sons, Inc.

New York • Chichester • Weinheim • Toronto • Singapore • Brisbane

This text is printed on acid-free paper.

Copyright © 1997 by John Wiley & Sons, Inc.

All rights reserved. Published simultaneously in Canada.

This publication is designed to provide accurate and authoritative information in regard to the subject matter covered. It is sold with the understanding that the publisher is not engaged in rendering legal, accounting, or other professional services. If legal advice or other expert assistance is required, the services of a competent professional person should be sought.

Library of Congress Cataloging-in-Publication Data:
Andersen, Arthur.
   Small store survival : success strategies for retailers / Arthur Andersen.
      p.   cm.—(National Retail Federation series)
   Includes bibliographical references.
   ISBN 0-471-16468-2 (cloth : alk. paper)
   1. Stores, Retail—Management.   2. Marketing—Management.
3. Small business—Management.   4. Retail trade—Management.
I. Title.   II. Series.
HF5429.A6628   1997
658.8'7—dc20   96-24438
                                                          CIP

Printed in the United States of America

10 9 8 7 6 5 4 3 2 1

CONTENTS

8 Case Studies

9 Management Tools

Appendix G: Survey Methodology   *371*

Bibliography   *377*

Index   *381*

ACKNOWLEDGMENTS

The concept and development of the study that led to the publication of *Small Store Survival* has been a team effort. We would like to acknowledge Jim Baum and David Vite, Illinois Retail Merchants Association, for their enthusiastic support of this project.

Particular thanks are due to the following at Arthur Andersen: Stan Logan for designing, leading, and keeping the study focused during the process; David Schwartz for his insight and counsel; and Mia Kreis, Gary Levin, and Pat Songer for their efforts during the implementation and reviewing stages of the study. Thanks are also due to A. McKinley Reynolds III of The Reynolds Communications Group, Evanston, Illinois, for his help and editorial assistance in the preparation of the original manuscript.

The Illinois Retail Merchants Association gratefully acknowledges the support of the Illinois departments of Commerce and Community Affairs and Employment Security for underwriting the study on which this book is based. We are also indebted to Arthur Andersen LLP for the time, talents, and efforts of its many experts in conducting this study.

We thank all the small-store retailers who so generously gave their time and shared confidential information for the benefit of their colleagues across the nation. This study would not have been possible without their participation in the surveys and site visits.

We are deeply indebted to the IRMA members who served on the project's Steering Committee, especially Beth Henderson Willey, who chaired it. All of them helped give the study its focus and ensured its success with their wholehearted support. They are:

Beth Henderson Willey
Vice President,
Henderson's Department Store
Sycamore, Illinois

George Kutsunis
President,
G.W.K. Enterprises, Inc.
Geneseo, Illinois

H. James Baum
President,
Baum's
Morris, Illinois

Terry McNeese
President,
Beard & Stovall, Inc.
Woodstock, Illinois

Jim Newman
President,
Martin Newman Shoe Co.
Jacksonville, Illinois

Brian Ziegler
President,
Ziegler Ace Hardware Co.
Elgin, Illinois

Keven Wilder
President,
Chiasso
Chicago, Illinois

We would also like to acknowledge the late William S. Peebles III, the National Retail Federation's 1988 Independent Retailer of the Year, for his valuable insights.

ABOUT ARTHUR ANDERSEN

Arthur Andersen is a multidisciplinary professional services firm that provides client service through economic and financial consulting, business consulting, tax and business advisory services, and audit and business advisory services. Its professionals combine extensive technical competence and industry experience with innovative and progressive thought to assist clients in improving business performance. Arthur Andersen is a business unit of Andersen Worldwide, the world's largest professional services provider, with more than 91,000 personnel in more than 76 countries. Its global practice is conducted by member firms in 371 locations.

ABOUT THE ILLINOIS RETAIL MERCHANTS ASSOCIATION

The Illinois Retail Merchants Association is a statewide professional organization representing more than 23,000 stores of all sizes and formats. Since its founding in 1957, IRMA has advocated the concerns of retailers in state government; helped store owners save money on essential services; and kept executives informed on the industry issues, laws, and regulations that directly impact on their companies' bottom lines. Small-store retailers, in particular, look to IRMA for assistance on legal, operational, and technical issues and developments in the industry. IRMA responds to their needs with a variety of programs that offer access to the kinds of resources that larger companies often have. These include legislative efforts, cooperative buying, publications, seminars, and workshops.

INTRODUCTION

This book is divided into easily digestible sections. Here is a brief overview of each:

- *Executive Summary.* Highlights key findings and their significance as well as action steps toward immediate improvement.
- *Economic and Retail Trends.* Provides an overview on the state of the retailing industry today.
- *Customers and Marketing, Merchandising, Store Operations, Management, Human Resources, and Finance.* These chapters offer in-depth analyses of six key areas of business practice that small-store retailers themselves consider most critical to success.

In addition to surveys and site visits, information was obtained from industry research contained in Arthur Andersen's knowledge base of retailing best practices and experience serving clients in the retail industry. From this information, specific recommendations on how small stores can adapt retailing best practices were developed for each area of business. These findings are highlighted in the recommendations sections of each of these chapters.

These sections make it even easier to reference a particular business strategy or technique.

In "Customers and Marketing," for example, you will find information on customer wants and satisfaction, competitive response, and image development. The business practices in each chapter are divided into first-tier and second-tier sections. The first-tier items are the most critical and will help you focus your efforts. The second-tier items are not listed in order of importance; the numbers are used to make them more readable.

- *Case Studies.* Developed from day-long site visits with ten of the survey participants, these case studies show how internal business practices and external factors affect other retailers' businesses. They also offer recommendations of what they should do to improve their businesses.

- *Management Tools.* This chapter includes a variety of tools, including operations-assessment questionnaires, that can help you evaluate your own performance and identify areas you need to improve. This chapter also includes a calendar to help you budget your time, as well as benchmark statistics. Developed from survey responses and research conducted by Arthur Andersen, these statistics let you compare your business practices to those of other retailers.
- *Resources.* This chapter offers comprehensive listings of books, associations, trade articles, and organizations.
- *Appendixes.* Useful background information is found in the back matter.

HOW TO GET STARTED

Though it may seem like an overwhelming task, evaluating your business practices and developing action plans to improve your operations are critical to surviving and prospering. Using this book can be the first step in that process. Here is how to make the most of the information in this book:

- *Familiarize yourself with the contents.* All sections are applicable to your business, but some will have a more significant and immediate impact than others. It depends on your business, the challenges you face, and the strengths or weaknesses of your capabilities in specific areas.
- *Have the members of your management team read the sections that are most pertinent to their responsibilities.* If, like most small-store retailers, everyone in the organization wears many hats, then each team member will likely review several sections. In that case, pick the one or two sections that address real problem areas in your business, and start with those. Arthur Andersen recommends that you begin with the chapter on customers and marketing.
- *Call a management meeting and discuss preliminary thoughts and impressions of the material the team members reviewed.* Have them express their feelings on the organization's strengths and weaknesses. Based on what they read, get their preliminary ideas on areas of the business that you and your team can improve.
- *Ask team members to fill out the operations assessment tools and review the benchmark statistics for their particular business practice area.* Have them take the time to critically analyze the organization's performance in each area and identify areas of opportunity for improvement. Ask each member to develop an action plan for

enhancing the strategies you already employ or implementing the strategies you have not tried. Participate in all areas and lead by example.

- *Review all the action plans with your management team.* From those plans, determine the ten issues most critical to your company's success, identify the opportunities for improvement, and refine an overall action plan for your business. Use the discussions to refine your objectives and your vision for the company. Obtain consensus from team members on the company's overall goals, but also encourage team members to implement their area-specific action plans and identify a timeline for execution.

Once you identify your opportunities and set an action plan in motion, keep up the momentum and stay on schedule. As you implement new practices and procedures, continually measure them against your objectives. Team members should regularly use the management tools to see how well new strategies and practices work against objectives. One of the most critical factors in achieving success is the need to continually challenge your organization and its status quo. Change is inevitable. To be successful, you must adapt to your customers and your community.

The information and recommendations outlined in this book can be invaluable in helping you adapt to the never-ending changes affecting small-store retailers during a time when survival depends on your ability to change.

EXECUTIVE SUMMARY

The essence of retailing is change. Never has this been more true than today.

Small-store retailers are facing the toughest series of changes since the introduction of the automobile and the advent of the mall. Cutthroat competition from mass merchants and other power formats, an uncertain economy, and changing demographics and consumer buying patterns dramatically affect the ways retailers conduct business. For many small-store retailers, these changes make survival difficult.

Yet with these changes come opportunities. The best small-store retailers can compete, succeed, and prosper financially. They can, that is, if they understand the implications of these changes; reevaluate every element of their business practices from the ground up; and craft action plans that continuously respond to these changes, enhance their competitive positions, and improve their stores.

In broad terms, every retailer must:

- Develop a continuous process to determine what his customers want and then meet or exceed those expectations at every turn.
- Identify and pursue a distinct customer market. Then offer it unique merchandise or value-added services.
- Design every aspect of store operations to enhance the shopping experience. This includes establishing labor-scheduling systems

to increase productivity and reevaluating the store layout to make sure it maximizes customer buying opportunities.

- Establish a vision and culture for the store, plan where the company needs to go, and execute the steps it takes to get there.
- Be prepared to compete more fiercely than ever for quality employees. Then make empowering, educating, and retaining them a top priority.
- Establish budgetary controls and cost-containment measures that enable him to manage frugally what can be measured and negotiate more aggressively for favorable terms from vendors and suppliers.

Small Store Survival was written to guide retailers in meeting these objectives. It is not, however, a trendy self-help book like *One Minute Manager* or *Life's Little Instruction Book.* It does not offer magic formulas or cookie-cutter recipes for success. It was written to help retailers find their own ways to achieve these objectives. There are hundreds of sound ideas presented in this book that are specific to small-store retailers. Most were developed and implemented to varying degrees by the industry's most successful retailers, accumulated and analyzed by Arthur Andersen and presented in its best practices knowledge base.

Though not every strategy or tactic will be appropriate for every retailer, the book offers ideas and direction.

Small Store Survival should challenge retailers' views of small-store retailing by questioning key areas of business. What is the vision for the store in ten years? How have the customers changed over the past few years? How current are the managers about what customers genuinely like and dislike? What is being done to attract, educate, and motivate the best retail talent in the area? How effective is the merchandising strategy? What plans exist for succession?

The real lesson of this study is that the best retailers never stop learning. They never stop growing. They never lose their enthusiasm for the customers and the business. And they never cease to revel in change and the chance to deal with it.

This book looks critically at key retailing strategies and practices, the relative importance that retailers assign to them, and how retailers deploy these practices in the face of increasing competition. Clearly, small-store retailers struggle with the changes. The financial statements of more than 150 respondents show that few small-store retailers are succeeding financially. Although many retailers reap financial benefits from real estate and other investments, most would enjoy a greater return on investment from well-managed mutual funds than they do from their stores.

In fact, these financial statements make a startling point: Of the respondents, one in five is losing money. And one in four registered pretax income of less than $10,000. Retailers suffering losses were not limited to the smaller stores, either. Of those recording losses, half had net sales of more than $1 million.

Retailers' comments support this evidence:

- "We are not successful. Success is increasing profitability dollars."
- "I should be earning much more on the basis of hours involved with my business."
- "Success during this current economy is still being in business."
- "Yes, we have been successful, but not in the last few years."
- "I feel over the last 25 years our business has been like a roller coaster, with good years and bad. . . . We have struggled and have had to put a lot of our own dollars back into the business to keep it afloat."
- "Profitability means success. We have few years in the last ten that have been profitable. Success is being a leader in one's profession. We have lost some of this. . . ."

This is not to say, however, that small-store retailers do not see themselves as successful. Many say they are very successful in qualitative terms. Even here, however, a financial qualifier frequently entered into the definitions:

- "Success at improving the bottom line is not nearly as important as providing a fun and exciting place for our customers and staff. . . ."
- "Success in business is paying your bills and making enough to support a good lifestyle. Success in life is love of family, good health, and ever-expanding knowledge."
- "The obvious definition of success would be that you are running a profitable business, but with a small business, there is a great satisfaction in making sure that your employees are making a comfortable living. You also are very pleased when the customer is satisfied."
- "We have an excellent customer base that we have serviced well. I feel that I am successful today but that I am putting too much of my life into my business and not taking time to smell the flowers."
- "Success today probably equates to survival. We have survived because of our customer service."
- "We have attained success in expanding the scale of our operation, but not in the profitability."
- "Success is being able to provide a quality product and service and still make money for the owners and investors."

To help small-store retailers better cope with the changes they face, the Illinois Retail Merchants Association, backed by a grant from the state of Illinois, collaborated with Arthur Andersen LLP to take a hard look at what Illinois retailers are doing, how they can improve, and where they might benefit from continuing education and training.

The purpose of the study was threefold:

- To identify successful practices retailers should use to manage change and improve performance.
- To develop case studies and practical tools for retailers to improve their competitive positions, enhance long-term growth, and maintain jobs.
- To identify critical areas where small-store retailers require additional training.

Although the study was conducted in Illinois, the results are applicable to retailers across the United States. Issues facing small-store retailers are addressed in the following chapters:

- "Economic and Retail Trends"
- "Customers and Marketing"
- "Merchandising"
- "Store Operations"
- "Management"
- "Human Resources"
- "Finance"

Readers should look through each section, then begin reading the one that interests them the most.

SUMMARY OF KEY CHAPTERS

Economic and Retail Trends

During the mid-1980s, the U.S. economy grew with a frenzy. Consumers spent more time and money shopping than ever before. They also increased their debt and depleted their savings.

When the surge ended in the late 1980s, many retailers—large and small—found themselves in precarious positions. Those that had expanded too quickly, let inventories grow, or assumed too much leverage watched cash flow slow to a trickle as consumers tightened their purse strings. Many stores were forced to close. Between 1990 and 1994, more than 71,000 retail businesses failed. Today, most experts predict that half of America's retail establishments will fold by 2000.

But the economy is showing signs of life. Low inflation and low interest rates continue to boost consumer purchasing power. Financing for new homes and other major purchases is more affordable. Increases in housing starts and consumer confidence signal a brighter economic future.

Even so, as this book goes to press, demographic, social, and economic factors continue to affect the state of retailing. Some may benefit retailers; others may not.

Industry consolidation. The last ten years have seen enormous consolidation in the retail industry. Of the top ten nonfood retailers in 1964, only five were still in the top ten by the end of 1992 (most current data available); most were victims of acquisition.

The larger retailers exert tremendous pressure on the marketplace. They attract more talented employees, and they drive the toughest bargains with vendors. And as the big retailers get bigger, they infiltrate and even dominate small towns. Sadly, in many cases, the need for small-store retailers diminishes.

Overstoring. Despite retail fallout and consolidation, America still has too many stores. Retailers today offer about 19 square feet of store space for every man, woman, and child in America. This overstoring stems from retailers' efforts to increase sales by expanding their market presence. There are a number of side effects to this, however. First, the resulting shifts in shopping patterns may force many stores to close or relocate. Second, customers now have many more options. The traditional small-store retailer may no longer be the logical choice, and this tests traditional customer loyalties.

Channel-blurring. As mentioned before, retailing in the United States is undergoing dramatic change, particularly in the non-durable-goods sector, which includes apparel, general merchandise, and food, both at home and away from home. Channel-blurring is on the increase as merchandise offerings of different retailing segments continue to overlap. Consumers, ever pressured for time, are growing increasingly tired of traditional shopping and more demanding than ever of "fair value." Thus, changes in retail formats are occurring rapidly. The nation's largest retailer, discount operator Wal-Mart Stores, has entered the grocery business with huge supercenters and a goal of becoming the leading grocer by the year 2000. To survive and grow in this challenging environment, retailers must have a clear value proposition defining which customer segments to target, how to differentiate from competitors, and which channels to use to sell products and/or services.

Value-conscious customers. Consumers today are more tight-fisted than they were in the 1980s, yet they no longer view value solely in terms of price. They realize that mass merchants, category killers, and other national chains have the purchasing power to buy direct from the manufacturer, offer high quality, and sell at low price. Small stores are clearly disadvantaged here. Many buy through distributors, receive smaller rebates and discounts, and sell at a higher price. Small-store retailers need to reevaluate their market niches, merchandise assortments, and pricing strategies in light of this trend.

The changing population. Small-store retailers need to keep a close eye on the dramatic changes taking place in America's population. The U.S. population, currently 263 million, is increasing at a rate of approximately 1 percent (or about 2.5 million people) per year. Much of the increase is due to immigration, both legal and illegal. Slow population growth contributes to a highly competitive retailing environment wherein significant sales growth can only come by taking market share from competitors. The makeup of the population is also rapidly shifting from white to multicultural. By the year 2050, the Census Bureau projects that nearly half the U.S. population will be "minorities." This change in the population mix also will require changes in marketing strategy. As the boomers move into the 50 and older category, they will require changes in marketing approaches, as they are better educated than their forebears and, as a result, will be more demanding and discriminating.

Today, the number of working women continues to increase, from 31.5 million in 1970 to 57.5 million in 1995, or 47.3 percent of the workforce (an increase of 1.6 percent from 1994).

Shrinking labor pool. The young labor pool, traditionally well-stocked for retailers, will not grow as quickly. Scarce labor will increase labor costs. Larger retailers will likely offer more attractive career opportunities and compensation and benefits packages, which will make it even tougher for small stores to attract talent.

Time-constrained consumers. As more women work, time becomes more precious to the dual-income family, and "going shopping" becomes progressively less attractive. Many people simply don't have time to shop. This challenges retailers still further as they struggle to create and maintain loyal customers.

Time-constrained consumers have neither the time nor the inclination to visit multiple stores. They want a one-stop experience. Small-store retailers will need to accurately target the right customers. Then they must make sure that they deliver value, selection, quality, convenience, and service when the customer comes to call. It's likely that this new generation of customers will give few stores a second chance.

Public policy and the costs of doing business. The unknown costs and impacts of health care reform, higher taxes, and the increasingly higher cost of doing business will likely hit small-business owners the hardest.

Methodology and Profile of Respondents

More than 1,500 Illinois retailers were surveyed during the course of the study on which this book is based; approximately 150 completed the full battery of three surveys.

In Survey I, retailers were asked to describe their stores and articulate their competitive advantages, disadvantages, and primary business concerns. Respondents came from all over the state of Illinois, and their respective formats were representative of all stores:

- Apparel
- Appliances
- Books
- Department
- Drugs, health care, and beauty care
- Electronics
- Florists
- Specialty

In Survey II, retailers were asked to evaluate which areas of the business they felt were critical to success and rate how well they were performing in each.

In Survey III, respondents to either of the first two surveys were asked to evaluate those practices they use in their businesses. To validate the information received in Survey III, a team of Arthur Andersen consultants visited ten retailers throughout the state to assess respective competitive positions and the business practices used.

OVERVIEW OF RETAIL BEST PRACTICES

Following is a summary of six core chapters that retailers should read before they take action. The best practices recommended in each chapter provide tried and proven tactics that small-store retailers should consider implementing. Then retailers should work through the chapter on management tools, which includes a series of diagnostic tests created to help isolate weaknesses in a business and identify where gaps exist between recommended practices and actual practices. After that, retailers should develop an action plan to begin to close the gaps. Retailers seeking additional information are urged to browse through the chapter on resources.

Customers and Marketing

Marshall Field was right. Retailers must "give the lady what she wants." If they don't, she will go somewhere else. Satisfying the customer is the

Profile of the Typical Respondent	
Net Sales:	$1.8 million (50% have net sales of less than $950,000)
Gross Margin:	40%*
Pretax Income:	$39,000
Sales per Square Foot:	$206†
Number of Stores:	2 (68% have only one store)
Years Company in Business:	43 (range from 1 to 150)
Full-Time Store Employees:	11 (46% have five or less)
Use of Automated POS Systems:	39%
Legal Status:	
Subchapter C:	51%
Subchapter S:	27%
Sole Proprietorship:	19%
Partnership:	3%
Principal's Years with Company:	24

* Except for gross margin and sales per square foot, no major differences existed between hard-goods and soft-goods retailers surveyed. Hard-goods retailers typically have a gross margin of 36 percent and soft-goods retailers typically have a gross margin of 42 percent. (Source: Dun & Bradstreet Information Services.)

† Hard-goods retailers typically have sales per square foot of $350 and soft-goods retailers typically have sales per square foot of $150.

heart of retailing. Yet many small-store retailers do not identify customer wants; nor do many continually and aggressively respond to those wants. They don't use available techniques such as interviews, comment cards, focus groups, and surveys. Why not? Many small-store retailers feel uncomfortable executing these techniques; many others do not allow the time to execute them. Retailers need to identify customer wants and link this knowledge to everything they do. If they do not, a current customer may quickly become a former customer.

Customers expect small-store retailers to excel at understanding and satisfying their needs. After all, many customers are friends and neighbors. And it is precisely because of this comfort level that 63 percent of the respondents said they "just know" what their customers want. The disappointing fact is, however, that beyond just knowing, few small-store retailers have developed a continuous process to glean information about customer satisfaction and what customers like and dislike.

The success of any small store begins and ends with the ability of the owner, manager, and employees to do everything in their power to make sure the customer returns. Studies show that for every dissatisfied customer who complains to management, 26 disenchanted customers never make it back to the store.

The chapter on customers and marketing discusses this in greater detail. It also provides best practices to closely monitor what customers want, such as:

- *Walk the floor.* Retailers should actively interview customers, either in the store or over the phone. Customers' candid comments about such issues as merchandise, service, pricing, and hours are key to serving them better.
- *Create and provide comment cards.* Retailers should urge customers to complete them and note if they enjoyed the shopping experience, found what they needed, and were satisfied with the service.
- *Conduct focus groups with a mix of customers and noncustomers.* Small-store owners should choose seven or eight candid and discriminating participants. Questions should be open-ended, but can come from previously developed customer comment cards or phone surveys.
- *Empower employees.* Successful retailers teach employees to solicit and manage customer complaints and then train and empower the staff to respond on the spot.

Competition and encroachment from mass merchants, category killers, and other chain formats will only intensify with changes in the market. Small-store retailers who seek to survive beyond the turn of the century must be prepared to respond to competitors. It is surprising, then, that the study found 30 percent of Illinois small-store retailers have no strategy to respond to competitors. In fact, only about half ever ask their customers where else they shop.

Retailers lack formal competitive response strategies for several reasons. Some lack the knowledge of how to respond properly to their competition. Others think they know their customers better than they do. Still others have simply failed to make this strategy a priority. Yet any laissez-faire attitude or false sense of security is risky, and retailers without a strategy for competitive response should be wary. Customers are fickle, and it takes little enticement for them to try an alternative.

The chapter discusses more fully key competitive issues and includes best practices on how to:

- *Continually study the competition and evaluate options.* Retailers should review competitors' ads, shop their stores, examine their merchandise, visit with their sales associates, and talk with their customers. Small-store owners should identify weaknesses or areas where they already have a competitive advantage or can create one. This might be in merchandise, the quality of sales associates, or in value-added services.
- *Respond with strength.* Retailers should carry a product line or offer a service that is not available at the competition and then promote that advantage. Providing customized at-home or at-

work services or same-day alterations; or offering special hours for time-constrained, valued customers can also work.

If small-store retailers expect to protect their turf, they better focus more attention on their marketing efforts and the returns on those investments. Almost half rank their performance as only fair when it comes to analyzing the effectiveness of their advertising. Few devote much effort to cultivating the free media exposure available in the local press, and a third of those retailers who maintain a customer database do not use it to market their stores.

Among retailers surveyed, fewer than one in four actually measure the effectiveness of their ads. Most retailers not only lack the know-how to measure advertising effectiveness but also fail to maintain the proper information to do so.

The survey also indicates that retailers rely heavily on newspaper advertising and may overlook opportunities in both radio and direct mail. Many large retailers successfully use direct mail to target well-defined customer markets. With the availability of simple, off-the-shelf database management software and the impact of a targeted message, retailers should take a closer look at this. Over a period of time, a list of customers and qualified prospects is not difficult to accumulate.

The chapter discusses more fully key advertising issues and includes best practices on how to:

- *Build measurement criteria into every effort.* In every ad, brochure, or direct mailing, retailers should include a message that asks the customer to mention how (or where) she heard about the store. Memories are faulty, however, and retailers should understand that results should be used as a guide, not an absolute.
- *Establish contacts with the local news media.* Reporters frequently need local sources to comment on events in the business community and local examples of national trends. An aggressive, savvy retailer can be that source.
- *Purchase a mailing list of target customers in the market area.* Retailers should experiment with sending brochures and new product information on a regular basis.

Merchandising

The most critical activities of retailing revolve around buying and displaying the goods. Though this study deals with five areas of merchandising, it emphasizes three areas where retailers must focus more attention: niching, pricing strategies, and vendors.

Niching means targeting a market or customer group with a unique mix of merchandise or services that compels customers to shop at the store. The study discovered that many small-store retailers do not realize that they need to differentiate themselves through some element of niching. In fact, while 88 percent of retailers surveyed said niching was important, 35 percent said their performance was fair or poor. This is a genuine short-coming for many retailers. Proper niching can be the salvation for small-store retailers trapped by the temptation to be all things to all people.

By niching, Arthur Andersen believes small-store retailers can truly distinguish themselves from their larger competitors. After all, who better than the small-store retailer to understand and respond to the local trade area? Who better to identify pockets of opportunity where large chain stores (with what are often described as "cookie cutter" concepts) cannot or will not compete?

To niche effectively, first and foremost, small-store retailers must understand their customers and the marketplace. Then they must analyze their strengths, look for weaknesses in the competition, and hone in on their own personal "power categories" or departments where they can differentiate themselves.

The chapter on merchandising discusses more fully key niching strategies and includes best practices on how to:

- *Better understand the customers and what they want.* This is the foundation of effective retailing.
- *Better understand what the store is and what it is not.* Sound niching begins with a plan that capitalizes on strengths.
- *Identify voids in the competition.* Savvy retailers will add depth to their strongest areas and expand their vendor base. More vendors can mean more exciting products.
- *Target specific markets.* Is there a group of customers that other retailers may not adequately serve?

Pricing is another merchandising area that deserves serious attention. Slightly more than one-third of the respondents said they are not performing well in this area. Many small-store retailers fail here because they employ a scattershot approach: too many conflicting pricing strategies in one store.

Pricing problems are often exacerbated because these retailers wait too long to move merchandise through promotional and clearance markdowns. This results in even greater margin erosion or carryover merchandise and can create confusion and mistrust in the local trade area. Although customers may occasionally overlook the lowest price, they never forget being deceived. The retail landscape is littered with retailers who try to salvage declining businesses with higher prices and bigger margins. Usually they fail because ultimately they alienate most of their customers.

Indeed, one reason customers are attracted to chain stores is because of the promise of consistency, not only in the merchandise offering but also in the pricing. Fairness and value are what customers seek. The key for small retailers is to find the point where price and quality intersect.

The chapter discusses more fully effective pricing strategies and includes best practices on how to:

- Identify the break-even point, where one additional dollar of incremental gross profit less all operating costs begins to generate pretax income.
- Track historical sell-through rates at various price points. Smart retailers test price points.
- Schedule markdowns. Retailers should bring goods in at a set price. After a period of time, they should begin to take a series of planned markdowns until all of the merchandise is sold.

The third key element in a sound merchandising strategy involves vendors. No retailer can survive for long without solid vendor relationships. The key to a successful relationship is trust. For any relationship to work, however, vendors must meet retailers' needs, comply with terms in delivering orders, and work with retailers to meet mutual goals. Retailers, for their part, must work with vendors to make sure that happens.

A failing of many small-store retailers, however, is that they are either unwilling or unmotivated to build vendor relationships: Nearly one in five said they have a fair or poor performance when it comes to vendor relations; and one in four said they share very little sales information with their vendors. Further, they don't always select their vendors by objective criteria. Vendors, in turn, need to pay more attention to the small store and share information in return.

The chapter discusses more fully effective vendor relations and includes best practices on how to:

- Communicate and share information whenever it is practical to do so.
- Keep vendors current on the business. Well-informed vendors are a great help. Uninformed vendors are not.
- Develop a vendor scorecard with merchandise, pricing, and delivery criteria weighted as a customer would weight them. Retailers can use this card to evaluate vendors and make purchasing decisions.
- Establish a performance monitoring system. Smart retailers let vendors know in advance what is important and how they will be evaluated.

Store Operations

The strongest marketing program and the finest goods in town will mean little if store operations fail to meet customers' expectations.

Store operations link the merchandise to the customer. That's why it is vital that retailers build programs that deliver exactly what customers want: efficient, attentive, friendly service.

Many of the small-store retailers surveyed lack efficiency. More than three-fourths, for example, have no formal labor-scheduling system. So while store operations may have some semblance of order when the owner is in the store, procedures and productivity quickly collapse when he leaves because there is no schedule in place.

Of the 12 categories discussed in the chapter on store operations, customer service, store staffing and labor productivity, and store layout most significantly affect customers' experiences.

In theory, customer service is an area where small-store retailers ought to outperform their larger counterparts. Indeed, 92 percent of those surveyed rated their customer-service performance as good or excellent. Yet many small-store retailers may be getting complacent. Only one in five offers greeters, and only 53 percent say employees actively offer assistance to customers within their respective departments. And despite the frequent customer complaint about inconvenient store hours, only 57 percent ever open their stores during nonstore hours.

The chapter on store operations discusses more fully the importance of maximizing customer service and includes best practices on how to:

- Hire the right people the first time.
- Communicate service expectations to every employee. The best retailers take this further, however, and lead by example.
- Stay current on customer expectations. Retailers should ensure that all employees ask customers about their shopping experiences and respond on the spot.

As critical as superior customer service is, though, retailers must provide it while heeding costs. After merchandise, labor accounts for the largest operating expense in retailing (10 percent to 16 percent of net sales). Despite the investment, however, many retailers fail to give this area adequate attention. Barely one in five uses even a manual scheduling system, and only 2 percent use any kind of automated system. By relying chiefly on rule of thumb, many of these retailers may misallocate their associates' time.

One of the best practices retailers can use to staff their stores cost effectively is to match staffing with customer traffic. Retailers should track customer traffic by hour, day, and season to determine the busiest and slowest times. Then they should adjust labor hours accordingly.

Store layout is another issue that can make or break a store. Here, however, small-store retailers appear to be performing well. Eighty-four percent of those responding rated their store layout as good or excellent, with combination layout and free-flow cited as the two most popular patterns. Yet, shopping is a blend of experiences. It is the retailer's obligation to provide the customer with a pleasurable visit, so retailers should not be afraid to tinker with their layouts. To truly maximize the contribution of store layout to the business, the layout must work together with the retailer's merchandise, target audience, pricing, and advertising. The chapter on store operations discusses more fully the contributions store layout can make and includes best practices on how to:

- Learn more about creative layouts. Sharp retailers never stop looking for ways to improve.
- Maximize selling space and minimize nonselling space.
- Create consistency in store appearance. Retailers should make sure that all shelves and displays, signage, and advertising work together to deliver a consistent message and image.
- Shop other retailers. Successful retailers are never shy about adopting good ideas.

Management

Small-store owners often feel like firefighters, moving from one crisis situation to another. Yet for today's retailer, well-planned day-to-day management is not enough. Moving a small store forward during these rapidly changing times requires much more. It requires a thoughtful vision and a well-defined culture, a strategic plan for growth and a development of management capabilities in the owner and management team, which are the three key issues in the chapter on management.

Unfortunately, many retailers are caught up in the daily rigors of running a store. They have little time or inclination to look ahead. As one retailer said, "When you are up to your waist in alligators, it is tough to remember that your mission is to drain the swamp."

It is critical that leaders define and articulate a vision. Vision is the light that guides the company. Culture is the set of values that unifies the organization. Together, vision and culture provide the framework within which retailers should execute all strategies. And though three-fourths of retailers surveyed say they have a vision, more than half rate their performance as just fair or poor; and only about half drive their vision through all levels of the company.

With a vision and culture in place, retailers must develop and articulate a strategic plan for the organization. Here, many small-store retailers do themselves a disservice. Fewer than one in ten have a documented strategic plan. And nearly half have no plan at all. Clearly, many small-store retailers fail to realize the tremendous value inherent in a written plan of action. Yet to do nothing is to court failure. And small-store retailers need to consider this point: Of the hundreds of successful retailers Arthur Andersen counsels every year, not a single one operates without a strategic plan, whether formal or informal. Indeed, successful large retailers wouldn't consider operating without one. Many update—even dramatically alter—their plans regularly.

The chapter on management discusses more fully the importance of forward-thinking management and leadership as well as the value of a strategic plan, and includes several best practices on how to:

- *Brainstorm to begin crafting a vision.* The owner, management team, and sales associates should talk about their vision for the company. Then the owner should put the vision in writing and actively promote it internally and externally.
- *Objectively assess the company.* Retailers should take a good, hard look at who they are and who they want to be. Then they should develop action plans that help them achieve their goals.

No matter how clear the vision or how developed the strategic plan, no retailer can move forward without support from his manager. And here, many retailers shortchange themselves, for without knowledgeable and experienced people, a retailer's organization simply cannot grow. And while nearly every retailer considers management depth important, 40 percent of small-store retailers admit to doing only a fair or poor job educating their people. Clearly, they do not commit to training their managers or themselves.

Quality training almost always pays for itself in reduced costs, increased productivity, and better customer service. It is win-win for both the store owner and the manager. For retailers, then, it is simply a matter of making a commitment to training. Plenty of opportunities exist to train managers, including on-the-job training, management seminars, and vendor workshops. Retailers need to strike a healthy balance between internal and external training and between informal and formal training.

Human Resources

A good salesperson can sell anything. A poor salesperson can't.

Customers see store employees as store values personified. And nothing spoils a shopping experience—or store image—more quickly than a poorly informed, uncooperative, or surly employee. The most successful retailers in the world vow that their employees are key to their success. They cherish a golden rule of management: Treat employees as employees should treat customers.

Many small-store retailers, however, fail to devote adequate time and attention to developing employees to their full potential. Though nearly all say hiring and retention is important, more than one-fourth say their performance here is no better than fair.

There are a couple of reasons for this. Whereas sharp retailers build a profile of the best employees (key personality traits, type of experience, etc.), fewer than half of Illinois small-store retailers from the initial study claim to develop such a description. Many either fail to see the value in such a profile or fail to take the initiative to develop one.

Further, many retailers view their associates as mere workers in a store, not as ambassadors of the company. They view employees as just another cost of running the business. They do not offer employees the opportunity to attend outside seminars on topics such as motivation, selling skills, and product knowledge. This may be because of the cost or because retailers do not know where to go to get the proper training. Yet these courses enhance the skills of the employees, better prepare them to serve customers, and can pay off with increased sales.

Three elements of sound employee relations are discussed in the section on human resources, but clearly the most important challenge facing the retailer is hiring and retaining top-notch associates. Selective employee turnover is desirable, of course, when it relieves the store of employees who perform poorly or helps infuse fresh ideas. But most small retailers simply cannot afford to lose even one of their good employees.

Retailers can take steps to improve their hiring process. No set of personality characteristics will guarantee success, but every retailer should develop a personality profile. Once they hire individuals who fit the profile, the retailers must do everything possible to educate the associates and motivate them to succeed.

Employee motivation, satisfaction, and retention can be enhanced by simple recognition programs, yet only 42 percent of those surveyed offer incentives for superior service. Many small-store retailers do not offer incentives to their employees because they do not know what goals to set for employees or what rewards to offer those who succeed. The chapter on human resources discusses many options for employee recognition and incentives. Central to all of these, however, is the idea that incentives should be based on what an employee can control and be tied to the individual performance (e.g., a store manager's incentive may be based on store profitability).

Successful retailers agree that the best way to retain quality associates is to empower them. Indeed, executives across all industries embrace empowerment as the management style of the 1990s. And with good reason: The best retail employees will serve customers better, solve more problems, and enjoy their jobs more if they are encouraged and given the training and authority to respond to customer needs.

The chapter on human resources discusses the importance and benefits of finding, recruiting, educating, and rewarding good employees and includes several best practices on how to:

- Develop a personality and skills profile. Successful retailers agree that some of the most important attributes of the best employees are interest in retailing and selling, prior experience, product knowledge, and personality. New hires should match a retailer's personality and skills profile and the store's image as closely as possible.
- Offer external training to employees in areas such as selling skills, motivation, and product knowledge.
- Develop incentives for employees that are based on factors that the employee can control and that also are related to the store's goals.

Finance

It is this simple: Retailers cannot manage what they do not measure.

The only hope small-store retailers have of becoming lower-cost providers is to pay attention to finance. Regrettably, retailers lag far behind their chain-store counterparts in this area. Nearly half rate their cost-reduction skills as only fair or poor.

Certainly, small stores do not have the same opportunities to reduce costs as do the large chains. Yet small doesn't preclude thrifty. And while there are plenty of resources available to help retailers reduce costs, few retailers take advantage of them. Only one in four deals with the issue in team meetings, and fewer than one in five provides an employee suggestion box for cost-saving ideas.

Besides cost reduction, small-store retailers must pay close attention to budgeting. Here again, however, small-store retailers do not perform up to par. While 81 percent say budgeting is important, half of those surveyed have no budget. Clearly retailers don't recognize that operating a business today without a budget is asking for failure.

Budgeting is the benchmark against which retailers of any size can accurately forecast cash flow; track performance; and measure sales, expenses, and profits. And though many retailers fail to budget because they either do not know how or fail to see the benefits, those who work without a budget only delude themselves into thinking they have their stores under financial control.

The chapter on finance discusses thoroughly the key aspects to cost reduction and budget development and includes several best practices on how to:

- *Review and benchmark all costs.* The only way to manage costs is to measure them critically and continually. Every month retailers should challenge each line item.
- *Reevaluate all policies and procedures.* Retailers must continually look for ways to reduce costs while maintaining or improving efficiency. They should eliminate policies or procedures that do not add value for customers or enhance business controls.
- *Determine what areas can benefit most from a budget.* Some retailers will be able to budget both sales and margin, while others will be able to budget only operating expenses. A budget for one area is better than no budget at all.
- *Create a budget.* The easiest way to develop a budget is to start with last year's results. Adjust for known current-year changes, then compare numbers with industry statistics on a line-by-line basis. Retailers who do this will know immediately where they stand and where they need to improve.

Small Store Survival presents a great deal of material, but retailers should not be intimidated. This book is meant to be read in small amounts. It is a reference guide. A thought provoker. A challenge to the status quo.

Having completed this summary, retailers should look through the chapter on economic and retail trends and then read the section entitled "How to Use This Book."

TRAINING NEEDS

The following is a summary of training needs for small-store retailers to better manage and operate their businesses. Retailers' trade associations, buying cooperatives, and vendors can help small-store retailers provide these needs. Vendor training primarily covers product knowledge as well as assistance with store layout and assortment planning. Certain trade associations and buying cooperatives provide training in areas such as selling skills, motivation skills, and merchandising.

Small-store retailers often do not take advantage of these training courses. Some belong to groups that do not offer training, while others are hindered by the costs of trade association and buying group memberships or the cost of travel.

Training needs are broken down into the major areas listed below. They include:

Customers and Marketing
- Identify and meet customers' wants
- Deliver quality customer service
- Respond to competition
- Use various market techniques
- Develop an image, and the implications of doing so
- Promote value-added services
- Identify and implement alternative marketing strategies
- Profile customers

Merchandising
- Identify and serve market niches
- Evaluate alternative pricing strategies
- Develop and maintain positive vendor relations
- Negotiate successfully
- Use open-to-buy in merchandise planning
- Measure merchandising performance
- Use assortment planning

Store Operations
- Schedule store labor
- Address store location issues
- Design effective store layout and displays
- Implement loss-prevention techniques

Management
- Exhibit leadership in a small store
- Develop and communicate vision
- Foster corporate culture
- Develop a strategic plan
- Plan for wealth and succession
- Develop management training
- Manage change in the small store
- Establish effective business controls
- Network

Human Resources
- Hire and retain the best employees
- Develop effective selling skills
- Design effective benefit programs

Finance
- Control operating costs
- Develop effective budgets

- Identify and provide timely key management reports
- Finance the business
- Establish information systems

This training could include outside industry experts, role playing, workbooks, and a "train-the-trainer" element in which individuals who attend the seminars use the information to train their employees.

1

ECONOMIC AND RETAIL TRENDS

During the 1980s, the U.S. economy experienced unprecedented growth. Indeed, the theme for the '80s was "shop 'til you drop." Consumers spent more of their disposable income, increased their debt, and depleted their savings. A warning came in 1987 with the stock market crash. The actual drop came in 1990, when consumers decided they were full. Recessionary years followed. During 1990, real gross domestic product (GDP) grew by 1.2 percent, while in 1991 it shrank by 0.7 percent.[1]

During this time, many retailers found themselves in precarious positions. As consumers began to back off in 1990 and 1991, retailers who had expanded too quickly or assumed too much debt faced lower cash flows. Recognizing the market forces at work, many analysts began predicting significant "fallout." The optimists said 10 percent of retailers would be out of business by the year 2000. The pessimists said half of all U.S. retailers would be out of business.[2] Fortunately, the most dire prediction is not coming to pass. Although more than 43,000 retail businesses filed bankruptcy between 1990 and 1992, only some 28,000 did so in the succeeding two years (see Table 1-1).[3]

[1] Value Line. Sept. 24, 1993.
[2] "Retailing: Who Will Survive?" *Business Week*, Nov. 26, 1990.
[3] The Dun and Bradstreet Corporation, New York, NY. Business Failure Record.

Table 1-1   Retail businesses filing bankruptcy

1985	13,494
1986	13,620
1987	12,240
1988	11,487
1989	11,120
1990	11,120
1991	12,972
1992	19,005
1993	15,661
1994	12,575

Source: The Dun and Bradstreet Corporation, New York, NY. Business Failure Record.

The economy started to get back on track by the second half of 1992. After hobbling along for the first half of the year, consumer spending—the economy's engine and the single largest component of GDP—revved up during the second half of the year. In late 1992, the GDP growth rate picked up considerably (see Table 1-2). The 1992 holiday season saw retail sales up 8 percent from the previous year.

But exhausted shoppers took a breather at the beginning of 1993. The first-quarter GDP annual growth rate was less than 1 percent, while retail sales increased 4.9 percent. Beginning in the spring, however, sales began to revive. This trend continued into December, when retail sales increased almost 7 percent.[4] This increase in consumer spending was reflected in 1993's fourth-quarter GDP, which grew at an annual rate of 7.5 percent.[5]

[4] U.S. Dept. of Commerce. Bureau of the Census.
[5] U.S. Dept. of Commerce. Bureau of Economic Analysis.

Table 1-2   Total U.S. gross domestic product (in billions)

1960	$513
1970	$1,011
1980	$2,708
1989	$5,244
1990	$5,514
1991	$5,673
1992	$6,039
1993	$6,510
1994	$6,897

Source: U.S. Dept. of Commerce. Bureau of Labor Statistics. Also: Value Line Investment Survey.

Table 1-3   Consumer price index
(excludes food and energy prices)

1990	1991	1992	1993	1994
5.4%	4.2%	3.0%	2.7%	2.5%

Source: U.S. Dept. of Commerce. Bureau of Labor Statistics.

MANY FACTORS DRIVE ECONOMIC REBOUND

The rebound in sales that retailers experienced in 1992 and 1993 has several underlying economic causes:

- *Inflation.*   During the last several years, inflation has remained low. So long as personal income growth stays ahead of inflation, consumer buying power will continue to be bolstered. A modest increase in the inflation rate without comparable increases in wages will slow retail sales and hurt the economy as a whole. One good indicator for inflation is the cost of labor, which is expected to remain in check for the near term because of excess supply, productivity initiatives, and downward pressure on benefits costs. The consumer price index reflects the inflation rate (see Table 1-3).
- *Interest rates.*   From 1990 to 1993, interest rates declined steadily (see Table 1-4). Mortgage rates reached their lowest level in more than 20 years, and the pace of mortgage refinancing grew accordingly. Like low inflation rates, low interest rates put more buying power into consumers' hands.
- *Consumer confidence.*   How consumers feel about their present situations and their futures affects the way they spend their paychecks. *Business Week* reported in its Feb. 7, 1994, issue that the number of people who thought that jobs were "hard to get" fell to the lowest level in three years.[6] In January 1994, the consumer confidence index reached 83.2, its highest level in several years (see Table 1-5).[7]

[6] "The Cold Won't Stall This Revved-Up Economy." *Business Week,* Feb. 7, 1994.
[7] University of Michigan.

Table 1-4   Prime interest rate (at year end)

1990	1991	1992	1993	1994
10.0%	8.5%	6.3%	6.0%	8.1%

Source: U.S. Dept. of Commerce. Bureau of Labor Statistics. Also: Value Line Investment Survey, June 2, 1995.

Table 1-5   Consumer confidence index (at year end)

1990	1991	1992	1993	1994
61.2	52.5	78.1	79.8	96.3

Source: University of Michigan. Also: *Economic Times,* vol. 6, no. 3, March 1995.

- *Housing activity.*   New residential construction is a leading indicator for the economy. Construction is typically followed by spending on expensive items, such as home furnishings, appliances, and lawn and garden items. In 1994, housing construction increased by 7.4 percent from 1993, reaching its highest level since 1989 (see Table 1-6). Housing permits are also on the rise, and sales of existing homes have increased almost 8 percent from 1994.[8]
- *Unemployment.*   The recent period of modest unemployment is a good sign for retailers, because keeping people in the workforce also elevates spending. Average weekly unemployment claims reached a three-year low in December 1993. There were 310,000 weekly claims that month, compared to weekly claims of more than 500,000 in early 1991.[9] The unemployment rate dropped from 7.4 percent in 1992 to 6.8 percent in 1993 to 6.1 percent in 1994 (see Table 1-7).
- *Personal incomes.*   Despite improvements in many areas, personal income growth has been limited. The *Wall Street Journal* reported that, after adjusting for the effects of inflation, disposable incomes rose at an annual rate of 1.9 percent in 1993 (see Table 1-8). This is low compared to the 2.9 percent growth rate in 1992. The only good news here is that inflation is not outpacing nominal increases in personal incomes.[10]

---

[8] U.S. Dept. of Commerce. Bureau of the Census.
[9] U.S. Dept. of Commerce. Bureau of Labor Statistics.
[10] U.S. Dept. of Commerce. Bureau of Economic Analysis.

Table 1-6   New housing construction (percent change)

1990	1991	1992	1993	1994
(13.0)%	(15.8)%	19.8%	7.0%	7.4%

Source: U.S. Dept. of Commerce. Bureau of the Census. Also: Economic Indicators by Joint Economic Committee, Sept. 1995.

Table 1-7   U.S. unemployment rate

1990	1991	1992	1993	1994
5.5%	6.7%	7.4%	6.8%	6.1%

Source: U.S. Dept. of Commerce. Bureau of Labor
Statistics. Also: *Monthly Labor Review,* Aug. 1995.

CONSUMERS SPEND MORE ON SERVICES, LESS ON GOODS

If consumers do have more money to spend, retailers want them to spend it on merchandise. However, over the past 24 years, more of the average consumer's paycheck has been spent on services and less on durable and nondurable retail goods (see Table 1-9).

One cause of this trend is the aging population—senior citizens tend to spend more of their disposable income on health care and recreation. Another cause: Through 1992, the rate of inflation on health-care services was two to three times the normal rate of inflation. The message is clear— retailers compete not only against each other for the consumer's dollar but also against other services.

Despite the trend toward greater spending on services, 1992 retail sales grew 3.3 percent to $1.96 trillion. While that seems modest, it followed a dismal 1991, when growth was at a mere 0.9 percent.[11] The 1992 comeback was led by the sporting goods group, which showed a 13.5 percent increase from 1991. Bookstores followed, up 12.5 percent. The popularity of outdoor activities and reading contributed to the strong increases. The big loser in 1992 was the jewelry group, hurt by lack of strong trends in the fashion business. The 1995 leader was the furniture group, up 8.8 percent, followed by automotive, up 8.1 percent.[12]

Many economists saw 1992 as a correction in which consumers unleashed their pent-up demand, leading economists to conclude that the

[11] U.S. Dept. of Commerce. Bureau of the Census.
[12] Market Statistics, 1993. 1993 Demographics, USA-County Edition.

Table 1-8   Disposable income (percent change)

1990	1991	1992	1993	1994
1.7%	0.1%	2.9%	1.9%	3.6%

Source: U.S. Dept. of Commerce. Bureau of Economic
Analysis. Also: Value Line Investment Survey, June 2,
1995.

Table 1-9   Components of consumer spending, 1960–1994

	1960	1970	1980	1990	1991	1992	1993	1994
Nondurable goods	52%	42%	39%	33%	32%	32%	31%	31%
Durable goods	8%	13%	12%	12%	12%	11%	14%	15%
Services	40%	45%	49%	55%	56%	57%	55%	54%
Total	100%	100%	100%	100%	100%	100%	100%	100%

Source: U.S. Dept. of Commerce. Bureau of Economic Analysis. Also: Value Line Investment Survey, June 2, 1995.

trend may not continue. In 1993 and 1995, the amount of U.S. retail sales grew 6.3 percent and 4.9 percent, respectively, to $2.074 trillion and $2.346 trillion, respectively (Table 1-10).[13] This performance has left many analysts guessing about what may happen next.

But as long as people are working, they will continue to spend their earnings. The key for small-store retailers is to make sure they garner their share.

IN RETAILING, ILLINOIS IS A MICROCOSM OF AMERICA

Small-store retailing in Illinois serves as an effective model for studying independent retailing across America. Illinois has elements of the

[13] U.S. Dept. of Commerce. Bureau of the Census.

Table 1-10   Retail Sales in the United States, 1988–1995 (in billions)

	1988	1992	1995	Increase from 1988	
				Amount	Percent
Durable goods					
Building materials	$84.0	$100.8	$124.1	$40.1	47.7%
Automotive dealers	357.0	406.9	568.8	211.8	59.3%
Furniture and home furnishings	92.0	97.0	130.1	38.1	41.4%
Other	75.0	98.9	117.7	42.7	56.9%
Total	$608.0	$703.6	$940.7	$332.7	54.7%
Non-durable goods					
General merchandise stores	$184.0	$246.4	$296.0	$112.0	60.9%
Food stores	331.0	377.1	408.4	77.4	23.4%
Gasoline service stations	107.0	137.0	147.6	40.6	37.9%
Apparel and accessory stores	83.0	104.2	109.5	26.5	31.9%
Eating and drinking places	157.0	200.2	239.9	82.9	52.8%
Drug and proprietary	60.0	70.0	84.4	24.4	40.7%
Other	81.0	113.1	119.8	38.8	47.9%
Total non-durable	$1,003.0	$1,248.0	$1,405.6	$402.6	40.1%
Total retail sales	$1,611.0	$1,951.6	$2,346.3	$735.3	45.6%

Source: U.S. Department of Commerce, Bureau of Census

economies and demographics of most states. Certainly the size is there. Based on total 1994 retail sales, Illinois' market is the fifth largest in the nation (see Figure 1-1).

In 1995, Illinois retailers generated approximately $105 billion in sales, or 4.5 percent of total U.S. retail sales. This reflects a 5.0 percent increase over 1994, versus the 4.9 percent increase at the national level (see Table 1-11). Through 1997, however, the outlook is better: Analysts predict Illinois retail sales will increase 31.4 percent to $138 billion, while total U.S. retail sales will increase only 14.8 percent to $2.7 trillion.[14]

Consider for a moment the size of the U.S. retail market, which is $2.237 trillion, and the relative share that the top 100 chain stores control, which is 27.5 percent, or $615 billion. The good news is that plenty of market opportunity exists for the middle-market chains and small stores. The bad news is that many middle markets and small-store retailers are chasing that market share along with the national chains. The top 100 retailers each generate about $5.81 million per establishment, while the other players each bring in $1.24 million in sales (see Table 1-12).[15]

Extrapolating these ratios to the Illinois market indicates that the market share available to the middle-market chains and small stores is

[14] Market Statistics, 1993. 1993 Demographics, USA-County Edition.
[15] "The Top 100 Retailers." *Stores,* July 1993.

Figure 1-1   Illinois represents the fifth largest state in retail sales in the United States. Of the top five states, Illinois has the second highest per capita retail sales, behind only Florida.

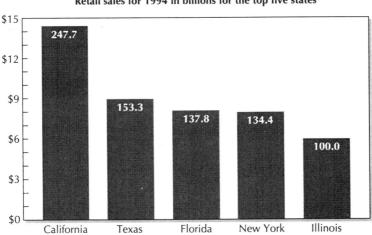

Retail sales for 1994 in billions for the top five states

Source: *Market Statistics,* 1995. 1995 Demographics USA County Edition.

Table 1-11   Dollar sales and percent change, 1985–1995

	U.S. (in billions)	Percent change	Illinois (in billions)	Percent change
1985	$1,375	6.8%	$66	7.4%
1986	$1,450	5.4%	$70	6.0%
1987	$1,541	6.3%	$75	7.1%
1988	$1,611	4.5%	$78	4.0%
1989	$1,747	8.4%	$82	5.1%
1990	$1,826	4.5%	$88	7.3%
1991	$1,843	0.9%	$92	4.5%
1992	$1,951	5.9%	$93	1.1%
1993	$2,074	6.3%	$95	2.2%
1994	$2,237	7.9%	$100	5.3%
1995	$2,346	4.9%	$105	5.0%

Source: Illinois Dept. of Commerce and Community Affairs.

about $72 billion. Illinois is not as overstored as the rest of the nation, but per-store figures are comparable. The top 100 retailers each generate about $5.6 million per store, while the others each bring in $1.24 million (see Table 1-13).

Challenges

Just as the Illinois market is a microcosm of the larger U.S. market in terms of sales, the Illinois market is also indicative of economic challenges facing the nation.

Rural retailers suffer most. Changes in the population cause fluctuations in the economy. While analysts predict zero population growth in many nonmetro areas, there are exceptions. For example, McHenry County, bordering Wisconsin, is expected to expand the most—by 15 percent, in fact— to 230,000. The population of Cook County, which includes Chicago, is expected to increase by 1.6 percent to 5.23 million.[16]

[16] Market Statistics, 1993. 1993 Demographics, USA-County Edition.

Table 1-12   U.S. retail market: total and top 100 chains

	Retail sales (in billions)	Percent	Number of establishments (in thousands)	Percent
Total retail sales	$2,237	100%	1,413	100%
Sales of the top 100 chains	$616	27.5%	106	7.5%
Other stores	$1,621	72.5%	1,307	92.5%

Source: U.S. Dept. of Labor. Bureau of Statistics.

Table 1-13   Illinois Retail Market: Total and Top 100 Chains

	Retail sales (in billions)	Percent	Number of establishments (in thousands)	Percent
Total retail sales	$100	100%	63	100%
Sales of the top 100 chains	$28	28.0%	5	7.9%
Other stores	$72	72.0%	58	92.1%

Conversely, rural areas are experiencing population declines. The loss of agricultural jobs in central and eastern Illinois, mining jobs in southern Illinois, and manufacturing jobs in northern Illinois is driving more and more people from rural areas to suburban and urban areas.[17]

A side effect of these population shifts is that many rural downtown business districts are dying. Many cities, including Chicago, are continually reviewing programs to revitalize their downtown in efforts to boost shopping, and other towns have simply resigned themselves to the reality that their downtown areas will not be the central shopping districts. These towns are converting what was once prime retail space to other uses. But rural towns are only beginning to go through these centrifugal forces. Residents of these towns often engage in heated debates concerning whether to permit the development of alternate shopping centers.

But while rural residents are deciding whether to revitalize the downtown business district, mass merchants, national chains, and category killers are setting up shop on the outskirts of town. With the smaller population in a rural community, a mass merchant is a big fish in a very small pond. This makes it hard for the small-store retailers in the immediate area as well as in surrounding communities to survive. It also takes sales tax revenue from surrounding communities, which can devastate local government budgets.

Industry-wide trends affect retail success. Increased business competition from national chains is only one of several forces that have begun to shape today's retail landscape. Industry-wide trends make market share more precious and place still greater pressure on profits—especially for small-store retailers.

Industry consolidation: The go-go '80s ultimately led many retailers to ruin. As mentioned earlier, more than 47,000 retailers nationwide have filed for bankruptcy in the past three years.[18] The crippling effects of these bankruptcies reach suppliers, landlords, banks, creditors, employers, and employees. On a more positive note, however, business failures allow surviving retailers the opportunity to capture more market share.

[17] Walzer, Norman. Introduction. Illinois Institute for Rural Affairs Rural Research Report. Winter 1992.
[18] The Dun and Bradstreet Corporation, New York, NY. Business Failure Record.

Another contributor to the widespread industry consolidation is the expansion of mass merchants, national chains, and category killers. These stores continue to take market share from independents and middle-market chains. As a result, they often drive the weaker players out of business. No small-store retailer is immune to the effects of mass merchants and other discounters, but independent grocers have proved to be particularly vulnerable. During the last two decades, the market share for independent grocers has fallen from 42 to 20 percent. Independent drugstores have not fared well either.

Overstoring: Today, retailers operate about 19 square feet of retail space for every man, woman, and child in America.[19] This is largely due to overzealous real-estate developers and anchor stores that collaborated on aggressive expansion campaigns in the '70s and '80s.[20] In fact, while population grew by 10 percent during the 1980s, retail square footage grew by more than 50 percent.[21] This overstoring is a symptom of retailers attempting to capture more market share, and it generally spreads customer traffic over more retail stores. Two side effects emerge: First, the resulting shift in shopping patterns may force some retailers to relocate or to close unprofitable stores. On the positive side, this trend may present small-store retailers with an opportunity to negotiate lower rents. Second, customers have more choices. The neighborhood retailer may no longer be their logical choice, and this tests traditional customer loyalties. This means that small-store retailers must establish themselves as destinations—preferred places to shop in their local communities.

Value-conscious consumers: The spending frenzy of the 1980s gave consumers a mall-sized shopping hangover. Disposable income declined, debt stayed high, and consumers found religion in value. Case in point: More than 50 percent of TJ Maxx customers come from households with incomes of $50,000 or more. Consumers no longer view quality solely in terms of price. And the stereotype that discounters sell cheap products is gone—blown apart by successful discount chains and category killers.

The changing population: By the year 2000, the entire baby-boom population—the 75 million Americans born between 1946 and 1964—will be between the ages of 36 and 54. This changing demographic presents both good and bad news to retailers. On the downside, the older consumers will begin to spend more of their money on travel, leisure, and college tuition. On the upside, they will spend more money on prescriptions, health care, and beauty care. In addition, the middle-aged segment will spend more on apparel for their children and furniture for their homes.

[19] "Who Will Survive?" *Business Week.*
[20] "Retailing Current Analysis." *Standard & Poor's Industry Surveys,* Sept. 16, 1993.
[21] *Inside Retailing,* October 1993.

And over the next 20 years, minority populations will expand rapidly; approximately 80 percent of all population growth is expected to come from African-American, Hispanic, and Asian segments. To continue to attract all of these consumers, retailers will need to tailor their service strategy, merchandise selection, and pricing policies. Small-store retailers have a distinct advantage—mass merchants have significantly less flexibility in catering to specific consumer segments.

Shrinking labor pool: Retailers employed over 20 million people and generated 390,000 new jobs in 1995 (see Figure 1-2).[22] But while baby boomers are graying, the size of the twentysomething crowd is shrinking. This means fewer young people will be in the workforce. Sadly, many of those new entrants will have limited oral and written skills. Since retailers traditionally rely on younger workers to satisfy part-time and seasonal employment needs, these trends could lead to higher payrolls because retailers will have to hire older, more experienced workers. The trends also could hinder customer-service efforts as retailers spend more of their available dollars on hiring and thus have less to devote to training.

Time-constrained consumers: More women are joining the workforce, and everyone is working longer hours. These trends make time a more precious commodity and shopping a less palatable experience; hence the sig-

[22] National Retail Federation.

Figure 1-2   Retailing provides a significant labor market for the U.S. economy. But as the twentysomething crowd shrinks, retailers may have difficulty filling their part-time and seasonal employment needs.

U.S. retail employment (in millions)

Source: National Retail Federation

nificant growth in nonstore retailing. Home shopping via TV, computer, and catalogs continues to grow each year.[23] To create store loyalty, retailers need to take a hard look at the convenience factor in their current strategies.

Public policy: The end of the Cold War allows the White House to focus more on domestic policy, most notably health-care reform and deficit reduction through higher taxes. The full impact of these and other policy decisions has yet to be seen. But the chance that any of these measures will put more money in the pockets of small-store retailers seems remote, at best.

These industry-wide trends have led many to conclude that, in the next decade, retailers will fall into two categories: those that are lean, mean, and customer-driven, and those that are gone. What will the survivors have in common? For small-store retailers, the implications are obvious:

- An owner who possesses a clear vision for the store backed by a strategic plan and a strong desire to improve the skills and capabilities of the organization.
- A clear focus on customers' wants and the store's service strategy, merchandise selection, and pricing policies, supported by effective advertising.
- A strong relationship with vendors, suppliers, employees, and community leaders.
- A demonstrated appreciation for training and retaining employees, treating them as valuable assets, and involving them in cost-reduction and operations-improvement issues.
- An ability to respond to dynamic external changes and the ability to plan for those changes, supporting retail decisions with facts learned through effective marketing research, budgeting, and financial analysis.
- A true entrepreneurial spirit in which innovation, creativity, and courage prevail in response to competitive threats.

These qualities are paramount to retail success. Of course, given the current economic backdrop, small-store retailers need to take some strong steps to ensure their survival in a constantly changing marketplace. Those not willing to make changes will likely fail. The results of this study show that small-store retailers can survive and prosper—but only if they are willing to work at it.

[23] *Inside Retailing,* October 1993.

2

CUSTOMERS AND MARKETING

Retailers Must Listen to Customers to Know How to Please Them

"Success is determining consumers' wants and needs and fulfilling those needs. . . . We are successful, but we certainly have room to improve . . . and the customer is a moving target," says a department-store retailer in northern Illinois.

Many small-store retailers echo this retailer's sentiments. Almost all retailers agree that understanding customers is critical to success. And with good reason: Today's customers expect more from retailers than ever before—and they are harder to please than ever before. To prevent customers from going to the competition, retailers have to devote considerable time and effort to determine what their customers want and whether retailers satisfy those wants. These are the two most critical priorities for retailers.

Unfortunately, the methods retailers use to address these priorities do not go far enough. The primary means the respondents use today to determine what their customers want are word of mouth and gut feeling. Retailers need facts to back up their instincts of what customers want and whether they are satisfied. They need to use focus groups, surveys, and comment cards to solicit comments from their customers. Monitoring customer attitudes can no longer be a part-time effort; it is a full-time commitment to a continuous process. Ultimately, to succeed, retailers need to develop strategies that will enable them to always meet or exceed their customers' expectations. To do so, however, they must first determine what their customers really expect.

This chapter discusses eight business issues (see Table 2-1). Although Arthur Andersen concurs with retailers about the relative importance of the top item (Figure 2-1), it believes retailers should place more emphasis on Arthur Andersen's first-tier items.

According to Arthur Andersen and small-store retailers, the most important aspect of customers and marketing is determining what customers want and how satisfied they are when they visit the store.

Research indicates that consumers today are looking for quick checkout, consistent—not necessarily low—prices, knowledgeable sales assistance, quality merchandise, convenience, and in-stock merchandise. These wants vary widely with the circumstances, however, and what customers want today may not be what they want tomorrow. Many small-store retailers look for quick answers or industry trends to determine what customers want. But no magic formula exists. Retailers need to find out this information for themselves by using more formal means to determine what their customers want and whether they are satisfied.

The two other critical areas identified by Arthur Andersen are competitive response and a combination of advertising, public relations, and direct mail. In contrast, retailers ranked competitive response sixth; and advertising, public relations, and direct mail fourth in importance. The definitions:

- *Competitive response.* Investigating and shopping your competition to understand and anticipate what competitors are doing.
- *Advertising, public relations, and direct mail.* Developing print, radio, and television advertising strategies to increase store traffic; effectively using the media to report positively on the business; and maintaining a database of customer information (e.g. age, address, family size, shopping frequency) to be used for direct-mail advertising.

Table 2-1   Tier rankings

Arthur Andersen's First Tier	Retailers' First Tier
1. Customer wants and satisfaction	1. Customer wants and satisfaction
2. Competitive response	2. Customer profiling
3. Advertising, public relations and direct mail	3. Image development
Second Tier	**Second Tier**
4. Image development	4. Advertising, public relations and direct mail
5. Value-added services	5. Value-added services
6. Alternative marketing strategies	6. Competitive response
7. Customer profiling	7. Alternative marketing strategies
8. Alternative delivery channels	8. Alternative delivery channels

Figure 2-1   Retailers need to improve their performance in identifying customer wants and meeting those wants. Competitive response, marketing strategy, advertising, and public relations are also critical marketing areas where the retailer should focus his attention first. How do you compare? Ask yourself how important each business practice is to you and how well you perform it. Then fill in the chart in the section on operations assessment.

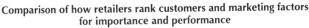

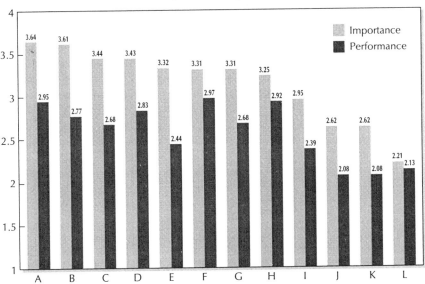

Comparison of how retailers rank customers and marketing factors
for importance and performance

A. Customer wants
B. Customer satisfaction
C. Customer profiling
D. Image development
E. Advertising strategy
F. Value-added services

G. Overall median for considerations of customers and marketing
H. Competitive response
I. Alternative marketing strategies
J. Customer database management
K. Public relations
L. Alternative delivery channels

These practices go hand in hand with delivering on customer wants and satisfaction. Retailers need to know who their competitors are and understand competitors' tactics if they want to maintain or enhance market share. The competition is not necessarily limited to retailers in the local community; it may also include those retailers an hour or two away. Retailers must continually study their competition's merchandise selection, services, pricing strategy, and sales support. To accomplish this, retailers can visit competitors' stores, talk with other retailers, and visit with consumers who shop the competition.

Retailers also need to develop a sound advertising, public relations, and direct-mail plan. Retailers often fall short when analyzing which advertisements generate the greatest increase in customer traffic. Indeed, a majority of retailers do not formally measure the effectiveness of their advertisements; they "just know." Retailers need to track the response to their advertisements to determine which forms of media and which advertisements work best. These advertising efforts should be supported with a combination of public relations and target marketing, which may include direct mailings to current and prospective customers based on their demographic profiles.

Collectively, these three issues—customer wants and satisfaction; competitive response; and the combination of advertising, public relations, and direct mail—represent Arthur Andersen's first-tier priorities for retailers.

The five remaining areas of customers and marketing are also important in helping retailers understand customers, enhance their store image, and improve their marketing efforts, but they are not as critical. These second-tier issues can be addressed after retailers have critically analyzed the first-tier items:

- *Image development.* Presenting customers with a distinct impression of the store.
- *Value-added services.* Providing services beyond customers' expectations.
- *Alternative marketing strategies.* Using target marketing and in-store promotions to increase traffic and sales.
- *Customer profiling.* Understanding customers in terms of what they are buying.
- *Alternative delivery channels.* Identifying and executing nontraditional distribution methods to sell merchandise.

In summary, retailers must first understand what their customers want and how satisfied customers are; then, they can begin to meet those wants and enhance that satisfaction. Retailers can then use other areas in this chapter to build on the practices already established. Understanding customers' wants and satisfaction will help retailers exceed customers' expectations and build a group of loyal customers.

CUSTOMER WANTS AND SATISFACTION

Marshall Field: "Give the Lady What She Wants"

Determining what customers want and how best to satisfy those wants is the basis for everything retailers do—from where they locate their stores to the merchandise they carry to the sales associates they hire.

Stanley Marcus of Neiman Marcus says it best: "Customer satisfaction is when you sell something that does not return to someone who does." And to make that sale—and satisfy customers—retailers must first

Figure 2-2   Retailers must continually seek information on what their customers want.

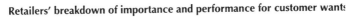

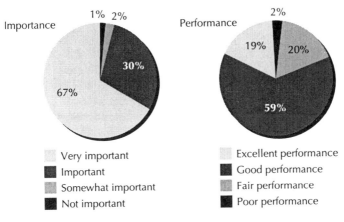

Retailers' breakdown of importance and performance for customer wants

determine what their customers want. Figure 2-2 suggests that while retailers appreciate the importance of customer wants, they lack a formal approach to continuously identify them. And while 97 percent of retailers think that customer satisfaction is important or very important, 86 percent say they aren't doing as well as they could at keeping their customers happy (see Figure 2-3). If this is true, it does not bode well for retailers. Obviously it is difficult to stay in business without satisfied customers.

Figure 2-3   Are customers truly satisfied with the store's services and merchandise? Most retailers cannot answer this important question. If customers are not satisfied, they may not give a store a second chance.

Retailers' breakdown of importance and performance for customer satisfactioi

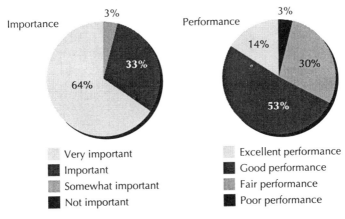

A good way to start is by listening to the customers themselves. Most owners personally respond to some complaints or comments that customers make while in the store; 62 percent respond to all customer complaints and comments in the store, by letter, or by phone (see Figure 2-4). So, on the one hand, most retailers react well and respond to complaints in some way. But on the other hand, retailers miss an opportunity by not calling customers frequently to see if they are satisfied with the store's merchandise and service. Retailers should actively seek customers' opinions, not wait for them to complain.

Market research studies indicate that, on average, customers expect knowledgeable assistance from the sales staff, fair treatment, consistent pricing, in-stock merchandise, and quick checkout, but this varies widely with the customer, the retail format, and the expected shopping experience. Still, this differs from what retailers think customers want (see Figure 2-5 on page 39).

Unfortunately, few retailers have a formal approach to keeping tabs on the changing needs and wants of customers. Word of mouth or gut instinct is how most small-store retailers determine their customers'

Figure 2-4   Most retailers successfully respond to customer complaints by acting on them immediately. Employees should have more authority to resolve complaints, and retailers should strive to seek customers' opinions and act on their suggestions before they become complaints.

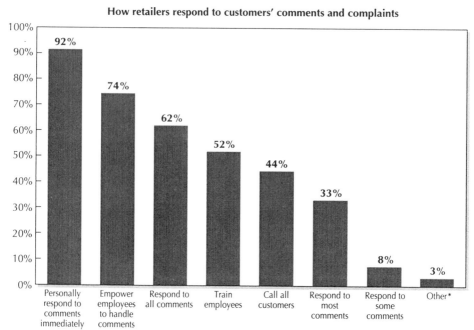

How retailers respond to customers' comments and complaints

* Includes prompt, gracious attention.

Figure 2-5 Retailers say friendliness and personal service top the list of customers' wants. But customers say they also value well-stocked stores, prompt customer service, quick check-out, and consistent pricing. Retailers who want the competitive edge should determine what their customers want and address those wants accordingly.

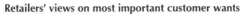

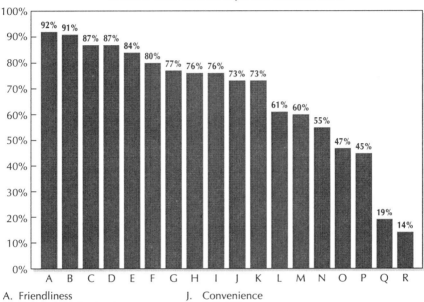

A. Friendliness
B. Personal service level
C. Fair price
D. Knowledgeable product assistance
E. Prompt customer service
F. All major credit cards accepted
G. Large selection (breadth)
H. High quality
I. Cleanliness

J. Convenience
K. Reliability
L. In stock
M. Hassle-free returns
N. Depth of inventory (quantity)
O. Personal charge accounts
P. Quick check-out
Q. Lowest price
R. Proprietary credit card

wants—in fact, 63 percent say they "just know." But, while instinct is important, these methods simply are not effective over the long term (see Figure 2-6). Instead, retailers need to turn to more organized and analytical approaches such as documented in-store interviews, focus groups, or mail surveys. These techniques generate cold, hard facts about what customers and potential customers want. It is this information, when compiled and reviewed regularly, that will enable small-store retailers to keep up with the changing marketplace.

Retailers must remember that for every complaint that management receives, 26 more disenchanted customers will never make it back to the store.[1] Bad experiences will fester in the minds—and on the tongues—of

[1] Technical Assistance Research Programs Institute, Washington, D.C., 1990.

Figure 2-6   Rather than relying on their instincts alone, retailers need to determine what their customers want through more analytical means such as documented in-store interviews, focus groups, surveys, and comment cards.

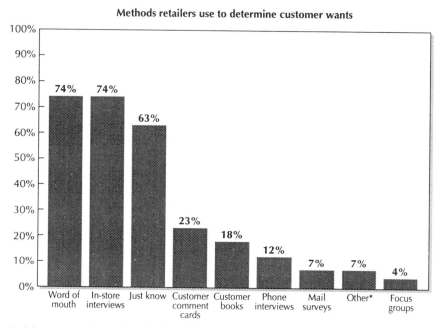

Methods retailers use to determine customer wants

* Includes personal experience and employee feedback.

ex-customers. Retailers must make determining customer wants and ensuring customer satisfaction their top priorities. In the process, retailers will reap many benefits, including greater store loyalty and more business.

Obviously, any information about customer wants must be current to be valuable, but simply tracking customer sentiments is not enough. Retailers need to interpret and act on this information to enhance services, improve merchandise, and ultimately increase store traffic and sales. They need to empower their employees to resolve customer complaints and suggestions. They need to formally train their employees to effectively address customers' needs and wants. And they should constantly communicate customers' expectations to employees at weekly meetings, in addition to recognizing and rewarding employees who demonstrate outstanding customer service (see Figure 2-7).

Best Practices You Can Use

To fully satisfy your customers, you need to find out what they really want. Does your store's merchandise quality, selection, and customer ser-

Figure 2-7   Holding weekly meetings with store employees and establishing a formal communication program will help focus the entire organization on meeting customer wants.

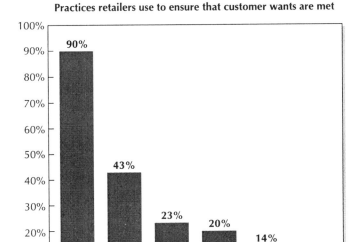

Practices retailers use to ensure that customer wants are met

* Includes monthly store meetings and recognition in newsletter.

vice meet—or exceed—their expectations? Try some of the following suggestions to gather customers' comments.

Interview customers.   Walk the floor and talk to them. Introduce yourself by name, ask for theirs, and thank them for their patronage. Customers are more than happy to tell you exactly what they think, and they will be impressed that an owner or manager takes time to listen. Talk to customers over the phone or in the store at all points of interaction—the sales floor, the cash register, and the door. Encourage other personnel to do so as well. Ask customers whether they would shop in your store again. Ask them what they like and don't like. If the customer has a complaint, listen carefully, ask what would satisfy her, and then respond in such a way as to exceed her expectations. Well-received responses usually include: apologizing, giving store credit, helping take packages to the customer's car, or sending a follow-up letter. Discuss customer concerns with your employees regularly during staff meetings. Then, determine what actions you need to take to exceed customers' wants and improve their level of satisfaction.

Document conversations.   Keep track of what individual customers have to say to you, your sales people, and your store managers, and regularly communicate these comments to the appropriate people.

Conduct telephone or mail surveys. Ask customers how they like the new merchandise, what other merchandise they would like you to carry, and if they are satisfied with the service level. Some useful questions include: Were the sales associates friendly and helpful? Did you find what you were looking for? Was there an ample supply of sale merchandise? Were sale items clearly identified and easy to find? What would you like to tell us about your shopping experience at our store? If this were your store, what would you like to see added or changed? Will you come back again? Offer customers a gift certificate or discount for responding to the surveys (see Table 2-2).

Conduct a focus group composed of customers and noncustomers. Ask each of them to bring a friend to round out the group. Invite all the participants to the store and start a lively discussion on why they do or do not shop at the store, what services they would like to see, and what shopping hours are best for them. Offer an incentive for participating. Focus groups should consist of six to eight customers or prospective customers and can be moderated by almost any objective leader or manager. The owner should not moderate the focus group because he may not be objective. Keep the discussion to 90 minutes or less and try to focus on only four or five topics. Choose subjects of greatest importance to your business and your customers, such as merchandise assortment, service levels, and advertising. Spend no more than 20 minutes on each topic and move on. Do not expect to solve all of the problems in one meeting.

Provide self-addressed, postage-paid comment cards at the checkout area. These can help gauge customer satisfaction levels. Customers can complete the cards while they wait or mail them later. Ask how they enjoyed their visit to the store, how the service could be improved, and if they found what they were looking for. Ask them what they liked as well as what they didn't like. You can use the questions in the sample comment card on page 43 to interview customers, conduct a focus group, or send a formal questionnaire. When customers request follow-up calls, respond immediately or customers may be disappointed further.

Use store signs. Place a sign near the checkout area encouraging customers to express their feelings about the store and merchandise. Use signs to encourage customers to ask about items they want and you don't have.

Place an employee suggestion box or idea board in the back room. This can be used to obtain ideas from employees who are shy or intimidated in group meetings. You need to respond to all suggestions—good and bad—so staff members know you are serious about listening to them. You can respond at employee meetings or in individual discussions with the person who submitted the idea. Consider rewarding employees for sharing

Table 2-2 Sample customer survey

PLEASE TELL US ABOUT YOUR EXPERIENCE . . . Are we Outstanding (O), Satisfactory (S) or Unsatisfactory (U)? Check the appropriate column.			
SERVICE	**O**	**S**	**U**
I was greeted promptly and courteously.	—	—	—
The sales associate was knowledgeable about the merchandise or services offered.	—	—	—
Sales transaction was handled accurately and efficiently.	—	—	—
There were enough sales associates on the floor to serve me.	—	—	—
The return policy is . . .	—	—	—
Overall I rate the service as . . .	—	—	—
MERCHANDISE			
The store's merchandise represents a good value for the money.	—	—	—
The store carries styles I like.	—	—	—
The store has a good selection in my size.	—	—	—
Advertised merchandise was sufficiently in stock.	—	—	—
OPERATIONS			
The store layout is easy to shop.	—	—	—
The fitting rooms are neat and clean.	—	—	—
Overall I rate the store . . .	—	—	—

Comments: _____

_____

_____

Sales Associate's Name: _____

Department Shopped: _____

Date and Time Shopped: _____

Customer's Name: _____

Address: _____

City, State, Zip: _____

Phone Number: _____

May we call you to discuss your comments?   Yes ___ No ___

THANK YOU FOR YOUR COMMENTS

their bright ideas. These rewards do not have to be monetary; they can be a certificate of recognition, a free lunch, or a day off.

After you gather information from customers, you and your employees need to do the following.

Review and discuss. Every week, try to meet with all of your employees at once, either first thing in the morning or at the end of the day. If your part-time employees are not able to attend, update them in informal discussions. The theme of the meetings should be to share customer satisfaction experiences from the past week—both positive and negative. You and your employees should also review customers' comments and brainstorm on better ways to meet their wants. Determine as a group what you can do to prevent negative situations from occurring in the future, but also emphasize positive scenarios so all employees can learn from one another how to satisfy customers. These meetings should last no longer than 30 minutes. Everyone should leave the meeting focused on how to satisfy the customer all the time.

Once you know what your customers want, you must take action to make sure they remain satisfied with their shopping experiences in your store:

Summarize and communicate recurring complaints to employees to keep them abreast of the situation. Determine the proper course of action needed to reduce the number of complaints. Maintain a log of complaints and how you responded to them; share this with all your employees. Trends in complaints may indicate a need for additional training, new store policies, or different business practices.

Teach employees how to respond to customer calls. Hold practice sessions for employees to brush up on their phone skills. Role-play with your employees to show them how to handle customer phone calls—especially dissatisfied customers. Role-playing should cover both positive and negative situations. The ultimate goal is to make all your employees comfortable dealing with customers.

Educate and empower your employees to act on customer complaints. When customers complain, they want immediate action. Develop a list of complaints and corresponding responses. Make sure that everyone is comfortable with the acceptable ways to resolve customer complaints.

Send personalized thank-you notes to customers who share their suggestions—positive and negative. These notes should be hand-written and come from the owner or manager. Notes should not only thank customers but also indicate what actions you are taking. Consider sending a gift certificate as a bonus.

Respond in writing to letters from customers. The owner should personally respond to people writing with complaints or suggestions and then call to reinforce the commitment. Indicate what actions you are taking, and be sure to thank customers for taking the time to write. The worst thing you can do is not respond to customers who took time from their busy lives to write.

Promote services. Hang signs around your store to highlight the services that you offer in response to customers' requests. Some commonly requested services are home delivery, custom orders, and same-day alterations. You should also promote any price-guarantee policy.

COMPETITIVE RESPONSE

Nothing Motivates Like Stiff Competition

Because of the influx of mass merchants, category killers, and other chain formats, small-store retailers need to constantly respond to competitive forces; otherwise they will not survive. The most important elements of competitive response, therefore, are the motivation and ability to change. Eighty-eight percent of Illinois small-store retailers ranked competitive response high in importance, and 79 percent ranked their performance as fair or good (see Figure 2-8).

To maintain a competitive advantage, however, small-store retailers must be prepared to respond quickly and decisively to moves by competitors. The survey reveals that many small-store retailers do not focus enough effort on their competition. While most retailers know their competition, 30 percent of the respondents say they have no strategy to respond. Their excuse: lack of time to design and execute a comprehensive strategy. And many retailers wrongly believe that customers will shop at a store today just because they did yesterday. Understanding the competition involves reading their ads, shopping their stores, and talking with

Figure 2-8 Most retailers know who their competition is, but many do not have a strategy to respond. When asked whether they have such a strategy, 30 percent of retailers said they do not.

Retailers' breakdown of importance and performance for competitive response

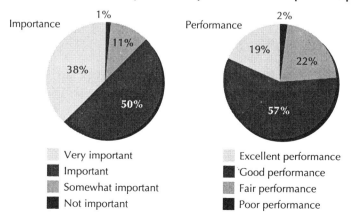

customers and other retailers, although only half of the retailers use the latter two methods (see Figure 2-9). If small-store retailers do not keep a watchful eye on the competition, they will lose to retailers who do a better job of serving customers.

Successful retailers constantly adopt ideas from others, tailor them to their own images, and use them to distinguish themselves from the competition. When a competitor acts, the retailer must analyze the implications to his business and respond, if appropriate. Of the 70 percent of retailers who do have a strategy to respond to competition, the most common tactics are to improve the service level and increase the merchandise selection (see Table 2-3).

Retailers need to keep in mind that just expanding their merchandise selection does not give them a competitive advantage—particularly if they end up carrying the same merchandise as the competition. In fact, they ultimately assume more risk because of the higher cost of carrying more inventory. A more effective technique is to offer some unique merchandise or services that the competition does not offer. The first key step is to understand the competition and why people shop there. The second is to put in place a plan that will create a competitive advantage for the retailer.

Figure 2-9   Only half of the respondents either ask customers where they shop or talk with other area retailers to obtain valuable information about competitors.

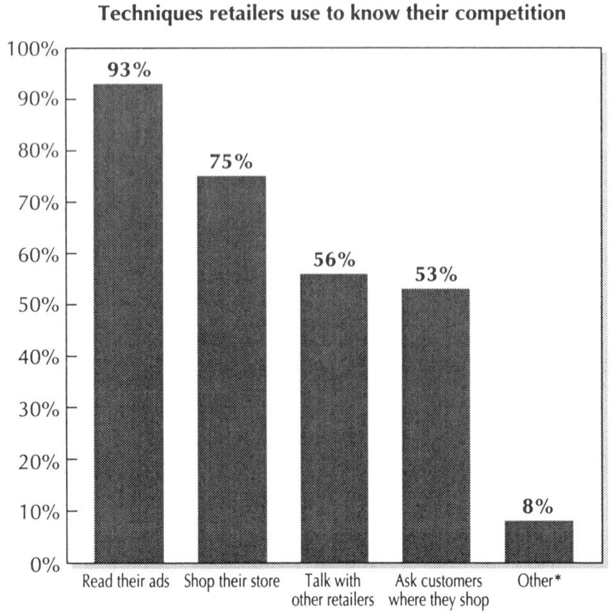

Techniques retailers use to know their competition

* Includes vendor and employee feedback.

Table 2-3   Retailers correctly identify ways to respond to competition. They should also emphasize unique merchandise and service.

Actions retailers take to respond to competitor tactics (in order of importance as ranked by retailers)

- Improve service level
- Increase merchandise selection
- Lower prices on selected items
- Increase merchandise depth
- Increase spending on advertising
- Increase store promotional events
- Add value-added services
- Increase merchandise categories
- Eliminate merchandise categories
- Expand store hours
- Increase number of sales events
- Raise prices on selected items
- Publicize price-match guarantees

Best Practices You Can Use

You can employ a number of techniques to understand your competition better and to respond more effectively:

Talk with customers.   Ask customers in the store or at focus groups about other places they shop and why. Also ask what merchandise and services competitors do or do not offer.

Shop the competition.   Pay close attention to price, merchandise variety, ambiance, employee attitude, and service. Plan to shop the competition on a regular basis—at least once a month. Remember that your competition is not just the stores in your local area but also at the mall that may be 60 miles away. Look for things they are doing and determine how you can do them better. For example, if no one greets you when you walk in the door of another store, be certain your employees greet all your customers.

Analyze competitors' advertisements.   How often do they advertise? In which media? What goods do they showcase? What services do they boast? What sales promotions do they run? Are they more appealing than yours? How many items are in their ad?

Talk with other retailers in your area.   Find out what they know about the competition and how they know it. How do they then respond? Share ideas. If the competitor is a major mass merchant, consider joining together as a team to respond.

Once you know what you're up against, you can respond accordingly. Here are some ways to defend or enhance your market share.

Improve the service level. Greet customers by name whenever possible. Make them feel welcome and at home. Help them find what they're looking for. Don't let the sales staff pass customers off from one salesperson to the next. Have salespeople help customers shop the entire store, not just the department they are assigned to. If customers pay by check or credit card, thank them by name for their purchase. Thank them for patronizing your store.

Stock unusual items and hard-to-find sizes of common items that competitors don't offer, or be willing to find such items through special ordering. Creating a unique niche will attract more customers. See the section on unique products in the merchandising chapter.

Lower prices on selected items. Compare the store's prices to the competition's and make adjustments if necessary. If you and your competition carry the same brands of basic merchandise (e.g., snow shovels) and their price is $2 less, lower your price to meet the competition. Unless you offer a value-added service beyond what the competition does, you must meet the competitor's price. Consider offering a well-publicized price-match guarantee.

Adapt store hours to customers' lifestyles. Find out from customers what hours they want the store to be open, and give time-constrained consumers those hours. If you decide to change store hours, make sure to advertise the change. See the section titled "Time-Constrained Consumers Want to Shop Around the Clock" in the chapter on store operations.

Spruce up the decor. A clean store, background music, and light fragrance can work wonders. Is the light bright enough? If your store looks rundown or "tired" compared to the competition, it could be time to add a fresh coat of paint and new carpeting.

Create pleasant surprises. Use small giveaways that surprise customers. Give a tie to everyone who purchases a suit. Give out free samples of that new private-label candy. Such personal touches provide opportunities to boost customer loyalty and liquidate seasonal or slow-moving merchandise.

Expand value-added services. Customers appreciate home delivery and special ordering, but ask them what other services they want. Think creatively. Many customers shop stores because they offer value-added services. See the section titled "Customers Appreciate Those Little Extras" in this chapter for more information on value-added services.

Focus your advertising on competitive advantages. Let customers know what your store offers in terms of merchandise and services that the competition doesn't offer. Tell them why you're different. If you offer custom-made suits or free alterations and your competition doesn't, be sure to advertise it.

Adjust merchandise categories within a department. Ask yourself whether too much floor space is devoted to slow-moving or low-margin items by comparing sales and margin per square foot to available square footage committed to the department. Try alternative merchandise presentations and formats to create some excitement. For example, instead of neatly stacking pens and selling them for 50 cents each, put them in a bin display and offer them at two for $1 or buy two and get one free. You will be surprised at the results a simple change can make.

Increase the breadth and depth of merchandise selection to go beyond what the competition carries in certain departments or categories. With a wider selection of merchandise, customers will have a better chance of finding what they seek. They will begin to identify your store with its power categories. If your competition only offers three brands of televisions, consider carrying more brands and different models. If the competition offers only 17- and 27-inch TVs, consider carrying 17-, 21-, 27-, 31-, and 35-inch TVs.

Offer an extended warranty or service contract—and advertise it. Customers want to know that you stand behind your merchandise.

Host in-store promotional events. Contests and prize drawings increase store traffic and can garner media attention. For example, the contest or prize drawing could be for a free shopping spree at your store. Promotions need to be advertised so they draw customers to the store.

ADVERTISING, PUBLIC RELATIONS, AND DIRECT MAIL

Extra! Extra! Advertising and PR Let Customers Read All about It

Most retailers agree that their advertising, public relations, and direct-mail strategies are important. But they fall short in performance: Almost half rank their performance in advertising as just fair (see Figure 2-10), few devote much effort to public relations (see Figure 2-11), and 53 percent of retailers either do not maintain customer database information or do not use available database information to market their products or services (see Figure 2-12 on page 51).

The simple fact is that most retailers do not recognize the potential benefits of implementing a comprehensive marketing strategy. The right mix of marketing efforts can make a big difference in a retailing business. It can boost store traffic, establish a store's personality and image, and distinguish the store from the competition.

Figure 2-10   Advertising can either boost business or financially drain the store. Retailers must measure the effectiveness of their ads so they know they are spending their advertising dollars wisely.

Retailers' breakdown of importance and performance for advertising strategy

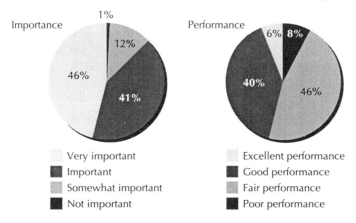

The most critical component of such an integrated marketing plan is advertising. A creative, well-executed ad will grab consumers' attention and pull them into the store. Today, an overwhelming number of advertising media exist, including local television, radio, newspaper, billboard, catalog, coupons, signage, and point of sale materials. Retailers sometimes overlook radio, which under the right circumstances can be more cost-effective than both print and television.

Figure 2-11   Public relations is often overlooked as an effective way to convey a store's message to existing and potential customers.

Retailers' breakdown of importance and performance for public relations

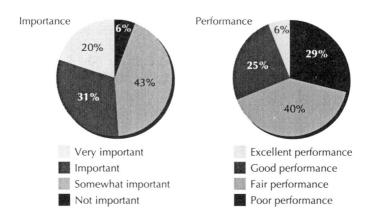

Figure 2-12 Fifty-three percent of retailers either do not maintain databases or do not use database information that is maintained for marketing products or services. Either they do not realize how this information can help them reach their customers or they do not know how to apply it to their operating decisions.

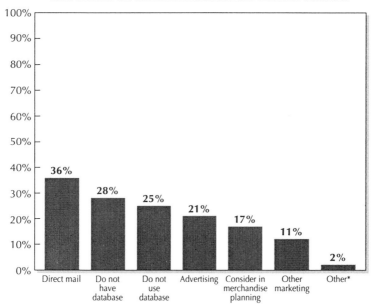

How retailers use information maintained in customer databases

* Includes calling customers to tell them about new merchandise.

Effective advertising requires creative and analytical thinking. In addition to developing the creative message, however, retailers need to choose the right advertising mix, decide the proper frequency, and measure the return rate. Many retailers are uncertain of the right medium because they don't know how to measure the effectiveness of their ads (see Figure 2-13). Almost 50 percent of retailers say they "just know" how effective their ads are, but, as retailer John Wanamaker once said, "I know only half of my advertising is working. The problem is, I don't know which half." There is no way to be certain unless retailers formally track increases in customer traffic or sales affected by different advertising formats, which is what successful retailers are doing. Retailers can also ask customers if they saw their ads or how they heard about the store, but neither of these methods is as reliable as tracking response rates based on the medium used. There is a simple way to evaluate the relative costs of like media. Cost per thousand (CPM) enables retailers to see which ad reaches the most potential customers in the target market at the lowest cost. CPM should be used to measure target audience reached, however, not total audience. For example:

	Cost of Ad	Circulation to Target Market	CPM
Newspaper X	$500	10,000	$500/10,000 $\times 1,000 = 50
Newspaper Y	$1,000	50,000	$1,000/50,000 $\times 1,000 = 20

This analysis shows that Newspaper Y is a more effective medium. But keep in mind that it does not take into account the effectiveness of the advertisement or the size of the retailer's target market. Using CPM is best when comparing identical media, such as which newspaper, radio station, or television program is a better bet.

Another way to make use of different media outlets is through a public-relations plan, but many retailers overlook this option. Coverage

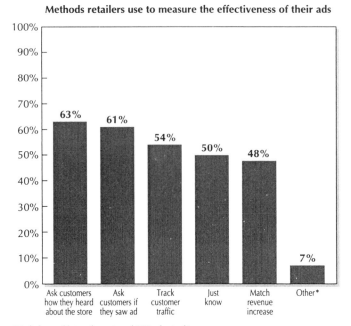

Figure 2-13   Advertising costs too much for retailers to waste money on ineffective ads, yet of the 78 percent of retailers who say they do measure the effectiveness of their ads, 50 percent say they "just know" and don't use any formal tracking.

Methods retailers use to measure the effectiveness of their ads

* Includes weekly trend reports and POS sales tracking.

by the news media of a store, retailer, or new product gives a store third-party objectivity and credibility. Public relations also can be a cost-effective way to reinforce the store's image through "free" advertising and can increase customer awareness and establish good community relations.

Of those retailers who do have public-relations strategies, however, only 56 percent maintain relationships with the local news media, and only 34 percent inform the news media of upcoming in-store events. The reason why so few retailers work with the media is because they have not considered the benefits the local news media can be in promoting their business (see Figure 2-14). Clearly, few retailers give enough consideration to the benefits of good, old-fashioned publicity. In truth, all retailers should have a relationship with the appropriate editors of the local newspaper. News reporters are always looking for stories, and retailers have the chance to prove themselves as "good sources." While conventional advertising and public-relations strategies are strong elements of a combined marketing effort, Figure 2-15 shows that retailers often ignore one of the most cost-effective marketing strategies—direct mail. Direct mail enables retailers to target a specific demographic market that is well

Figure 2-14   Not enough retailers recognize the benefits of maintaining relationships with local news media, among them promotion of in-store events. Retailers who do not feel public relations is important should consider how it can help develop a store's image.

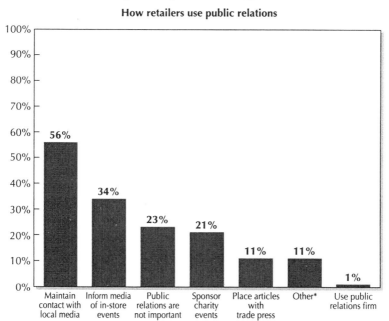

How retailers use public relations

* Includes sports sponsorships and vendor public relations programs.

Figure 2-15 Retailers must determine the effectiveness of their advertising and take that into account when creating an advertising strategy. One way for retailers to measure effectiveness is to make coupons available to customers. Direct mail will help retailers focus on target markets.

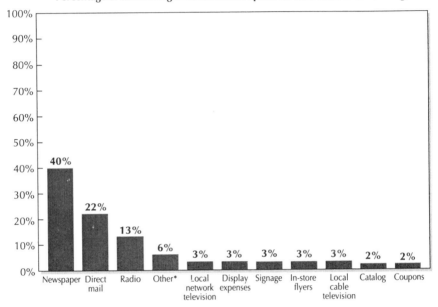

Percentage of advertising dollars retailers spend on each form of advertising

* Includes church bulletins, yellow pages, billboards, and magazines.

suited to the store and its merchandise. With the proper list, retailers can go directly to the homes of legitimate prospects and receive response rates between 3 and 12 percent.

Powerful direct-mail campaigns can be facilitated with the help of today's simple-to-use databases. But many small-store retailers do not take advantage of the marketing potential of basic customer information maintained in database form (see Figure 2-16).

Managing such a database will help retailers better understand customers' buying habits. This way, they can develop special promotions that cater to individual segments of the customer base. By identifying over a period of time those customers who are most likely to respond to direct mail, effective database management can also help reduce advertising and promotion expenses.

Seventy-two percent of retailers capture database information. According to retailers surveyed, the most important information is customer name, address, zip code, and phone number. Although this basic information is necessary, other data, such as what the customer purchased most recently and how often the customer makes a purchase, is just as important. This will tell the retailer how valuable that customer really is to

Figure 2-16 Gathering customer information does not require expensive, complicated systems. Personal computers and customer books work well.

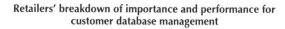

Retailers' breakdown of importance and performance for customer database management

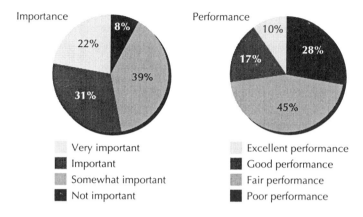

the business. And the customer's birthday, anniversary, and family size can help the retailer with additional direct-marketing efforts.

One example of a popular direct-mail technique is to send a card and coupon worth 20 percent off during the customer's birthday or anniversary month. Or retailers can invite their most frequent shoppers to join a frequent buyer program. Or retailers can send surveys to a random sampling of customers in an effort to determine customer wants and satisfaction.

Over the next several years, Arthur Andersen expects that a number of new software products to help retailers identify and attract customers will hit the market. Also, third-party companies with proprietary consumer databases are realizing they can sell access to these databases. Citibank, through a service called CitiProfile, offers data on 30 million Citibank Visa and MasterCard cardholders. This data contains valuable insight into consumers' buying behavior.

Best Practices You Can Use

An effective marketing strategy should include a combination of advertising, public relations, and database-driven direct mail. Successful retailers use the following practices.

Hire an advertising agency, public relations firm, or marketing specialist to analyze your current advertising strategy or develop one for you. An advertising agency can provide information on the demographics of your community, including age, family size, and income level. This information can then be used to create a focused advertising campaign to attract the greatest number of potential customers. Hiring an outside agency will free up your time and allow you to focus on customer service. Other community retailers or the local chamber of commerce may be able to refer you to an agency.

Ask customers to bring in the flyer or postcard they received in the mail. Track the number of mailings redeemed versus the number mailed. Every time you send out a flyer or any other form of mailing to your target customers, indicate that they need to bring in the mailing to receive the sale price. By doing so, you can measure the redemption rate. You will soon know what form of mailing or promotion generates the greatest response. The other benefit you receive is knowing what part of the community shops at your store. For example, if you sent out a mailing to the entire community and 90 percent of those returned were from the west side of town, you know to focus future similar mailings on that part of town. However, don't just rely on results of one mailing; watch for patterns to develop after sending out several mailings.

For every advertisement you place, whether it is print or broadcast, include a message that asks customers to mention the ad when they come in. At the point of sale, have sales employees ask customers if they saw your ad and if it drew them into the store. Keep in mind, however, that people may not always remember where they saw or heard the ad.

Monitor customer traffic based on the type of medium used. Do TV or print ads bring in more customers? To determine what medium brings in the greatest traffic, promote a sale the first week of the month using only one medium of advertising. Track the number of customers that come into your store and whether they buy anything. Then run the same promotion several weeks later using a different advertising medium, and again track customer traffic. This comparison method works best for promotions with specific beginning and ending dates. This will provide a comparison between two forms of advertising media and tell you which one generates more store traffic. You need to do this several times to get the true picture of which medium works best because other factors figure into the equation, such as weather, competitors' promotions, and seasonal factors.

Match revenue increases with the advertising medium and style of ad used during a particular time period. For example, don't just compare TV ads to newspaper ads; compare a quarter-page newspaper ad to a half-page ad. Run one type of ad during one month and another type during another month. During each time period, track total sales for the week and compare the two. This works best with promotions that have starting and ending periods. This will give you an indication of which type of advertisement generated the greatest sales. Again, do this comparison several times before you come to a concrete conclusion about which type of advertising to use.

Compute the CPM for different advertising media as indicated above. This will tell you which advertising medium potentially reaches the most consumers at the lowest cost.

Hire interns. Recruit marketing or advertising students from local universities to help create ads or handle mailings. They can also track response rates, so the owner or manager can focus time on customers and other aspects of the business.

Establish contacts with the local news media. Introduce yourself to local newspaper editors and television and radio news producers. Offer to take them to lunch and give them a "get acquainted" tour of your store. Show a genuine interest in their need for legitimate news, and, when the opportunity arises, editors will look to you for help. Editors often include mentions in feature articles and community calendars, so send them announcements whenever your store introduces new goods or sponsors an event.

Position the owner or store manager as a retailing expert. Local reporters often need community experts to comment on a local event or put a local twist on a national story. Offer to share with them what you expect to be the new style for spring, or the latest in lawn and garden equipment. Send the local news media interesting articles you see in trade journals that relate to your merchandise or industry trends.

Call local news editors or send news releases to inform them of upcoming in-store events, such as open houses, tent sales, product demonstrations, or your store's involvement in a charity or community activity. Remember to maintain a consumer-oriented news focus. Announcing a sale is self-serving; announcing a fun, educational event that benefits the community is more likely to receive coverage. News media may help drum up interest by including the information in community calendars. When a new full-time employee is hired or an existing employee is promoted, send an announcement to the local newspapers. It's good publicity for your store and boosts employee morale.

Establish a community-oriented strategy. Sponsor a sports clinic or cooking class to educate or entertain the community; such an event could qualify as a good story. Also try to link your event to a community activity like a Boy Scout trip or a Toys For Tots campaign. News media are generally interested in such stories—and your customers will appreciate your contributions.

Sponsor charity or community events—they frequently garner media attention. Contact local charities or the chamber of commerce to find out about upcoming events. Then inform the news media of your support.

Write a column for the local newspaper. Editors like articles on household hints, product safety tips, hot new fashions and products, and how customers can use and benefit from these new products. Of course, match such articles with your merchandise. Send announcements of new and unique merchandise. Pitch a story on consumer trends, based on your customers' buying habits and wants.

Create a database for use in direct mailing. See the section titled "Profiling Gives Retailers a Picture of Their Customers" in this chapter for information on how to start and manage a database. Use the data to send specially tailored offers. For example, a children's clothing retailer will save money and have a higher response rate if he sends flyers promoting a back-to-school sale only to parents of school children. With direct mail, retailers can afford to send customized direct-mail packages. The cost of sending a sample of a new perfume to women who have bought perfume from you before is a worthwhile expense, because these women are more likely to buy from you again.

IMAGE DEVELOPMENT

Store Image Lets Customers Know What to Expect

Image is one of the most important assets for retailers, say 92 percent of respondents to the Illinois survey (see Figure 2-17). Why? A store's image, incorporating its unique attributes and level of customer devotion, separates the retailer from the competition. If a store does not have a distinct image, customers will have no reason to remember why they should shop there. The principal elements that determine a retailer's image are price, selection, quality, service, and location. The external look and internal ambiance of the store are also important. But beware: Retailers must deliver on the image they develop. Not delivering on a projected image will create skepticism and mistrust among customers.

There are four perspectives of image. The actual image of the store may not be the same image the owner wants or thinks the store has[2]:

- The image the store wants to project
- The image customers and noncustomers now have of the store
- The image of the store held by its suppliers
- The image held by store employees

To develop or refine an image, retailers must determine the message they want to convey. How? They should build their image based on what

[2] O'Connor, Michael J., "On the Subject of Image." Arthur Andersen International Trends in Retailing.

Figure 2-17 Many small-store retailers need to accentuate their images so their customers have something specific and differentiating to remember after they leave the store.

Retailers' breakdown of importance and performance for image development

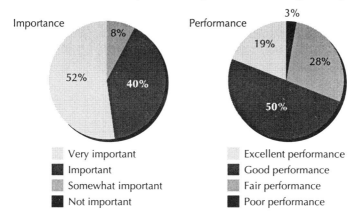

customer surveys indicate customers want. Because possible images run the gamut from low price to excellent service, retailers need to personally ask their customers and noncustomers what they want from the store. Image development begins with deciding what the store wants to project (e.g., its unique products or exciting atmosphere). The next step is communicating this image to customers. Retailers need to match all aspects of their business, including advertising, merchandising, displays, service, accommodations, and employee training, to the desired image (see Table 2-4). If a women's clothing retailer wants his store to be known as the one where customers are waited on hand and foot, he must advertise the store's services, such as personal shopping assistance and wardrobe consultation. He must create a comfortable, relaxing atmosphere with overstuffed chairs, halogen lights, and large fitting rooms. He must train his employees in color coordination, wardrobe planning, and accessorizing.

Owners need to use weekly meetings to communicate to their employees the image they want to portray. This way everyone can unite to give customers a clear idea of what to expect when they enter the store. Retailers must constantly reemphasize their desired image to their employees so the entire team can deliver on that image at every opportunity.

Demonstrating that customers are important is a key ingredient of any image, so retailers need to constantly communicate with their customers, and listen and respond to them. But as Figure 2-18 shows, retailers are severely lacking in this area. Retailers may say they are friendly to customers, but what does this mean? Smiling and genuine friendliness are two different things.

Table 2-4   Retailers need to send a consistent message
concerning their image. Some methods include
using music in the store, carefully designing ads,
promoting events, and hiring employees who reflect
the customer profile.

How retailers communicate their image (in order of importance as ranked by retailers)	
• Store ambiance	• Store frontage
• Visual merchandising	• Store signage
• Advertising	• Employee attire
• Depth and breadth of merchandise	• Price
• Employee communications	• Direct mail or catalog
• Location	• Public relations

Small-store retailers need to distinguish themselves to create loyal
customers. As evidenced in Figure 2-18, less than half of the respondents
tangibly express their appreciation. They fail to realize the long-term benefits this can bring in creating loyal customers. Salespeople should send
thank-you letters to frequent customers. Owners should send customer
appreciation letters to all their regular customers and Christmas gifts to
their top customers. They should also call their regular customers periodically, thank them for their patronage, and ask them what new merchandise or services they would like to see.

Managers must be role models for the sales staff. All store employees, from the owner to the newest sales associate, need to show they care
by continually seeking customer input and treating everyone who enters
the store like a longtime, valued customer. It takes a lot of time and effort
to gain a customer, but it is so easy to lose one by simply ignoring her
or not letting her know how important she is to you. The most successful retailers realize this and cater to their best customers at every opportunity.

Best Practices You Can Use

Several ways exist for you to communicate your store's image.

Visual merchandising. Display your merchandise in a way that customers
know what you carry. An electronics retailer that wants to be known for
televisions should have a wall display of TVs so customers immediately
know what the store image is. Visual merchandising can also accentuate

Figure 2-18 Giving gifts to the most important customers, calling customers, and sending them appreciation letters goes a long way toward enhancing customer satisfaction and creating loyal customers. If a retailer doesn't do these things, competitors will.

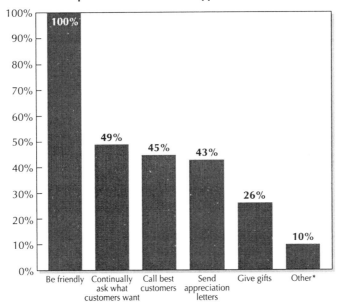

Techniques retailers use to show appreciation for customers

* Includes preferred customer programs.

the mood and romance of the merchandise. For example, good visual merchandising can turn ordinary blue jeans into a clothing adventure.

Advertising. Advertise the unique merchandise and services you offer. This should be done in every advertising medium used. If you promise same-day alterations, in-home fittings, or free pick-up and delivery, then advertise it, especially if it's a competitive advantage.

Depth and breadth of merchandise. If you want to be known for great depth or breadth of merchandise, be willing to invest in the inventory level needed to support that image.

Employee communications. Continually compare customers' comments, store policies, and merchandise with your desired store image. Communicate that information to your employees during weekly meetings, and emphasize the image you want to be known for. Use posters in break rooms that spell out your image so employees are constantly reminded of what is expected of them. Consider using in-house memos or newsletters to communicate image issues to employees.

Store design. Match exterior and interior designs and displays with merchandise offerings. If you offer unique merchandise that sets your store apart, make sure it is prominently displayed. If you want to be known for your men's suit selection instead of your sportswear, make sure customers can tell that immediately from your window displays and sales floor. Also, place signs in the storefront windows that announce your value-added services.

Store signs. Use in-store signs to let customers know what your store offers in terms of products and services. If you want to highlight your liberal return policy, place signs at each register. If you have a wide merchandise selection or various departments within your store, provide a store directory at each entrance and on each floor. Use hanging signs in each department. These signs should be large and positioned so that customers can quickly find the department they are looking for.

Employee attire, attitude, and behavior. Consider having employees wear the clothes that you sell if you are an apparel retailer. Have all employees wear name tags—including the owner and manager. The behavior you expect from your employees must be communicated through one-on-one training and meetings with the entire staff. The owner and manager must always lead by example.

Price. If you want to be known for low prices, make certain that you are in fact the area's low-price retailer on most items. This can only be accomplished by shopping the competition on a weekly basis. Then advertise this image and promote any low-price guarantee.

Direct mail or catalog. Send out mailings or catalogs that reflect your store's image. If your store is known for high-quality merchandise, your mailings must be of high quality in terms of design and printing. For example, a fur retailer would not send out photocopies of merchandise that is on sale.

Service level. You must deliver on your image at every opportunity. If you have a hardware store and want customers to come to you for practical, hands-on advice, you must educate your sales force because your customers' expectations will be high. The worst thing you can do is disappoint them.

Civic and charitable activities. Get involved in local charity events. Make sure your customers know about your community involvement by advertising it both in your store signs and in external advertising. Your involvement will help cement existing customer relationships and will likely attract new customers.

Location. Choose a location near other stores with images similar to yours. If you have the option of relocating, go where your customers are. Don't expect them to come to you.

Public relations. Have lunch with a public-relations professional to get ideas of ways others have enhanced their images. This is a low-cost way to get information from consultants.

VALUE-ADDED SERVICES

Customers Appreciate Those Little Extras

Almost 90 percent of respondents say value-added services are important or very important to their businesses (see Figure 2-19). Value-added services are important not only in drawing new customers into the store but also in maintaining the existing customer base. Despite the value retailers place on these services, only 72 percent say they are doing well in this area.

Retailers are not performing up to par because most don't actively seek out specifically what their customers want. In fact, more than 60 percent say they "just know" what their customers want (see Figure 2-20). But let's face it, with the rapid changes taking place today, small-store retailers can't afford to play psychic. And less than 20 percent use any quantifiable

Figure 2-19   Retailers need to better understand what value-added services their customers want and then implement those that are practical.

Retailers' breakdown of importance and performance for value-added services

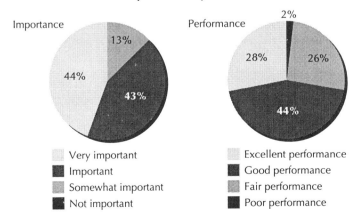

Figure 2-20   To determine what value-added services customers want, retailers need to rely on more than "just knowing." They should collect facts and opinions from focus groups, comment cards, and customer surveys.

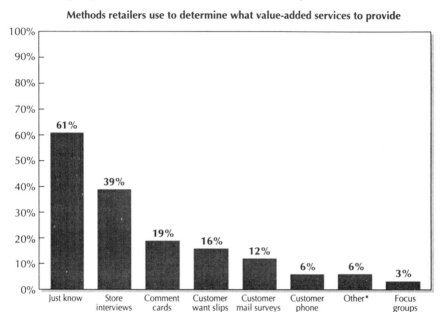

Methods retailers use to determine what value-added services to provide

* Includes employee feedback.

means to determine what value-added services their customers want. The reason: Most retailers do not consider comment cards, surveys, or focus groups to be valuable tools.

Successful retailers conduct focus groups, surveys, and interviews to find out what both their customers and noncustomers want. (For more ideas, see the section titled "Marshall Field: 'Give the Lady What She Wants' " in this chapter.) Retailers should also check out the competition to see what other stores do or do not offer. Retailers need to ask customers what services they want. They should compile customer wish lists and implement as many value-added services as they can. Arthur Andersen research indicates that the value-added services that customers most frequently request are those that save them time and money. Gift wrapping, at-home repair, and assembly are among such services.

Then retailers must use advertising and in-store signage to promote their value-added differences as aggressively as possible. Retailers also need to keep in mind that customers are willing to pay for certain services, such as delivery and gift wrapping, if they save the customer valuable time or effort.

The importance of value-added service cannot be over-emphasized; just selling merchandise is not enough. Undeniably, small-store retailers can distinguish themselves with value-added services, especially when competing against large retailers who don't personally know their customers. To do this, retailers must identify the services that customers want that are not being offered. For example, 86 percent of retailers feel their customers want knowledgeable product assistance, but only 38 percent try to educate the customers themselves. Of course, not every store can offer every service shown in Figure 2-21. The key services to offer are those that customers request the most. Appliance stores might offer free assembly, for example, or apparel stores might offer alterations.

Best Practices You Can Use

Some of the following suggestions may entice customers into your store. But remember that you will need to promote these services both internally and externally. Use signs and tell customers about the value-added services you offer.

Product education and knowledge classes. Hold how-to classes for your customers in which you teach them to cook, hang wallpaper, or draw.

Figure 2-21 Value-added services should correlate more closely with what customers want. Although 86 percent of retailers feel that customers want knowledgeable product assistance, only 38 percent offer this as a value-added service.

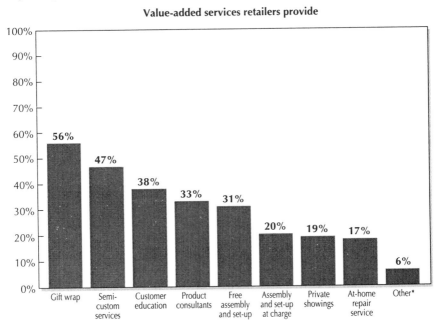

* Includes special orders, rentals, and in-store repair service.

These classes should take place in your store. This way you have a captive audience of customers and can get to know them personally. Highlight your new merchandise during the demonstration.

Product consultants. Interior decorators on staff can save home remodelers a lot of headaches—and win the store some happy and vocal customers. Have the product consultants meet customers at home at the customer's convenience. Make sure consultants have solid product knowledge and good people skills.

House calls. Send a technician to the customer's home or office to fix the vacuum instead of requiring the customer to bring the appliance into the store. Offer to bring the customer's purchases to their house so they don't have to carry them around.

Special ordering. Offer to order a different size shirt for a customer or to locate merchandise you normally don't carry. Or offer to service an appliance, even though the customer bought it somewhere else.

Assembly assistance. Consider preassembly and adjustment of bicycles, stereo components, and VCRs. Offer to demonstrate to the customer how to program, adjust, or use their new product.

Gift wrapping. Time-constrained consumers will always appreciate this service.

Mailing. Offer to send customers' purchases anywhere in the United States.

Private showings. Give preferred customers a sneak preview of new merchandise, showering them with personal attention. Call your preferred customers to invite them to these showings. They should be held at times convenient to the customers. You could even consider showing new merchandise at your customers' homes.

Gift registry. This is a common practice for brides and grooms, but it also works well for Mother's Day, Christmas, birthdays, and anniversaries. Customers can indicate what merchandise they would like to receive. Use this information to enhance your customer database and profiles, and use this information for direct-marketing efforts. When gift-buyers come in, they can choose something they know the receiver needs. Make sure to check off the merchandise bought to avoid duplicate gifts. You can even use preprinted forms with common gift items. For example, a successful hardware retailer uses a form that lists gift items such as power tools and gardening equipment. But leave room on the form for other items, too.

Storage. A customer may not have room for her new couch until she moves next month, so offer to store it for her. Although this is an expensive short-term cost, it may pay off in a grateful customer. You can offer free storage, or you can pass some of the expense on to the customer.

Personal shopping services. Some bookstores, for example, take customers' wish lists over the phone, find the books, and reserve them.

ALTERNATIVE MARKETING STRATEGIES

Product Demos and Fashion Shows Attract Customers

Alternative marketing strategies, especially target marketing and in-store promotions, can distinguish retailers, generate excitement, and increase customer traffic and sales. Retailers recognize this, as 73 percent of them feel nontraditional marketing techniques are important or very important (see Figure 2-22). But, as in other areas, most retailers say they could do better. Only half believe they are doing a good or excellent job.

Small-store retailers who value alternative marketing strategies try to focus on specific customer profiles, such as new parents or homeowners. Identifying and understanding different customer types and needs are the first steps in implementing alternative marketing strategies. The best prospects are existing customers, so retailers should use data collected from customer books as well as frequent-buyer programs. See the sections titled "Extra! Extra! Advertising and PR Let Customers Read All

Figure 2-22   "If you build it, they will come" does not apply here. Instead, retailers need to consider nontraditional methods of marketing to boost store traffic.

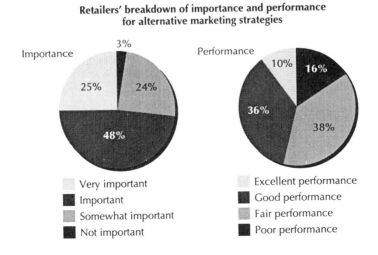

Retailers' breakdown of importance and performance for alternative marketing strategies

Importance
3%
25% 24%
48%

Performance
10% 16%
36% 38%

Very important
Important
Somewhat important
Not important

Excellent performance
Good performance
Fair performance
Poor performance

About It" and "Profiling Gives Retailers a Picture of Their Customers" in this chapter for information on how to establish customer databases and measure the effectiveness of target-marketing efforts.

Once retailers know what their customers are looking for, they can target those needs through target marketing and in-store promotions. More than 80 percent of small-store retailers use target marketing in one form or another. The most common techniques are supporting community organizations and advertising to target markets (see Figure 2-23). While these are steps in the right direction, many retailers fail to properly use target marketing to reach new customers. In many cases, retailers are not sure where or how to find those prospects. Yet many sources exist for such lists; retailers can begin by contacting advertising representatives from their local newspaper or Yellow Pages publisher. One example: A hardware store could send a flyer to every new homeowner in the area.

Likewise, the majority of retailers use some form of in-store promotions, such as drawings and product demonstrations, to increase customer traffic and awareness. But the 21 percent who don't are missing out on a great opportunity to create fun, exciting stores that will attract more customers and increase sales (see Figure 2-24). Examples of in-store events

Figure 2-23 Eighty percent of retailers use some form of target marketing. Contacting new residents and new homeowners deserves more consideration, however.

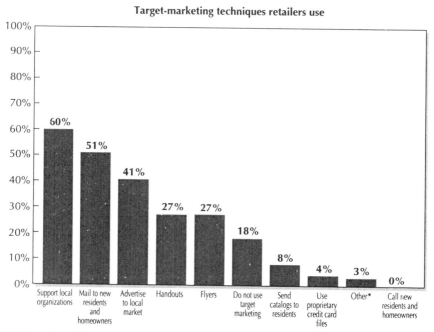

* Includes sending mailings to new parents and grandparents.

Figure 2-24 The 79 percent of retailers who do use in-store promotions create excitement and entice customers into their stores. Drawings are used by 67 percent of these respondents and are an effective promotional device.

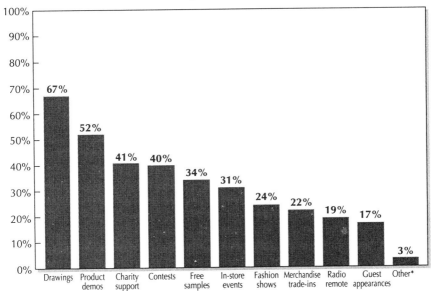

In-store promotions retailers use

* Includes book signings and trunk showings.

include Customer Appreciation Week, when customers get refreshments and a special gift, and Trade-In Day, when customers can trade in their old vacuums for new ones, for example.

To be fully effective, target marketing, advertising, signs, and publicity must support the in-store promotions. The promotion used should be a planned activity in which one or more products are given special sales support. The most common promotional methods are short-term price reductions and in-store events. The objectives of the promotion should be to increase customer traffic, increase transaction size, generate cash flow, enhance or reinforce customers' image of the store, or correct an inventory problem.

After each promotion, retailers should determine if they met their original objectives. If not, retailers must look for ways to improve their promotions by increasing advertising or using a different in-store event. Consistently offering the same in-store promotion will ultimately bore customers.

Best Practices You Can Use

The following are examples of target-marketing techniques.

Send flyers to new residents in the community, informing them of the store's services and merchandise. This provides you with a fresh, impressionable audience. You can obtain names and addresses of new residents from the local chamber of commerce, recorder of deeds, local newspaper, or welcome-wagon publication.

Send merchandise catalogs or flyers to households that reflect the demographic profile of your target customers. Purchase mailing lists from marketing companies, or begin to develop your own list. To determine the demographic profile of your target customer, ask for information on proprietary credit card applications, customer surveys, or comment cards.

Work with other retailers. Coordinate cross promotions with other retailers. For example, a fur retailer and a jewelry retailer can send a combined merchandise catalog or cosponsor a special event. A health club and shoe retailer can cross-market discounts on aerobics classes with athletic shoes. Examples of in-store promotions:

- *Product demonstrations (seasonally or when new products arrive).* Show customers how to use that handy new appliance.
- *Fashion shows.* Team up with a local club, like the Girl Scouts or PTA, and use members to model the store's new fashions. Offer discounts on the clothes the models are showing.
- *Special day or time promotions.* Invite senior citizens to have a shopping time all their own. Or invite store associates, friends, and family members to browse through the merchandise after hours.
- *Prize drawings.* With every $50 purchase, a customer can enter to win a gift certificate or free merchandise.
- *Contests.* Ask customers to submit their children's artwork in a contest. The child with the winning picture gets a new toy, and the parents win a shopping spree.
- *Free samples.* Surprise customers with purse-sized samples of that hot new fragrance.
- *Charity events.* For every $25 a customer spends, give $1 to a local hospital.
- *Local guest appearances.* Ask a local author to autograph copies of his book in the store.
- *Merchandise trade-ins.* Have customers bring in their oldest, dirtiest pair of shoes and give them a 25 percent discount on a new pair.
- *Gifts with purchase.* Put a sharp handkerchief in the pocket of a customer's new suit.
- *Bundling.* If a mop and cleaning fluid would cost $6 when purchased separately, sell them for $5 when purchased together.
- *Radio remotes.* Call a favorite radio station and ask them about broadcasting live from the store. The station will help with the promotion, but be prepared to pay.

- *Cross-promote.* The cross-promotional marketing idea mentioned earlier also works with in-store promotions. An apparel store and a shoe store located near each other can run a joint promotion, such as a fashion show.

CUSTOMER PROFILING

Profiling Gives Retailers a Picture of Their Customers

Getting an idea of the store's typical customer, commonly called customer profiling, can be achieved in a relatively short time (six to nine months). Most retailers, 92 percent, say customer profiling is important or very important, but only 64 percent say they are doing it well (see Figure 2-25). Most of the retailers who successfully profile their customers capture the information at the point of purchase.

The reason retailers lag in performance is because almost half of them do not recognize the benefits of tracking customers' purchases by store, department, category, class, or SKU (see Figure 2-26). Yet, as successful retailers are quick to point out, "You can't manage what you can't measure." A formal tracking system helps retailers decide how to merchandise their stores and target their customers. It can also aid in identifying the best customers—who should be catered to in every possible way. And though computerization does aid in tracking sales by customer, it's

Figure 2-25 Although many retailers don't have the technological resources for customer profiling, several low-tech alternatives exist, such as customer books and frequent-buyer programs.

Retailers' breakdown of importance and performance for customer profiling

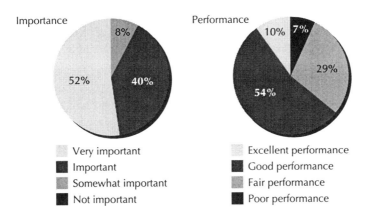

Figure 2-26   Retailers are unable to focus properly on their target customers because they do not track or understand what individual customers are buying. They should record individual purchases to increase sales to these customers and to better merchandise their stores.

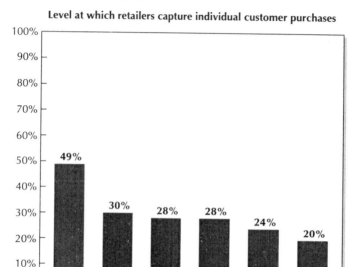

not necessary. Tracking can also be done manually by using customer books, accumulating sales slips by customer, or establishing frequent-buyer programs.

As one respondent said, "Once you understand your customers' tastes and interests, you can tailor your inventory to meet their preferences." This is exactly what successful retailers do. Retailers can also target specific customers with sales promotions. For example, if a retailer knows Megan Reynolds' reading habits, he can call Megan when her favorite author's new book arrives.

Best Practices You Can Use

A variety of ways exist for you to monitor your customers' buying habits, and none of them necessarily require a computer. However, a computer does facilitate the process; it also enables you to manage the information better. Here are some methods of capturing profile information either manually or electronically.

Ask for information to contribute to your database at point of sale. Have customers provide information on index cards while they wait in line, or give them a self-addressed postage-paid card to fill out at home. Consider raffling off a prize to customers who have completed the requested information. Information cards should request the following:

- Customer name
- Address and phone number
- Size of family and ages of family members
- Birthday and anniversary
- Type of merchandise most often purchased at the store

Each time a customer visits your store, write down what she purchased and the date of the visit. Maintain the information on a computer or in customer books.

Track sales slips by customer. If you are running a promotion on a specific department, contact the customers who have bought merchandise from that department.

Maintain customer books. Use index cards to manually track what regular customers are buying.

Analyze sales slips. File sales slips by customer name and take a look at what each customer purchased this month, season, or year.

Institute frequent-buyer programs. Such programs ask customers to complete an application that asks for name, address, phone number, family size, and merchandise preference. Every time a customer makes a purchase, she gets her frequent-buyer card punched. When the card is full, the customer receives a gift certificate based on the volume of purchases in a given calendar year. This type of program provides you with a fairly complete profile of your customers, but you need to consider the costs of such a program, including merchandise costs.

Implement a proprietary credit-card program. Talk to your local bank about getting a store credit card. Private credit cards provide demographic information from the customer's application and make it easy to monitor all credit-card purchases. But before you implement a proprietary credit-card program, evaluate the economics. You will have to compare the benefit of the customer accommodation and increased income with the internal administrative costs, such as payroll cost, processing, and mailing, as well as the cost of financing customer receivables.

ALTERNATIVE DELIVERY CHANNELS

Retailers Must Try to Go Where the Customers Are: Home, Work, Mall

Identifying and executing alternative delivery methods to sell merchandise, such as in-home sales or mail order, is not considered very important by small-store retailers. More than 60 percent of retailers say this is not important or only somewhat important (see Figure 2-27).

Retailers may be on the right track here. Although large-format stores will probably increase their use of alternative delivery channels, most smaller retailers do not have the financial resources to use any high-tech alternative channels such as computer networks or televised home-shopping programs. But in-home presentations, flea markets, and kiosks offer significant cost-effective opportunities for small-store retailers. Still, small-store retailers should first devote their resources to improving their stores.

But there's no denying that opportunities exist here to increase sales. Retailers who have the resources to use alternative delivery channels must talk with their customers and look at what their competition is doing to determine which methods to consider implementing. Retailers need to ask customers, "How can I make your life easier?" Some men's apparel stores, for example, are returning to the good old days of fitting the customer for suits at the customer's home or office.

In addition to giving time-constrained consumers what they want, alternative delivery channels also enable retailers to reach more con-

Figure 2-27   Alternative delivery channels, such as kiosks, leased departments, and catalogs, help retailers snare consumers who are pressed for time.

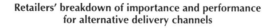

Retailers' breakdown of importance and performance
for alternative delivery channels

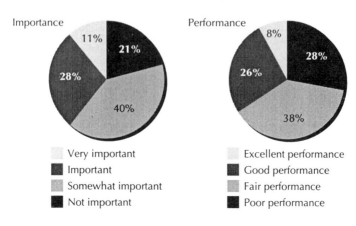

Importance	Performance
11%	8%
21%	28%
28%	26%
40%	38%

Very important — Excellent performance
Important — Good performance
Somewhat important — Fair performance
Not important — Poor performance

sumers (e.g., kiosks or catalogs) and liquidate slow-moving merchandise (e.g., flea markets). As Figure 2-28 shows, some retailers are using a few of the more common alternative delivery methods. To determine what's right for a particular business, retailers should consider anticipated costs, including fixtures, staffing requirements, and inventory. They should also consider potential benefits, including increased sales, profitability, and exposure to new customers.

Home shopping will eventually be a competitive threat to store retailing, but probably not in any significant way for at least 10 to 15 years. Teleshopping, infomercials, and computer shopping still only account for 1 percent of total retail sales.

Best Practices You Can Use

Today's frenzied consumers don't always have the time or the energy to shop in the traditional way. Retailers who have the necessary resources should consider which alternative delivery channels may enable them to meet their customers' needs.

Direct mail and catalogs. Develop a catalog that showcases your merchandise offerings. Purchase a mailing list that matches your customer

Figure 2-28 Other than direct mail, no alternative delivery channels are widely used. However, some low-cost, low-tech options, such as home shopping and kiosks, offer unique opportunities.

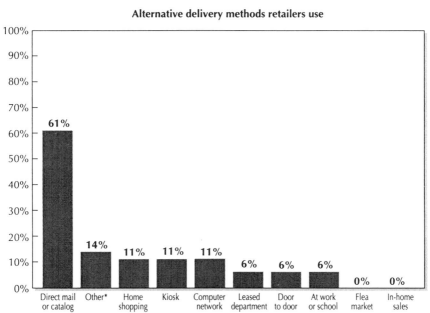

Alternative delivery methods retailers use

* Includes local street fairs.

profile from a direct-marketing database-management company. Ask your local chamber of commerce or other retailers in your area to recommend a direct-marketing company.

In-home shopping. Offer customers an opportunity to shop from the comfort of their home and at their convenience. This is especially effective for targeting housebound customers such as parents with young children, the elderly, and the handicapped.

Leased departments. A department store that carries luggage can contact a local travel agency about the opportunity to set up a luggage display and sell the goods, for example. Offer the travel agency the opportunity to set up a desk in your store so you both receive a mutual benefit and commission for selling each others' products and services.

Kiosks. To boost holiday sales, many retailers open temporary kiosks or rent push carts in malls or at other retail establishments. These are less expensive alternatives to opening up a new store. Not only is the capital requirement less for fixture costs, but also the inventory investment and staffing requirements are much less than a full-line store.

Sidewalk sales. Coordinate a community sidewalk sale with other retailers. This is also a good way to liquidate slow-moving merchandise.

Charity functions. Set up displays at charity functions. Contact the local chamber of commerce to find out about upcoming charity events, and then contact the local charity about the possibility of selling your merchandise at the event. You may be asked to donate a portion of your sale proceeds.

Flea markets. Rent space at the local flea market and set up a display of your merchandise. This is another great way to liquidate slow-moving merchandise.

Door to door. Go to potential customers who can't visit your store. For example, showcase your new robes and slippers at the local nursing home.

At work or school. Work with local businesses and schools to offer product demonstrations.

LESSONS LEARNED FROM CASE STUDIES

Special Attention to Customers Strengthens Retailers' Lifelines

A retailer's lifeline is his customers. That's why the father-and-son team at a paint and wallpaper store in suburban Illinois does everything it can to show customers how much it cares.[3] The best way to do this, according to Richard Snow and his son Dave[4] is to offer unique value-added services—ones that the competition does not offer—that make for satisfied, loyal customers.

Services include on-staff decorating consultants who provide free in-store and in-home consultations and customer education. The services also include in-store seminars and how-to articles they publish in local newspapers.

Of course, to keep customers—even the most loyal ones—retailers need to fight the competition. To this end, keen competitive analysis and quick response are critical, says Kevin Keller, manager of an appliance and electronics store.[5] In addition to visiting local competition, Kevin travels anywhere within 100 miles to glean ideas from other retailers. He pays close attention to customer service, advertising, store layout, and merchandise assortment; these are the areas that can provide the best competitive advantages.

Kevin shares the ideas with his management team, and together they decide how to implement them. Recently they have changed their customer comment cards and advertising and have introduced several unique products.

[3] See Chapter 8 for a complete case study.
[4] Names used are pseudonyms.
[5] See Chapter 8 for a complete case study.

3

MERCHANDISING

Niching, Pricing, and Vendors Should Be Key Merchandising Strategies

Next to customers and marketing, Arthur Andersen and retailers alike believe that the most critical business practice is merchandising. Every activity that a retailer performs has to support merchandising—buying and displaying the goods. As one retailer said, "Merchandising is critical, but the challenges are making time to do it right and knowing where to begin."

To succeed and prosper in the marketplace today, small-store retailers must be more than scaled-down versions of their national chain-store competitors. They must have good quality, selection, service, and price. Small stores must be destinations, attractions unto themselves, where customer wants are met at fair prices and without hassles.

In Arthur Andersen's view, one of the best ways for small-store retailers in Illinois to succeed is through unique, creative, and targeted merchandising. The retailing industry boasts a number of success stories featuring companies that carved their own niches and then grew rapidly. The Gap, The Bombay Company, and Williams-Sonoma are good examples. In all cases, the concepts are simple. And although the stores position their merchandise as specialty goods, they sell essentially commodities or basic goods.

So what makes these retailers successful? Each has developed a niche by displaying the merchandise in a creative way. Small-store retailers can apply these same concepts to their stores. Once a retailer develops a niching strategy, he must execute it with constant attention to detail and changing customer wants.

In today's increasingly competitive environment, merchandising means more than offering the right products at the right price and time and in the right quantities. It means meeting customers' wants and needs by buying and displaying unique products in exciting and creative ways (see Figure 3-1). According to Arthur Andersen, niching, pricing strategy, and vendors are the top issues on which retailers should focus their time and resources over the next year (see Table 3-1):

- *Niching.* Successfully targeting a market segment or specific customer group with a unique mix of merchandise or services that customers see as important.
- *Pricing strategy.* Establishing a set of pricing parameters that meets customer wants and company profit objectives.

Figure 3-1   Retailers need to reprioritize and improve performance levels with niching, pricing strategy, and vendor relations. Open-to-buy has the largest performance gap and is also an area that needs more attention. How do you compare? Ask yourself how important each business practice is to you and how well you perform it. Then fill in the chart in the section on operations assessment.

Comparison of how retailers rank merchandising areas for importance and performance

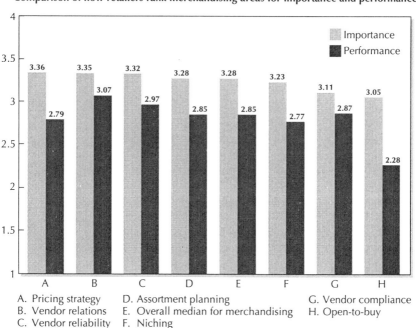

A. Pricing strategy   D. Assortment planning   G. Vendor compliance
B. Vendor relations   E. Overall median for merchandising   H. Open-to-buy
C. Vendor reliability   F. Niching

Table 3-1   Tier rankings

Arthur Andersen's First Tier	Retailers' First Tier
1. Niching	1. Pricing strategy
2. Pricing strategy	2. Vendors
3. Vendors	3. Assortment planning
Second Tier	**Second Tier**
4. Open-to-buy	4. Niching
5. Assortment planning	5. Open-to-buy

- *Vendors.* Developing a trusting relationship in which vendors meet retailers' needs, comply with their terms in delivering merchandise, and work with retailers to meet mutual goals, including vendor relations, compliance and reliability.

Niching represents the single best opportunity for small stores to distinguish themselves. But many retailers do not adequately exploit specific merchandise niches and have trouble pricing merchandise to achieve the ideal sell-through rate. But niching cannot be successful if the strategy only encompasses price, convenience, or service. Rather, successful retailers base their niching strategies on the merchandise itself and the way they display it. Thus, a hardware retailer can carve a niche by presenting every SKU of quality nuts and bolts in a well-organized and user-friendly merchandise display. Many home centers would find it hard to manage such a depth and breadth of items.

National chains, including mass merchants, category killers, and other discounters or specialists, are placing intense pressure on small-store retailers, forcing them to act quickly or lose the bulk of their customer base. Customers today have so many retail choices available to them and so little time to shop. Yet if retailers can offer something that their trade area perceives as unique—either products or services—they can set themselves apart from their larger competitors and exceed customer expectations. Arthur Andersen believes that customers focus their shopping trips to those stores that they are confident will have exactly the items for which they are looking. They know their needs will be met. Other times, their confidence is in the fact that, although they might not know what they want right now, they know they will find something they want once they get into the store. Small-store retailers need to fill voids with merchandise that customers cannot find anywhere else.

For customers to be loyal, they need a retailer they can depend on from the very first shopping experience. Too often, however, customers are disappointed with the shopping experience at one store, so they divide their loyalties among many shopping alternatives. By focusing on a defined niche in the marketplace, retailers can create loyalty by having the right merchandise. That effort, along with an effective pricing strategy consistent with the store's image and good vendor selection to help find the right goods, can go a long way toward building successful merchandising strategies.

Because retailers do not use niching enough, all areas of merchandising may be out of focus. Retailers should rethink their priorities of first-tier and second-tier items accordingly. Second-tier merchandising items include:

- *Open-to-buy (OTB).* Using budgets to control buying activities and merchandise levels.
- *Assortment planning.* Determining classes, styles, colors, and sizes to carry in each category or department.

NICHING

Unique Products and Services Carve Market Niches

In less than 20 years, Gordon Segal of Crate & Barrel turned his one-store, husband-and-wife enterprise into a thriving multistore business that spans the nation. His secret: targeting a niche. As he said recently in a retail trade publication:

> "The excitement in retailing springs from the merchandise. The specialty retailer must have a focused outlook, offer unique merchandise that represents good value, and present it in an environment that is continually exciting. The very essence of retailing is change. Excitement in retailing comes from the search for uniqueness. The fun is not selling what everyone sells. It comes from selling a unique assortment."[1]

Niching is a major merchandising opportunity for small-store retailers, and it affords them greater price flexibility. Unfortunately, according to Arthur Andersen, most retailers do not recognize the potential. Although 88 percent say niching is important or very important, retailers still rank it fourth overall in importance (see Figure 3-2). And 79 percent say their performance is only fair or good.

Arthur Andersen believes that small-store retailers must focus on niching with target markets and key categories if they intend to survive and prosper. Some small-store retailers will find it difficult to niche, but they should see if some elements of niching could help their businesses. Successful retailers differentiate themselves through at least one of the following elements:

[1] *Inside Retailing,* December 1993.

Figure 3-2   The full potential for niching is not recognized by most retailers. Retailers may not be able to keep up with mass merchants' low prices, but they can earn their higher prices by targeting specific groups or by offering better products and services.

Retailers' breakdown of importance and performance for niching

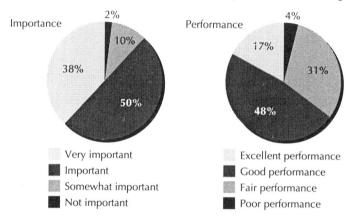

- *Marketing.* Targeting a specific group of customers to serve.
- *Selection.* Consistently offering customers unique products, specialty merchandise, or a breadth or depth of merchandise that is greater than what competitors offer.
- *Quality.* Offering merchandise superior in quality to that of the competition.
- *Service.* Providing customers with trained sales associates who are friendlier and more knowledgeable and helpful than those at the competition.
- *Price.* Offering products at prices as low or lower than those offered by the competition for similar merchandise, or offering greater value with higher prices.
- *Fashion.* Offering fashion-forward merchandise.

As Table 3-2 shows, most retailers rely on service, including customer service and value-added services, to differentiate themselves through value merchandising. Here retailers are moving in the right direction. As noted in the chapter on customers and marketing, customers rank service as one of their primary wants.

Retailers also use quality and selection to differentiate themselves, but they do not feel that fashion is critical to value merchandising. Respondents rank price near the bottom. Small-store retailers will never compete with discounters on price. But that does not mean that they can ignore price as an issue and continue to pass on high prices just because

Table 3-2 Most retailers realize that
they cannot win price wars with mass
merchants and category killers. Instead
they should work for unique selection,
good quality, and value-added services.

**Attributes of value merchandising
(in order of importance as ranked by retailers)**

- Service
- Quality
- Selection
- Price
- Fashion

---

they are downtown and active in the community. Instead, retailers must earn their higher prices by going above and beyond the norm with value-added services, unique products, and a commitment to serve loyal customers.

"The customers eventually reward the store that gives satisfaction, that is more fun to shop in, that doesn't play it safe all the time, that makes it possible for the customer to find an out-of-the-ordinary dress or tie that their friends will notice and ask where they bought it," says Stanley Marcus of Neiman Marcus.[2] Retailers need to consider what is unique to their markets and customers and focus on providing uniqueness within their categories. But it does not appear to Arthur Andersen that small-store retailers have fully embraced the concept of developing niching strategies, perhaps because they do not understand the positive repercussions to their businesses. Figure 3-3 shows that most survey respondents who niche do so by offering unique merchandise. But the definition of unique merchandise varies not only among retailers but also between retailers and customers. Some retailers say their niche is breadth and depth. But if retailers offer the same merchandise as everyone else, they will not stand out regardless of how many colors or sizes they carry (see Figure 3-4, page 85)—that is, unless they are able to display the merchandise in an exciting way or are willing to price lower than their competition.

Other respondents say offering unique merchandise means carrying an expanded assortment of products that appeals more to customer wants. Today's consumers are buying based on wants and needs. Most retailers can satisfy basic needs. Those who can also satisfy wants will have the upper hand.

But customers are finding the same merchandise everywhere they shop. This has caused a significant drop in customer loyalty, particularly among department stores. The problem is buyers' mentality: They want to

---

[2] Marcus, Stanley. *Arthur Andersen Retailing Issues Newsletter.*

Figure 3-3 Although only 38 percent of retailers feel niching is very important to their success, a majority claim they use some niching tactics. To compete more effectively, retailers should target a specific audience and carry unique items.

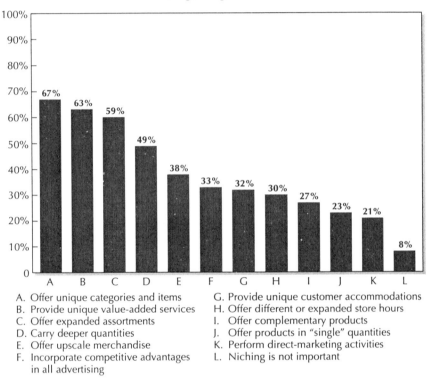

A. Offer unique categories and items
B. Provide unique value-added services
C. Offer expanded assortments
D. Carry deeper quantities
E. Offer upscale merchandise
F. Incorporate competitive advantages in all advertising

G. Provide unique customer accommodations
H. Offer different or expanded store hours
I. Offer complementary products
J. Offer products in "single" quantities
K. Perform direct-marketing activities
L. Niching is not important

play it safe, so they buy low-risk, fast-moving goods from a limited number of vendors, many of whom sell the same assortment of merchandise to all of their accounts. For the creative buyer, unique products may take the form of private-label or imported products, and they may be geared toward specific age groups. Buying groups and co-ops allow greater access to small-store retailers to purchase these goods.

Other ways exist for retailers to carve niches. Ideas might include providing unique services to the customer group that supports a target marketing strategy. Retailers must be sure to incorporate any competitive advantages into their advertising and give consumers a reason to choose their stores over the competition. A shoe retailer on a busy suburban thoroughfare, for example, has a single, oversized storefront sign that proclaims WIDE SHOES. Every person who drives by that store knows exactly what merchandise it carries and what to expect when they step through the door.

Figure 3-4   Setting a store apart from its competition is a key factor in niching. Retailers should offer nationally recognized brands if it makes sense to do so, but private-label merchandise is an important opportunity for retailers. Retailers must work harder to find exciting and unique products. Small-store retailers lack buying power and have difficulty gaining access to these markets for private-label or unique goods.

Factors retailers see as important to competitive advantage

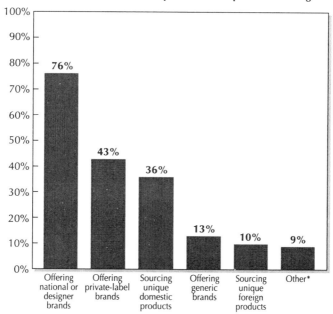

* Includes offering higher quality products.

Another option is to target population niches. In Illinois, African-Americans comprise 15 percent of the population, Hispanics comprise 8 percent, and Asian-Americans comprise 2 percent.[3] Such population segments present prime niching opportunities for Illinois retailers.

Best Practices You Can Use

To carve the right niche for your customers and differentiate yourself from the competition, you first need to develop a plan of attack.

Recognize what you really are.   Assess your store to find out what kind of store image you portray and what your customers truly think. Also take a

[3] Adapted from *Market Statistics*, 1993. 1993 Demographics, USA-County Edition.

look at your strengths and weaknesses. Look for independent and objective thinking from customers, other local noncompeting retailers, and your business advisers. Bring in your management team and sales associates. Measure your business against criteria your customers establish. Successful retailers accumulate specific data on their stores on a continual basis but perform a formal assessment at least once a year.

Commit to and develop a niching strategy. Decide where you want to improve and where you want to excel. You need to focus on your strengths and what you can do well. Work with your store team to create a timeline and responsibility chart that highlights key dates when and by whom niching strategies are to be implemented. Get buyers and sales associates involved. Soon you will distinguish your store from the market-hungry competitors.

You can choose from a variety of niching tactics. You must, however, differentiate yourself in your customers' eyes, so make sure you incorporate their thoughts into your efforts.

Target specific markets. Is there a group of customers or type of customer that other retailers in the market are not servicing adequately? Form a store image and merchandising strategy to focus on that target group.

Increase selection. Identify voids in your competitors' product lines, then fill those voids. Offering more selection and one-stop shopping gives customers a reason to shop at your store. For example, if a mass merchant is offering soap in multipacks, you can expand your offering of single units. The key is to have depth in the categories that you consider to be your most powerful. Focus on your strengths, but be careful. If you expand your merchandise in one department, you may have to cut back in another. One more idea: Work with a variety of vendors. More vendors can mean more new, exciting products. Ask them about new selection ideas. This may be difficult if you are like many small-store retailers, who would rather consolidate their purchases among fewer vendors. But Arthur Andersen believes more vendors mean more opportunities to niche during a time when larger national chains are reducing the number of vendors they use.

Improve quality. If a competitor has a few low-quality products, advertise your high-quality counterparts. This is a common and effective practice for electronics retailers, where many small-store retailers emphasize their high-end national brands.

Offer friendly, knowledgeable service. Many consumers view discounters as cold, impersonal, and uninformed. Successful small-store retailers actively try to fill that gap with great service. One Illinois paint and wallpaper retailer advertises the fact that his salespeople are trained interior decorators who provide free in-home and in-store consultation. Another way to improve service is to change or expand store hours.

Emphasize price integrity. Lowering your prices across the board to compete effectively against mass merchants is a strategy for financial suicide. But emphasizing price integrity and consistency can distinguish you from a chain store if you offer better value. Genuine value, not low price, creates loyal customers.

Carry up-to-date fashions. Ask your vendors what's in style. Check around at buying and trade shows for the unusual products that are not usually available in your trading area. Browse through consumer magazines. Travel and expose yourself to the world beyond Illinois. Get the merchandise that your customers crave. Remember, retailing is fashion. And that applies to everything from hardware to books—not just apparel.

PRICING STRATEGY

Consumers Look for Value, Not Always Price

Gone are the days when high price automatically meant high quality. Today's consumers are looking for something called *value*. But they may define value in a variety of ways: high quality, selection, service, convenience. Usually, it is a combination of factors. Retailers need to ask their customers how they define value. Then they need to establish a merchandising and pricing strategy that will lead to loyal customers who will return time and again—without the enticement of weekly price cuts and markdowns.

Retailers recognize that how they price their products has a direct impact on their image and profitability: 92 percent rate pricing strategy as important or very important (see Figure 3-5). Still, the question persists whether retailers have a merchandising and pricing strategy that equates to value. The performance gap indicates that retailers may not be adjusting their pricing strategies to the current environment. A smart retailer once said, "Deal in commodities, and you deal in price. Deal in specialty goods, and you deal in price-value."

The problem in retailing is that customers are tired of the high-low, flip-flop pricing so common in the market today. This has created a serious pricing credibility problem. Customers want consistency and fair play.

Time-constrained shoppers simply do not store-hop like they used to. They prefer one-stop shopping. So customers reward those retailers who promise them the merchandise they want at a fair price every day. A recent Grey Advertising study indicated that only 37 percent of respondents compare prices anymore, down from 54 percent in 1991.

Figure 3-5   Prices dramatically affect a store's image as well as profitability, retailers say. Now they need to adjust their pricing strategy to a concept called *value*.

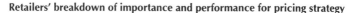

Retailers' breakdown of importance and performance for pricing strategy

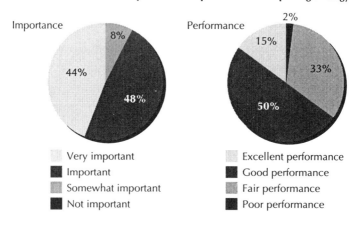

Unfortunately, not enough retailers consider their customers' perception of value in their pricing strategies (see Figure 3-6). Instead, as Table 3-3 (page 90) shows, most survey respondents determine their prices based on their expected margin, the competition's prices and the manufacturer's suggested retail price (MSRP)—not on customers' expectations. Relying on the MSRP at least provides a frame of reference for other prices. Retailers can price unique products and branded products higher than off-brand and private-label products.

Still retailers need to graduate from traditional pricing methods and try to match prices with their store image, the uniqueness of their merchandise and the customers' perceptions of value. This will differ between retail formats, but the concept applies to both hard- and soft-goods retailers. For example, a specialty home-furnishings store will likely have a higher price for a lamp than a mass merchant, but a lamp at a specialty store is perceived as being of higher quality, higher value, and more unique because of the better selection, service, and ambiance of the store.

Many retailers use everyday low pricing (EDLP) for basic products and full-price promotional pricing for fashion and seasonal merchandise (see Figure 3-7, page 90). Retailers at least should consider EDLP as a strategy in select categories because today's consumers are very attracted to value pricing.

However, EDLP is not possible for many retailers because it requires a lower cost of merchandise and overhead structure. Everyday fair pricing (EDFP) is a term that was introduced by Walter Salmon in a 1991 *Sloan Management Review* article:

Figure 3-6 Shopping smart is here to stay.

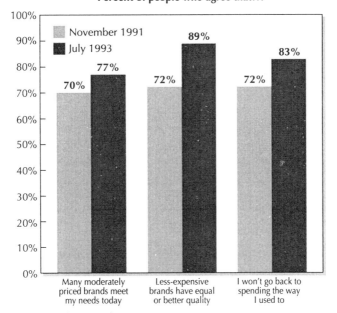

Percent of people who agree that...

Source: Grey Advertising and Fortune, Autumn/Winter 1993.

"EDFP means a restoration of everyday prices to levels that represent good value to customers even though they do not purport to be the lowest in town; fewer sales events; and, most importantly, excellence in other differentiating elements of the merchandising mix, such as service and assortment."[4]

Almost any retailer can use an EDFP strategy that offers value to customers, is easy to understand, and involves fewer (and more legitimate) sales events. Arthur Andersen believes retailers should use a consistent mix of full-price, promotional, and EDFP, depending on whether the merchandise is fashion, seasonal, or basic and on retailers' relative strengths in these categories. These strategies increase traffic and build credibility among customers. Customers want pricing that is consistent with value, and retailers must deliver value if they want to regain their credibility.

Retailers need to remember that consumers quickly lose faith in stores with inflated retail prices and deep markdowns, though an occasional use of this "high-low" tactic may be necessary to boost store traffic during slow periods. Regular seasonal promotions, such as after-Christmas

[4] *Arthur Andersen Retailing Issues Newsletter.*

Table 3-3   Retailers need to link their pricing strategies to their customers' perceptions of value, not their own.

Factors retailers consider when establishing prices (in order of importance as ranked by retailers)
• Expected margin
• Competitors' prices
• Manufacturer's suggested retail price
• Customers' perceptions of value
• Perceived demand
• Landed cost
• Company image
• Fashion vs. seasonal vs. basic
• In-stock position

and back-to-school sales, can be much more effective in maintaining pricing credibility.

Regarding markdowns, most retailers wait too long to discount goods and rely too heavily on end-of-season campaigns (see Figure 3-8). But retailers must not wait this long to promote slow-moving merchan-

Figure 3-7   Retailers will build credibility by sticking to one pricing strategy. High-low pricing can erode consumers' trust and keep customers away.

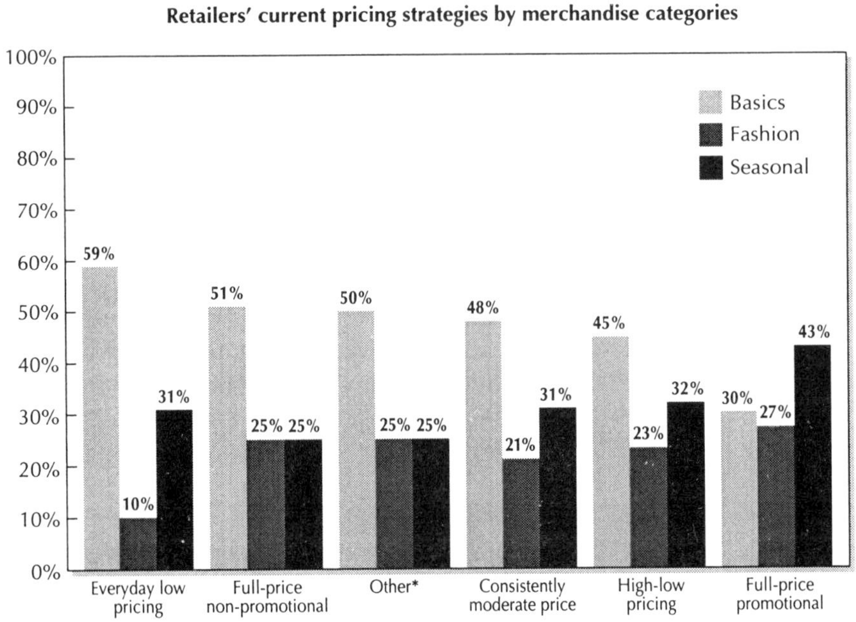

Retailers' current pricing strategies by merchandise categories

* Includes prices set by manufacturer.

dise. They cannot risk carrying inventory into the next season. Nor can retailers rely on across-the-board or rule-of-thumb markdowns; they need to focus on gross profit dollars, not only gross margin percents. Inventory aging information, item-level movement, and predetermined markdown formulas are more effective tools for improving inventory management. Retailers must strive to find out why goods aren't selling. Is the merchandise appropriately displayed and priced?

Reducing markdowns overall, though, would help increase gross margins, according to many retailers (see Table 3-4). More than half of retailers believe that gross margins will increase over the next three years. These retailers attribute this projected increase not only to reducing markdowns but also to purchasing at lower cost and changing the product mix. If they are wrong, these retailers will be in for some trouble—and recent history does not support their prediction.

The overall trend in retailing is for continual erosion of gross margins. Those retailers expecting this decrease cite increased competition as the primary reason. Large retailers implement quick-response strategies driven at the point of sale to replenish basic and fashion merchandise on a

Figure 3-8 Most retailers mark down merchandise at the end of the season, but they should shift their focus to inventory aging information, sales movement and progressive markdown formulas early in the season. Rule-of-thumb and across-the-board markdowns are not adequate tactics in a complex retail environment.

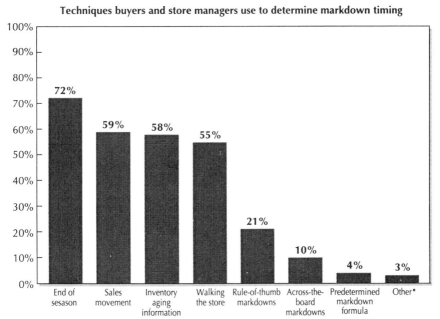

Techniques buyers and store managers use to determine markdown timing

* Includes semi-annual sales.

Table 3-4   Retailers can reverse the trend of eroding gross margins by offering unique products that customers want.

Factors retailers feel will increase gross margin in the future (in order of importance as ranked by retailers)

- Purchasing at a lower cost
- Changing mix of products sold
- Reducing markdowns
- Charging customers higher prices
- Pricing services more profitably
- More fashion or seasonal merchandise
- Offering fewer SKUs

Factors retailers feel will decrease gross margin in the future (in order of importance as ranked by retailers)

- Competition
- Overcapacity in retail industry
- Higher purchasing prices
- Change in customer preferences
- Change in mix of products sold
- Lower-cost merchandise

continuous basis. This has proven effective in reducing markdowns but requires technological investments. Common pricing tactics retailers use include:

- *Price pointing and lining.* Many retailers establish a range of prices for all items in a department or category, which simplifies the consumer's selection process and creates value breaks. For example, some retailers mark all men's dress shirts at $39.99, $29.99, and $19.99.
- *Price ends.* Retailers also establish different price ends for different products. Nonsale items may be priced at $35, sale items at $27.99, and promotional items at $24.95. This enables retailers to track and compare sales at different value points.
- *Scheduled markdowns.* Successful apparel retailers are masters of this technique. The company brings in the goods at a set price, takes the first markdown after 30 days, the second after 45 days, and the final markdown after 60 days. This tactic focuses on keeping the traffic and inventory moving and leaves minimal carryover stock. It also forces customers to decide whether to pay the asking price now or risk missing out on the goods.
- *Price comparisons.* The practice of displaying the original price and the new price after the markdown shows the customer exactly what she is saving. The practice of showing prices of comparable brands emphasizes what a customer can save by not being

brand-loyal. And the multitiered pricing tactics show the customer three products from the same manufacturer and emphasize the concept of paying a premium for higher-quality products.

Arthur Andersen believes that the best way to increase gross margin is to change the product mix to include unique products at higher price points and to use sound pricing tactics. Retailers need to focus their merchandise on those profitable products that customers want. At the same time, retailers also may have to satisfy customer needs with less profitable products. Another good way to improve margins is by providing value-added services, which enable retailers to have higher price points. "Don't give away the store" is a good maxim. Most customers appreciate value-added services and—depending on the services offered—are willing to pay for them.

Best Practices You Can Use

Establish a pricing strategy. Separate your customer base into buyer value segments. This will give you a better understanding of who frequents your store. This aids with marketing, merchandising, and determining whether customers are price shoppers, convenience shoppers, or loyal customers. Try to answer the following questions about your customers and your business to decide which overall pricing strategy is right for you:

- What percent of your customers fall into each category (price shoppers, convenience shoppers, and loyal customers)?
- How satisfied are your customers in each of these segments?
- What percent of your main competitor's total sales fall into the same categories?
- What do your customers (not just the price shoppers) like best about your store? Your main competitor's store?
- What would your customers like to see more of in your store? What would they like to see changed?
- What type of sales appeal most to your customers (not just the price shoppers)? What items at what prices appeal to them most?
- What is your store's image? What is your primary competitor's image?
- What are your employees' images of your store? Your customers' images of your store?
- What would you have to do to attract more loyal customers?
- What do you think your main competitor's strategies and tactics will be for the next several years? What is your strategy?

Match pricing tactics with profit goals and customers' perceptions of value. If your value strategies seem to conflict with your profit goals, try to cut expenses even more and then decide how many gross margin dollars you need to make the targeted profit.

Three ways exist to increase your gross profit: (1) increase the volume of units sold; (2) increase the mark-up percentage; or (3) shift the merchandise mix to higher-margin items. These alternatives sound simple, but achieving an optimum balance may be difficult.

Increase the volume of units sold. Many items influence sales volume, including merchandise, customer service, location, demographics, image, convenience, advertising, promotions, the local economy, and sales-force effectiveness. One more critical factor is price. Discount retailing has shown that low prices can lead to higher volumes. The quandary arises from trying to determine if the higher volume will generate enough margin dollars to offset the lower mark-up and the higher labor costs. Unfortunately, no model exists to accurately forecast the impact of lower prices on volume. But you can do some basic breakeven analysis of your own and look at your historical figures to gain some insight. Here is an example:

- Identify the break-even point. Imagine that last year you sold 100 T-shirts at $10 each and achieved a gross margin of $5 each. If you lower the unit price to $7.50, you will have to sell 200 T-shirts to generate the same number of margin dollars. Remember: Focus on dollars in this analysis. You pay your bills with dollars, not percentage points.
- Track historical sell-through rates at various price points. As you tinker with the prices of specific items, track the sell-through rates over certain periods. For example, if you normally sell hammers at $10 each and you put them on sale for $7.50 each, you need to track how consumers respond to the sale, how many units it takes, and how long it takes to generate the planned amount of gross-margin dollars. How quickly those gross-margin dollars are generated will help quantify the impact on volume that may come from lowering prices.

Increase mark-up percentage. To achieve this, you can increase the prices on existing goods or you can maintain the regular prices on lower-cost (not discount) goods.

- *Source at lower cost.* Participate in a buying group or cooperative. Identify sources for seconds or closeouts. Limit the branded products in your inventory. Finding low-cost suppliers takes time and research, but plenty of sources do exist. Start with your retailing network.

- *Sell at higher prices.* Discover unique products and bring them to the market before the competitors. Improve your customer service level and visual merchandising efforts to complement the higher-priced merchandise.
- *Reduce markdowns.* Don't succumb to vendor pressures, don't accept substitutes at any time, and don't take deliveries too late in a season. Don't mix discounted goods with full-price goods; instead, use discreet liquidation tables and prominently display new goods. Track the receipt date on tickets to know when products are getting old. This helps you accelerate markdowns and prevent deeper markdowns later. Establish a specified day in each month or season when the owner and store manager review the inventory to pinpoint the slow movers. Consider changing the floor plan; slow movers may not be getting the right positioning in the store. Test new merchandise before you overstock, then reorder if it sells well. Try to get vendors to guarantee margins or accept returns.

Shift the mix to higher-margin items. You can accomplish this through improved in-store merchandising, a two-part project:

- First, work with your vendors to bring in higher-margin items (e.g. private labels for apparel stores and generic drugs for drugstores).
- Second, persuade your customers to buy these items. Concentrate on these items for promotions, in-store demonstrations, and special advertising, because these are your highest-margin goods.

Balance promotional with permanent markdowns. Tie a promotional markdown to a sales event and restore full price after the event. Permanently mark down merchandise to move the goods out of stock, and do not restore the original price. In a perfect world, you would not need permanent markdowns. But permanent markdowns will always be necessary to move goods out the door and deplete excess stock. The key to remember is to take permanent markdowns on a more timely basis, which will increase your gross margin return on investment. At the same time, you can create some real excitement and synergy between your permanent and promotional markdowns by bringing in promotional goods at marked-down prices. This will increase store traffic and move merchandise, whether it is marked down promotionally or permanently. You also need to avoid broken assortments and low-stock situations. Isolate low-stock goods in a bin or on a table and sell them as soon as possible. If you are low on your best stock or have ordered wrong assortments, you clearly need to take a hard look at the replenishment practices of your store. This is more of a buying than a pricing issue. It is also acceptable to run a clearance sale to promote permanently marked down merchandise if it helps to sell the goods and does not damage your store's image. A cardinal sin is to restore a permanent markdown after a promotional event. Customers know the difference between new goods and goods you are trying to eliminate. Never try to fool your customer.

Overlay pricing strategy against selling velocity of specific merchandise. For instance, price items of steady demand at full-price nonpromotional, price fast-selling items at everyday fair prices, and price slow sellers at full-promotional or with high-low tactics.

Formulate a markdown strategy. The key to formulating an effective markdown strategy is to base it on the date you receive and display the merchandise, not the order date. For example, if the display date is January 1 and the merchandise isn't moving 30 days later, mark it down 20 to 30 percent. If it still isn't moving by the middle of February, mark it down 40 percent. Reposition the display and continue to mark down the price until customers start buying the merchandise. Don't carry it over to the next season. This is bad for cash flow, and it doesn't fool your customers. Successful retailers know that there is usually more value in selling discounted merchandise today than in carrying it over to next year at the same or even a moderately higher margin.

VENDORS

Good Relationships Lead to Good Buys

Retailers say finding trustworthy vendors with whom they can work and communicate expectations is an important merchandising practice. In the Illinois study, retailers evaluated this practice for three different categories: vendor relations, vendor reliability, and vendor compliance.

Vendor relations involves identifying the right vendors and developing those relationships. Ninety-one percent of retailers say it is important or very important, and 81 percent view their performance as good or excellent (see Figure 3-9). Straight-talking, cooperative vendor allies are those who show interest in retailers' customers and who support their products through value-added services, timely receipts, and quality merchandising ideas.

Most retailers obtain their merchandise from a variety of vendors. The process of reaching that decision, however, is often subjective and dependent upon "gut instinct" or personalities. A hardware retailer, for example, may buy red-handled screwdrivers from a vendor simply because he likes the salesperson, or perhaps because he perceives that red is more appealing to his customers.

Retailers should consider their instincts, but they should not lose their focus during the sourcing decision and become vendor-driven rather

Figure 3-9　Retailers correctly rank vendor relations as one of the most important success factors. They can improve performance here by selecting vendors based on objective criteria rather than making decisions based on intuition.

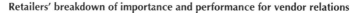

Retailers' breakdown of importance and performance for vendor relations

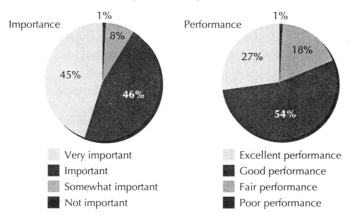

than customer-driven. This may lead to some bad buys. Retailers sometimes also buy what they like, not necessarily what their customers want. This can happen when a retailer, desperate to replace a basic item quickly, uses an inferior vendor. Bad buys will occur frequently when retailers forget that they are buying the merchandise for the customers and not for themselves. Bad buys also occur when retailers rely too much on vendors' judgments of what will sell and not enough on their own knowledge of what customers want.

Retailers must go beyond subjectivity and consider objective criteria in buying decisions. In choosing vendors, retailers say they look for some of the same qualities a customer wants in a retailer: product quality, price for value, and timely delivery (see Table 3-5). These are all important items, but so are honesty and integrity, which retailers rank only ninth overall in terms of importance.

Working with vendors who want to be allies makes it easier for retailers to share sales information and learn what other retailers are doing. This is crucial to any sound working relationship. Yet many small-store retailers fall down in this area. They either fail to ask vendors for the proper information or they do not know what information to seek. The fact that 28 percent of retailers surveyed do not share information with their vendors indicates that they do not view vendors as allies or do not appreciate the importance of vendor-retailer relations (see Figure 3-10, page 99). Perhaps this is because their vendors treat them poorly or give them little attention. Perhaps it is simply because many small-store retailers do not trust their vendors.

Table 3-5 The criteria retailers use to select vendors should be consistent with criteria customers use to select retailers. Above all, customers want price for value, quality, and product availability.

Criteria retailers use in selecting vendors (in order of importance ranked by retailers)	
• Product quality	• Honesty and integrity
• Price for value	• Sales representative skills and expertise
• On-time delivery	• Reputation of vendor
• Product availability	• Credit terms
• Delivery accuracy	• Product support
• Breadth of product line	• Hot item
• Brand-name reputation	• Lead times
• Return privileges	• Other value-added services

Of those retailers who have healthy communications with vendors, 63 percent share sales information, but Arthur Andersen believes this figure would be higher if retailers simply asked vendors what benefits they would derive from sharing sales information. More retailers should also consider sharing on-hand inventory levels and gross margin information. This will help vendors better understand retailers' businesses so they can better plan shipments and avoid overstocked positions.

Reliability is also an integral element in retailers' relationships with vendors. Small-store retailers, however, have little control over vendors' reliability. Without complete confidence that a vendor will deliver the promised goods on time, a retailer cannot meet his customers' needs, maintain his reputation, or protect his market share. It's no surprise, then, that 88 percent of retailers say vendor reliability is important or very important (see Figure 3-11), but only half of the retailers rank their vendors as reliable.

Why the disparity? Unfortunately, many retailers and vendors harbor an "us vs. them" mindset when it comes to working with each other. How retailers evaluate reliability is subjective, but, as Table 3-6 (page 100) shows, they are correct to place a premium on vendor follow-through and responsiveness to their specific needs. Retailers should also consider increasing the frequency of their communications. Though communication ranks last, it is the most effective way to build trust. Successful relationships depend on achieving mutual goals, and those goals must be communicated at the beginning of the relationship and continuously throughout.

Building trust and sharing information will eventually pay off for both the retailer and the vendor. Vendors will begin to view the universe

Figure 3-10 Sharing certain sales information with vendors builds trust and can enhance retailers' relationships with vendors, according to 72 percent of respondents. Those retailers who share no information with their vendors should consider doing so in certain cases as a first step to building vendor alliances.

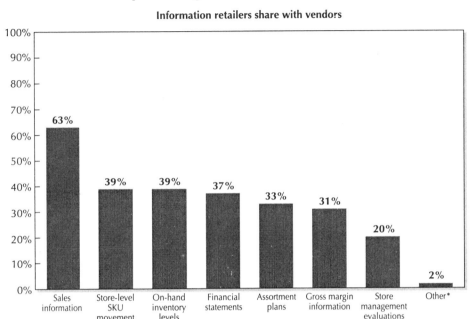

Information retailers share with vendors

* Includes providing other information vendors request.

Figure 3-11 Too many retailers have an "us vs. them" attitude when it comes to vendors. Retailers should consider not only vendors' follow-through and responsiveness, but also communications as the most important factors in selecting vendors.

Retailers' breakdown of importance and performance for vendor reliability

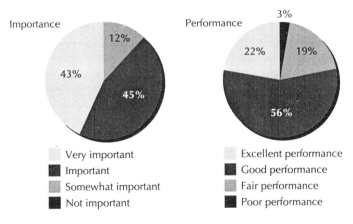

Table 3-6 Communication should be the most important criterion to develop trusting relations with vendors. Retailers need to work with vendors to make them more responsive and committed to retailers' success.

Qualities retailers look for in evaluating vendors' level of trust (in order of importance ranked by retailers)

- Responsiveness (meeting specific retailer needs)
- Commitment (follow-through)
- Flexibility
- On-time delivery
- Integrity and honesty
- Communications

---

of small-store retailers as a significant source of revenue growth and will want to work with retailers to micromarket.

Why? As increased competition, customer fragmentation, and changing consumer buying patterns continue to be strong forces in the next century, middle-market and small retailers may have a greater voice in influencing sales, prices, and margins of manufacturers and wholesalers of apparel and consumer products. Small-store retailers should look particularly hard at forming alliances with wholesalers. Wholesalers and small-store retailers would make natural allies, since they share a common competitive threat: the chain store that buys directly from a manufacturer.

By turning vendors into allies, retailers can achieve greater effectiveness in their merchandising strategies. This in turn can help decrease markdowns, increase margins, improve customer satisfaction, and enhance store image. Small-store retailers need to limit their vendors only to those willing to cooperate with them.

"If you don't ask, you won't get it," said one appliance retailer about vendor cooperation and compliance. If only more retailers shared this view. While retailers rank vendor relations, trust, and reliability as the more important areas of merchandising, 79 percent of retailers say compliance is important or very important (see Figure 3-12). Vendor compliance goes hand-in-hand with vendor relations and reliability, and retailers need to overcome the common presumption that small-store retailers cannot influence their vendors' behavior. Again, they need to communicate with their vendors more regularly and negotiate ways to improve compliance with retailer wants.

However, only 59 percent of retailers establish a performance standard for their vendors. Successful retailers monitor their vendors' performance for two reasons: First, to make certain that the vendors deliver what they promised; and second, to develop benchmarks for the next time

Figure 3-12 Retailers need to improve the practices they use to regulate vendor compliance.

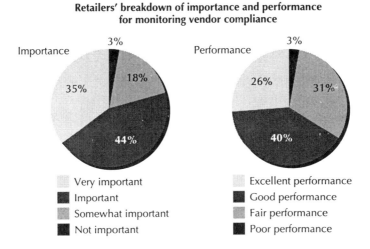

they need to go through the vendor selection and negotiation process. Retailers who do not monitor vendor performance cannot measure how well they are being served; over 50 percent of retailers fall into this category. Those with performance standards usually include adherence to delivery dates and order completeness (see Figure 3-13). Retailers should also evaluate their achieved gross margin by specific vendors and use this information as a negotiating tool.

An alarming detail is that more than half of the retailers who establish performance criteria do not monitor their vendors against those criteria (see Figure 3-14). Of the retailers who actually monitor the standards they establish, most rely on buyers' opinions and sales by vendor. Buyers should keep vendor correspondence files, both to track compliance by vendor and to track maintained margins by vendor for renegotiation purposes.

Best Practices You Can Use

A proven way to determine what vendors will receive your orders is to develop a rational and systematic vendor scorecard.[5] Keep in mind that this scorecard is not intended to replace your judgment; it is merely another subjective tool to enhance your effectiveness.

---

[5] Davidson, William, et al. *Retailing Management*, 6th ed.

Figure 3-13 By communicating their expected delivery dates to vendors, 95 percent of retailers strengthen the relationships. Although retailers see the importance of discussing their expectations of delivery dates, only 67 percent relay expectations of order completeness.

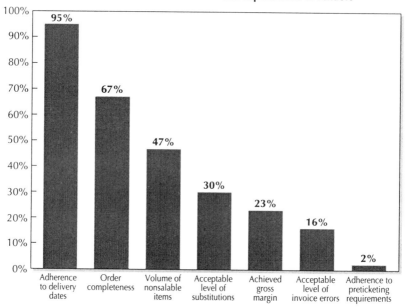

Areas where retailers communicate expectations to vendors

Develop scorecard criteria and score your vendors. First identify the most important selection criteria. Assign each quality a weight based on the number of criteria identified, in this case on a scale from 1 to 8, with 8 being the most important. Focus on the top five or ten criteria from the list in Table 3-5 (shown previously) and the vendor scorecard shown in Table 3-7 (page 104). To score the vendors, assess how well the vendor meets each quality on a scale of 0 to 4, with 4 being the highest. Multiply the weight by the achievement score. then add up the points and select the vendor with the highest score. Also consider your company's image, strategy, and customer satisfaction goals. In the sample below, Vendor C ranks highest overall. Above all, ask yourself if this is a vendor you trust and with whom you want to work, and whether he wants to work with you. The scorecard shown is just an example. You need to tailor your scorecard to your own unique circumstances and add more quantitative and qualitative criteria.

Negotiate, consolidate, or replace vendors. After scoring your vendors, you will have a clear picture of how to proceed. Clearly you should continue to work with high-scoring vendors. You should also consider increasing your sourcing from those vendors. You can negotiate with midrange performers. A spotty performance record can be a useful nego-

Figure 3-14 Monitoring vendor performance is a key factor in improving vendor compliance and improving profits. The 47 percent of retailers who do monitor vendor performance rely on buyer opinion and sales by vendor. Tracking margins and markdowns and documenting notes on invoices are helpful in developing a vendor history and in reordering and renegotiating with vendors.

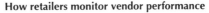

How retailers monitor vendor performance

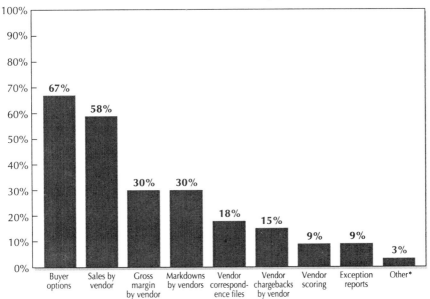

* Includes daily communications with vendors.

tiating tool, especially if you can show the supporting documentation. And consider reducing the number of midrange performers by consolidating some of your sourcing needs. Consider dropping the vendors who flunk if they offer no value to your business; they waste valuable time and money. A word of caution: Try to replace dropped vendors with top-of-the-line vendors as soon as it is practical. You cannot afford to be restricted by too few vendors. An important point here is that you must use the information that you collect to negotiate with vendors. Get vendors to commit to improving or get them to agree to concessions if they don't comply.

Establish a performance monitoring system. Set up a file for each vendor and consider maintaining the following information:

- *Sales and margin data.* Keep a copy of summary sales and margin reports in each file. Compare this information with those statistics presented by the vendors. Another way to do this is to make notes on invoices and file the invoices by vendor.

Table 3-7   Sample vendor scorecard

Retailers' Criteria	Weight	Vendor A		Vendor B		Vendor C		Vendor D	
		Score	Total pts.	Score	Total pts.	Score	Total pts.	Score	Total pts.
Vendor can fill reorders	4	1	4	2	8	4	16	0	0
Markup is adequate	5	2	10	4	20	3	15	1	5
Customers ask for the line	8	3	24	2	16	4	32	0	0
Vendor's line has significant seasonal changes	3	3	9	4	12	2	6	0	0
Vendor's line contributes to fashion leadership	6	2	12	1	6	0	0	4	24
Vendor accepts returns	2	1	2	0	0	3	6	2	4
Vendor provides co-op advertising	1	0	0	1	1	2	2	3	3
Vendor appears willing to work with store in helpful and honest manner	7	1	7	0	0	4	28	3	21
Total scores (Multiply weight by score to get total points.)			68		63		105		57

- *Open purchase orders.* After you place an order, put a copy in the corresponding vendor file. This helps you remember to what terms the vendor agreed. Use this information to ensure compliance with agreed-upon terms.
- *Closed purchase orders.* Once an order is closed out, remove it from the active section of the file.
- *Exception reports from store and warehouse personnel.* Ask your employees to use the receiving report to document every discrepancy. This will help you assess the administrative costs of doing business with a specific vendor. You should always discuss issues with vendors and try to resolve them without doing something that would hurt the relationship.
- *Markdown reports.* Maintain markdowns by vendor. Every time you mark down merchandise, note the amount by vendor. Having this in the file will help you assess the profitability of the vendor and the merchandise sold compared with assertions previously made by the vendor. Use this information to negotiate a guaranteed margin.

- *Debit and credit memos.* Retain copies in your vendor correspondence files.
- *Vendor letters.* Retain copies of all correspondence between you and the vendor.
- *Scorecard.* Keep the vendor's scorecard in the file.

Understand vendor philosophies and practices. Ask your vendors their position on doing business with small stores. How many stores in the region do they currently supply? What special programs or deals do they have for small stores? How do they specifically respond to the need for product support and timely receipts?

Meet face to face with key vendors. Share key elements of your merchandising plan with them and find out how they can help with marketing, advertising, and other value-added activities. Discuss your performance expectations with them. Ask for some assurances in the form of guaranteed margins, allowable returns, or markdown allowances.

Confirm agreements in writing. Using a purchase order in which vendor allowances, such as co-ops and cash allowances, are clearly spelled out is the best way to avoid misunderstandings.

Share customer-satisfaction information. If customer satisfaction is a high priority for your vendor—and it should be—consider sharing customer feedback with him regarding his merchandise lines.

Educate the sales force. Ask the vendor to meet with your salespeople or send product materials or videos. Topics should include product functionality, features, and benefits, as well as how to position the product in the store.

Inform vendors. When you promote a specific product, consider sending the vendor a note detailing your efforts. This will reinforce the commitment you made to your mutual success and should lead to greater flexibility in future negotiations.

Pay your most important vendors first when cash flow is tight. If you won't be able to pay by the due date, call your vendors before they call you. Don't tell them that the check is in the mail—unless it really is.

Don't take undocumented deductions. If an invoice has an error, contact the vendor to get the adjustment authorized.

Update vendors on potential order cancellations. If order cancellations are necessary, give the vendor as much notice as possible. If you must pay restocking charges or return freight, make those payments timely. Include a personal note emphasizing the importance of your relationship. If you track open-to-buy and you know that an order will put you in an overbought position, alert your vendor that your commitment level may change if the merchandise doesn't move quickly. This is a good time to ask for extra promotional assistance.

Learn negotiation skills. There are a number of training workshops available on developing negotiation skills. Check with your state's chamber of commerce for references.

OPEN-TO-BUY

Inventory Control Is the Best Way to Increase Profits

Though most retailers say open-to-buy (OTB) is important, it remains an underrated and underused management tool (see Figure 3-15). Nearly half of retailers say they do not use it.

The overall objectives of merchandise planning are to control the flow of merchandise and to optimize gross margin return on inventory (see the benchmarks in the resource section for calculation). Inventory control is critical to meeting this objective because it greatly influences sales and cash flow. Too much of the wrong inventory could lead to slow-moving goods and a tight cash situation, not to mention dissatisfied customers and heavy markdowns.

That is why OTB, which determines the budgeted dollars to commit to purchases, is critical to managing inventory and preventing overbuying and out-of-stock merchandise. OTB refers to the quantity of merchandise a store should receive into inventory during a month to keep inventories

Figure 3-15   While many retailers say their performance is good or excellent for open-to-buy, all must take advantage of OTB as a way to manage merchandise levels.

Retailers' breakdown of importance and performance for open-to-buy

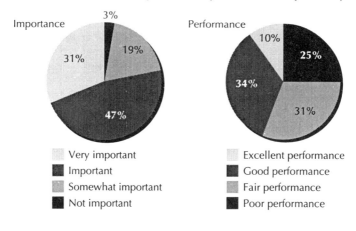

in line with sales plans. These are the reasons why small-store retailers need to devote more attention to merchandise planning.

Although larger retailers commonly use OTB to guide the management of inventory—and have done so for years—many small-store retailers have not yet embraced this technique. Those who do use OTB mostly use it at the store or department level (see Figure 3-16). Store level is a good start, but OTB is more effective when done at a more detailed level, such as department, category, class, or price line.

Retailers not using this tactic are missing out on an important practice to manage their inventory. A good rule of sound merchandising is to maintain some OTB at all times. Why? First, the wholesale market is characterized by a constant stream of new merchandise. The prompt procurement and promotion of such goods helps keep customers interested. It can also be an important source of additional volume and profits. Second, by keeping the purchase limit open, the retailer can take advantage of special prices and other promotions vendors occasionally offer. Third, retailers often must order a certain amount of fill-in merchandise to maintain complete assortments.

Figure 3-16 Nearly half of all retailers, 46 percent, do not use open-to-buy. Of those retailers who do use OTB, most monitor reporting at the store and department level. OTB reporting should occur at least at the department and class level for greater accuracy.

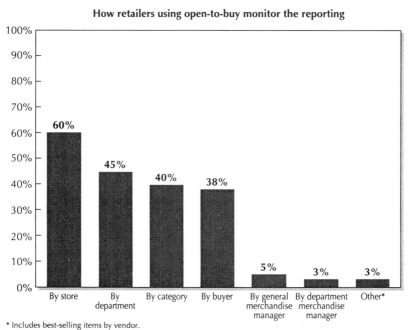

How retailers using open-to-buy monitor the reporting

* Includes best-selling items by vendor.

To put it simply, effective use of OTB planning helps retailers determine how much to buy. It also helps determine when to buy merchandise, cancel orders, take markdowns, and plan receipts. Ultimately, this all leads to lower markdowns, improved margins, lower interest costs, better cash flow, tighter inventory control, improved store image, and happier customers.

Other facets of inventory control include monitoring inventory levels and ordering. Figure 3-17 shows that most retailers perform physical counts or other forms of observation to determine whether to reorder merchandise. This is fine for those with one or two stores, but larger retailers need to do more. Computerized perpetual inventory systems may be an effective alternative, but they require a lot of maintenance.

Computers can also help with determining reorder points, although manual alternatives also work. But retailers need to come up with more effective ways of determining when to reorder, especially when reorders are a key part of the business. Many small retailers do not want to reorder merchandise except for basics. More than half reorder only when an item is out of stock (see Figure 3-18). Retailers must realize that customers have to be able to find what they want when they want it, or they won't return.

Figure 3-17   For retailers with one or two stores, physical counts are an effective way of monitoring inventory levels. Retailers with three or more stores need to use more sophisticated systems.

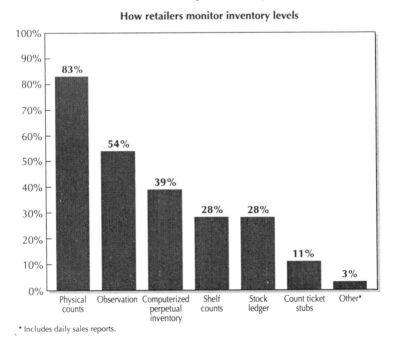

How retailers monitor inventory levels

* Includes daily sales reports.

Figure 3-18 By ordering only when items are out of stock, 54 percent of all retailers may be letting customers leave with empty arms and unfulfilled wants. Giving customers what they want when they want it is critical. Retailers should move toward minimum and maximum parameters, model stocks, and never-out lists.

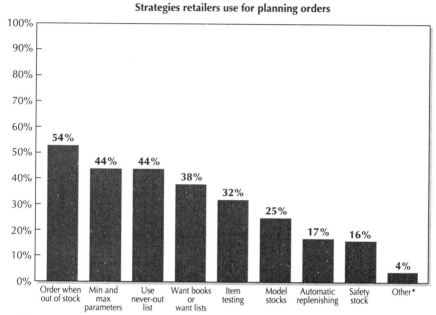

Strategies retailers use for planning orders

* Includes "gut feeling" and weekly sales reports.

Ordering only when merchandise is out of stock is simply not acceptable. At the same time, ordering too much will create an inventory problem. More effective planning tactics include model stocks (replenish to a predetermined assortment), minimum and maximum parameters, and never-out merchandise.

Best Practices You Can Use

You need to consider a formal OTB calculation to control your inventory and spending. Several key elements are involved in developing an OTB, including the following:

Last year's purchases. Look at last year's monthly purchases. Did you buy too much or too little compared with sales in the same period?

Last year's sales and promotion calendar. Ask yourself if the promotions generated the sales you expected. Will you run the same promotions at the same time this year?

Current inventory levels. What merchandise do you need to get immediately? Based on anticipated sales and markdowns, what can you plan to order for the next six months?

Customer wants. Consider what customers have told you about your merchandise. You may want to add or delete some lines or styles.

Competitor actions. Take a look at your competitors and the changes they have recently made. Decide what you need to do to maintain your niche.

Current economic and demographic trends. Is a new housing development ready to market homes to people? Should you expand your furniture offerings in anticipation of increased sales? If the answer is yes, you may want to pursue these new high-potential customers. Keep track of economic and demographic trends.

Once you have considered all of these factors, you should determine your formal OTB as follows:

Develop your overall sales plan for the next season. Incorporate planned markdowns.

Divide the sales plan into merchandise classifications or departments—the narrower the better. Otherwise, you could end up with too much inventory in one category and not enough in another. Don't forget anticipated markdowns. You want to record the net sales you realize.

Break the sales plan into months. It is easier to plan a month at a time than a season or year at a time.

Determine the inventory levels necessary to achieve the targeted sales level. This will give you the level of inventory you need to meet targeted monthly sales.

Subtract on-hand inventory. What's left is the level of monthly purchases needed to meet the planned inventory and sales levels. If one month you don't meet the planned sales level, you may need to reduce your planned purchases the next month. Notify your vendors of canceled or postponed orders as soon as you can.

An example of a simple OTB plan is shown in Table 3-8. At the end of the month, you should perform the same calculation on an actual basis. The following represents conditions in a certain department as of June 30. All figures are at retail value.

It's logical to begin the solution with the June planned-purchases figures since you should have made this calculation before June 1. For simplicity's sake, assume that the actual beginning inventory is the same as the planned figure. This is computed as:

Table 3-8 Sample OTB plan

Assumptions		Retail OTB Plan	
Beginning-of-month inventory	$205,000	Beginning-of-month inventory	$205,000
Planned sales for June	90,000	Less budgeted retail reductions	
Planned markdowns for June	17,000	*Sales*	*90,000*
Planned shrinkage	0	*Markdowns*	*17,000*
Planned end-of-month inventory	180,000	*Shrinkage*	*0*
Merchandise received to date	50,000	Total reductions	107,000
On order, June delivery	18,000	Plus planned purchases at retail	82,000
		Planned end-of-month inventory	$180,000
		Planned purchases at retail	$ 82,000
		Less merchandise received to date	50,000
		Less on order, June delivery	18,000
		Open-to-buy	$14,000

$$\text{June planned purchases} =$$
$$\$90{,}000 + \$17{,}000 + \$180{,}000 - \$205{,}000 = \$82{,}000$$

Planned purchases for June are $82,000 at retail. Now, in order to determine the OTB on June 30, the planned-purchase figure for the month must be reduced by merchandise received to date and on-order goods yet to be received. This is computed as:

$$\$82{,}000 - \$50{,}000 - \$18{,}000 = \$14{,}000 \text{ (the retail OTB on June 30)}$$

You can compute the OTB at cost value, which is the amount that your buyer can spend, by multiplying the retail figure by the complement of the initial markup percentage by merchandise classification or department. If the budget calls for an initial markup of 40 percent, the cost multiplier is 100 minus 40, or 60 percent. Thus the OTB at cost is:

$$\$14{,}000 \times 0.60 = \$8{,}400$$

From time to time, you will have to revise your budget estimates. This means that you must make some adjustments in the OTB calculation. To illustrate, a cancellation of $2,000 in the markdown allowance will reduce the amount of value that is added through purchasing. If the purchase requirement is $200 less at retail, then logically you must reduce the OTB at retail by that amount. In summary, any increase in the budgeted figures for sales, reductions, or end-of-the-month stocks will expand the purchase limit. Conversely, any decrease in any of these factors will lessen the purchase limit.

If your actual end-of-month inventory is greater than your planned inventory, you are in an overbought position. When this occurs, you need to mark down the goods to sell them, which will free your OTB to purchase more stock. Otherwise, you may end up with aged merchandise.

ASSORTMENT PLANNING

Facts Must Back Owners' Instincts

Many retailers make the mistake of carrying overly broad merchandise assortments of items, styles, sizes, colors, and brands. This often results in too few quantities of too many items. Small-store retailers should focus their assortments to free up inventory dollars for new items.

More than 90 percent of retailers rank assortment planning as important or very important, and they are performing reasonably well (see Figure 3-19). Many retailers successfully rely on their instincts or historical sales patterns and purchases to determine the appropriate merchandise assortment. However, they need to focus more on what customers are saying and on what the external world is telling them (see Table 3-9). Retailers often fail in this area because they rely too much on last year and lack the time or discipline to focus on what factors or conditions may have changed since those sales were generated. Instincts may not be good enough in today's environment, and what sold last year may not sell this year.

Successful retailers are those who constantly corroborate their instincts with analysis and peer input. They have an understanding of their customers and merchandise. They review in detail current and historical sales patterns and item level movement. They obtain input from their store managers, buyers, and sales associates—the ones interacting with the vendors and customers. They communicate with vendors to see what is hot. They view their sales associates as the customers' purchasing agents. They talk directly with their customers to find out what assortments they want, and they talk to new vendors to find out what items are available.

Figure 3-19 Retailers recognize the importance of assortment planning, but to improve their performance levels they must focus on historical sales patterns and vendor input.

Retailers' breakdown of importance and performance for assortment planning

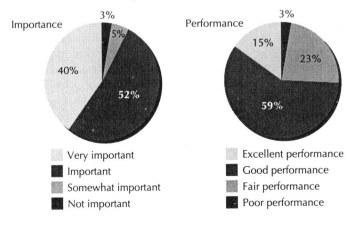

Table 3-9 Relying on owner instincts is a start for assortment planning, but retailers need to back their instincts with facts.

Information retailers use in assortment planning (in order of importance as ranked by retailers)

- Historical sales patterns
- Owner instincts
- Historical purchases
- Historical customer feedback
- Sales representative suggestions
- Store manager input
- Buyer input
- Vendor-supplied profiles

Table 3-10 provides additional insight into respondents' planning processes. Here one of the most important tactics, responding to competitor actions, ranks at the bottom. Many retailers do not make time to shop the competition and assess the impact on their own merchandise assortments. Retailers need to properly niche, anticipate their competitors' plans, act first with new, exciting merchandise assortments and complement the merchandise with effective advertising.

Best Practices You Can Use

Focus your assortments. Assortments evolve over time. Concentrate your assortments in the areas where you are strong. Examine what customers buy. Talk to your customers at the point of sale and ask them what they like, or conduct surveys and focus groups composed of customers and noncus-

Table 3-10 Retailers need to supplement their instincts with external factors, such as customer buying trends and competitor actions to decide what merchandise to carry.

Types of information retailers use in merchandise planning (in order of importance as ranked by retailers)

- Prior year sales
- Current inventory levels
- Buyer instincts
- Overall financial goals and strategies
- Current local economic trends
- Prior year promotion
- Vendor performance records
- Current demographic and psychographic trends
- Competitor actions
- Merchandise samples
- Market research studies

tomers. (See the section titled "Marshall Field: 'Give the Lady What She Wants' " in the chapter on customers and marketing.) Talk with your employees to find out what they hear from customers. Find out what styles, sizes, colors, and brands your customers want you to carry and at what price. Look at marked-down goods for any trends. Your customers are your most valuable resource for merchandising tips. Regardless of whether you are a soft-goods or hard-goods retailer, you need to take time to talk with your customers. (Don't assume that you know what they want.)

Observe people who come in the store. Spend time on the sales floor. Categorize customers by characteristics such as gender and clothes size. Then see how these categories match up with your merchandise offering.

Obtain vendor input. Vendors typically provide suggested assortments based on their category performance studies.

Link your merchandise with your image and corporate vision; that is, who you want to be and how you want to be known by your customers. Your merchandise assortment should reflect your store's image and be greatly influenced by your customers' perceptions. There must also be consistency in your offering.

Investigate and shop the competition. Offer assortments that include products, brands, and sizes that your primary competitor doesn't have. Make your store look different from the competition, or neutralize competitors by copying their best ideas. A common complaint of customers is that merchandise in most stores looks the same. If that's true, how can you entice customers into your store? One recommendation is to buy an assortment of unique, high-style merchandise for windows and front displays. Push yourself to be different. Plan to lose some money on these products, about 2 percent of total purchases. But that's the price of standing apart from the crowd.

Find out what's hot. Watch for fads and fashion trends. Shop the fashion leader. Attend buying shows and trade shows. Read trade journals and consumer magazines, and make them available to your buyers and customers. Proudly display reviews of new products. Talk with your vendors and ask them what's in style. Experiment. If you're not certain how well the product will sell, ask the vendor if he will provide markdown allowances or offer it on consignment to you.

Review last year's sales. Look at what sold best: colors, sizes, brands, styles. But be prepared to make adjustments. Ask yourself, "If I had more extra-large shirts, would I have met or exceeded my sales goal?" Review your out-of-stock frequency to see where your assortments did not reflect what the customer wanted. Also look at your end-of-season markdowns to see what didn't sell well.

Consider response time and how quickly you can replenish merchandise. If you can fax orders to manufacturers who offer next-day delivery, then you don't have to tie up your capital resources by carrying large quantities of these products.

Develop a way to track lost sales. Document every time a customer walks out of your store because you don't have the right size, color, or merchandise. Track returns by reason code. This should help provide information on which to base your assortments.

Develop a merchandise plan. An example of a monthly sales plan by classification only is shown below. You should develop this by size, color, vendor, and so on to assist you in planning your assortments. Start with total sales by season and plan by merchandise class. Then break it into months, as shown in Table 3-11.

LESSONS LEARNED FROM CASE STUDIES

Layout and Assortment Are the Key to an Effective Image

The importance of promoting and projecting a consistent store image cannot be stressed enough, as one menswear retailer is realizing. John Smith[6] wants his niche to be customers' first choice for quality suits.[7] But instead of proudly displaying his special-ordered, custom-tailored suits in the front of the store, John relegates them to the rear and fills the front—and the display windows—with sportswear. In fact, he dedicates three times more floor space to sportswear than he does to suits.

[6] John Smith is a pseudonym.
[7] See Chapter 8, "Poor Financial Performance, Declining Store Traffic Hinder Lifestyle Goals for Menswear Retailer," for complete case study.

Table 3-11   Sample of monthly sales plan by classification

Class	% of total season	Total season $ sales	Aug. (14%)	Sept. (14.5%)	Oct. (15%)	Nov. (17.5%)	Dec. (27%)	Jan. (12%)
A	19	$19,000	$2,660	$2,755	$2,850	$3,325	$5,130	$2,280
B	25	25,000	3,500	3,625	3,750	4,375	6,750	3,000
C	6	6,000	840	870	900	1,050	1,620	720
D	12	12,000	1,680	1,740	1,800	2,100	3,240	1,440
E	15	15,000	2,100	2,175	2,250	2,625	4,050	1,800
F	23	23,000	3,220	3,335	3,450	4,025	6,210	2,760
Total	100	$100,000	$14,000	$14,500	$15,000	$17,500	$27,000	$12,000

The result: The store layout and merchandise assortment do not support John's desired niche. First-time customers—and even some return customers—do not identify the store as having tailored clothing. Moving the suits to the front of the store, displaying them in the store windows, decreasing the sportswear assortment, and increasing the suit assortment would help John make his store into what he really wants it to be.

A department-store retailer, Brent Johnson,[8] uses a unique line of sportswear to differentiate his store from the competition.[9] Brent's unique merchandise is backed by a reputable vendor, who gives Brent exclusive rights to sell the merchandise in the community. The retailer emphasizes this unique merchandise through window displays, advertising, and in-store signs. The unique merchandise does not end there. Over the holidays, John carried a test run of gourmet, private-label coffee and candy. The trial run met with success; now John carries the coffee and candy year-round.

[8] Brent Johnson is a pseudonym.
[9] See Chapter 8, "Even After 100 Years, Department Store Cannot Rest on Laurels," for a complete case study.

4

STORE OPERATIONS

Once Inside, Customers Want Prompt, Royal Treatment

It's time for retailers to roll out the red carpet for customers. It's also time for retailers to sharpen up several other areas of store operations. Optimizing store operational performance is critical to retailing success. No matter how exciting the merchandise is or how effective the advertising is at getting customers into the store, if retailers don't provide customers with enjoyable shopping experiences, customers will not come back.

Because of consumers' high expectations and sophistication, retailers must generate synergy between their merchandise and promotion strategy and their store location, layout, and customer service. The challenge is to provide this synergy within an operating cost structure that permits store profitability.

This chapter focuses on 12 primary areas. Arthur Andersen and the retailers agree on the two most important functions of store operations. While they differ in the rankings of other categories, the difference in importance that retailers assigned to the remaining ten areas is slight (see Table 4-1).

Arthur Andersen and small-store retailers agree that the two most important aspects of store operations are customer service and store staffing and labor productivity:

- *Customer service.* Assisting customers in a timely and courteous fashion, making customers feel welcome and exceeding their expectations.

Table 4-1   Tier rankings

Arthur Andersen's First Tier	Retailers' First Tier
1. Customer service	1. Customer service
2. Store staffing and labor productivity	2. Store staffing and labor productivity
3. Store layout	3. Cleanliness
Second Tier	**Second Tier**
4. Customer accommodations	4. Shelf and display management
5. Store location	5. Store location
6. Shelf and display management	6. Receiving, stocking, and distribution
7. Store hours	7. Loss prevention
8. Loss prevention	8. Store layout
9. Utility management	9. Store hours
10. Cleanliness	10. Utility management
11. Register functionality	11. Register functionality
12. Receiving, stocking, and distribution	12. Customer accommodations

- *Store staffing and labor productivity.* Matching the quantity and quality of store staffing with customer traffic and needs.

Customers are more sensitive than ever. They want fast, friendly service on their terms every time they come into a store. If they do not get it, they will abandon that establishment in search of another one.

Although top-quality customer service originated with the small-store retailer, performance has been waning lately. Complacency, sales pressure, and margin pressure have caused many small-store retailers to sacrifice service.

The next most important area of store operations is store labor. Maximizing labor productivity and minimizing labor cost is key to achieving success. Retailers must strike a balance between having employees available to help customers when needed and reducing payroll costs. Most retailers generally have no method for assuring this balance.

In Arthur Andersen's view, store design and layout is the third most important factor in effective store operations. Retailers ranked cleanliness third and store layout eighth; however, the margin of difference was insignificant (see Figure 4-1).

Store layout is vital to maintaining the proper flow of traffic and making merchandise visible throughout the store. The coordination of store design and layout with the overall merchandise strategy sends a cohesive message to customers, and it is also a way to create an exciting atmosphere. Additionally, organizing the merchandise within the store to make shopping easier can increase store traffic and improve profits.

While respondents identified cleanliness as the third most important area, Arthur Andersen believes that cleanliness, while important, is a technical function. A simple adjustment of policy and procedures can ensure that a store is clean and orderly. Therefore, this book will discuss tech-

Figure 4-1 Retailers need to focus primarily on improving performance in customer service, store staffing, labor productivity, and store layout to enhance the customers' shopping experience. How do you compare? Ask yourself how important each business practice is to you and how well you perform it. Then fill in the chart in the section on operations assessment.

Comparison of how retailers rank store operations categories for importance and performance

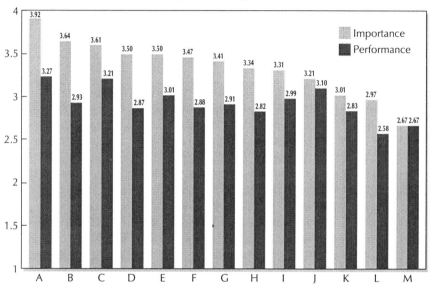

A. Customer service
B. Store staffing and labor productivity
C. Cleanliness
D. Shelf and display management
E. Store location
F. Receiving, stocking, and distribution
G. Overall median for store operations
H. Loss prevention
I. Store layout
J. Store hours
K. Utility management
L. Register functionality
M. Customer accommodations

niques to ensure cleanliness in lesser detail, along with other functions that Arthur Andersen considers second-tier:

- *Customer accommodations.* Providing conveniences customers desire, such as chairs, changing tables, and validated parking.
- *Store location.* Locating stores in the best places and knowing when to move.
- *Shelf and display management.* Displaying merchandise effectively.
- *Store hours.* Adjusting store hours to meet customer demands.
- *Loss prevention.* Controlling shoplifting, employee theft, and employee/customer team theft.
- *Utility management.* Controlling costs of heat, light, and common areas.

- *Register functionality.* Effectively using the cash register for sales reports, inventory, management, and the like.
- *Receiving, stocking, and distribution.* Managing the flow of merchandise from the vendor through the store to the customer in a quick and cost-efficient way.

CUSTOMER SERVICE

Smiles Are Not Enough When It Comes to Serving Customers

Author, professor, and management consultant Peter Drucker wrote, "The purpose of a business is to create customers and keep them." This charge is difficult in today's retail environment. In almost all retail formats, today's consumers are demanding higher service levels. Determining what service elements customers value and delivering those elements without fail is the hallmark of successful retailers. Survey respondents realize this, and an overwhelming 93 percent say that customer service is very important (see Figure 4-2). Retailers rate their performance in this area very high—36 percent believe they are excellent at delivering quality customer service, and 56 percent believe they are good.

Although customer service has its roots in small-store retailing, many small retailers today do not devote adequate attention to delivering quality customer service. Failure to deliver quality customer service will

Figure 4-2   As customers demand increasingly higher service levels, retailers must take every opportunity to deliver excellent customer service.

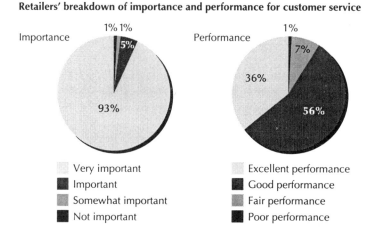

Retailers' breakdown of importance and performance for customer service

result in increased customer complaints, merchandise returns, and, ultimately, lost customers. It is more cost efficient to keep an existing customer than to find a new one.

It is in customer service that small-store retailers hold what is potentially a major competitive advantage over mass merchants and national chains. These retailers have an opportunity to know their customers better than their chain counterparts do. Chains, which are generally larger and located on the fringe of town, offer more of a cookie cutter approach to dealing with customers rather than a focused, personal approach.

But many small-store retailers have become complacent. Gone are the days when retailers greeted customers by first name at the door and escorted them through the store. Today only 53 percent of respondents say their employees offer assistance within their assigned departments (see Figure 4-3). Many retailers do not pay attention to the value of these details anymore, perhaps because they do not understand their importance.

Additionally, the economic and retail climates have made the task of offering top-notch customer service more difficult because of a shrinking and more expensive labor pool. Often, one of the first moves to control

Figure 4-3 Employee name tags are an easy way to give the store a more personal touch. Employees should smile and say hello. Greeters can help with loss prevention.

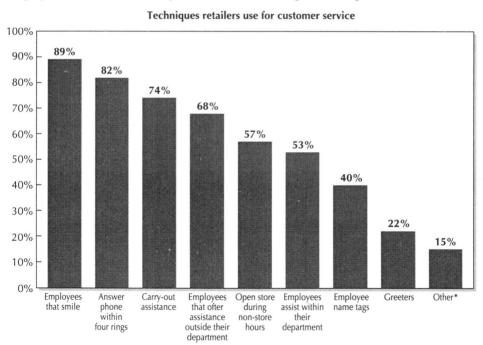

Techniques retailers use for customer service

* Includes delivery, house calls, and special orders.

costs is to reduce staff. But retailers must maintain a balance between controlling payroll cost and delivering outstanding customer service. For example, cutting back on staff may mean that customers have to wait longer to check out. To remedy such a situation, employees should acknowledge customers' presence and ask them to wait for just a minute. That way, customers will not feel ignored and leave.

There are several general techniques retailers can employ to win customers' loyalty. According to respondents, smiling employees and promptly answered phones are the two techniques that most effectively engender customer loyalty (see Figure 4-3 on the previous page). But there are other contributors. One effective technique that 57 percent of retailers use is to open stores on a "by appointment only" basis beyond normal store hours. This gives preferred customers a special opportunity to shop. In addition, retailers should offer to help customers carry their purchases to their cars and walk customers to their cars with an umbrella on rainy days. Although 74 percent say they do this, this percentage should be in the high 90s. Employees also should wear name tags to help bridge the distance between them and customers. Retailers should be sure that employees act as greeters near the front of the store. This orients customers, makes them feel welcome, and helps to prevent loss.

Leonard L. Berry, director of the Center for Retail Studies at Texas A&M University, says there are seven principles of quality service:[1]

- *Quality is defined by customers.* Improving service begins with determining the most important service characteristics customers want, measuring the store's performance against those characteristics, and increasing retailers' efforts in areas where performance falls short. This should be remembered during customer research.
- *Quality is a journey.* Quality service is a commitment, a mind-set. There are no quick fixes or permanent answers. Excellent service must be one of the retailers' priorities in good times and bad. Retailers and employees must do as much as possible to foster this mind-set.
- *Quality is everyone's job.* All employees must believe that their most important priority is to deliver outstanding customer service, regardless of each employee's specific position with the company. Retailers must provide specific examples to employees on how to deliver quality service.
- *Quality, leadership, and communication are inseparable.* Constant communication between the owner, managers, buyers, and salespeople—whether coaching or praising—is critical for quality cus-

---

[1] Berry, Leonard L. "Delivering Excellent Service in Retailing." *Arthur Andersen Retailing Issues Newsletter.* April 1988.

tomer service. Retailers should talk to employees during store hours and hold meetings before the store opens.

- *Quality and integrity are inseparable.* Fairness as an element of the corporate value system is essential to providing outstanding customer service. Employees who see management sacrifice the customers' interests for the sake of a quick profit will not take pride in the store. And pride is necessary to deliver superior service. Retailers should emphasize the importance of fairness in dealing with customers.
- *Quality is a design issue.* Customer service requires planning. It is a way of thinking that influences how retailers develop and implement new services and product lines.
- *Quality is keeping the service promise.* Delivering excellent service is not a part-time proposition. Retailers must strive for zero defects. Studies have shown that a customer will tell many more friends about a bad experience than about a good one. Retailers cannot afford to overpromise or underdeliver on customer expectations.

The best retailers use a variety of methods to ensure quality customer service, but all respond to employees' and customers' wants. Kathleen Alexander of Marriott Corp. writes that "taking responsibility for service is a willful act."[2] Employees will not take responsibility if they do not recognize the benefit, and they cannot take responsibility if they do not have the authority.

The challenge to customer service, Alexander states, is "to create an environment in which employees are committed to the success of the business and conduct themselves accordingly." This requires a significant time commitment on the retailer's part.

Best Practices You Can Use

Alexander indicates that, in addition to time, several key concepts will build employees' commitment to delivering excellent customer service (see also Chapter 6):

Employ the right people. Look for individuals who are enthusiastic, bright, and eager.

Orient employees. Educate them on the full experience of your business, including company culture and values. Show them all areas of the operation. They will feel trusted and capable, and this confidence will be evident in their performance.

---

[2] *Arthur Andersen Retailing Issues Newsletter.*

Communicate service expectations. Tell employees what you expect of them and, more importantly, lead by example. These are highly effective ways to communicate your vision. Instill in your employees the importance of listening to customers; it is the only way to determine what the customer wants.

Give employees authority. For employees to take responsibility for customer service, you must empower them to make decisions on how to remedy customers' concerns. Provide employees with guidance about when to waive a delivery charge or when to service equipment that you don't carry.

Motivate employees. Use incentives to encourage them. The key to successful incentives is making them commensurate with delivering good service. And incentives do not have to be financial. Recent studies conclude that employees rank money near the bottom of a list of incentives. Sometimes just a note of thanks or a public thank-you is enough. Establish a method of measuring success. Employees need to know if they are succeeding. So set a goal, make it known, and let employees know their influence in attaining it. Measures of performance, such as number of complaints or number of new ideas, are a good method for evaluating performance and encouraging self-correction.

Treat employees fairly and with respect. Interacting frequently and personally with employees is critical to developing loyalty and commitment. Also, instill trust in them. Generally, employees will treat customers the way they are treated. If they feel good about you, they will feel good about the store, and it will show.

Once you have laid the groundwork by building employees' commitment to excellent customer service, you need to determine what customers want (see the section titled "Marshall Field: 'Give the Lady What She Wants' " in Chapter 2. To do this:

- Encourage employees to ask customers what services they value and what other services they would like to see.
- Use comment cards or conduct periodic (at least annual) telephone surveys or focus groups.
- Ask employees what they would value as customers.
- Document all comments received, and analyze the information you collect.
- Determine the things you are doing right and the things you need to improve.
- Share these comments and the new policies they inspire with employees through regular meetings and day-to-day contact.

- Inform customers about how you plan to respond to their comments and complaints.
- As much as possible, strive to anticipate the customer's next point of interaction with the store and create the opportunity to resolve problems before they become complaints. For example, an appliance retailer should call customers to make certain that everything went well with the delivery. If a customer is pleased with the delivery and assembly, she will simply appreciate the call. If something went awry during the service, your call will give her the opportunity to bring it to your attention—and you the chance to smooth the waters and retain the customer.

STORE STAFFING AND LABOR PRODUCTIVITY

Proper Labor Scheduling Is the Key to Controlling Costs

Labor is the largest operating cost in retailing. In most retail formats, labor costs represent at least 10 percent of net sales. An effective labor-scheduling methodology maximizes the productivity of store labor by matching labor needs with qualified employees. Sixty-eight percent of respondents think store staffing and labor productivity are very important to the success of their businesses (see Figure 4-4).

Figure 4-4   To use labor resources effectively, retailers must know the tasks employees perform and the time required to complete them.

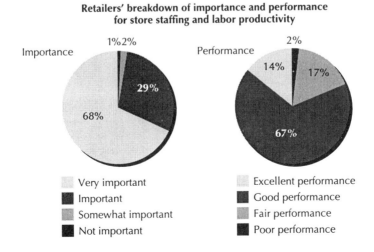

Retailers' breakdown of importance and performance for store staffing and labor productivity

Despite the fact that 81 percent say they are doing an excellent or good job maximizing labor productivity and controlling labor costs, most small-store retailers do not have a formal method. In fact, 78 percent either have no scheduling system at all or just use "rule of thumb" (see Figure 4-5). Why? Many retailers lack the knowledge necessary to develop an effective labor-scheduling system.

An ineffective labor-scheduling system leads to under- or over-staffing with unqualified or overqualified employees. Overstaffing results in unproductive employees and unnecessary use of labor dollars, and understaffing leads to poor customer service and loss of sales and customers. A recent National Retail Federation/MasterCard study found that 62 percent of customers who decided to buy a product while in a store left empty-handed because adequate sales assistance was not available.

Many small-store retailers think that available labor scheduling software is too expensive. Arthur Andersen agrees that the cost of sophisticated labor-scheduling software often outweighs the benefits for small-store retailers. However, retailers can implement a cost-effective system to schedule store labor using manual systems or simpler retail automation packages.

The key to a labor-scheduling system is to gather information on store traffic patterns and other labor needs (buying, receiving, stocking, and so on) and to use that information to optimize store staffing and cost. To develop an effective system, retailers must gather information about

Figure 4-5   To control labor costs, retailers need to know sales and traffic patterns by day of week and time of day.

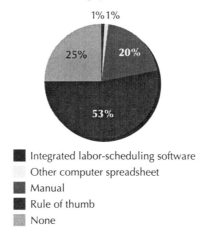

Labor-scheduling systems retailers use

■ Integrated labor-scheduling software
□ Other computer spreadsheet
■ Manual
■ Rule of thumb
▨ None

store traffic patterns, timing of other store labor needs and dates of promotions, holidays, and other special circumstances. Store owners and managers should also consider what areas of their stores require more experienced and skilled salespeople. For example, the furniture department of a department store should be staffed with those sales associates who have the most product knowledge—not with a salesperson from the fragrance department.

Lack of a formal scheduling method also can lead to employees performing tasks inconsistent with their positions and responsibilities. Figure 4-6 shows how owners, store managers, assistant managers, and sales

Figure 4-6 Properly allocating employees' time is important for retailers. Managers should spend more time with customers. Owners need to decrease their time allotments for administrative duties—leave that to the managers and sales employees—and spend more time on analyzing the business and planning ahead.

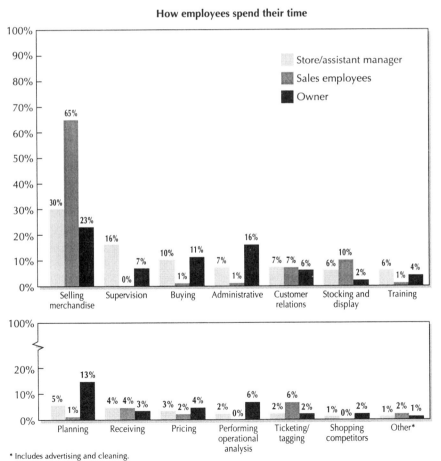

employees spend their time. Overall, small-store owners need to reassess how they spend their time. Arthur Andersen research indicates that successful owners divide their time equally among planning, customer relations, and supervising. Survey results indicate that small-store owners are spending an appropriate portion of their time on planning and customer relations; however, they are spending too much time with administrative and operating functions and not enough time with employees. Owners must decrease the time they spend on administrative duties like pricing and ticketing.

It is true that owners, like everyone else in small businesses, wear many hats. In fact, 62 percent of small-store owners are also store managers. But employees are stores' most valuable assets, and their development must be a priority; it appears that owners do not fully realize this. Owners should delegate administrative tasks to make time for training and supervising their employees, because ultimately this will lead to more loyal customers and greater sales.

While owners need to spend more time with their employees, managers need to spend more time with customers. Store managers and assistant managers should spend at least 50 percent of their time selling merchandise and interacting with customers, especially during high-traffic periods. Managers instead are spending time performing tasks that owners should be doing, like planning, buying, and analyzing operations. Store managers are on the front line and can provide valuable input in these areas, but these are really owner functions.

In stores where the owner is also the manager and buyer, time obviously must be allocated differently. In these situations, the owner must delegate functions such as ordering to trusted associates and instead focus on more critical areas such as leadership, merchandise strategy, vendor relations, and customers.

In contrast to owners and managers, sales associates appropriately allocate their time. Salespeople spend 72 percent of their time on the floor selling merchandise and interacting with customers. Considering that these employees perform a variety of other tasks, this percentage is right on the money. But store employees, as well as managers and owners, must make the most of their time on the sales floor; merchandise and displays can wait, but customers will not. Are managers and owners spending quality time with their customers? Are they greeting everyone who walks through the door? Are they providing helpful, knowledgeable assistance? Are they finding the right merchandise for their customers? Owners should focus on these issues when training and supervising employees.

Figure 4-7 shows how buyers spend their time. The good news is that they correctly spend about half of their time communicating with customers and other store employees. Communication is key to understanding what customers really want and translating those wants into merchandise plans. But the bad news is that buyers spend only 5 percent of their time planning. Buyers should spend up to 20 percent of their time planning, depending on the store's format. In addition, buyers in small stores must allocate more time to formulating and executing focused advertising plans. Currently they devote only 2 percent of their time to this task; they should spend between 5 percent and 10 percent.

But because small stores often lack sufficient technology, basic tasks take up larger chunks of buyers' time. For instance, buyers have to spend 20 percent of their time reordering and reviewing product availability. If retailers automated their merchandising systems or used open-to-buy, these basic tasks would require less time from buyers.

Buyers have one more weak area: competitive response. Buyers spend only 6 percent of their time attending buying markets and identifying new vendors and merchandise to respond to what competitors are offering. But these are the best ways to find unique merchandise that will give their stores an edge over the competition. Owners and buyers need to get out into the marketplace, see what is available at buying markets, shop competitors, and seek out new vendors. The buyer must be proactive in these areas (see the section titled "Unique Products and Services Carve Market Niches" in Chapter 3).

Figure 4-7 Buyers need to spend more time with vendors to identify new merchandise opportunities. They should spend more time planning as well.

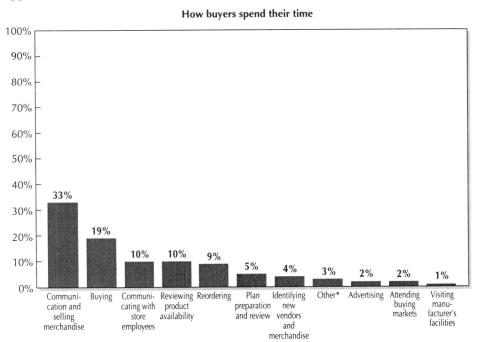

How buyers spend their time

* Includes training, inventory control, and administration.

Best Practices You Can Use

If you're like most small-store retailers, you probably cannot justify purchasing sophisticated software. But you still can develop an effective labor scheduling system.

Track customer traffic and number of transactions per hour by department for a sample period, such as two or three weeks. Include every day of the week, as well as days with and without promotions.

Solicit customers' input. Talk to customers as they enter or leave the store. Ask if they consider staffing to be adequate. Talk with them while you ring up their purchases. Or get the information from customer-service surveys and focus groups (see "Marshall Field: 'Give the Lady What She Wants' " in Chapter Two). Assign an employee to be a greeter who welcomes customers on their way in and thanks customers—and asks them about the service—on their way out. The employee, or roving service provider, should cover his department and perform other tasks when store traffic is slow, such as pricing merchandise, straightening displays, and cleaning.

Develop a simplified forecast of labor-hour requirements. Take, for instance, the following method:

- Calculate a forecast of weekly sales volume within 5 percent (use historical sales patterns to assist you). You should develop this forecast at least one month in advance.
- Correlate historical sales with the hours sales employees worked to determine the sales per person per hour (SPH) rate.
- Establish a benchmark of SPH based on historical data and industry benchmarks (call your trade association for industry-specific measures). If your store labor cost is too high, gradually work toward your goal.
- Using the forecasted sales and the desired SPH calculated previously, determine the number of hours to schedule your sales employees for the upcoming week. For example:

Forecasted sales for upcoming week:
$20,000

Desired sales per hour:
$100 per salesperson per hour

Salesperson hours required for week:
$20,000 (forecasted sales)/
100 (SPH) = 200 hours

- Next, determine how many sales employee hours you need to staff per day of the week. Use historical sales trends. Anticipate weekly sales as shown in Table 4-2.

Table 4-2   Weekly sales chart

Day of the week	(A) Percentage of weekly sales	(B) Total hours for the week	(C) Hours needed per day (A × B)
Monday	5%	200	10
Tuesday	5	200	10
Wednesday	10	200	20
Thursday	20	200	40
Friday	15	200	30
Saturday	25	200	50
Sunday	20	200	40
Total:	100%	200	200

Keep in mind that promotions, seasons, weather, day of the week, and time of day can affect requirements, as can nonselling activities such as receiving, ticketing, and restocking. Offer flexible scheduling for senior citizens or mothers with school-age children. Hire part-time employees to assist during peak hours and with promotions, but make sure they receive adequate training to provide top-quality customer service. The last thing a customer wants when in a rush or you are running a popular promotion is a sales associate who is not knowledgeable about your merchandise or operating policies.

Continually benchmark store labor as a percentage of net sales by comparing performance against your goals and industry results. See Chapter 9 for benchmark statistics.

Periodically update your staffing to be responsive to changes in the business. Such changes include the reorganization of departments or evolving traffic patterns.

For store owners, managers, and buyers, determine the most important business functions required by these roles and reprioritize everyone's time. Delegate administrative and operating tasks (such as marking merchandise) to trusted store associates so that you and your management team can focus on critical elements.

STORE LAYOUT

Audience Plays a Key Role in Aisle Style

Retail success depends on location, merchandise, price, and service. But even the best merchandise cannot ensure success if retailers do not effectively present it to customers. Stores must be both easy to shop and inviting to customers. The way retailers use floor space and display merchandise can make or break their stores. The majority of retailers feel that store layout is important, and they rate their layouts as good (see Figure 4-8). But Arthur Andersen research indicates that few small-store retailers take full advantage of using store design and layout to influence their image. As previously mentioned, store layout can increase customer traffic and store profits if used effectively. This is especially true when retailers pay close attention to the allocation of space to departments; arrangement of departments; and location of registers, customer-service offices, and receiving.

To be successful, this layout strategy must work in tandem with retailers' merchandise, target markets, and other marketing strategies such as pricing and advertising. For example, an apparel store specializing in infant and toddler clothes must make sure that the aisles are wide enough for strollers and the restrooms contain changing tables. Retailers also must remember that the demographics and lifestyles of customers influence their preferences and expectations, and retailers must be willing to change their layouts to keep up with customers' changing buying habits.

As Figure 4-9 indicates, the most common store layout is a combination of the basic layouts, which are free-flow and gridiron aisles. This reflects the trend in retailing to incorporate as much merchandise as possible into one store. Figure 4-10 (page 134) shows examples of the most common types of layouts.

In addition to selecting the best layout for their stores' formats, retailers should also follow a practice that their successful peers use: allocating space based on productivity ratios (e.g., gross margin and sales per square foot) so that the most profitable merchandise gets the most room. Determine profit contribution by items, categories, or departments, and use that measure when allocating space. Gross margin or sales are also good.

Figure 4-8   An effective store layout enhances a store's ambiance.

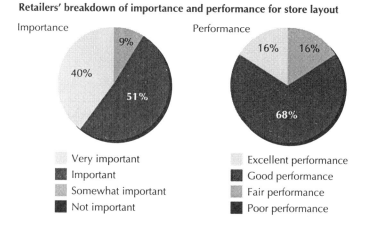

Retailers' breakdown of importance and performance for store layout

Importance

9%
40%
51%

Performance

16%   16%
68%

Very important
Important
Somewhat important
Not important

Excellent performance
Good performance
Fair performance
Poor performance

Figure 4-9 Use of the combination layout reflects a trend among retailers to organize their stores to incorporate a wide variety of merchandise. Retailers should make it easy to shop by ensuring wide, congestion-free aisles.

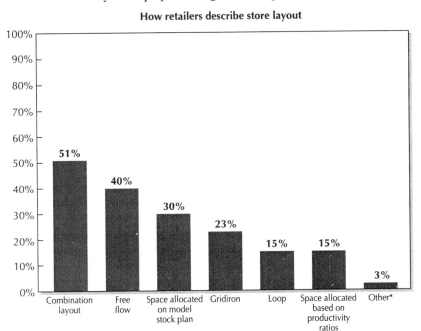

How retailers describe store layout

* Includes salon selling and no special plan in use.

The effectiveness of any of these arrangements, however, depends on the type of merchandise offered. Free-flow patterns work well in apparel and furniture stores, while the gridiron layout works well with food, drug, and general merchandise stores. The free-flow arrangement allows customers to move freely throughout the store and gives them convenient access to all items. This format encourages browsing and impulse buying, but it also takes up more space. Whether retailers need to get outside advice before changing store designs depends on the significance of the remodeling effort. Retailers undertaking major remodeling efforts, including painting, flooring, and structural changes, may want to hire professional store designers to assist in the planning process. But retailers who are just rearranging their stores, adjusting space allocation or conducting minor remodeling (e.g., coat of paint) should be able to handle the changes themselves using sales, item movement, and gross profit information.

Best Practices You Can Use

Consistency in store appearance, merchandise, advertising, and price are critical. You must make them consistent not only with one another but

Figure 4-10   The most common style of store layout retailers use is a combination of free-flow and gridiron. This reflects the retailers' desire to maximize the amount of merchandise they can place in the store.

Common store layouts

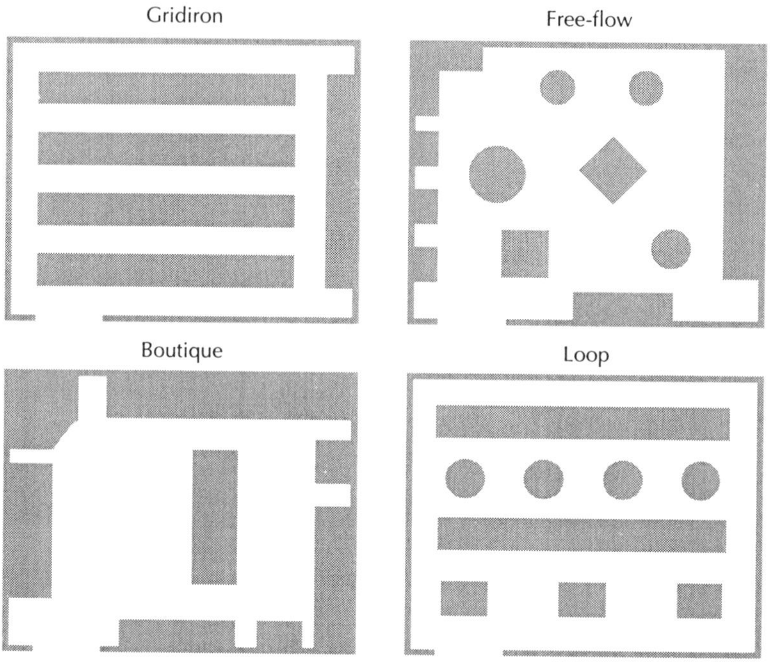

also with the image you want your store to portray. Display windows, interior signage, and exterior signage should reinforce your advertising strategy (see "Extra! Extra! Advertising and PR! Let Customers Read All About It" in Chapter 2) and the type of merchandise you offer (see "Facts Must Back Owners' Instincts" in Chapter 3).

Use background music and fragrance to improve the overall ambiance of the store. Obviously, you need to consider the overall message and image you want to convey in deciding whether to use either of these techniques.

Use in-store signage and directories to help customers find their way through your store. Place directories near each entrance and on each floor.

If you decide to hire an outside store designer, provide that individual with your overall merchandise plan and an indication of the arrangement and space allocation you have in mind. The designer should then be able to provide additional ideas.

If you elect to plan your own store design, consider the following steps:

Educate yourself. Shop other retailers with similar formats, especially successful chains. Chain stores typically devote significant internal resources to analyzing and developing store design. Additionally, they have been able to refine their design over time to maximize store profitability. Contact your commodity-specific trade association for general examples of effective store designs. Buy a retailing book; many exist that describe the ins and outs of store design. Keep in mind, however, that even though you can adopt general concepts for store design from other retailers, you need to develop a unique image. So use these resources as general guides, not cookie-cutter models.

Keep in mind the general rule for an effective layout. Always have a clean, organized store that encourages customers to shop.

Allocate as much space as possible to the selling floor. Nonselling space (e.g., offices, receiving, stocking) should take up no more than 10 to 15 percent of the total store space. While having a large office may appeal to you, it will cost you money in the long run. Keep offices and storage space to a minimum. Small-store retailers need to maximize space productivity. One exception is fitting rooms; in specialty apparel and upscale department stores, their size should not be minimized. For those formats, fitting rooms can be productive selling areas where sales associates offer personalized service.

Balance space allocation with customer needs and wants, so keep related departments together. To help boost your profits, keep clearance areas away from regular stock, and put impulse items like accessories near the registers.

Organize shelving, racks, and fixtures based on how you want customer traffic to flow. Remember the importance of a good layout.

Don't underestimate the power of color. Color can have a tremendous effect on the feel of the store. For instance, bright and dark colors will make a space seem smaller, and white or neutral shades will create the illusion of more space. Mirrors on the walls also make a space seem larger. You may also find it helpful to distinguish departments by slightly contrasting the color of the decor from department to department, though this results in less flexibility for changes in space allocation.

Flooring should be consistent with the color scheme and the overall image of the store. Tiles are cheap and easy to maintain, but they portray a no-frills image. Carpet is more expensive to maintain, but thanks to the longer lasting carpets on the market today, carpeting is generally a good investment for an upscale store image. One way to make carpet a more cost-effective option is to use carpet squares that you can replace on a square-by-square basis. Except near entrances, you should not combine tiles and carpet because it limits you in reallocating space. Wood flooring is the most expensive flooring option and should be considered only for more upscale stores.

Lighting also affects the image of a store. It should vary depending on location within the store and on the size and shape of the space being lit. Fluorescent lighting is harsh and best used in discount stores with higher ceilings. Halogen fixtures closely resemble natural light and create dramatic spotlights that are highly effective in specialty and upscale stores.

Fixtures must also be consistent with the overall image. For instance, in an apparel store, use waterfalls and four-arm displays for higher-end apparel and rounders for low-end and clearance merchandise. Also consider how much of the merchandise a fixture allows the customer to see, how much merchandise the fixture holds, how much the fixture costs, how flexible it is (adjustability, portability, etc.) and how the fixture fits into the overall shape of your store. You can usually buy good, inexpensive fixtures from vendors or from retailers going out of business. For high-end stores, consider antique shops for furniture and fixtures.

CUSTOMER ACCOMMODATIONS

Accommodations Can Distinguish Stores from Competitors

Survey respondents say that excelling at customer service and meeting customer wants are two of the most critical factors to their success. Yet customer accommodations, which should go hand in hand with those practices, rank last, according to retailers. Almost 70 percent say customer accommodations, which enhance customers' shopping experiences, are important or somewhat important, and 78 percent rate their accommodations as only fair or good (see Figure 4-11).

Clearly, small-store retailers fall short in emphasizing accommodations as a way to create greater customer loyalty. But customers continue to increase their expectations in the areas of service and accommodations. Small stores can meet and exceed those expectations by taking advantage of an area that large national chains miss—personal service accommodations. These accommodations are necessary to attract new customers and keep existing ones.

Because retailers underestimate the importance of accommodations, they do not invest the time and effort needed to determine their customers' needs and expectations regarding accommodations. Retailers tend to rely on their ideas of what customers want, which often are not the accommodations most highly valued by consumers. The importance of accommodations varies across formats. For instance, if the store targets males between the ages of 25 and 40, having a changing table in the restroom is probably not an accommodation that is important to the con-

Figure 4-11 As customer expectations rise, retailers need to increase the level of importance they give to customer accommodations.

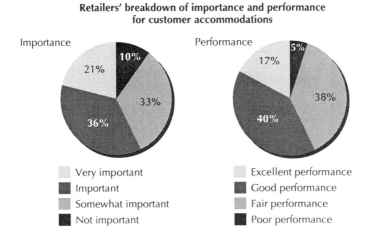

Retailers' breakdown of importance and performance for customer accommodations

Importance

10%
21%
33%
36%

Performance

5%
17%
38%
40%

Very important   Excellent performance
Important   Good performance
Somewhat important   Fair performance
Not important   Poor performance

sumer. The key is to determine the accommodations customers want and then to provide them.

As Figure 4-12 shows, many retailers accept major credit cards, take phone orders, and have layaway plans. However, if these retailers offer the same accommodations as other stores, they will not create a competitive advantage but will merely be following the norm. Successful retailers provide unique customer accommodations valued by their customers, including home delivery, home shopping, refreshments, gift registries, free trials, personal shoppers, seating, in-store postal service, and special parking for the elderly. It only takes a small investment to provide some of these unique accommodations, and the return on that investment can be great. But retailers need to make consumers aware of their stores' accommodations by citing them in all types of media and on in-store signage to generate more store traffic.

Generally, customers say one of the most important accommodations is a hassle-free return policy. Customer returns can provide helpful feedback, so they require constant attention from the retailer. The most common reasons customers return merchandise, according to retailers, are that an item is defective or that the customer did not want it (see Table 4-3, page 139). Defective merchandise may indicate that the retailer is not paying enough attention to details. To remedy this situation, retailers need to inspect all merchandise closely as it is put on the sales floor or delivered to the customer and negotiate more liberal return policies with the vendors.

To reduce the volume of returns, retailers need to monitor customers' reasons for returning merchandise and use this information to

Figure 4-12   Retailers should try to offer as many customer accommodations as possible. Parking and public washrooms are important. Retailers need to promote the accommodations they offer.

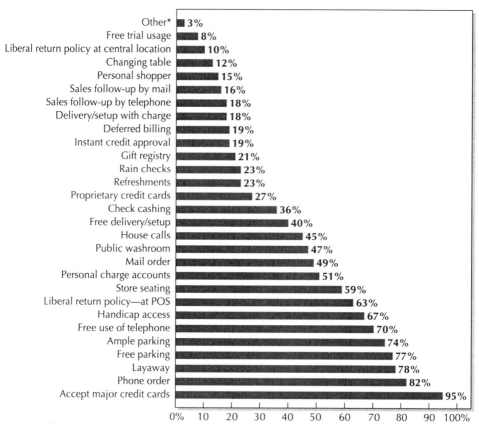

Customer accommodation techniques used by retailers

Accommodation	%
Other*	3%
Free trial usage	8%
Liberal return policy at central location	10%
Changing table	12%
Personal shopper	15%
Sales follow-up by mail	16%
Sales follow-up by telephone	18%
Delivery/setup with charge	18%
Deferred billing	19%
Instant credit approval	19%
Gift registry	21%
Rain checks	23%
Refreshments	23%
Proprietary credit cards	27%
Check cashing	36%
Free delivery/setup	40%
House calls	45%
Public washroom	47%
Mail order	49%
Personal charge accounts	51%
Store seating	59%
Liberal return policy—at POS	63%
Handicap access	67%
Free use of telephone	70%
Ample parking	74%
Free parking	77%
Layaway	78%
Phone order	82%
Accept major credit cards	95%

* Includes alterations.

take corrective action. One response might be to drop a perpetually problematic vendor. Another is to improve customer service so that customers purchase the right merchandise the first time. For example, retailers should encourage customers to try on clothes before purchasing them. But as Figure 4-13 shows, more than a third of retailers do not record or monitor reasons for return, let alone analyze them.

Since returns are an indication of a dissatisfied customer, retailers also need to provide hassle-free return service to make the resolution simple and to regain the customer's loyalty. Policies vary from "we accept all merchandise returns and give cash back" to "all sales are final" (see Figure 4-14). The most common return practices small-store retailers use are cash

Table 4-3 Retailers could prevent many returns by inspecting merchandise before putting it on the sales floor or delivering it.

Reasons why customers return merchandise (in order of importance as ranked by retailers)	
1. Defective merchandise	6. Wrong color
2. Did not want	7. Damaged merchandise
3. Wrong size	8. Wrong style
4. Wrong item	9. Price lower elsewhere
5. Gift return	10. Inferior quality

refunds with a receipt, merchandise credit with a receipt, and merchandise credit without a receipt. An alternative is to give only merchandise credit with or without a receipt. That way, retailers will not lose the sale. But, before using this method, the retailer must evaluate how customers will react—if they opt not to shop a store with a less liberal return policy,

Figure 4-13 Talking to store personnel is a good way to find out why customers return merchandise, but tracking reasons why merchandise is returned gives retailers the ability to analyze problems and serve customers better.

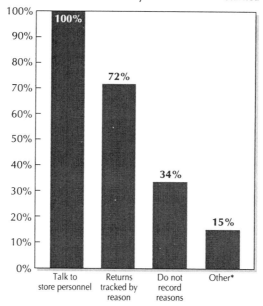

How retailers learn why merchandise is returned

* Includes stating reasons for return on refund slip and talking directly to customers.

Figure 4-14   While offering store credit for returns with a receipt prevents the retailer from losing the sale, many customers may view it as a hassle. Solicit customer opinions on all accommodations before instituting them. Additionally, reassess customer reactions to accommodations already in place to determine whether continuing them is worthwhile.

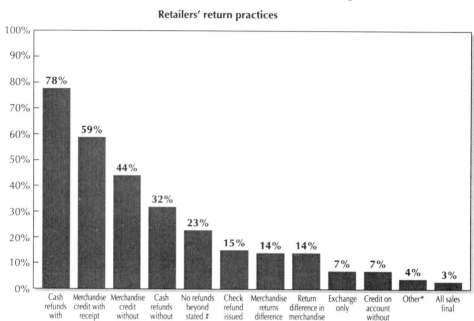

Retailers' return practices

* Includes merchandise exchange within 30 days of purchase.

more sales may be lost than by granting cash for returns. From a loss-prevention perspective, the most successful retailers give only store credit when customers return merchandise without a receipt unless a gift sticker is attached.

Best Practices You Can Use

The right accommodations vary among stores, depending on format and customer base. Some things are given, such as compliance with the Americans with Disabilities Act. But beyond that, there are no easy answers. You must determine what your customers value most. To select what accommodations to provide, you should do the following:

Ask customers what they want. Talk to them at all natural points of interaction such as at the register and on the sales floor. Also use surveys, comment cards, or focus groups to determine what accommodations your customers and potential customers want (see "Marshall Field: 'Give the Lady What She Wants' " in Chapter 2).

Shop the competition. See what accommodations—unique and otherwise—they offer.

Make your store customer-friendly. Think about how they will use your merchandise and how you can accommodate their lifestyles. A toy store, which obviously attracts parents and children, should provide tester toys and changing rooms.

Use other resources such as trade associations, publications, and seminars to get ideas for accommodations. Benefit from the experience of others.

Evaluate what you learn from your customers, your competitors, and other resources, and decide what you will provide. Then implement those accommodations and maintain their quality—if you are going to provide store seating, make sure the chairs are not in disrepair. Some customer accommodations you can provide are shown in Figure 4-12.

To establish a convenient return policy, you should consider the following.

Determine how liberal you want your return policy to be. Weigh that against customer service and loss prevention. Keep in mind that offering only merchandise credit is a way to avoid losing the sale, but you need to ask customers returning merchandise if that is acceptable.

Consider the policies of your competitors. Since hassle-free returns are so important to customers, consider making your policy as customer-friendly as possible.

STORE LOCATION

Real-Estate Rules Apply: Location, Location, Location

The majority of retailers feel that store location is very important, and they rate their location as effective (see Figure 4-15). But many small-store retailers, even those who are expanding or looking at other sites, often fail to consider all of the critical factors in maintaining or selecting sites. They view their current location as fixed and do not feel they can consider alternate sites; they either own the real estate or simply cannot afford to sell or move.

Figure 4-15   A store's location is critical for its success. Retailers must consider all factors, including occupancy costs and parking accessibility, in deciding to move or expand their businesses.

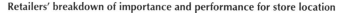

Retailers' breakdown of importance and performance for store location

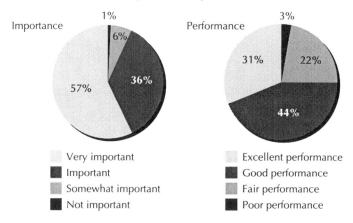

Analysis of demographic and location factors is critical to selecting a new site and reevaluating an existing site. Effective selection requires the retailer to first identify a trade area that contains a substantial proportion of his target customers. For example, an upscale sporting-goods store should look for a community filled with middle- to upper-income individuals between the ages of 25 and 40.

The retailer must then analyze the type of location by asking some questions: Is the store a destination where people will come regardless of surrounding retailers, or does it need to be near other traffic-generating complementary stores? Does the store rely heavily on convenience business and thus need to be near a busy intersection with easy-in, easy-out parking? These types of questions are critical to determining the most effective location. An important note: Most small-store retailers need to be near other retailers.

Another location factor to consider is the proximity of the proposed site to competing retailers, which retailers rank seventh in importance (see Table 4-4). Arthur Andersen's experience indicates that successful retailers identify the number of competitors within their market area and assess the relative strength of each potential competitor. The key is to identify the location that still will set them apart from the competition.

Square footage is also critical. One of the worst things a retailer can do when identifying store sites is to ignore the amount of square footage needed to effectively display merchandise. If the store is too large, it will look as if it is going out of business. If the store is too small, it will look crowded. When investigating locations, retailers need to visualize how their products will look within the available square footage.

Table 4-4 "Do my customers want to shop where my store is?" Retailers need to ask themselves this question and consider the kind of retailer they want to be and the kind of customer they want to attract.

Factors retailers consider in determining store location (in order of importance as ranked by retailers)

- Occupancy costs
- Convenience
- Demographics
- Parking accessibility
- Square footage
- Location to other major retailers
- Proximity of competition
- Free standing vs. mall vs. strip
- Own vs. lease
- Zoning regulations

Retailers also need to consider whether to own or lease. However, this is only a financing decision and should not influence where the store is located. But this element greatly affects cash flow. A number of factors influence this decision, including available capital, taxes, return on investment, cost of capital, age and condition of the building, and the length and terms of the lease. Currently, substantial excess retail space exists in the market. Even one-store retailers have some negotiating power these days.

Small-store retailers should avoid form leases because, for them, flexibility is key. Generally, a shorter fixed term with more option periods provides that flexibility. Buy-out clauses are also helpful, though not cheap. Small-store retailers, most of whom lack the time and expertise to determine new sites, should also take advantage of third-party real-estate companies that specialize in site selection and lease negotiation. Consultants can be expensive, and some are better than others, but a good consultant is invaluable. A retailer will find it difficult to overcome a poorly negotiated lease.

Best Practices You Can Use

Recognize mistakes. If you are in a location that once made sense but no longer does, get out. If you do not, you could lose your entire investment. One of the downfalls of small-store retailers is being enticed by free rent offered by real-estate developers and shopping-center owners. Many times retailers accept these offers and end up with bad store locations.

Hire a site selection consultant. Some are better than others. If you are considering hiring a consultant, call the National Retail Federation for a list of preferred consultants.

Recognize conflicting priorities. If you own the store, try to divorce your real-estate decisions from your retailing ones. If the store is not performing, look for alternative uses for your facility and move your retail operations elsewhere.

You should consider a variety of factors when assessing the adequacy of an existing location and determining where to locate a new store or relocate an existing store, including:

Occupancy costs. Does the cost of rent and utilities comprise a disproportionately high percentage of your net operating profit (i.e., profit before you deduct these costs)? A good rule of thumb is that occupancy costs should not exceed 7 percent of net profit. If you have healthy sales and gross profits relative to your peers (using industry benchmarks) and still cannot overcome your rent structure, this is a sure sign that you need a new location. Other important items:

- Avoid a lease that requires your personal guarantee of payment. You don't want to risk your personal wealth.
- Require the landlord to provide estimates for any common-area maintenance and real-estate costs you may encounter.
- Inspect the most recent real-estate tax bill.

Zoning regulations. What regulations exist that would restrict accessibility, expandability, and other such considerations. Call the local zoning board to find out both current and proposed laws.

Demographics. Do the demographics of the market area match those of your target market? Contact your local newspaper, chamber of commerce, planning board, or economic development organization for demographic information about your community. Or you can purchase census information from a variety of companies.

Proximity of traffic generators. Is the market saturated? Is there a grocery store or mass merchant in the area that will increase or decrease your store traffic? If so, find out how long they have been there and if they may be leaving the location soon. Depending on the format of your store, you may need help from other stores to generate traffic.

Proximity of competition. Is the competition close by? If so, is your store so unique in its service level and merchandise offering that you will be able to take market share away from the competition?

Free-standing vs. mall vs. strip. Do you need to be in a high-traffic area, or will your merchandise and service attract customers? Ask your existing and potential customers where they shop and why, and what attracts them to particular locations.

Convenience. Will customers only shop in your store if you're close by? Ask customers and noncustomers if the store is convenient to them.

Parking accessibility. Can customers get in and out easily and safely?

Availability of labor. What is the quantity and quality of the local labor force? Talk with other retailers and the local chamber of commerce.

Own vs. lease. If you are thinking of buying, can the funds be put to better use?

Store configuration and storefront. Does the store's layout fit with the way you anticipate displaying the merchandise? Is it responsive to your back-office needs? Does the storefront have enough windows or the right character?

Landlord support. If you are considering a mall location, does the management company provide adequate support in the areas of maintenance, marketing, and promotion? Strip-center locations should provide similar services, although the quality may not be as high.

Receiving. Can you bring goods into the store efficiently?

SHELF AND DISPLAY MANAGEMENT

Dynamic Displays Generate Traffic and Sales

Effective merchandise presentation and display, commonly referred to as visual merchandising, are closely related to store layout. This subject also relates closely with merchandising. The primary purpose of a display is to attract attention to the merchandise, which leads to a sale. Displays may also reinforce the store's image. As a result, effective shelf displays of both basic and special items can dramatically influence customers and their purchasing behavior. That's probably why 94 percent of survey respondents say this is an important or very important task (see Figure 4-16). But only half rate their displays as good, and a quarter say that they are only fair.

Perhaps these respondents realize that small-store retailers often display merchandise in a manner inconsistent with their store image and advertising promotion strategy. For instance, a small-store retailer advertising his store as an upscale women's specialty store should not display merchandise (except clearance) on tables. Consistency among displays, advertising, and image is critical for effective selling, although many retailers do not understand this. In fact, 40 percent of retailers say they do not use any techniques to ensure that their shelf and display management strategies are consistent with their other marketing techniques. Successful retailers make this a foundation of their merchandising strategy.

Figure 4-16   Shelf displays, when carefully aligned with a store's advertising strategy and image, can influence customers and their purchasing. Retailers need to strive for consistency between displays, advertising and image.

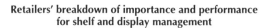

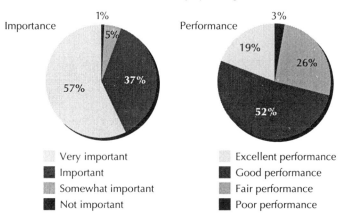

Of those retailers who do use techniques to ensure consistency, only 43 percent match their displays with their advertised items, and only 30 percent of buyers work with store managers to ensure consistency with displays of stock and promotional items—two important practices of successful retailers (see Figure 4-17). Retailers who do not do this are setting themselves up for failure. Customers who cannot quickly find the advertised merchandise they want can become noncustomers.

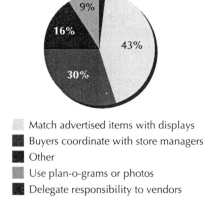

Figure 4-17   Only 60 percent of retailers use any techniques to create consistency between their displays and other marketing strategies. Yet, shelf and display management can enhance a store's performance.

How frequently retailers reset displays

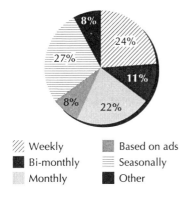

Weekly
Bi-monthly
Monthly
Based on ads
Seasonally
Other

Figure 4-18 Although many retailers change displays monthly or seasonally depending on the merchandise, they should consider resetting displays more often to create excitement for the consumer and encourage impulse buys.

Another area that retailers should address is the frequency with which they reset their displays. As Figure 4-18 shows, 27 percent of respondents say they change their displays seasonally, 24 percent change them weekly, and 22 percent change them monthly. Retailers should change displays often to create excitement in the store, pique customers' interests with new items, increase shopping frequency, and promote impulse buying. But the exact timing varies depending on format. Hardware stores, for example, should vary their displays at least every season, while drugstores should do it weekly, based on promotions.

Best Practices You Can Use

There are numerous things you can do to attract customers' attention through smart visual merchandising. How you display a product greatly influences how quickly it moves off the shelves. In apparel stores, this may mean grouping higher-end items together, away from the lower-end merchandise. Special signage and glitzy displays can attract customers to these items. If you sell apparel, do not display your high-end merchandise on rounders. Instead, use T-stands or pyramid displays. In drugstores, this may mean placing high-margin items toward the ends of the aisles where they are more prominent. Some general best practices include the following.

Match your displays with the items you advertise, and build displays around high-margin or fast-moving items. Make sure adequate signage accompanies the displays. Display the best sale items near the front of the store. Except during storewide sales, avoid having too many marked-down goods in the same display.

Display large items at the front of the store. This encourages the customer to take a cart.

Give ample amounts of display space to impulse buys. Display items such as candy, magazines, and sundries near the register.

Keep displays simple. Don't cram them with too many items or display so many items that customers cannot walk around easily, and feature seasonal, up-to-date goods.

Use color or props. These factors—especially moving props—attract attention, establish the tone of the display, and tell a story. Use props to show the merchandise in use.

Make sure the displays are well-lit. High-intensity halogen fixtures or track lights can add drama to displays.

Have a theme for each display. These can be communicated with signage that reads NEW AND IMPROVED, NEW, LOW PRICE, CLEARANCE, or whatever else is appropriate.

Cross-merchandise displays. Display garden tools and grass seeds, suntan lotion and sunglasses. In furniture stores, display room settings.

Use waterfall fixtures to display featured apparel items and position them in the front of the store. For hardware, use bins, baskets, or pallets.

Do not use handmade signs on your displays. Handmade signs are unprofessional—they are a turn-off to customers. Generally a local print shop can make signs for you cost efficiently, or you can purchase a color printer and computer graphics package and produce them yourself. Enhance signage by using colors to highlight key information (e.g., 30 PERCENT OFF in red). Details matter—this is not the area to be overly frugal.

STORE HOURS

Time-Constrained Customers Want to Shop around the Clock

Consumers today are busier than ever. The number of dual-income households and single-parent families has increased dramatically over the past 10 years. Quite simply, many—if not most—consumers do not have time to shop during the traditional store hours of 9 A.M. to 5 P.M. Retailers need to establish store hours that are sensitive to today's hurried customers. Large retailers, including mass merchants and national chains, realize this and offer expanded store hours or special shopping arrangements, such as mail-order shopping. Some retailers even open their stores during non-store hours for their preferred customers. Small-store retailers say they realize that store hours are important. More than 80 percent rank store hours as important or very important (see Figure 4-19). They also rank their performance high. But retailers may need to reevaluate their performance. Most small-store retailers have limited hours. They generally close at 5 P.M. or 6 P.M. weekdays and Saturdays and rarely open on Sunday. In fact, of the 50 hours or so that most small-store retailers are open each week, only 10 do not fall during the traditional hours of 9 to 5.

Figure 4-19 Retailers need to match store hours with customers' lifestyles. Not opening stores on Sunday frequently means missed opportunities.

Retailers' breakdown of importance and performance for store hours

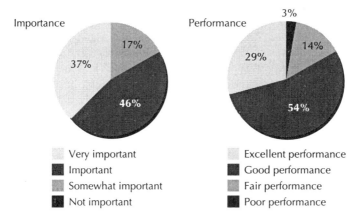

Still, respondents insist that they establish their store hours based on customer feedback, other retailers' hours, and the competition's hours (see Table 4-5). And Arthur Andersen research indicates that most customers are searching for retailers with extended hours. Customers want to shop on the way to work or in the evenings. Sunday is also a popular day—many retailers who are open Sunday say it is their second busiest day of the week. Small-store retailers need to realize that time-constrained customers need to shop when it is convenient to them, not to the retailer. One respondent recently decided to open his store from noon until 4 p.m. on Sundays. He says the increased sales are more than enough to cover the costs, and he has found an entirely new group of customers.

Best Practices You Can Use

Understand and monitor your store's traffic patterns. Purchase an inexpensive hand-held traffic counter. Then, over several weeks, count the number of customers that enter your store every hour. Once you have this information, determine the percentage of customers that enter your store on an hourly basis by day and the percentage that enter your store each day of the week. Then analyze your store hours. For example, if you find out that only 2 percent of your customers shop between 9 A.M. and 10 A.M., ask yourself if you really need to open at 9 A.M.

Make sure you advertise before you change your hours so your customers and potential customers know. Then monitor store traffic during those hours to determine if the traffic and gross-margin dollars generated are

Table 4-5   Retailers should experiment with store hours. Opening on Sunday may be one way to increase customer traffic. Closing or reducing store hours on the slowest weekday (usually Tuesday or Wednesday) is another consideration. Retailers should advertise any changes.

Factors retailers consider in establishing store hours (in order of importance as ranked by retailers)

- Customer feedback
- Competition
- Other retailers
- Traffic patterns
- Employee feedback
- Local laws

beneficial, considering the additional costs of opening (labor, utilities, and so on). Be patient; it will take several weeks or months for customers to change their shopping habits.

Consider decreasing your store hours on the slowest day of the week (traditionally Tuesday or Wednesday for small-store retailers) and increasing them on other days, especially Sundays and weekday evenings. These hours are less convenient for employees, though. You may need to offer incentives or develop rotation schedules.

Ask your customers when they like to shop. Use comment cards, focus groups, or interviews to find out what hours your target market wants (see "Marshall Field: 'Give the Lady What She Wants' " in Chapter 2 for information on developing comment cards and conducting focus groups). You need to talk to people who do not shop your store as well as those who do. Some noncustomers might come to your store if you offered hours convenient to them.

Consider other retailers' hours. You need to coordinate hours with other community retailers, especially if your store is not a destination shop.

Consider having by-appointment-only hours and promote them as competitive advantages. You can offer this service to preferred customers at the register or through a targeted mailing.

LOSS PREVENTION

Reducing Theft and Shrinkage Adds to the Bottom Line

More than half of retailers feel that loss prevention is very important, and almost half rank their performance as good (see Figure 4-20). However,

Figure 4-20 Overall, retailers feel they do a good job in the area of loss prevention, but they take little direct action to prevent theft.

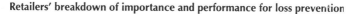

Retailers' breakdown of importance and performance for loss prevention

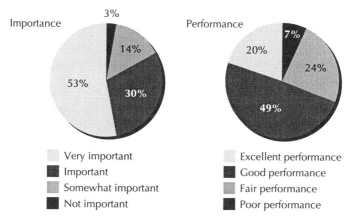

Importance
3%
14%
53%
30%

Performance
7%
20%
24%
49%

Very important — Excellent performance
Important — Good performance
Somewhat important — Fair performance
Not important — Poor performance

most respondents do not consider theft to be a significant risk and so do little more than lock the store at night and take an annual physical inventory.

While some small-store retailers indicate that they do not want to encourage employees to mistrust customers or other employees, the fact is that shoplifting is the largest monetary crime in the United States and comprises as much as 7.5 percent of sales.[3] Shoplifters come in all ages, races, and genders. Although professional shoplifting circles exist, most shoplifting is conducted by amateurs and store employees. Professionals hit small stores with a vengeance because these stores are generally easy targets due to lack of loss prevention controls. Employees steal by purchasing merchandise at a discount for friends and family, conspiring with customers and vendors, and stealing merchandise and cash.

As Figure 4-21 shows, retailers are missing out on some effective ways to minimize their losses. Successful retailers have awareness programs, but only 67 percent of small-store retailers have such programs. And 64 percent rely on the store manager to monitor and prevent merchandise losses.

Best Practices You Can Use

Some techniques to control theft include the following.

Educate employees. Be open with them about the dollar impact of theft. Discuss high-loss areas and ways to protect the merchandise. Create awareness and concern and emphasize the cost of getting caught. One

[3] Mason, J. Barney, et al. *Retailing*, 4th ed.

Figure 4-21 One of the most effective ways for retailers to prevent losses is an awareness program for employees. Other useful methods include background checks on new hires and inexpensive items such as fake cameras and two-way glass.

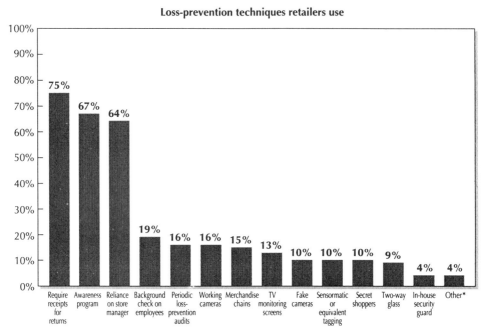

Loss-prevention techniques retailers use

* Includes mirrors and working closely beside the customer.

successful retailer keeps employees aware of shoplifting with a Wall of Shame—a break-room wall covered with pictures of previously apprehended shoplifters. Provide training on how to recognize shoplifters and respond to shoplifting incidents. Institute a recognition and award program to prevent shoplifting. Encourage employees to greet everyone; thieves hate to be noticed. The best deterrents to shoplifting are alert, assertive employees.

Increase accountability of store managers to focus on controllable profit, which includes shrinkage in addition to sales. Base your manager's incentive compensation on this measure.

Prosecute all shoplifters—including friends, acquaintances, and employees. One Illinois retailer prosecuted a local minister. Set a precedent to deter theft. In Illinois, a first-time offender's maximum sentence is a year in jail and a $1,000 fine. Prosecution for repeat offenders is an automatic class-four felony and can include as much as three years in jail. Take advantage of civil recovery laws, which allow retailers to pursue thieves and bad check writers for the amount stolen plus monetary damages up to three times the value of the loss plus attorney fees and court costs. Contact your local police department or the Illinois Retail Merchants Association for more information.

Plan the store layout to deter shoplifting by using the following techniques:

- Maintain adequate lighting in all areas of the store.
- Keep displays at eye level. If this is not possible, use mirrors or surveillance cameras.
- Maintain neat merchandise displays.
- Keep small items of high value (e.g., film, cigarettes, and small appliances) behind a counter or in a locked case.
- Lock all entrances and exits that customers don't use or that you cannot keep an eye on. Make excess doors emergency exits only.
- Attach noisemakers to unlocked exits.

Consider an anonymous witness program. In such a program, an employee may anonymously call another retailer or answering service to report internal theft.

Position people in the store. Instruct them to keep their eyes on all aisles or hidden areas of the store.

Use protective equipment and hire an outside security service if necessary. Other theft-deterring possibilities include:

- Two-way mirrors
- Observation booths
- Visible cameras (real or dummy)
- Concealed cameras
- Dressing room attendants
- Merchandise chains and cables
- Electronic article surveillance devices or ink tags

Vendors and reputable consultants will help you assess your areas of greatest exposure. Limit security tagging and chains to high-value items such as furs and leathers. You could also use pull tags, whereby the customer redeems a ticket for the merchandise at the register. The pull tags should be located next to a sample of the merchandise.

Be cautious when receiving merchandise. The receiving door should be supervised by a store manager or assistant manager.

For new employees, perform background checks and call their references. Many organizations, such as the Employers Mutual Association in Chicago, offer negative data pools of apprehended dishonest employees.

Require receipts or gift tags for merchandise returns. Review refunds weekly to ensure that they are properly authorized.

Call your local police force. Often the police provide seminars on how to spot shoplifters and what to do if one is identified and apprehended. Coordinate this effort with other local retailers.

Learn to look for these common behavior traits of shoplifters. Teach employees to do the same:[4]

- Shoplifters use their hands to steal; if you are suspicious of someone, watch that person's hands.
- Shoplifters are looking constantly to see if they are being watched. They have a tendency to look quickly from one direction to another.
- Shoplifters often exhibit quick, jerky movements in an attempt to conceal merchandise on their person.
- Shoplifters use diversionary tactics, such as fainting, while their accomplices grab merchandise.
- Shoplifters may pretend to be clumsy, repeatedly dropping items on the floor, or they may make repeated trips to the same area of the store until the coast is clear to steal.
- Shoplifters may carry large shopping bags.

Recognize the tactics thieves use to rob stores.[5]

- Palming small objects with a handkerchief or glove
- Crowding behind customers to avoid being seen by store employees
- Handling three or four objects at a time, returning some and stealing some
- Layering store clothes under their clothes in a fitting room or rest room
- Switching tickets from less expensive to more expensive merchandise
- Concealing merchandise in coats and jackets with large pockets
- Grabbing any item near the front of the store and leaving quickly
- Placing a coat on top of an item on the counter and picking up the coat and item together

Lock unattended registers.

Require sign-on passwords for cash registers.

Perform periodic cash counts for all cashiers throughout the day.

Review cash over/short at least every month.

Be alert of the behavior patterns of employees. Some behaviors could be an indication of employee theft, such as:

---

[4] Cash, H. Patrick and Frankel, Harold H. *Improving Apparel Shop Profits: A Professional Approach.*
[5] Ibid.

- Friends who come to the store often to visit employees
- Employees who always carry bags to and from work
- Employees who are consistently the last to leave the store or the first to arrive in the morning

UTILITY MANAGEMENT

Retailers May Miss Out on Opportunities to Control Costs

Seventy-two percent of retailers feel that utility management is important or very important (see Figure 4-22). And most retailers rank their performance as fair or good. In fact, many small-store retailers take measures to control utility costs. Few, however, challenge utility-company charges (see Table 4-6). Nor do they take advantage of consulting services that local utility companies offer.

Best Practices You Can Use

If you pay the utility bill directly, contact your local chamber of commerce to obtain a list of utility auditors. Ask the auditor to conduct a thorough evaluation of your utility-management strategy and recommend ways to improve it. Then implement the auditor's suggestions, including retrofitting your store, if necessary.

If you pay your utility bill indirectly (e.g., the cost is included in a lease), challenge your rent and attempt to obtain concessions from your

Figure 4-22   Retailers need to look for different ways to reduce utility costs.

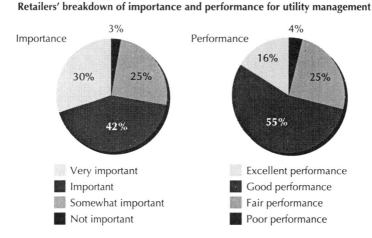

Retailers' breakdown of importance and performance for utility management

Importance — 3%, 30%, 25%, 42%

Performance — 4%, 16%, 25%, 55%

Very important
Important
Somewhat important
Not important

Excellent performance
Good performance
Fair performance
Poor performance

Table 4-6   Retailers should ask local utility companies to help identify cost-saving opportunities.

Methods retailers use to control utility costs
(in order of importance as ranked by retailers)

- Employee education on effective usage
- Use of timers
- Programmed thermostats
- Capital improvements and investments
- Energy consultants
- Modify store hours
- Negotiate with landlord
- Common-area maintenance audits
- Utility auditors

---

landlord for structural and design elements that contribute to inefficient energy usage.

If your store is in a mall, conduct a common-area maintenance audit. Based on an article by Michael Hartnett for *Stores* magazine, you will recover, on average, $2 for every $1 invested in auditing common-area charges. Common errors in these charges include not receiving credit for past payments, being overcharged for the space occupied, being charged for insurance that is not part of the common area (e.g., boiler and/or glass insurance) and having real-estate taxes allocated incorrectly. You should analyze and challenge all common-area charges by performing the following steps:

- Analyze monthly charges over the past several years and ask the landlord about increases.
- Recalculate the percentage of square footage of your store to the percentage of the total mall square footage. If the mall has increased in size but your allocated percentage has not changed, you could be overcharged.
- Recalculate or compare the monthly charges for each item, based on the total square footage of your store as compared to the total mall square footage.
- Talk with other retailers in the mall to determine if the common-area charges are consistently allocated and calculated. Consider working together to challenge the total common-area charges.
- Benchmark utility costs against industry performance, using the ratios on page 332 and information from resources such as the National Retail Federation's *Financial and Operating Results* and studies sponsored by your commodity-line trade organization.
- Consider applying for a grant from the Illinois Department of Energy and Natural Resources to install more energy-efficient equipment.

CLEANLINESS

Stores Must Clean Up Their Acts

Although retailers do not feel customers place a high premium on cleanliness, the retailers themselves value it highly. More than 65 percent of retailers say cleanliness is very important, and 85 percent rank their performance as good or excellent (see Figure 4-23). On the other hand, customers do not place a high premium on cleanliness because they have come to expect a clean store, and they will quickly reject an unclean store.

The reality, though, is that most retailers do not perform the cleaning tasks as frequently as they should (see Figure 4-24 on the following page). Mass merchants and national chains excel in cleanliness, so small stores need to keep pace. Every day retailers should clean the bathrooms, sweep the floor, empty the trash, dust and clean the fixtures, and straighten or face the merchandise.

They also need to keep their stores orderly. The store is a stage for the merchandise; detracting from the customer's focus on the product could result in lost sales. Yet many retailers have overstocked stores with cluttered aisles and shelves. This not only turns off customers because they feel like the store is not clean, but it may also create safety hazards. Moreover, stale displays and dated window arrangements will drive away customers.

And because of the poor economy the last few years, many retailers have postponed remodeling their stores. Not only can this reduce effectiveness of layout and displays, it can also make the store look unclean, drab, and outdated. While some retailers remodel significantly every one

Figure 4-23   Retailers understand the importance of having a clean store, but they seem to recognize that there is room for improvement.

Retailers' breakdown of importance and performance for cleanliness

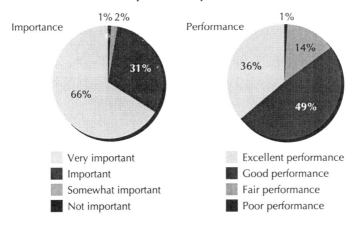

Figure 4-24 Retailers should be aware that national chains excel in cleanliness. Even though the bathrooms in small stores are mostly for employee convenience rather than customer use, they should be cleaned daily.

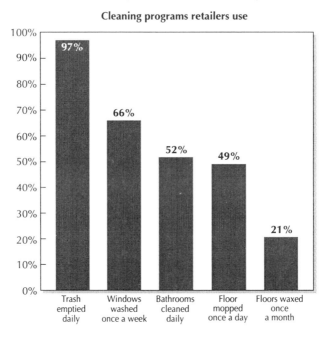

Cleaning programs retailers use

to five years, most wait longer; 47 percent remodel every five to eight years, and 35 percent wait more than eight years to remodel. Successful retailers usually perform significant remodeling every five to seven years.

Best Practices You Can Use

Establish a cleaning schedule. Include such tasks as mopping and waxing floors (at least once per month), washing windows once per week, emptying trash and cleaning bathrooms daily, and cleaning displays weekly.

Straighten displays every day. During busy seasons, you may need to do this several times each day. Keep window displays free of cobwebs and flies.

Clear the aisles. Don't keep empty boxes or excess merchandise in the aisles. Stock shelves and racks when customer traffic is at its lowest point.

Inspect the store regularly. Make sure lighting is adequate, and replace bulbs immediately when they burn out. Make sure the floor is clean and free from objects that might cause an accident. Make repairs as soon as possible.

Keep a clean store. An unclean store may present safety problems. Educate employees about the importance of safety. Education is much less expensive than insurance and attorney fees for customers or employees who hurt themselves. Meetings, employee newsletters, and employee bulletin boards are all good vehicles for safety education. Keep good records of safety, cleanliness, maintenance policies, and employee education programs. They will be instrumental in case of a lawsuit after an accident.[6]

Apply a fresh coat of paint. A good rule of thumb is to remodel every five to seven years. Between major remodels, you can repaint, recarpet, or change the layout and signage to improve your store's appearance. See the section entitled "Audience Plays Key Role in Aisle Style" in this chapter for some ways to develop effective store designs.

Schedule maintenance for nonbusiness hours. If this isn't possible, clearly mark all work areas. Make sure that contractors are covered by a certificate of insurance for general liability.

Keep the floors dry. Use nonskid mats or carpeting in entranceways. Mop up rainwater or snow that customers track into the store. Put up caution signs when the floors are wet.

Clearly mark changes in floor levels with signs.

Hire a maintenance service to keep the parking lot clear of debris and snow.

Properly apply floor wax. Be sure the wax is nonskid, and don't overapply it.

REGISTER FUNCTIONALITY

Computers Are Necessary to Keep Up with the Joneses

Retailers not willing to embrace—or at least consider—technology at the register are at distinct disadvantages when it comes to servicing customers and managing their businesses. Customers are no longer willing to wait in line for manual price checks or lengthy credit authorizations. And management needs accurate sales information every day. Vendors are using bar codes in more commodity lines. Luckily, the personal computer revolution has reached the retail market, and retailers easily can take advantage of relatively inexpensive hardware and software to meet almost every need.

But small-store retailers have not embraced this technology as quickly as their larger counterparts, perhaps because they do not fully understand the benefits or because they feel point-of-sale (POS) technol-

[6] Perry, Phillip, "How to prevent slips and falls." *Stores.* June 1993.

ogy is too expensive. In fact, most respondents feel register functionality, which enables retailers to use the cash register in sales reporting and inventory management, is only somewhat important or important (see Figure 4-25). Only half of retailers believe their systems are up-to-date.

Nonautomated retailers need to realize that electronic POS is no longer limited to the national chains. As one shoe retailer said, "I have been a holdout for years, but I'm not sure how much longer I can hold out." Many computer companies have developed affordable retail software that expands the common features of point-of-sale (POS) registers to include such things as scanning, perpetual inventory, customer profiling, sales reports, and labor scheduling. And because small-store retailers by definition have few stores, they can implement systems more easily than can large chains.

But small-store retailers still shy away from this technology. In fact, a disappointing 61 percent do not have an electronic POS system. Those who do mostly use it to authorize credit cards and record customer purchases (see Figure 4-26). Retailers need to use their computerized systems to eliminate manual tasks, such as sales reports and inventory tracking.

Best Practices You Can Use

Before you purchase a computer system and software, you need to assess what features and functions you want. (See "Computer Revolution Changing the Way Retailing is Done" in Chapter 7.) Ways to do this include:

Figure 4-25   Retailers need to accept that in order to remain competitive, they need to consider updating their register technology. High-tech registers aren't just for big chains anymore.

Retailers' breakdown of importance and performance for register functionality

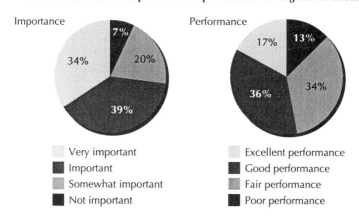

Figure 4-26 Retailers with POS systems should use them for the generation of sales reports, merchandising data, labor management, and much more. Retailers who have yet to implement POS should reconsider, as it is less expensive now and performs many more functions.

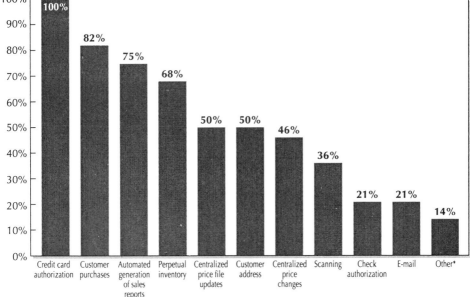

Ways retailers use POS systems

* Includes special order tracking, receiving at POS, and purchase orders generation.

- *Talk with your employees.* Ask store managers what information they need to run day-to-day operations. Ask others what they need to help with merchandising, inventory control, and accounting. To make a change as significant as automating, you need to have your employees' full support.
- *Talk with other retailers.* Ask noncompeting retailers detailed questions about their POS systems.
- *Shop your competition.* Find out what they are using and how it facilitates the checkout process.
- *Talk with hardware and software vendors.* Find out what products they recommend for small-store retailers.
- *Talk with your customers.* Ask them what they like or dislike about the checkout process.

After you determine what systems you can automate, you need to take a look at the associated costs and benefits.

Talk with manufacturers, vendors, and people at trade associations and technology shows.

Perform a cost/benefit analysis. Benefits of a POS system may include faster processing of customer sales, which in turn may reduce labor. Make sure you include short-term and long-term benefits as well as tangible and intangible ones.

Develop a timeline. Determine when to purchase the equipment, learn the system, and train your associates. Recognize that you and your employees will have a period of adjustment during which you may question your decision, but soon everyone will be adept.

RECEIVING, STOCKING, AND DISTRIBUTION

Profitability Depends on Moving Goods to the Floor Quickly

While Arthur Andersen ranks receiving, stocking, and distribution as the least important store-operations function, retailers say it is the sixth most important store-operations practice, with 53 percent saying it is very important and 41 percent saying it is important (see Figure 4-27).

The relatively low level of importance Arthur Andersen ascribes to this practice is based on the fact that a majority of respondents have only one store and no distribution center. Still, developing an effective system

Figure 4-27   The critical aspect of receiving, stocking, and distribution is getting merchandise on the floor, so that the customer can buy it as soon as possible.

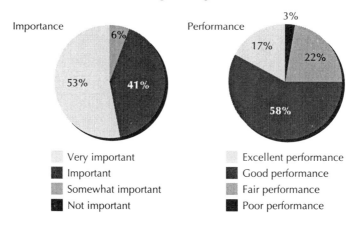

Retailers' breakdown of importance and performance for receiving, stocking, and distribution

Importance

6%
53%   41%

Performance

3%
17%   22%
58%

Very important
Important
Somewhat important
Not important

Excellent performance
Good performance
Fair performance
Poor performance

to manage the flow of goods from the vendor to the customer is important to profitability and competitive advantage.

Very few small-store retailers have vendors preticket the merchandise. While preticketing helps to decrease labor costs and increase employees' productivity at other tasks, most small-store retailers are not able to arrange cost-effective methods for vendors to ticket the merchandise. As a result, most retailers rely on ticketing at the store level. Not ticketing merchandise is acceptable as a labor-saver—provided that retailers use signs that clearly state the prices.

The bottom line, however, is that retailers need to get the merchandise into a presentable condition and to the right location as quickly as possible. Successful retailers have implemented a policy of getting merchandise to the shelf the same day it arrives and limiting the amount of merchandise in the back room. As the saying goes, "You cannot sell what your customers cannot see."

Best Practices You Can Use

You should consider the following procedures to increase efficiency in merchandise flow, which includes receiving, checking, marking, and stocking merchandise:

- *Plan ahead.* Anticipate new shipments and plan where, when, and how you will display the merchandise.
- *Look at your existing receiving area and determine if delivery vehicles can easily access it.* Also make sure the area is clean, organized, and secure.
- *Analyze your existing receiving and stocking space.* Determine if you can reduce this space and add more selling space to your store.
- *Depending on the kind of goods, consider locating the receiving, checking, and marking area close to the sales floor or stockrooms.* Handling costs are high, so you must consider ways to minimize them.
- *Use specialized equipment to facilitate unloading and processing merchandise.* Ideas include flexible conveyors, specialized marking and processing stations, ticketing guns, and pricing machines.
- *Schedule your deliveries with common carriers to arrive at times that are convenient to you, generally during slow-traffic hours.*

Upon receiving merchandise, do the following:

- Check the merchandise against the store's purchase order and the vendor's invoice. Look at quality and quantity. Mark exceptions on the invoice and have your buyer contact the vendor immediately. For those vendors with good track records, consider only spot-checking the goods.

- Compare the actual count with the count on the invoice before payment. For items that do not match the purchase order (substitutes, wrong quantities, and so on), have the buyer work with the vendor to rectify the situation.
- Mark and stock merchandise during slow-traffic times. Don't leave merchandise or empty boxes in aisles.

LESSONS LEARNED FROM CASE STUDIES

Convenient Hours and Attractive Displays Are Vital

Today's time-constrained consumers want to shop around the clock, and malls are doing their best to accommodate them. That's why Pete Gates,[7] who owns a women's apparel store, needs to reevaluate his store hours.[8] He does not open his store on Sundays or weeknights. Pete should monitor store traffic to determine the best hours, ask his customers what hours they want, and then test different hours. He could offset the costs of these additional hours by opening later in the mornings or by closing on a slow weekday, like Tuesdays. Pete also needs to work on his displays. He should showcase his high-margin merchandise on T-stands or pyramid displays instead of the rounders he now uses. Rounders are best for low-end or clearance merchandise.

[7] Pete Gates is a pseudonym.
[8] See Chapter 8 for a complete case study.

5

MANAGEMENT

When Walt Disney founded his first theme park 39 years ago, his vision was simple: to create a fun environment for customers and employees. Walt was able to achieve this vision by incorporating it into the company's operating principles:

> "At Disney, all new employees receive training which emphasizes the Disney heritage. They are taught important slogans such as 'Don't take yourself seriously, take your job seriously,' and 'What does Disney make? It makes people happy.' These slogans are part of the pixie dust formula which consists of 'training,' 'communications' and 'care.' The formula creates a culture that fosters excellent customer service without a high level of (management) supervision."
> —*Arthur Andersen Retailing Issues Newsletter*, January 1990

Small-store retailers can learn a lot from Walt, especially when it comes to managing their businesses.

The role of management in a small retail establishment consists of providing overall stewardship for the organization, setting direction by establishing a vision and a strategy, leading the employees, and creating a culture that enhances the company's image.

Many small-store retailers, however, have trouble focusing on these broader responsibilities. "Fighting fires" on a daily basis leaves many retailers with little time or energy to attend to these issues. But these management objectives are critical; a strong management ultimately drives the organization toward success. Accordingly, retailers cannot afford to get bogged down in the details. Although managing a business effectively is easier said than done, retailers can look at eight key management practices for direction (see Table 5-1). Retailers ascribe the most importance to increasing the flexibility of the owner, focusing more time on strategic planning, and enhancing business capabilities. Although retailers' performance in the flexibility of owner or operator category is consistent with that category's importance, the gaps between importance and performance for strategic planning and capabilities are wide (see Figure 5-1).

However, the best practices of successful companies indicate that having a vision is the critical first step in designing and implementing winning strategies, according to Arthur Andersen research. Strategic planning and capabilities are the other two first-tier issues on which retailers should spend more time and resources. What do these issues mean?

- *Vision and culture.* Communicating to the organization what the company should be and encouraging employees to embody that vision
- *Strategic planning.* Establishing strategies for achieving goals and objectives by understanding the company's strengths, weaknesses, opportunities, and threats
- *Capabilities.* Developing the skills and knowledge of the management team. Without a clear vision for the future, retailers will find it difficult, if not impossible, to focus their efforts or formulate successful strategies. Vision and culture ultimately give purpose to every business activity.

Let's return to the Disney example mentioned earlier. Making people happy is the goal of all business activities, and the company's operating principles—training, communication, and care—are fashioned to meet this goal. Those who have not visited the Magic Kingdom lately, should. Aside from moderate waits for rides during peak season, it is difficult to get frus-

Table 5-1 Tier rankings

Arthur Andersen's First Tier	Retailer's First Tier
1. Vision and culture	1. Flexibility of owner or operator
2. Strategic planning	2. Strategic planning
3. Capabilities	3. Capabilities
Second Tier	**Second Tier**
4. Flexibility of owner or operator	4. Management and business controls
5. Depth	5. Vision and culture
6. Wealth and succession planning	6. Depth
7. Management and business controls	7. Wealth and succession planning
8. Retailer cooperation and networking	8. Retailer cooperation and networking

Figure 5-1   Retailers need to improve management performance levels. They should especially focus on improvement in the areas of vision, strategic planning, and capabilities. How do you compare? Ask yourself how important each business practice is to you and how well you perform it. Then fill in the chart in the section on operations assessment.

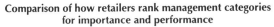

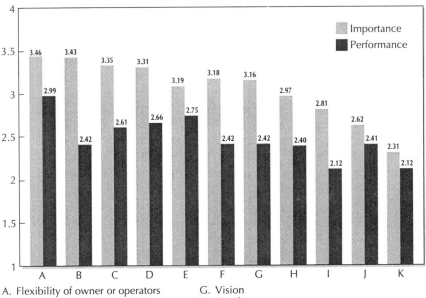

Comparison of how retailers rank management categories for importance and performance

A. Flexibility of owner or operators
B. Strategic planning
C. Capabilities
D. Management and business controls
E. Culture
F. Overall median for management

G. Vision
H. Depth
I. Succession and wealth planning
J. Retailer cooperation
K. Retailer networking

trated in the Disney environment. This is because the company attempts to eliminate the frustrations of visiting a vast entertainment complex.

Accommodations such as monorail service from hotels to the park, accessible rest rooms, convenient water fountains, and wide sidewalks consistently support Walt's vision. But the reason that families flock to the theme park is for the journey through their imaginations. Disney attractions are tantalizing, not terrorizing. And Disney customers are satisfied, not stressed.

Establishing vision and culture facilitates developing the strategic plan. The strategic plan provides the framework for action. The process of strategic planning should ultimately lead to a documented plan and a prioritized list of projects for the owner, management team, and employees. The plan does not have to be lengthy; it can be as simple as one page. In the face of day-to-day fire fighting, the strategic plan becomes a tool to track progress so the vision can become a reality.

Forming a vision and strategic planning are sound business practices. To follow through effectively on these initiatives, the owner and management team need to possess the appropriate capabilities. A great plan poorly executed is as good as no plan at all.

Management, for many small-store retailers, is composed of the owner and a few key employees. In larger organizations, management comprises a team of individuals, each with specialized skills. But on smaller teams, each member must wear many hats. This means that the brunt of management decisions falls on the owner, who must deal with issues concerning merchandising, store operations, customer service, finance, and human resources. Consequently, the owner and key employees need to continuously assess their capabilities and then take action to enhance them.

But how do retailers fulfill all their responsibilities with their limited time and resources? No set timeline exists, but retailers need to focus their efforts on the things that really matter and eliminate other activities. Those retailers who have a plan and set priorities for themselves know how to spend their time.

After establishing a vision for the company, building a strategic plan to accomplish that vision, and assessing the capabilities of the organization, retailers can address second-tier issues. Most of these business practices are a natural outcome of addressing the first-tier business practices. Arthur Andersen's second-tier issues are:

- *Flexibility of owner or operator.* Showing the willingness and ability to change
- *Depth.* Creating an organization that can assume some of the owner's daily responsibilities
- *Wealth and succession planning.* Preparing for the owner's retirement and the succession of ownership
- *Management and business controls.* Safeguarding assets and operations with people, policies, and practices.
- *Retailer cooperation and networking.* Collaborating with local retailers on specific activities as well as joining co-ops or buying groups to achieve mutual goals.

VISION AND CULTURE

Retailers Need a Clear Sense of Who They Are and Where They Are Headed

Vision and culture are two factors that can dramatically shape a retailer and his bottom line—for better or for worse. Vision is the owner's view of what the organization will be in five to ten years. Culture is the set of commonly held beliefs, behaviors, and attitudes of most employees in an organization. Together, they help shape the destiny of any company—large or small.

Without question, success for any organization requires a leader who has vision, or one who can create enthusiasm so that all employees embrace that culture and vision.

Companies without vision limit their ability to succeed. Vision binds strategy, leadership, culture, and people. Vision creates direction for the company and provides a sense of purpose for the organization. Having purpose gives employees a greater sense of reward as they and their company move closer to the vision. In fact, companies with a clear vision often find that their employees go above and beyond their day-to-day responsibilities in pursuit of achieving common goals. These intangible benefits ultimately lead to improved employee performance, more satisfied customers, and a stronger bottom line.

Surprisingly, many small-store retailers fail to appreciate the significance of vision. They rank it fifth overall out of eight management issues. Only 64 percent feel it is somewhat important or important, and 57 percent say their performance is poor or fair (see Figure 5-2). The reason for the low importance rating may be that most small-store retailers do not fully understand or appreciate the benefits of vision. Even those who do may fail to take the time to formalize and communicate a specific company vision.

Of the 77 percent of respondents who do have an established vision, 82 percent say the owner thinks about his company's future, 63 percent say the owner champions the vision, and 58 percent say the owner incorporates the vision into all modes of communications, including staff meetings and correspondence (see Figure 5-3). These are steps in the right direction, but all of these percentages should be higher.

Figure 5-2 Retailers need a vision to bring into focus how they operate their stores and serve their customers.

Retailers' breakdown of importance and performance for vision

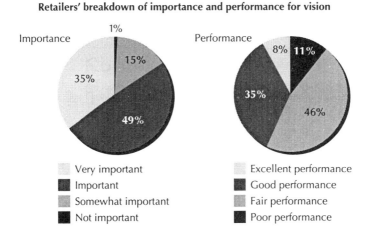

Importance

Performance

- Very important
- Important
- Somewhat important
- Not important

- Excellent performance
- Good performance
- Fair performance
- Poor performance

Retailers placed significantly less emphasis on culture, though 82 percent feel they are doing a good or fair job at promoting a culture throughout their organization (see Figure 5-4). The influence of a store's culture on its employees and customers can be widespread and dramatic. Culture gives employees a sense of unity and belonging. Culture shapes (and in some cases, dictates) employee performance. If honesty and integrity are held sacred and demonstrated by the retailer, these characteristics will make themselves evident in the employees. If serving the customer with tender loving care is a value, then that is how customers will be treated.

Retailers need to influence the culture of their organization. Many ways exist to do this, but the most common is for the owner and top managers to serve as role models (see Figure 5-5). Discussing expectations and conveying consistent values are other ways to influence culture. But, according to the survey results, only 25 percent of retailers encourage their management teams to participate in conveying consistent values, which can hinder retailers' efforts to communicate and incorporate their vision.

Figure 5-3   Establishing a vision is important for retailers so everyone will know where the company is headed. It is equally important that employees take ownership of the vision since they will move the company toward its goals.

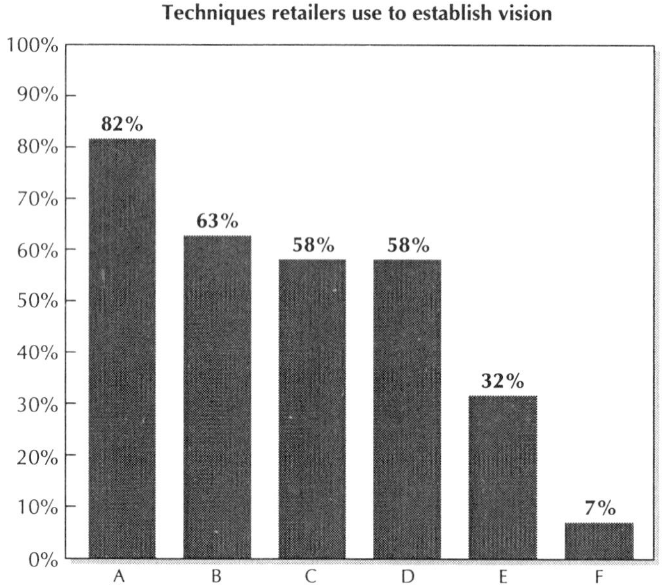

Techniques retailers use to establish vision

A. Owner or operator thinks about company's future
B. Owner or operator champions the initiative
C. Owner or operator incorporates vision in all modes of communication
D. Vision communicated to all employees
E. Participation by management team
F. Vision communicated to key employees only

Figure 5-4   Every company should have its own culture. Retailers need to shape the culture of their businesses to make it productive and customer-friendly.

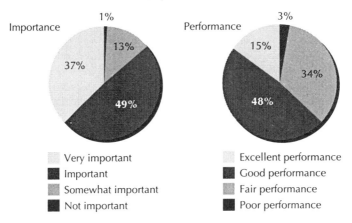

Retailers' breakdown of importance and performance for culture

Figure 5-5   Retailers must take important steps to create consistent values within the company. These values should be responsive to customer expectations and feedback. All owners and top managers should serve as role models. Discussing expectations with new employees is a good practice, but periodic performance reviews will reinforce these expectations.

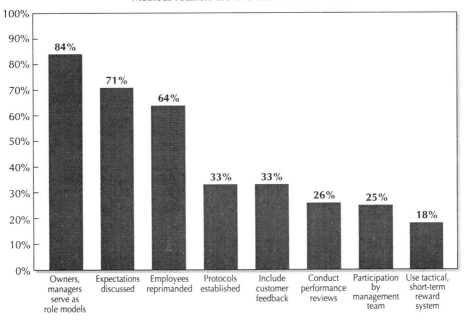

Methods retailers use to create consistent values

Figure 5-6 On-the-job training is a must for employees. Incentives and rewards are also valuable tools retailers can use to encourage employees to strive for consistent quality service.

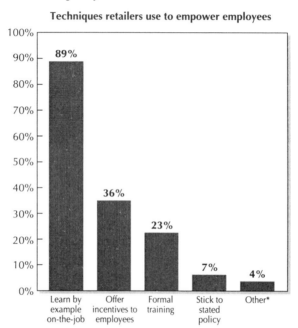

Techniques retailers use to empower employees

* Includes "produce or get fired."

Most of the retailers who do convey consistent values have employees learn by example while on the job (see Figure 5-6). Retailers can reinforce this training with rewards like a free lunch or a day off in appreciation. Employees will treat customers the way that retailers treat employees.

Best Practices You Can Use

Developing a vision isn't easy. Before you begin, consider what you want your company to be. That vision does not need to be unique, revolutionary, or so futuristic that it is unrealistic. On the contrary, it should be simple and clear. In creating your vision, you need to let go of any traditional rules you may have about who you are and what you are capable of doing. Disregard other perceived constraints for the time being.

Think through critical issues such as:

- *Customer perspectives.* What would you like your customers to say about their shopping experiences? What would you like them to say about the merchandise? The price? The service? What do you want customers to say about the layout of the store?

- *Employee perspectives.* What would you like your employees to say about your company? The work environment? The compensation and benefits? The culture? The career opportunities?
- *Owner perspectives.* How should you feel about your business and your job? Your compensation? Your time invested?
- *Community perspectives.* What do you want people in the community to say about your business?
- *Other perspectives.* What would you like key third parties, such as vendors, landlords, and banks, to say about your relationships?

As you brainstorm, document the vision by converting these questions into formal statements about how you see your business in the future. Next, narrow the statements down to a brief summary. At this point, you should have a working draft of a vision statement.

You can only realize the full benefit of a vision when your employees understand and embrace the vision. Getting employees to do this can be accomplished through several practices:

- *Involve your employees in the process of developing the vision.* Conduct meetings in which you solicit their views on where the company should be headed.
- *Show an appropriate level of enthusiasm for the vision.* Employees look to the owner to set the level of motivation.
- *Promote the vision.* Emblazon it on your letterhead or on a sign in the break room. Your statement might say, for example:

  "Our goal is to be the preferred women's apparel boutique. We will provide quality merchandise and service for our customers and an exceptional work environment for our associates."

Developing a culture is not a quick task, either. And changing it can be a challenge. A simple approach that you can use to develop an understanding of your culture and identify where modifications may be needed is discussed below. Given the potential benefits of culture, you should perform the first two steps in the process. If significant gaps exist between the two steps, you should proceed with the third step. Remember, more culture is not necessarily better culture.

Step 1: Situation assessment—who you are. Prepare a list of the values, protocols, behaviors, and philosophies that collectively make up your company's existing culture. Include examples of how you and your employees demonstrate or practice those values. Start this list at the beginning of the week. As each day passes, observe your employees' actions, attitudes, and demeanors. Are their values evident in how they interact with customers and fellow workers? How do customers respond to them? Spend a few minutes each day building the list until you feel it is reasonably complete.

Step 2: Vision—what you want to be. Identify the culture you would like to see within the organization by modifying the list prepared above. Delete the undesirable values and add desirable ones. As you go through this process, consider the following questions:

- What are the expectations and values of your target customers?
- How will your cultural identity affect the community's perception of your company?
- How capable are you and your employees of "delivering" your culture?
- How will your cultural identity affect your relationships with key stockholders, employees, and vendors?
- Can your cultural identity improve your competitive position?

Step 3: Course of action—how you can initiate change. Strategies that successful retailers use to develop and communicate their culture include:

- *Reward and recognition programs.* Reward the type of behavior that improves organizational performance. Examples of rewards include personal notes from the owner or president, newsletters heralding employee performance, special awards or trophies, and incentive compensation.
- *Leadership by example.* Be the quintessential model for expected behavior.
- *Training.* Use training sessions to tell employees what is expected of them in terms of behavior and demeanor. Discuss specific situations in staff meetings to determine how to portray the store culture.
- *Corporate mission statement.* Display the company credo in your back office for employees to see and near the cash register for customers to see.
- *Performance reviews.* Incorporate cultural values into the performance appraisal process.
- *Screening.* Hire people who share your values and beliefs.

STRATEGIC PLANNING

Reaching Your Destiny Is Easier with a Road Map for the Future

Strategic planning is the process by which retailers chart a road map for the future. With this road map, they can achieve their objectives more easily, particularly in today's highly competitive environment of small-store retailing. The strategic plan becomes the foundation for all other business activities. Retailers should link their plans of merchandising, customer service, marketing, human resources, and finance, and make them consistent with the overall business strategies and vision. A properly designed and executed strategic plan will accomplish this objective.

For these reasons, retailers are right in ranking strategic planning so high in the management section. As Figure 5-7 shows, 95 percent of retailers rank strategic planning as important or very important. Their performance, however, leaves much to be desired; more than half rank their performance as poor or fair. Why the breakdown? Many small-store retailers do not formulate strategic plans because they do not have company visions to guide their strategies. Some underestimate the value of having a plan, some lack the know-how to put one together, and some think it takes too much time given their daily pressures. In fact, 46 percent of retailers do not have a strategic plan, and another 44 percent do not have a documented plan (see Figure 5-8). This leaves 10 percent who actually have a specific, measurable plan of action.

One technique of successful strategic planning is employee brainstorming (see Table 5-2). The presumption that the owner has all of the answers is unrealistic. Employees likely will have different experiences and perspectives on various aspects of the business, including what is important to the customer, what tactics are working, and ways to improve.

Employees who are involved in the process of developing the company's strategy will also be more inclined to embrace that strategy. For some employees, a natural reaction to having a strategy handed to them is to challenge or disregard it immediately. By being involved in the process,

Figure 5-7   Planning ensures that the store will have a future.

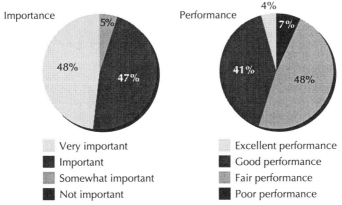

Retailers' breakdown of importance and performance for strategic planning

Retailers' use of strategic planning

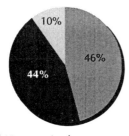

No strategic plan
Strategic plan not documented
Strategic plan documented

Figure 5-8   Without a clear vision and documented strategic plan, retailers cannot effectively move their businesses toward success.

employees sense that their views are important and that they can influence the company's future.

One benefit of strategic planning is certainly the plan itself, but it is the process of team problem-solving and challenging old thinking that produces the greatest organizational benefits. It also creates a framework against which retailers can measure their performance.

These benefits become even more important when considering the number of issues that will influence retailing over the next five years. Retailers feel, and Arthur Andersen concurs, that declining margins will have the greatest impact on their businesses, followed by lower consumer spending and rising health-care costs (see Table 5-3). To combat these complex issues, retailers need to incorporate strong actions into their strategic plans. They need to carry higher-margin goods, look for ways to decrease operating costs, and question everything they are doing, from the type of bags they use to the way they replenish merchandise.

Table 5-2   Internal and external resources can prove valuable in formulating a strategic plan.

Techniques that retailers use to understand strengths and weaknesses (in order of importance as ranked by retailers)

- Management brainstorming
- Seminars and outside publications
- Asking other retailers
- Asking suppliers
- Competitor benchmarking
- Asking friends and family members
- Asking outside advisers
- Market research

Table 5-3 To combat the factors affecting their businesses, retailers need to incorporate strong action into their strategic plans.

Factors retailers believe will have the greatest impact on their businesses (in order of importance as ranked by retailers)

- Declining margin
- Lower consumer spending
- Healthcare costs
- Declining sales
- Payroll costs
- Shortage of qualified employees
- New competitors
- Fewer shoppers
- Consumer confidence
- Excess retail space and overstoring
- Continuing recession
- Insurance costs
- Tax legislation
- Time-constrained consumers
- Growth in non-store retailing
- Interest rates
- Succession issues

Best Practices You Can Use

Strategic planning doesn't have to take up large amounts of time, and you can gradually develop a plan over an extended period. For the process to be effective, it should consist of the following phases:

Phase 1: Define your business and establish your vision. Start the process by asking a few critical questions. Who is your customer? What is your business? Why are you in the business? What do you want to be? What do you have to do to get there? This is the most critical part of the planning process because it drives all other elements of the plan. Your answers to the last two questions indicate what your vision and mission statements should be.

Brainstorm. Many small businesses have success with using brainstorming sessions to flesh out strategic issues. Include all key employees in these sessions, which should be conducted off-site in a relaxed environment.

Phase 2: Self-assessment of your organization and your current position in the local market. Understand the market in which you operate. Who are your potential customers? What are their wants and needs? How big is your market area? Is it growing or shrinking? How much of the market area do you reach? What are the demographics of your market area? Who are your primary and secondary competitors? What do your competitors do well? What do they do poorly? What is your competition doing better than you?

Evaluate your organization's strengths and weaknesses. What are you good at? What do you need to improve? What sets you apart from the competition? Are your sales associates capable? Does your buyer have adequate experience or training? Have you achieved optimal store productivity? How effective are you at meeting customers' wants and needs? Why do customers shop at your store instead of at the competitor's? Do the members of your management team have adequate financial and operating information to execute their responsibilities effectively? How are your relationships with employees, suppliers, bankers, and other advisers?

Assess the potential impact of uncontrollable factors on your business. How will new tax legislation impact your business? How will the proposed health-care reform affect your payroll costs? How will zoning changes in your community affect you? How will you respond to a shrinking labor pool? How will you respond to the impact of an aging population?

Phase 3: Establish objectives and goals

- Refine or modify your vision and mission statements.
- Identify the strategies necessary to achieve your objectives and goals.
- Develop guiding principles for your organization.
- Establish near-term (within the next six months), mid-term (within 12 months), and long-term (within 18 months) objectives and goals for your organization.
- Identify specific tactics for accomplishing the objectives and goals and determine who will execute them and in what time frame.

Phase 4: Establish a timeline. Generally speaking, your strategic plan should cover three years, and you should update it annually. Management personnel should refer regularly to a well-developed plan. The following is a handy guide to simplify strategic planning:

- *Vision.* What you want to be (for example, to be the preferred boutique of women's apparel).
- *Mission.* What you have to do to get there (provide outstanding customer service and unique, high-quality merchandise).
- *Goals.* How much you want to accomplish and how soon you want to accomplish it (increase sales to $5 million by 1996).

- *Strategies.* What approaches you have to take to achieve objectives and goals (track employees' customer-service techniques and source unique products).
- *Tactics.* What specific actions you have to take to implement your strategies (conduct training seminars and attend buying shows semiannually).

CAPABILITIES

Skills Signify Success for Small Stores

The skills of the retail organization significantly influence prospects for small-store success, which is why 91 percent of small-store retailers say their management capabilities are important or very important (see Figure 5-9). But their management performance is not something in which very many retailers take pride; 87 percent of respondents say they do only a fair or good job.

Retailers do not provide enough training and education for their management teams. As Figure 5-10 shows, 76 percent of retailers use on-the-job training. While this is an effective way to educate employees about business practices, it lacks objectivity and, by definition, is limited to the capabilities of the existing employees and the experience that the store provides. On-the-job training is also task-oriented; it tends to focus on

Figure 5-9   Retailers rank the capabilities of managers as important. However, the poor showing in performance shows that capabilities need enhancement. Retailers can accomplish this through skill development, training, and education.

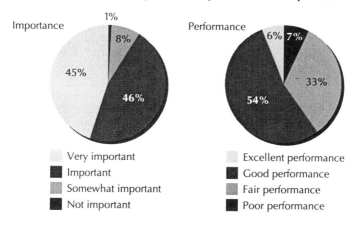

Retailers' breakdown of importance and performance for capabilities

Figure 5-10   Good management training is an indication of the owner's commitment to developing people, but it requires a balance of internal and external training. Not enough retailers are making an effort to understand managers' needs.

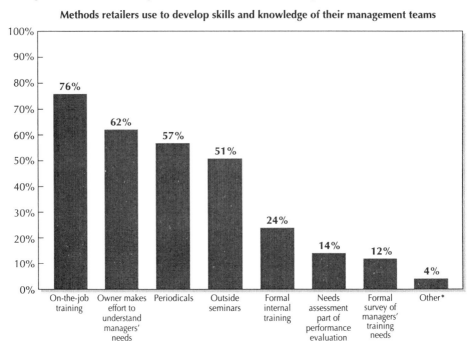

Methods retailers use to develop skills and knowledge of their management teams

* Includes occasional outside training opportunities.

functional skills. In contrast, management training is the process of giving employees a well-rounded education in the business and the retailing industry as a whole. Unfortunately, only 24 percent of respondents say they use formal internal training.

Small-store retailers must recognize that the more knowledge and experience management has, the higher the chance for management to excel.

A combination of on-the-job training, outside seminars, formal training programs, and informal training is critical to success. Such a combination shows employees that owners care about them and also want to invest in their continuing education.

Training is a win-win concept, because it benefits both the employee and the employer. Most management employees want to experience prosperity in their careers. Prosperity comes from having the right skills and the right knowledge. Skills are developed from practical experience. Knowledge comes from training. Employees who want to prosper need the opportunity to develop the skills and obtain the necessary training.

Retailers who afford these opportunities to their employees will create good will and, in effect, facilitate the employee's prosperity. Satisfied employees will lead to satisfied customers.

These methods enable retailers, whose skill levels should always be improving, to maximize the potential of their organization. Most people can perform at higher levels with the right leadership and a healthy dose of training and coaching. Building the skills of a management team requires recognition of expected benefits, good planning, awareness of available resources, and personal and financial commitment.

The key to achieving competitive advantage in any business is first to understand what skills are required to succeed in the business. With a vision in place and a strategic plan developed, the retailer must then evaluate his skills and those of his employees. He also must ask himself whether the capabilities are adequate to achieve the vision. If the answer is no, the retailer must identify what skills he needs to develop in order to improve his capabilities and those of his management team.

Successful retailers have programs in place that focus on training people in the core competencies of the organization. Deficient skills require extra training; proficient skills require less training. Before small-store retailers can become more successful, they need to embrace skill development as a continuous management process.

Overcoming the barriers to progress in the area of training will lead to smarter, more capable managers, which in turn will lead to more productive and empowered employees. Some examples of how training can enhance success include:

- A store manager with training in labor scheduling can reduce payroll costs by better matching store labor with customer activity and merchandise movement.
- A buyer with training in open-to-buy can better manage inventory levels, which should help sales and cash flow.
- An owner or manager with an appreciation for strategic planning can set the company in the right direction and communicate his vision to the entire organization.
- A sales associate who understands customer-satisfaction concepts can develop strategies for better understanding and meeting customers' wants and needs.
- An owner with training in advertising is more likely to improve advertising effectiveness.

The best companies have long recognized that their greatest asset is their people. Training becomes an investment or enhancement of that asset. Retailers who make the necessary investments in their people will reap the rewards.

Best Practices You Can Use

The following are common objections you may have to making the necessary commitment to management training and some practices that can be implemented to overcome them.

Training costs too much money. Various techniques control the cost of training:

- *Train the trainer.* The manufacturer's representative provides product training to the buyer, who in turn provides that training to sales associates.
- *Issue follow-up reports.* If you cannot afford to send all of your managers to a trade seminar, have those who do attend prepare a follow-up report and present it to the organization.
- *Videotape if possible.* Videotape the group providing the training seminar. Share the tape with other managers in your organization.
- *Supplement your education.* Read trade periodicals and other literature. General business videotapes and audiotapes are also available.
- *Get personally involved.* On-the-job and internal training can be effective and relatively inexpensive alternatives when the owner is committed to leading his team.
- *Split the cost of bringing a training program to your town with other local retailers.*
- *Rotate jobs.* This version of on-the-job training gives employees different perspectives of the business.

You do not know what kind of training your managers really need. You can identify what training your management team needs in a variety of ways:

- *Conduct a survey.* In a formal or informal survey, ask your management team what training they think they need—then respond.
- *Assess your employees' needs during regular performance appraisals.* Together you and your employees can determine the most appropriate training program.
- *Consider your company's core competencies and evaluate your management team's capabilities in each of them.* Your core competencies should include merchandise buying, assortment planning, visual merchandising, time management, leadership, employee relations, labor scheduling, customer satisfaction, basic marketing and advertising, accounting, and finance. One good way to brush up on these core areas is to review college courses on related topics. Talk with the instructors about the skills taught in specific areas. You will quickly recognize any gaps between the skills you and your employees have and the skills you need.

Training material is not available, and developing a training program is too expensive. Consult your trade association or local chamber of commerce. The Illinois Retail Merchants Association and National Retail Federation, for example, offer a variety of videos and books. Other possibilities include:

- Vendor-supplied training materials, such as videotapes.
- Trade association seminars.
- Educational programs at conventions and expos.
- Basic management books at your local bookstore or library.
- Community college courses.

Training takes too much time. Develop a training calendar and stick to it. At the beginning of each year, create a list of needed skills for your employees (see the response to the second objection for how to accomplish this). Also make a calendar of upcoming seminars that you would like to attend and discuss them with your employees. A list of events can be obtained well in advance from trade groups such as the National Retail Federation. In terms of timing, consider the following best practices:

- Train sales associates right before your peak selling season.
- Train buyers right before your peak buying season.
- Use off-peak time for general management training.

Managers loathe the idea of attending "training." Don't force-feed training—it will be a waste of time and money for you and your team. But do encourage your team to appreciate training:

- Create a reward or recognition program for training successes. Many retailers successfully use certificates of accomplishment or recognition pins.
- Share the benefits of training with your managers. Lighten up the training with a fun event, such as dinner, bowling, or golf.
- Include an objective for obtaining training in your manager's annual goals and assess performance against the goal during annual performance reviews.

FLEXIBILITY OF THE OWNER OR OPERATOR

Owners Must Always Be Willing to Change

In the dynamic world of retailing, successful companies must constantly adapt to changing conditions. The faster a retailer can respond with strategies for dealing with these changes, the greater his chances for success.

Survey respondents realize this, as an overwhelming 93 percent rank it important or very important (see Figure 5-11). Given this high ranking, one should expect a correspondingly high ranking in performance. But that is not the case; about half of retailers rate their performance as only good and a quarter as excellent.

Retailers recognize that if they cannot change or do not change quickly enough, they will miss opportunities. The best example of this situation is when a new national chain store enters the market. Customer loyalty is immediately challenged because people have a compulsion to visit any new store.

In this situation, small-store retailers need to defend their territory against the competition by changing or improving their advertising, merchandise, or service, for example. In these situations, owners can anticipate and plan for specific changes. In other situations, like when a competitor changes his pricing strategy, the changes are unexpected and place retailers in reactionary modes.

Flexibility is a mind-set that gives the owner strength to address almost any situation because he is constantly anticipating change and planning strategies to deal with it. People who make money in retailing are the ones who are nimble enough to respond quickly to change.

The owner's ability to adapt to change is a skill that employees value. Employees want to follow a leader who they respect and trust. One way to build that respect and trust is to demonstrate great management skills by anticipating and responding to changing conditions, including simple day-to-day tactical changes and long-term strategic changes.

Figure 5-11   Retailers rightly place high importance on flexibility; failure to adapt or respond effectively to change limits success.

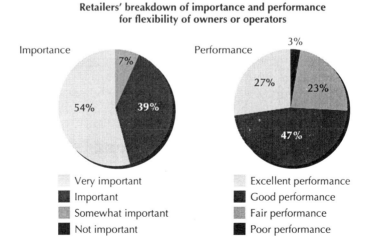

Retailers' breakdown of importance and performance
for flexibility of owners or operators

Importance

7%
54%   39%

Performance
3%
27%   23%
47%

Very important

Important

Somewhat important

Not important

Excellent performance

Good performance

Fair performance

Poor performance

Making changes that work and then ensuring that employees are aware of the success will increase employees' confidence in the owner's ability. Once the confidence is gained, employees themselves will be inspired to raise their own performance levels. For example, if the retailer modifies merchandise selection and customers respond well to the change, the salespeople will recognize this success. They will have greater confidence in the owner's skills as a retailer and will be encouraged to present new and unique merchandise to customers.

Retailers say the most common factors requiring them to alter their strategies are increasing local market competition and shifting customer wants (see Table 5-4).

While these retailers may understand the forces that drive their businesses, when it comes to making strategic changes, they do not fare as well. The low performance rating is likely due to four critical barriers:

- *A lack of leadership.* To implement changes, retailers need strong leadership skills. Unfortunately, some retailers simply do not have these skills.
- *A lack of knowledge.* Some retailers feel that they lack the knowledge to effectively implement changes. A lack of knowledge can create a fear factor, which in turn makes people accept the status quo.
- *A lack of time.* Many small-store retailers do not commit enough time to respond to changing conditions. Once again it becomes easy to get caught up in the day-to-day fire fighting. This, of course, is counterproductive.
- *A lack of money.* If remodeling or expanding the merchandise offering is necessary, it will certainly require additional capital, which is a common barrier for making change.

As Figure 5-12 on the next page shows, 85 percent of retailers rely on owner leadership. While this percentage may seem high, it really should

Table 5-4   Retailers need to keep a close eye on their competition and customers and quickly adapt to changes

Factors that cause retailers to change strategy or tactics (in order of importance as ranked by retailers)

- Local market competition
- Shift in customer wants
- Direct competition
- Overall economy
- Competitive formats
- Overall retail industry
- Shift in customer demographics
- Personal financial situation

Figure 5-12   Effective flexible management requires strong leadership, good communication, and strong project management skills.

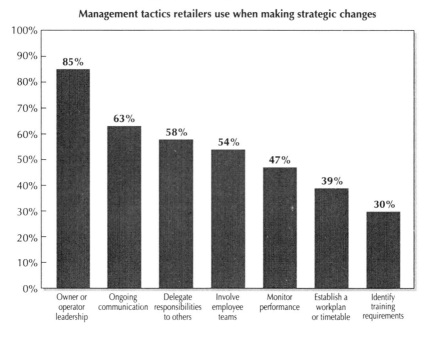

Management tactics retailers use when making strategic changes

be near 100. In addition, involving the management team in the process of making strategic changes, which only 54 percent of the retailers do, is critical and should be closer to 100 percent.

For the most part, teams develop more ideas of better quality than individuals. Whenever possible, retailers should try to get teams of people involved in problem solving. Teamwork also increases employees' communication skills. Other critical elements of managing change are establishing work plans and timetables and monitoring performance. Unfortunately for small-store retailers, only about half of the respondents use these tactics.

Best Practices You Can Use

Know where you are going. The best way to adapt to changing conditions is to anticipate those changes. This gives you the ability to think through alternatives and develop the best strategy. Hold a strategic planning session.

Know where you have been. Anticipate and respond to changing conditions by assessing your track record. Look back on the past three to five years and ask yourself what you would have done differently given what you know today. Would you have offered more or different merchandise lines? Would you have invested in different technology? Would you have moved to a different location? Would you have opened a second store? Would you have offered additional or different accommodations or services?

Be objective. Consider what others are saying about the future. While no one understands the specifics of your business as well as you do, industry experts have a good track record for identifying the forces of change in the industry. Sources include seminars and conferences, industry and general business literature, and peer review groups offered by national associations. Consult with local businesses or with your trusted business advisers. Find out how other businesses handle industrywide changes. What do your advisers think you should be doing? What are their thoughts on what you could have done differently or what action steps you should take now?

Be courageous. Taking some level of risk is necessary, so have courage as you tackle change—and never quit. Challenge your assumptions. Question every business practice, no matter how long you have done it. Perform the following key action steps prior to implementing changes in your business:

Perform a cost-benefit analysis and support your findings with facts. Prepare a list of the quantifiable costs and benefits in implementing a change. For example, the cost of a new computer system would include software and hardware costs, labor costs for maintaining the new system, and training costs. The benefits would include quicker access to better information and reduced office labor in the maintenance of sales records. If the computer is a POS system, your benefits would also include better tracking of sales movement, price management, and inventory control. After you perform a cost-benefit analysis, document the intangible benefits. What are some of the soft issues that you cannot quantify in terms of dollars and cents? If the benefits exceed the costs and there is a long-term strategic value to change, then the owner should go forward.

Consider training requirements. If anticipated change requires added training for employees, it should be well thought out to enhance your chances for success. The best strategies can be counterproductive if employees are not adequately trained and prepared. The cost of such training, including your personal time, should be considered in the cost-benefit analysis.

Anticipate varying attitudes. The next most important issue after your own flexibility is the flexibility of your employees. People inherently do not like change, but employee acceptance of your plan is critical to its success. In order to achieve acceptance from the group, you should include employees in the decision-making and strategy-formation processes as early as possible. Some effort should be made to communicate to employees what the benefits of the changes will mean to your organization and, in particular, to them individually. For example, a new POS system will initially require more time for the sales associates to use, but it will quickly reduce transaction processing time and give associates more time for selling.

Develop feedback loops. If changes will affect your customers, you should carefully monitor their reactions. Ideas for compiling customer feedback can be found in Chapter 2 in the section "Marshall Field: 'Give the Lady What She Wants.' " If changes will affect your employees, you must develop some form of feedback loop for them as well. This could take the form of weekly or monthly meetings.

Establish an overall work plan. Your plan should include a timetable for completion of portions of the work, detailed "to do" lists, objectives, and responsibility assignments.

Track performance by periodically assessing the status of implementation against the work plan. Revise your work plan when appropriate.

DEPTH

Grooming Promotable People Makes the Business Stronger

Small-store retailers often face an obstacle that the chain stores do not: lack of a clear career track for employees. For the larger retailer, a store's assistant manager recognizes that outstanding performance should provide an opportunity to move up to store manager, district manager, and potentially a corporate office position.

In the small-store environment, the organizational chart tends to be flat. The opportunity to advance to store manager does not occur very frequently, and the opportunity to advance to a level higher than store manager is almost nonexistent. For this very reason, almost 70 percent of the respondents rank depth as only somewhat important or important, and more than 50 percent rank their performance as poor or fair (see Figure 5-13).

To encourage employees to remain with the company and increase their productivity, small-store retailers need to create an environment that challenges and encourages people to continually improve their skills. One

Figure 5-13 Management needs to increase organizational depth by creating an environment that encourages employees to develop their full potential.

Retailers' breakdown of importance and performance for depth

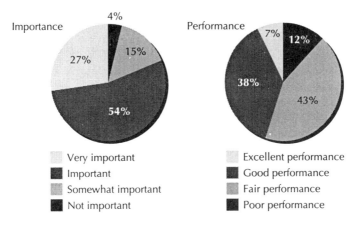

of the most critical strategies retailers can use to build depth is to rotate people in and out of positions, which very few retailers do (see Figure 5-14). This is surprising, given the fact that most small-store retailers operate with a shoestring staff.

Rotation can improve employees' productivity. It also gives retailers greater flexibility to fill temporary voids. When key employees are absent, there should be a sense of confidence that other employees can step in and perform necessary responsibilities. If a key employee leaves the company, or the retailer decides to open a new or larger store, the depth created in the ranks will allow for promotion from within.

Best Practices You Can Use

Empower your employees. Create a culture that encourages creativity and some risk-taking. Employees who are given this latitude will revel in their successes and learn from their mistakes. As a result, they will grow into smarter, more promotable people. Owners and managers should hold accountable people at any level for making decisions that they are required and qualified to make.

Expand the realm of experience. Challenge your employees with new experiences by rotating their responsibilities. For example, require your buyer to work the sales floor. This experience will give your buyer valuable insight into customer wants and needs, and he/she can incorporate this insight into buying activities.

Figure 5-14   Too few retailers—64 percent—see the importance of building management depth. Rotating employees increases their interest and grooms them for promotions. Retailers should create challenging careers for managers and employees and establish plans for the future.

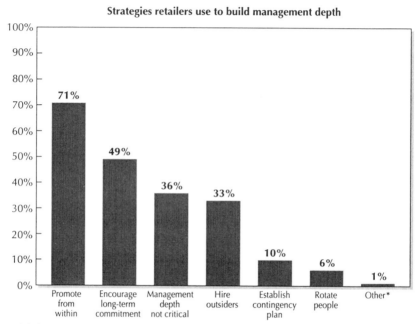

Strategies retailers use to build management depth

* Includes hiring new employees.

Solicit involvement. Use monthly meetings with all employees to discuss the state of the business, problems they are facing, and positive experiences that they have encountered. Then solicit their input for resolving problems and creating new strategies.

Demonstrate your loyalty. Promote from within whenever possible. Build loyalty in your associates by first demonstrating your loyalty to them. Also consider job-sharing and flex-time as vehicles for showing your employees that you have respect and concern for them.

Encourage training. Strongly encourage your employees to seek out the training they need. Guide them through the process, and give them recognition when they complete the training.

Coach, lead, and mentor. The best manager is one from whom employees can always learn. People can be greatly inspired to perform at their highest level if they have a leader to emulate. But be careful: Being a good manager does not make you a good leader. You can enhance the level of trust in your relationships with your employees if you coach them on the dos and don'ts of your business during day-to-day operations. As your relationship grows, you will effectively pass your knowledge on to your employees. As a result, you will increase your depth in promotable people.

Create financial incentives. While money may not be a top motivation for some employees, financial incentives do create some enthusiasm for improving individual performance. Sharing the prosperity of your company with your employees will create an environment of long-term commitment and increase the depth of your organization.

WEALTH AND SUCCESSION PLANNING

Retailers Need to Plan for the Next Generation

Small-store retailing is traditionally a family affair, but many retailers do not consider their families in their long-term plans. As Figure 5-15 shows, 76 percent of retailers consider wealth and succession planning as important at best. And an overwhelming 66 percent rate their performance as poor or fair.

Today's retailers cannot ignore subsequent generations in their plans. Retailers can ensure their families' financial futures with estate planning, which is the process of preparing for the owner's retirement and succession of ownership. In order to manage wealth, retailers must have a plan to meet the needs of the family as well as those of the business, while balancing the plan with tax laws.

Figure 5-15 Retailers can avoid unnecessary taxation by planning for the succession of the business.

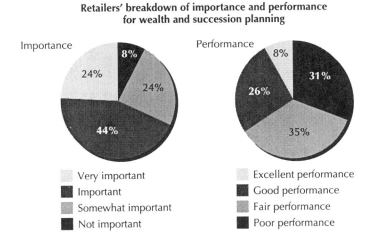

Retailers' breakdown of importance and performance for wealth and succession planning

Importance

Performance

Often retailers overlook the importance of formulating a strategy that integrates both personal and business objectives and thus miss many tax planning opportunities. Failure to understand and deal with these interrelationships early can often jeopardize financial success and family relationships.

Unfortunately, many retailers are headed for trouble in wealth planning. Although 97 percent indicate they have taken steps to preserve their wealth both now and in the future, only 86 percent maintain life insurance. Eighty-one percent have a will, and 74 percent maintain business liability insurance (see Figure 5-16). The lack of life insurance, a will, and business liability insurance has led many businesses (not just small-store retailers) to failure.

Nearly all retailers should be taking these steps. They should also maintain short-term and long-term disability insurance. Retailers also

Figure 5-16   Almost all retailers (97 percent) have taken steps to preserve their wealth. All retailers should execute wills, maintain business liability insurance, and consult with professional advisers to preserve their wealth.

Steps retailers take to preserve wealth

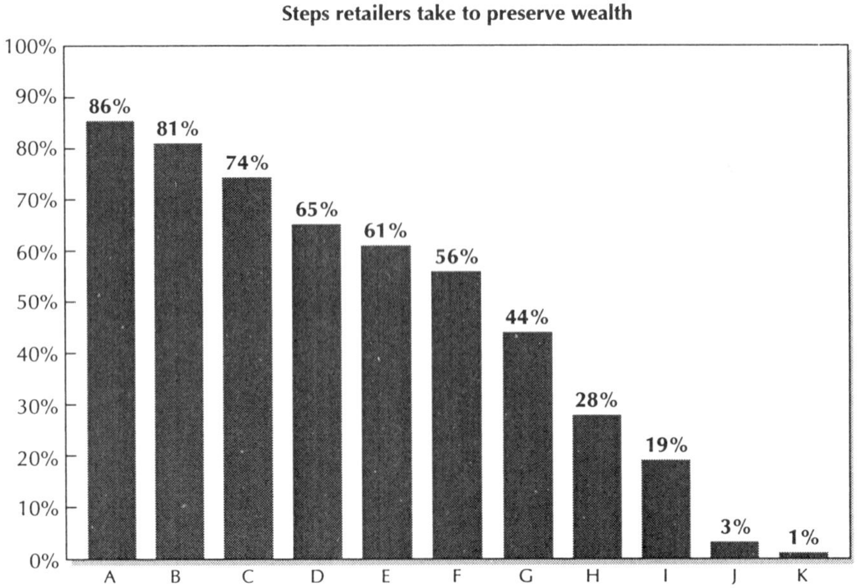

A. Maintain life insurance
B. Execute a will or living trust
C. Maintain business liability insurance
D. Maintain personal liability insurance
E. Investment diversification
F. Consult with professional advisers

G. Appoint estate executor and trustee
H. Appoint guardian for children
I. Family gifting program
J. Have not taken any steps
K. Other*

* Includes preparing buy/sell agreement.

Retailers' intentions for their businesses

Transfer business to children
Sell business to employees
Sell business to outside buyers
Operate business until die/leave
Have not developed succession plan

Figure 5-17 Retailers must be prepared for the future. The 28 percent of retailers who have not developed succession plans should consult with advisers immediately.

need to consult with professional advisers on an ongoing basis to learn new ways to preserve their wealth in the ever changing world.

These steps are especially critical, considering that 40 percent of retailers intend to transfer their businesses to their children (see Figure 5-17). But as the graph shows, 28 percent of retailers have not even developed a succession plan.

Best Practices You Can Use

Wealth- and succession-planning are evolving processes. You must alter your strategies as business conditions and family objectives change. To be most effective, you must initiate your planning process early. The following steps can contribute to the design and implementation of effective wealth and succession strategies:

- Consult with professional advisers.
- Prepare for an orderly administration of personal affairs by executing a will and updating it periodically. You should do this every three years.
- Prepare for an orderly administration of business affairs in the event of an emergency. This will guard against asset loss and deterioration of business value. You must formulate a plan and communicate it to all relevant parties.
- Guard against asset loss, both business and personal, by maintaining the proper type and appropriate amount of insurance cov-

erage (especially life and disability). Meet and take bids from several insurance agents to determine the appropriate insurance and related costs.

- Formally appoint a successor, guardian, executor, and/or trustee.
- Advise your estate planner of changes in your business or personal life that may affect your plans.

MANAGEMENT AND BUSINESS CONTROLS

Keeping Your Investment in Top Condition

Most retailers have a significant investment in their business. Maximizing the value of that investment is critical. This is true for large public companies as well as small-store enterprises. And small-store retailers seem to recognize this: 88 percent say it is important or very important to have effective management and business controls; 60 percent say their performance is good or excellent (see Figure 5-18).

Best management and business practices enable an owner and his management team to monitor the company's activities effectively, control the level of business risk assumed, and limit the likelihood that an illegal act or error, intentional or otherwise, will damage the business and its reputation. Strong business controls lead to better management and financial performance.

Although retailers rate their performance fairly high, they can do more to control assets and business operations. Most retailers balance the cash register daily and take physical inventories annually, but these tech-

Figure 5-18   Preserving retailers' investment in their businesses requires effective management and business controls.

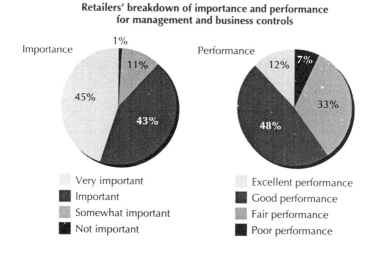

Retailers' breakdown of importance and performance
for management and business controls

niques are not enough (see Figure 5-19). Retailers need to use budgets and monthly account reconciliations to highlight problem areas, such as missing bank deposits or ghost vendors (when merchandise payments exceed the budget and inventory records do not match the inventory on hand).

Only 78 percent of owners say they are personally involved in all areas of the business, which may indicate a substantial percentage of owners who are not involved in the day-to-day store operations, perhaps because they focus on other business ventures or because they rely heavily on management. The graph also indicates that skepticism is present within management, because only 23 percent feel their work environment encourages self-control among employees.

Establishing good business controls is in the owner's best interest. Other benefits of strong business controls include peace of mind, better

Figure 5-19 Most retailers see the importance of employee training as a means to control assets and business operations. But monthly account reconciliation is a key business practice that nearly 50 percent of all retailers ignore. More retailers need to be personally involved in all critical areas of their businesses and foster a culture that encourages self-control.

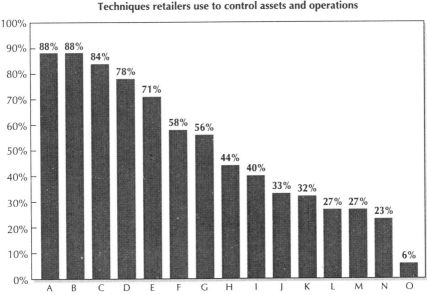

Techniques retailers use to control assets and operations

A. Daily register cash balancing
B. Annual physical inventories
C. Property and casualty insurance
D. Personal involvement in all areas
E. Train and educate employees
F. Monthly account reconciliation
G. Use of vaults or safes
H. Segregation of duties

I. Budget controls
J. Periodic consultation with outside counsel
K. Computer passwords and user IDs
L. Use of security service
M. Annual outside audit or review
N. Culture and environment encourages self-control
O. Conflict-of-interest or ethics questions

integrity of the company's financial information, increased ability to respond to and control issues before they become problems, and deterrence against theft or misappropriation. Overall retailers need to balance controls against the benefits they create. Controls should not prevent employees from doing their jobs.

Best Practices You Can Use

Be a hands-on owner. Effective business controls begin with the proper mind-set at the top. Your attitude about management and business controls will largely influence your employees' behavior. Your close personal and visible involvement, in day-to-day activities or that of your immediate family, is typically a very pervasive and effective business control, since it promotes self-control among employees. For example, if you are involved in the day-to-day operations of your business, you should approve invoices, sign checks, and compare budgeted to actual results. Also ask your management team to explain variations from the plan.

Establish budgets and interim reports. Budgets serve as accountability tools. You can compare actual performance against the budget and quickly identify areas of potential concern (such as unauthorized spending). The best retailers review the check register weekly and actual operating performance monthly. See "Measuring, Managing Go Hand in Hand" in Chapter 7 for more details.

Institute risk-management controls. You should manage exposure to risks by obtaining the right property and casualty insurance and periodically consulting with outside legal and tax counsel.

Safeguard assets. Use safes or vaults to safeguard assets; also use a security service during non-business hours. See "Reducing Theft, Shrinkage Adds to Bottom Line" in Chapter 4 for further discussion.

Establish and use financial records. Use various controls to assess the integrity of your financial records. The best example is a physical inventory. Other examples include:

- Annual outside audits or reviews
- Daily cash-register balancing
- Monthly account reconciliation
- Monthly explanations of expense variations from budget and prior year results

Use other general business practices. Widely used practices include:

- Conflict of interest and ethics questionnaires
- Mandatory vacation policies

- Periodic rotation of positions
- Computer passwords
- Segregation of duties for critical high-risk functions, such as daily cash balancing and daily bank deposits
- Manager or owner approval on such items as merchandise returns, capital expenditures, check disbursements, and purchase orders
- Use of preprinted and prenumbered forms for expense requests, markdown sheets, sales slips, and purchase orders.

RETAILER COOPERATION AND NETWORKING

Working With Other Retailers Makes Cents

Successful retailers leverage relationships with others to keep business costs down. Many small-store retailers, though, do not realize the benefits of such relationships. Only half feel retailer cooperation is important or very important or that they do a good or excellent job at it (see Figure 5-20).

Retailers must work with each other to increase exposure of their shopping area to the community at a low cost. While retailers who operate in a large mall typically receive good support from their landlord in promoting the shopping center, those operating in downtown areas or strip centers must initiate the cooperation, which few do. As Figure 5-21 shows, 22 percent of retailers do not participate in coordinated activities with other retailers. Of those who do, the top-ranking events are sidewalk sales and group advertising.

Figure 5-20 Many retailers fail to recognize the benefits that lie in cooperating with their fellow retailers.

Retailers' breakdown of importance and performance for retailer cooperation

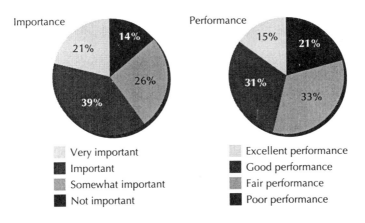

Figure 5-21   Retailer cooperation can lower costs for retailers, yet only 78 percent of retailers participate in any form of cooperation. Of those who do, 79 percent use group advertising.

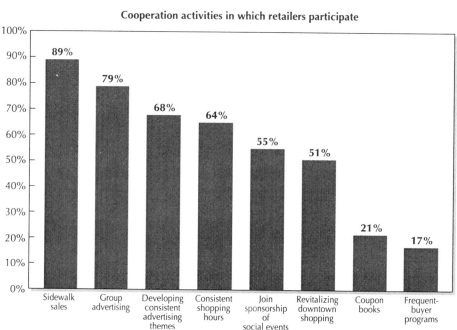

Cooperation activities in which retailers participate

Regardless of their location—downtown or strip mall, hometown or neighboring community—small-store retailers need to band together to effectively promote their shopping area and increase traffic, even if the stores are of similar formats. At relatively low cost, retailer cooperation creates goodwill and community spirit not found in the mass-merchant environment. Such downtown revitalization ultimately attracts more customers.

Fifty-six percent of retailers say retailer networking is not important or only somewhat important, and 65 percent say they do a poor or fair job at it (see Figure 5-22). Although it ranks last in the management category, networking does have its benefits. Foremost among them: It enables small-store retailers to operate more cost effectively by taking advantage of economies of a scale that larger chains enjoy.

By combining resources, retailers achieve lower costs in various areas, including advertising and buying. But as Figure 5-23 shows, only 38 percent are members of buying groups, 23 percent cooperatives, and 8 percent seek out advertising cooperatives. This is a clear example of how small-store retailers miss out on solid business practices that can reduce their costs and enhance their success.

Figure 5-22   Small-store retailers need to band together to help each other. Potential areas of cooperation include buying, sharing costs, and advertising.

Retailers' breakdown of importance and performance for networking

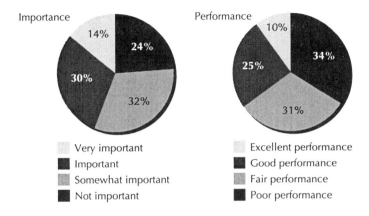

Retailers can participate in a variety of networking activities, as Figure 5-24 shows. Sharing office equipment and clerical personnel is a good way to reduce operating costs. Perhaps the most important networking technique, though, is for retailers to evaluate each other, which only 21 percent do. Many entrepreneurs may not appreciate being told what to do, but to survive they need to obtain advice from noncompeting retailers as to how they can improve their businesses. Apparel and hardware stores, for example, have nothing to lose and everything to gain from sharing information.

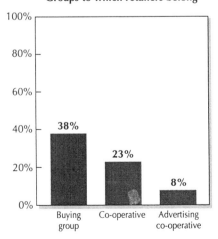

Groups to which retailers belong

Figure 5-23   Retailers should consider networking as a way to lower costs and increase leverage when advertising and buying merchandise.

Best Practices You Can Use

You can cooperate with other retailers in a variety of ways:

Retailer-sponsored social events. Such events are fairly common and often partially funded by the town. Examples include festivals and carnivals, live musical entertainment, dinners, dances, and auctions.

Sidewalk sales. Some small-store retailers think such sales are inconsistent with their image, while others view them as positive community activities. Many use this technique as an opportunity to liquidate slow-moving merchandise.

Figure 5-24   While retailers may not like the idea of getting suggestions from other retailers, they can learn valuable information from retailers in noncompetitive formats. For example, a men's clothing store and hardware retailer have nothing to lose and everything to gain from networking with each other.

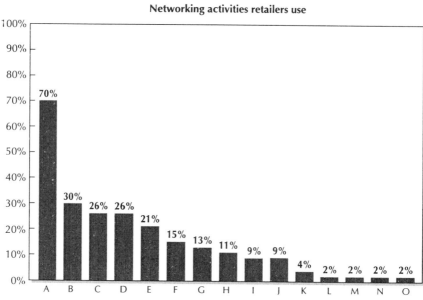

Networking activities retailers use

A. Meeting with other retailers
B. Offering reciprocal discounts
C. Working with retailers to develop catalogs
D. Offering barter transactions
E. Working together in evaluating each other
F. Consolidating purchase orders
G. Working together in price shopping competition
H. Developing market demographics
I. Working with retailers to combine store deliveries
J. Working together in identifying and developing training
K. Working with retailers in negotiating in-bound transportation
L. Time-sharing of office equipment
M. Sharing office space
N. Sharing clerical staff
O. Sharing distribution center or warehouse

Trade-area coupon books. Costs for this kind of activity would include printing, distribution, and redemption costs. With the abundance of coupons in the Sunday paper, you should consider alternative distribution methods.

Trade-area raffles and drawings. These activities are sometimes sponsored by the local chamber of commerce. To lower costs, use local retailers' products and services as prizes, which might include vacations, appliances, or shopping sprees. You need to consider local laws.

Charity fashion shows. Apparel retailers should consider fashion shows. Work with school districts and women's organizations to coordinate them.

You can also network in a variety of ways:

Strategize. Develop solid professional relationships with two or three noncompeting retailers with whom you can discuss industry issues and company problems. You can also help each other formulate competitive response strategies.

Buying groups and cooperatives. The most common networking practice is the use of buying groups or buying offices. Buying groups typically offer a program, which is an assortment of products for a particular category or season. The buying group consists of experienced buyers who go to market in search of products that meet the needs of the group's customers. By consolidating the procurement process into a buying group, you avoid the time and cost of managing the relationship side of securing these goods. For example, group buyers often go overseas to buy merchandise. Group members then share the costs of these buying trips and can often achieve lower invoice prices, sometimes volume discounts or rebates, and lower distribution costs. Buying groups provide other benefits, including training, site-selection assistance, centralized accounting, key factor reporting, group advertising, and promotional activity. If buying groups are not available for the products you carry, you should at least consider identifying other retailers with whom consolidating purchase orders or inbound transportation would be feasible.

Joint sponsorship of economic development initiatives. Such activities have received great attention in the press recently. Downtown revitalization programs seem to dominate. The truth is that businesses survive only if the community does, not vice versa. Therefore, all businesses need to band together to promote community events and support the downtown area through revitalization and renovation programs. Downtown businesses must view their stores as an alternative to malls in the surrounding locales. Communities that successfully undertake downtown revitalization efforts learn that they must stop mourning the loss of department stores and begin to view the downtown as a coordinated cluster of interdependent units. Some best practices are:

- Take an active role in local events and organizations.
- Invite an economic developer or local banker to speak to your community leaders.
- Research economic development initiatives of other communities, particularly those affiliated with the National Trust for Historic Preservation's Main Street program.

Catalogs. The best way to explain this networking strategy is by example. A small Illinois bookstore developed a catalog that contained a broad assortment of general books. Several publishers subsidized the cost of the catalog through a co-op advertising arrangement under which the publishers paid for space in the catalog. Several retailers in noncompeting markets participated in the group. In return for a fee, these retailers received a four-color catalog with their trade name and address printed on the front cover. The retailer in charge of the catalog handled all of negotiations with the publishers and printers, performed all of the administrative aspects, developed the catalog, and oversaw distribution. You can use the same concept with other forms of direct mail.

Group sourcing of advertising. One strategy to lower your advertising costs or start an advertising program is to purchase print space with other retailers. This allows the members to share costs. For example, a shoe retailer and a men's apparel retailer could develop an ad displaying both shoes and suits and invite customers to both stores. Like the buying group mentioned previously, the members of this advertising group would appoint an administrator for the group who would handle all of the negotiations and paperwork. Full-page ads cost less per column inch than half-page ads. With this in mind, networking with other retailers should lower costs and increase exposure to customers.

Here is another example of leveraging advertising costs: Several retailers planned a sidewalk sale. One of the retailers had a lower cost than the others for print space because of his high usage. The group used this rate and shared the costs. Often small-store retailers are not aware of the cooperative advertising allowances that are available from their manufacturers. You should investigate the availability of these allowances in an effort to cut costs.

Bartering and reciprocal discounts. Retailers often overlook the benefits of bartering. For example, an apparel retailer who achieves a gross profit of 40 percent and gives a $100 gift certificate to its cleaning service for $100 of services in effect achieves a savings equal to $40. Reciprocal discounts create similar benefits. For example, a gift-store operator and a florist agree to give each other a 10 percent discount on all purchases. This technique encourages retailers to shop locally. Check with your tax adviser before entering into any such transactions.

Market research. Work together to subsidize the cost of developing market demographic information. Many small-store retailers are inhibited by the scope and the cost of gathering baseline demographic information. By making this a joint effort, you can spread the cost, both in terms of your time and your money.

Share office equipment or personnel. For example, all the members of your strip mall could share the cost of renting or buying copiers, fax machines, and other office equipment. You can also share staff or services of a nonsensitive nature, such as clerical or maintenance.

Training. Collaborate with noncompeting retailers on joint training with outside consultants. As discussed in the capabilities section, costs are a common barrier to training. Networking with other retailers allows you to lower this cost.

LESSONS LEARNED FROM CASE STUDIES

Drugstore Adrift without Strategic Plan

All successful retailers have documented, well-defined strategic plans. Such plans have many purposes, not the least of which is defining the owner's goals and vision for his or her business. This purpose is critical when partners have different ideas for their store, as Mike Sylvester and Andrew Kates[1] are realizing.[2] Mike is not active in store operations, and he is not interested in expanding the business. Andrew, however, is fairly committed to the business. Together the two need to formulate a specific strategic plan that maps out exactly where the business is going and how they plan to get there.

Market changes, including vicious competition and the closing of a neighboring traffic-generator, mean that time is of the essence for these drugstore owners. Mike and Andrew's strategic plan may lead to moving the store, changing the merchandise assortment, or dissolving the business. The key is that they need a plan soon or they will continue to drift.

Another key management issue is that of developing depth, which is especially important when a management change is imminent. Case in

---

[1] Mike Sylvester and Andrew Kates are pseudonyms.
[2] See Chapter 8 for a complete case study.

point: Jay Robinson,[3] who owns 10 shoe stores, wants to retire soon, and no one in his family is interested in taking over the business.[4] Jay's alternative, as he sees it, is to sell his stores to various store managers. To prepare them, he empowers selected managers to take on all management responsibilities, including buying, human resources, and promotions, at their stores.

---

[3] Jay Robinson is a pseudonym.
[4] See Chapter 8 for a complete case study.

6

HUMAN RESOURCES

Employees Should Be Treated as Customers

"Employee loyalty and commitment depend on a personal relationship with you. In essence, employees treat customers the way the company treats them," according to an article in a recent issue of Arthur Andersen Retailing Issues Newsletter.

If only more retailers recognized this fact. Instead retailers' most valuable—and expensive—asset does not even appear on the balance sheet. Next to the cost of merchandise, labor represents the highest single cost element of running a store. The only way to make the most of this asset is through an effective human-resource strategy, which is the practice of hiring, training, motivating, and managing the right people for the right jobs.

Managing human resources may be the most critical challenge of the next century for small-store retailers, who have to develop strategies for human resources that are at least as creative and effective as those developed for other parts of their businesses. Owners will have to devote a significant part of their day to managing this area. This requires a major change in traditional thinking (see Table 6-1).

Arthur Andersen concurs with retailers that hiring and retention—carefully selecting competent employees and keeping them satisfied to reduce turnover—are the most important aspects of managing human resources.

The problem most often noted with retailers of every size—not just with small stores—is that the best practices often do not extend beyond

Table 6-1   Tier Rankings

Arthur Andersen's First Tier	Retailers' First Tier
1. Hiring and retention	1. Hiring and retention
Second Tier	**Second Tier**
2. Sales training	2. Sales training
3. Compensation and benefits	3. Compensation and benefits

the hiring process or on-the-job training. As a result, retailers may do a good job hiring the right people but do not do as well retaining them. The reason: Their human-resource practices fall short in developing and motivating those people.

In several national retail chains, employee turnover annually can exceed 75 percent of the store's workforce. This generates incredible inefficiencies because of the low return on training investment dollars. This problem is particularly critical for small stores. Retailers cannot afford to lose their good employees. Even though some turnover is good for bringing in new ideas, the management cost to develop new people is much too high; it is less expensive in terms of both money and time not to lose the employees in the first place.

Many retailers may find it difficult to meet the human-resource challenge. Although retailers know what is important, they need to increase their knowledge and update their practices in this area. Owners need to spend more time motivating and developing their employees. They must commit adequate time and financial resources to programs within their stores that focus on developing skills, building teamwork, empowering people, and encouraging and rewarding employees (see Figure 6-1).

Arthur Andersen research indicates that national chains are raising the performance bar with improved sales training, compensation, and benefits, and small-store retailers are struggling to meet the higher standards. As competition for the shrinking labor pool heats up, small-store retailers may find themselves at a distinct disadvantage.

The second-tier issues dealt with later in this chapter include:

- *Sales training.* Educating employees by providing appropriate instruction
- *Compensation and benefits.* Providing competitive incentives, health insurance, vacation, retirement, and other benefits to employees

Retailing has developed a poor reputation as an industry in which to build a career. Yet Arthur Andersen believes increased industry demand and fewer jobs elsewhere will make retailing careers increasingly attractive to new graduates. So retailers need to attract and retain the best and brightest talent

Figure 6-1 Retailers need to raise human resources performance levels in all areas. They need to focus their attention first on hiring and retaining top-notch employees. How do you compare? Ask yourself how important each business practice is to you and how well you perform it. Then fill in the chart in the section on operations assessment.

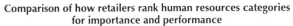

Comparison of how retailers rank human resources categories for importance and performance

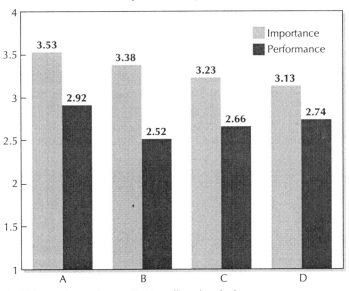

A. Hiring and retention C. Overall median for human resources
B. Sales training D. Compensation and benefits

because better people will lead to better business strategies and greater customer satisfaction. How do small-store retailers do this? First through effective hiring and retention, then through improved sales training, and finally through competitive, cost-effective compensation and benefits.

This section is not a training or how-to guide for a human-resources department; rather, it is a general guide to help small-store retailers better manage their most valuable assets.

HIRING AND RETENTION

Motivation Keeps Employees on the Team

Hiring and retaining quality employees is critical to retailers' success for two reasons. First, customers view employees as embodying the retailer's image. Second, employee turnover is very costly to retailers, in terms of both increased costs of retraining and decreased sales. After all, inexperienced and ill-trained salespeople can lead to customer dissatisfaction.

Given its importance, it is comforting to know that survey respondents rank this category their number-one human-resources priority.

In fact, 98 percent of respondents indicate that hiring and retention is important or very important (see Figure 6-2). When it comes to performance, though, retailers lag. Only 25 percent feel their performance is excellent; 48 percent, good; and 22 percent, fair.

Why the disparity? Retailers believe they are not doing enough to attract and retain top performers. How do retailers hire, develop, and retain top-notch employees? Arthur Andersen believes the secret lies in creating motivated, empowered, and involved employees who believe in the company's image and mission. It is critical to develop these skills in new and seasoned employees. Michael J. O'Connor, a retailing consultant for Arthur Andersen and contributor to International Trends in Retailing, tells about an experiment with employee attitudes as they relate to customers' evaluation of the store: A retailer installed a voting machine at the front of his store to let customers indicate whether they had a good or bad shopping experience. About one month into the experiment, management announced to sales employees that they were going to remodel portions of the store. Before work began in the back rooms of the store, management invited employees to a meeting to discuss the remodeling plans for the lockers, lunchroom, and employee restrooms. As work progressed in the employee areas, customers' rat-

Figure 6-2   Employees are retailers' most important assets, but it is difficult to find and retain good people.

Retailers' breakdown of importance and performance for hiring and retention

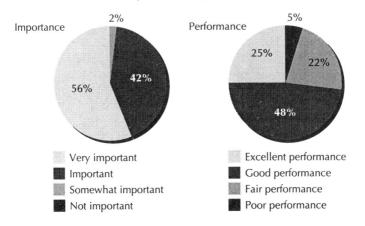

ings of the store improved dramatically. Yet none of the customers knew of the remodeling. Customers were only reacting to the employees' improved attitudes.

Retailers also need to do a better job of screening applicants: 56 percent do not have a personality profile for screening applicants. Why? Many retailers do not recognize the importance of such profiles and thus do not take the time to develop them.

Retailers need to develop a composite of attributes for hires to ensure that new employees have the personality and skills that the company—and customers—need. Retailers need to apply these standards consistently. Figure 6-3 shows some of the most important attributes, according to retailers. Chief among them are attitude, friendliness, prior experience, common sense, and selling ability. Retailers should remember, however, that no set pattern of employee characteristics exists that will guarantee success. Instead, retailers must rely on their own instincts and a combination of proven characteristics that make sense for their retail format.

Once employers hire the employees they want and need, they must try to keep them. The first step in retaining employees is to recognize the

Figure 6-3 Of the 44 percent of retailers who have identified desired traits of potential employees, most rank attitude and friendliness as most important. Retailers should also seek common sense and assertiveness in new hires.

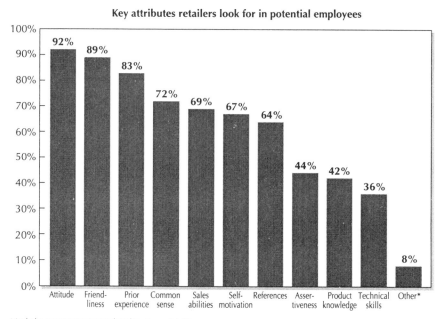

* Includes competency test and applicant's availability.

factors that lead to high turnover. Table 6-2 shows that the number-one reason for turnover, according to retailers, is higher pay outside retail. Other reasons include dissatisfaction with retail, higher pay in another retail establishment, dissatisfaction with job role, and night and weekend hours. But according to Arthur Andersen research, the overriding reason for employee turnover is that employees become dissatisfied with their jobs because their employers do not empower them to make their own decisions, make them feel part of the team, or give them increased responsibilities.

Fortunately, retailers can take actions to combat these factors. Though retailers can increase employees' base pay and must be willing to pay as much as their competitors, they must also recognize that pay is not the only motivation (see Figure 6-4). Employees want more involvement in the business, more variety in their daily work schedules, and more feedback from employers, especially on a job well done. To achieve the first two objectives, retailers need to cross train their employees. Department managers can move to new departments, and store managers can periodically perform some of the buyers' tasks. To achieve the third objective, the store manager or owner must spend time providing helpful input and positive reinforcement to employees.

Retailers might also consider employee recognition programs. Examples of recognition programs that enhance employees' satisfaction include giving credit for outstanding customer service and for suggestions that enhance the business (see Figure 6-5, page 212). However, 54 percent of retailers do not recognize their employees in any of the key areas shown in the graph. This is probably because many retailers simply do not know exactly what employee acts to reward or exactly what recognition and incentive programs will best enhance the business. According

Table 6-2   To reduce turnover, retailers need to foster motivation and involvement in employees. Retailers should also make pay scales competitive with those of other retailers and consider lifestyle issues when scheduling hours.

Reasons for high turnover (in order of importance as ranked by retailers)

- Higher pay outside retail
- Dissatisfaction with retailing
- Higher pay in other retail establishment
- Dissatisfaction with job role
- No opportunity for advancement
- Dissatisfaction with company
- Termination
- Dissatisfaction with management

Figure 6-4 Retailers recognize that willingness to pay as much as competitors is a key factor in reducing turnover, but money is not the only incentive. Retailers should consider employee recognition programs, employee empowerment, and lifestyle scheduling. For example, a young mother with school-age children could work a 10 A.M. to 3 P.M. shift.

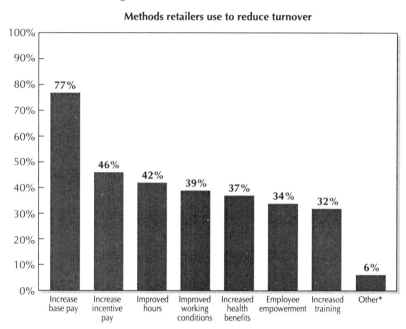

Methods retailers use to reduce turnover

* Includes flexible scheduling.

to Arthur Andersen research, though, recognition and incentives are the most effective steps retailers can take to retain employees, increase productivity, and foster team spirit.

Figure 6-6 (page 213) shows some of the incentives retailers use to reward and encourage their employees, although most retailers do not offer incentives simply because they do not understand what goals and corresponding incentives are most effective to enhance the business. Of the 42 percent who do offer incentives, 36 percent offer luncheons, and 32 percent offer paid days off. All the incentives listed are effective; retailers just need to remember to base them on quantifiable items, such as performance in achieved net sales and gross margin dollars. Employers should work together with their employees to set achievable goals and desired rewards. Retailers should also consider publishing recognition programs and incentives in employee newsletters, posting them in break rooms, or talking about them at weekly company meetings.

In addition, retailers must empower employees to make them feel like part of the team. Empowerment means authorizing and encouraging

Figure 6-5   Employee recognition for top sales performance or outstanding customer service is a proven way to enhance employee satisfaction. Retailers need to recognize employees for active performance, such as outstanding customer service, instead of passive performance, such as attendance or length of service. Yet only 46 percent of retailers offer programs to enhance employee satisfaction. Those who do not should adopt some of these most-used programs.

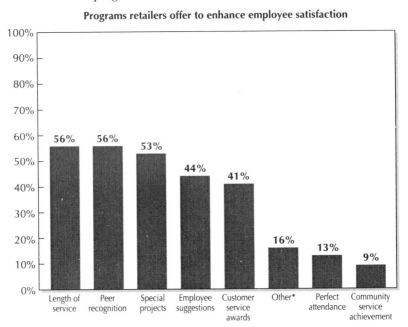

Programs retailers offer to enhance employee satisfaction

* Includes birthday lunches and newsletters.

store employees to resolve customer satisfaction issues using management guidelines as references. The bottom line, which Arthur Andersen research supports, is that employers must treat their employees in the manner of valued customers. Employees want to be empowered and rewarded when appropriate. They want to be treated with respect. They need to hear that they are valuable and do a good job.

Best Practices You Can Use

Hiring the right people can be a challenge. The following are some steps you can take to improve your chances of finding qualified employees:

Determine the requirements and duties of the vacancy or new position. While the requirements differ greatly from job to job and format to format, some common points for a store manager, for example, are:

Figure 6-6 Forty-two percent of retailers feel that offering incentives is an important part of hiring and retaining quality employees. Retailers should base their incentives on measurable criteria, and incentives should correlate with employees' performance.

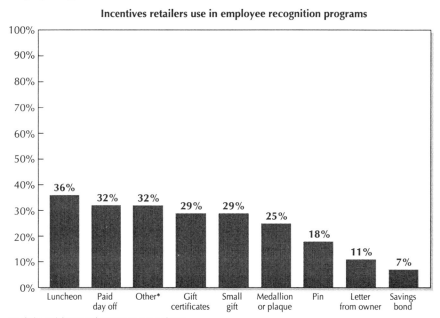

Incentives retailers use in employee recognition programs

* Includes cash bonus and recognition in newsletter.

- Minimum of five years of progressive hard-line, variety or mass merchandising retail management experience.
- Profit and loss responsibility and accountability.
- Hands-on management experience with all phases of retail, including merchandising, inventory control, human resources, customer service, product ordering, competitive strategies, and budgeting.

Make a list of the skills needed. Revisit your skills profile periodically to see what changes you should make. No perfect formula exists, but some of the attributes you should look for are:

- Interest in retailing
- Assertiveness
- Attitude
- Friendliness
- Prior experience
- Interest in selling
- Product knowledge

- Common sense
- Aptitude
- Enthusiasm for store's merchandise
- Eagerness to learn

Consider analyzing your best employees and determine the attributes they have that you would like new hires to have. Look for these characteristics during the interview process.

Match the applicants with your store and customer profile. If you manage a record store that caters to young adults, you should staff your store with young adults. If you are a hardware retailer and part of your image is to have employees with superior product knowledge, then the people you hire should be people who like to remodel or build or former tradespeople who are experts in carpentry, plumbing, or electricity. These people will likely have a wealth of product knowledge.

Once you hire the right people for the right job, you need to do your best to retain them. To reduce turnover, which can be caused by a variety of things, you need to properly motivate, empower, and recognize your employees, according to Arthur Andersen.

- Empower your employees to respond to customers and to act on their wants. Formally recognize them for exemplary efforts.
- Develop your own set of human-resource values and document them in a statement of philosophy. Post this statement in a visible area of the store for employees to see. An example from a successful retailer reads:

    "Our associates are our greatest asset. . . . We will be a store with talented and motivated associates who are interested in serving our customers and in implementing our strategies for success. We will do this through our focus on developing our people and by providing recognition and rewards for their accomplishments."

- Say thank you, write a note, or otherwise recognize your employees for a job well done; it will go a long way. If appropriate, thank your employees' families for supporting them.
- Make the work environment fun. Reinforce the behavior you expect with a smile instead of an order. Combine long meetings with a fun event. Host group lunches or dinners. Show employees that you care about their welfare. Make sure employees are clear about your expectations and goals for them.

Provide leadership. You must always demonstrate your total commitment to the business and your conviction to consistently execute the store's strategies. Your message must be that customer satisfaction, not profit, is your number-one priority. Lead by positive example and associates will follow. If you have multiple stores, spend at least one day each month in each store.

Involve employees and make them feel they are part of the team. Encourage employees to ask questions about their activities and to communicate ideas. Employees need to feel you appreciate their questions and value their input. Highlight their ideas, actions, and achievements through recognition and rewards. Share their ideas with all the store employees, and let everyone know who came up with a bright idea. Reinforce behavior through two-way communication and feedback. The best companies communicate what they are trying to accomplish and why. Let employees know what changes you are making in the store and why. Solicit their opinions and make them part of the process. For example, give a new employee a two-week trial period and ask existing employees for their feedback on the new hire's performance. When you achieve your goals, you need to provide feedback on the success factors and the lessons you learned so that all employees can benefit.

Train your employees. You must recognize that you have a responsibility to help your employees succeed at their jobs. Employees are much happier when they know they are prepared for anything. You must identify training needs in areas like customer service, product knowledge, telephone skills, and register proficiency. Do this with all your employees, and then follow through to make certain that they are trained. Monitor performance with the training provided, and identify whether employees' confidence is improving.

Evaluate employees on a regular basis. At least once every six months, you should formally evaluate your employees on objective performance measures. Evaluations should be in writing and in face-to-face meetings. You should also determine if employees are exhibiting the qualities for which you hired them. Employees desire and deserve timely, objective feedback. Use exit interviews to determine strengths and weaknesses in the company. Use the information to change or improve daily operations as well as to help reduce turnover.

Create an entrepreneurial environment. Encourage your employees to experiment, and show a willingness to accept failure. Set up suggestion boxes in the break room and ask your employees to submit ideas to improve the business. Then let your people implement and "own" the projects. So many of the great ideas in retailing have come from trial and error. Macy's Thanksgiving Day Parade began as an experiment.

Provide a workplace that reflects your diverse community. Provide career opportunities in an environment that is free from discrimination and harassment of any kind. Be firm in your actions and words that you will not tolerate such activities.

If you properly empower, motivate, and recognize your employees, they will go beyond the company policy in satisfying customers and performing tasks. You will also encourage good people to stay. Talk to your employees and other retailers in your area to determine what they offer and develop the proper mix of incentive and recognition programs for you.

Reasons to recognize
- Customer recognition of superior service
- High sales
- Top performance
- High productivity (especially for clerks and cashiers)
- Community service
- Employee suggestions
- Loss prevention
- Special projects (like developing customer database, shopping the competition)

Ways to reward
- Paid day off
- Gift certificate or merchandise gift
- Medallion, pin, or plaque
- Savings bond
- Letter from the owner
- Luncheon
- Cash bonus
- Weekday work schedule vs. evening or weekend schedule
- Recognition in company newsletter
- Customer service awards

SALES TRAINING

Star Sellers Keep Customers Coming Back for More

Sales associates are the retailer's direct link with customers. These employees are the ones who must embody the store's vision and promote the store's culture. If sales associates and other employees are not adequately trained, they cannot deliver quality customer service. This is probably why 92 percent of survey respondents say sales training is important or very important (see Figure 6-7). Unfortunately, almost half of retailers say their performance is only fair or poor.

Why the shortcoming? The reason is obvious: 30 percent of retailers do not have formal training programs other than on-the-job training. All retailers need to recognize the fact that employees need to be trained. For

Figure 6-7   Retailers do not devote adequate resources to training sales associates, although training is critical to serving customers.

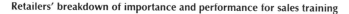

Retailers' breakdown of importance and performance for sales training

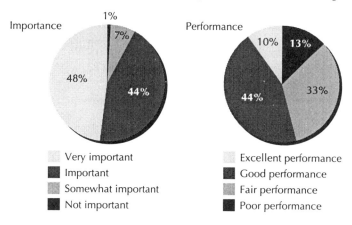

retailers to improve their bottom lines, they must train salespeople in critical areas like customer service and product knowledge. (Although this section focuses on sales associates, the information is applicable to other employees.) A recent National Retail Federation/MasterCard study reported that 60 percent of shoppers leave the store without their needs being met because salespeople lack product knowledge. All employees—from the part-time sales associate to the store manager—need formal, ongoing training. This training should cover everything from the company's image to its customer profile, phone skills to loss-prevention techniques, customer service to product knowledge.

Of the 70 percent of retailers who have formal internal training programs, most conduct separate programs for their new employees (see Figure 6-8). Obviously, newcomers need formal training to perform their jobs well. Surprisingly, 25 percent of retailers spend less than eight hours a year training their salespeople, mostly through on-the-job training. In contrast, many successful retailers—large and small—require their new sales employees to complete 45 hours of training before they even reach the floor and interact with customers.

Arthur Andersen notes that star sellers are those people with outgoing personalities, strong ethics, a sense of the company's culture, and plenty of product knowledge. While personality and ethics are intrinsic qualities, a retailer can instill the company's culture and provide product training. Retailers need to have knowledgeable, service-driven salespeople who are willing to learn about all the store's merchandise—not just goods in their own departments. Retailers also need employees who are

Figure 6-8   Although 30 percent of retailers do not formally train employees, most retailers understand the importance of teaching associates how to interact with customers. The 70 percent of retailers who formally train employees do so on the job. All employees—new, existing, or temporary—should receive training.

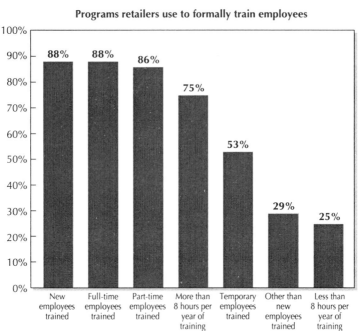

Programs retailers use to formally train employees

not afraid to approach customers and sell. Case in point: It's Christmastime. In the first scenario, a woman goes to a gift boutique to do all her holiday shopping. She has 10 gifts to buy and $50 to spend on each gift. Within an hour she picks out her gifts, pays her $500, and leaves.

In the second scenario, a woman goes to the local jewelry store to buy her husband a gift. As soon as she steps through the door, a salesperson greets her and asks how he may be of service. The woman says she only has half an hour, but she wants to buy her husband something nice for about $100. Thirty minutes later, after being sold up and spending $200, the pleased customer is on her way.

The first scenario was passive selling; the second was active selling by an assertive employee. That's what employers must train their employees to do. Training also needs to teach associates relationship selling, according to Sharon Beatty, a marketing professor at the University of Alabama.[1] One sales associate explains relationship selling in this way:

[1] Beatty, Sharon. *Relationship Selling in Retailing.* Also: *Arthur Andersen Retailing Issues Newsletter,* November 1993.

"The secret of selling is getting to know the person to the point that you have a friendship-type relationship, because that makes the person relax more and open up. You are able to find out their needs, and they tend to accept things a lot easier if they don't feel like you're being pushy. You can suggest things and sell more, because they are not on the defensive."[2]

In relationship selling, salespeople seek to strengthen customer loyalties through managed personal service, which includes informing customers of new merchandise, reminding them of important dates (such as birthdays and anniversaries), and pulling merchandise for customers before they arrive. One Illinois retailer has each of his salespeople work closely with 50 customers; employees send flyers to these customers and act as their personal shoppers. Arthur Andersen believes more small-store retailers need to educate their employees on relationship selling and use role-playing to teach them how to do it. Additionally, retailers need to empower their sales associates to solve customers' problems. If employees do not feel valued and empowered, they will be poor relationship sellers. To encourage and implement relationship selling throughout their companies, retailers must make a conscious commitment to it.[3]

One way to foster relationship selling is through on-the-job training, which all retailers offer (see Figure 6-9). But retailers should also offer other formal in-house training to teach employees more about customer service and the products they offer. Only 23 percent of retailers take advantage of

[2] Ibid.
[3] Ibid.

Figure 6-9   Retailers who are willing to send employees to out-of-store training seminars demonstrate interest in their employees' careers, which results in more capable, motivated staffs.

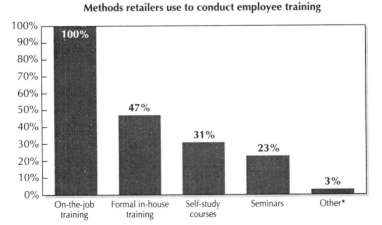

Methods retailers use to conduct employee training

* Includes training by trial and error.

outside seminars or courses offered by trade organizations, vendors, or manufacturers. Why? Some retailers do not know that these groups offer training; others do not feel that the benefits will outweigh the costs.

Outside seminars, however, can provide a wealth of new ideas on everything from exciting merchandise displays to effective customer-service techniques. They also increase employee productivity because employees see that their employer cares about them and their self-improvement, believes in their abilities, and is willing to make a financial investment in them. The challenge for small-store retailers is to select effective outside training that will benefit both their employees and their stores.

By annually devoting a percentage of training dollars to outside training, retailers can realize a variety of benefits. Effective training can decrease employee turnover and increase morale, job satisfaction, customer satisfaction, and, ultimately, profitability.

Best Practices You Can Use

Make your organization thoroughly committed to customers by showing employees that decisions are made with customers' best interests in mind. The customer is the reason why you are in retailing. The income statement only measures how good you are. Act ethically, and do not conduct business with people who aren't ethical. Always comply with all federal, state, and local laws. Your employees will live by the examples you set. "Customers are most likely to form relationships with companies whose practices are beyond reproach," says Barbara Caplan of Yankelovich Partners.[4]

Regardless of the type of training you choose to offer, your training should include product knowledge, ways to satisfy customers, and your company's vision and culture. Your training should also respond to your employees' needs. Perform an informal survey to pinpoint what skills your employees need to improve. Some effective training options include:

- *Train employees by role-playing.* This fosters interaction and is usually the best form of training. It is an effective way to teach employees how to resolve customer complaints and answer product questions. Memos or manuals are less effective; they represent one-way communication with limited opportunity for questions, practice, or discussion of the issues.
- *On-the-job training.* You need to spend time with your staff on the floor. Role-play customers and sales employees in a variety of circumstances. Observe your employees and critique and compliment them regularly in real situations (away from customers). Test employee product and service knowledge and reward their mastery of that knowledge.

[4] *Arthur Andersen Retailing Issues Newsletter,* July 1993.

- *Seminars taught by noncompany personnel.* Many seminars are available from trade organizations and small-business associations. Some programs are designed specifically for small-store retailers. The self-administered programs teach the fundamentals of good salesmanship for new and experienced associates and are available for less than $25 each in some areas. In addition, many consulting organizations exist that could help you to develop a one- or two-day seminar. You can start with the National Retail Federation.
- *Formal in-house training.* You can accrue significant benefits from the development of your own in-house training program. With the help of outside consultants, you can tailor the program to your store, employees, and customers. It will also be less expensive in the long run.
- *Videotapes.* These can be effective in a group setting if you lead a discussion immediately afterward. Because videos themselves do not facilitate interaction, they are less effective if employees view them individually. Ask your trade association what videos they provide.

COMPENSATION AND BENEFITS

Employee Retention Hinges on Healthy Packages

"Retailers' cash and images are in the hands of low-paid, poorly trained, temporary employees," write Harvard business professors Leonard Schlesinger and James Haskett in *Breaking the Cycle of Failure.*[5] Customers tend to react negatively to poor service, and this negative reaction tends to reinforce the sales associate's negative opinion of his job. A bad attitude encourages customers' negative reaction. The cycle goes on. The research by Schlesinger and Haskett identified all of the frequently heard arguments, which include:

- "We can't find good people these days."
- "People don't want to work."
- "We can't afford to pay for better people."
- "We can't afford to train people when the turnover is so high."
- "We just have to live with the situation."

But the two professors also found people in some companies who were not buying into these excuses. They cited two banks, a department store, a quick-serve French bakery, and a janitorial and food service company. In

[5] O'Connor, Michael. *How Much to Take and How Much to Leave?*

every case, better pay and more management involvement decreased employee turnover. In the case of small-store retailers, giving more responsibility, better compensation, and more benefits to store employees may ultimately bring more to the bottom line, although turnover may not be as great of an issue in rural and suburban communities as it is in urban areas.

Today's sales associates—especially those from dual-income households—are concerned about having time for themselves and their families. They are also concerned about income taxes, health care costs, and flexible hours. Most survey respondents recognize these fears and consequently view compensation and benefits as an important part of their human-resources strategies (see Figure 6-10). Successful retailers also pay close attention to what the competition offers. Arthur Andersen believes that small-store retailers need to incorporate more attractive features into their compensation and benefits packages.

Arthur Andersen, though, believes that dramatic changes will affect all employees and their employers. National chains will drive this change. They will make investments in technology that will turn sales associates into sales "executives" who are highly educated, systems literate, and skilled in sales. Successful retailers in the 21st century will give their employees more responsibility while making new and increasing demands on them. So to retain employees, all retailers—small and large—will have to offer comprehensive compensation and benefits packages. The implication for small-store retailers is that they will have to give more to get more. Since large retailers frequently offer more lucrative benefits

Figure 6-10 Although compensation and benefits are important, retailers need to continually analyze whether they are competitive with the market.

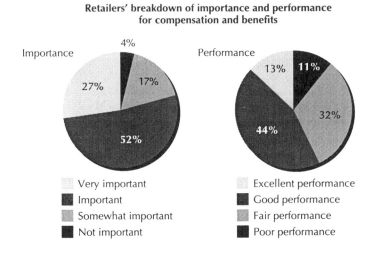

Retailers' breakdown of importance and performance
for compensation and benefits

packages than small-store retailers, especially for store managers, retailers without deep pockets will have to be smarter with their benefit dollars.

Figure 6-11 shows benefits for all retail employees: store managers, assistant store managers, department managers, buyers, full-time salespeople and part-time salespeople, as provided by survey respondents.

Figure 6-11 A great opportunity exists for retailers to offer benefits that work in the best interest of the retailer as well as the employee. Benefits such as profit sharing and flex hours will improve employees' attitudes and work habits.

Compensation and benefits provided to employees (in percents)

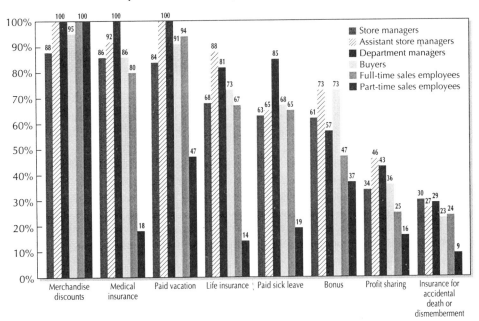

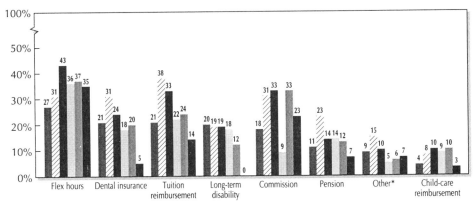

* Includes employee stock ownership programs, transportation allowances, and 401 K plan.

The alternatives run the gamut from child-care reimbursement to accidental death insurance. Although retailers are able to offer all these benefits at a cost, small-store retailers should consider sharing costs with employees. For example, retailers may want to let employees participate in a group life insurance plan in which they could deduct monthly charges from employees' paychecks. The figure also shows that most employees receive merchandise discounts.

A surprising finding is that a high percentage of employees receive life insurance, but very few receive long-term disability coverage. Considering that most employees are five to seven times more likely to become disabled than to die while working, retailers should consider offering this benefit as an alternative.

Retailers should consider profit-sharing plans to foster long-term commitment from employees. Given the changing nature of American families, they should also consider offering child-care reimbursement and flex time. Benefits such as these can go a long way toward building goodwill with employees.

Managers should receive at least two weeks of paid vacation and a reasonable level of paid sick leave (five to seven days). In many cases they should receive bonuses based on individual or group performance related to net sales and gross margins, which will help retailers bolster their profits.

In an unusual twist, respondents say fewer store managers than buyers receive bonuses. This is out of kilter. Store managers, especially if they function as business managers rather than caretakers, are just as responsible for net sales as buyers are. Both should receive bonuses in return for their contributions to increasing revenue or reducing costs.

To increase net sales, retailers should consider using commissions based on unit sales, straight sales, or monthly sales. A commission structure drives employees to act as purchasing agents for their customers and encourages them to contact their personal customers about upcoming events and new merchandise. Although the industry of late has experienced some movement away from commissions, they remain a critical part of the compensation mix. Some retailers may resist commission because they feel it does not foster teamwork or customer service. These retailers should consider a commission pool based on total store sales and profitability, so that everyone benefits.

Employers offering commission-based pay must also institute sales training for employees to teach them how to work effectively with their customers and colleagues. Commission is much more than a financial issue.

Part-time sales associates should only receive base pay, commission, and merchandise discounts, provided this is competitive with the market. Retailers should reexamine one of their more common practices: awarding paid vacation time to part-time and seasonal employees who are not permanent. Retailers indicate that many of these people are not around long enough for employers to realize any return on their investment.

Figure 6-12   Retailers can foster teamwork by setting common goals for all employees. Establishing individual sales goals for each employee and rewarding achievers will increase net sales.

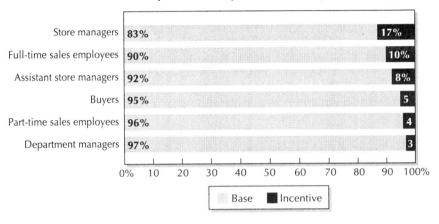

Figure 6-12 shows the percentage of compensation that is base pay and the percentage that is incentives for all employees. Most retailers seem to employ the proper mix of base and incentive pay. This is evident because employees who can have a bigger impact on sales and profits appear to have a higher portion of pay provided through incentives. To increase net sales, retailers must establish sales goals for their individual employees and for the company as a whole. They then need to offer incentives and recognition to encourage their employees to meet and surpass these goals.

For incentives to be effective, however, retailers must continually evaluate their store managers and buyers. Figure 6-13 shows that most managers and buyers are evaluated on the same criteria: sales and inventory turnover. The primary focus of managers should be sales, customer service, and store profits (excluding uncontrollable items like rent and depreciation), and the incentives should motivate accordingly. And retailers should reward buyers based on what buyers can control: achieved margin dollars, inventory turnover, and their ability to find new and unique merchandise for the target market.

Unfortunately, more than 25 percent of retailers do not offer any incentive compensation for either their managers or their buyers. These retailers need to realize that store managers and buyers have enormous impact on the sales and profitability of the store, and they should reward them accordingly (see Figure 6-14).

Best Practices You Can Use

Determine what compensation and benefits to provide. To find out what is competitive, ask your employees and fellow retailers what local com-

Figure 6-13   Buyers should be evaluated on criteria they can directly affect: achieved margins, inventory turnover, and ability to find merchandise unique to their trade areas. Store managers should be evaluated on sales and store profits (excluding those costs that the store manager cannot control, such as rent), two areas on which they have the greatest impact.

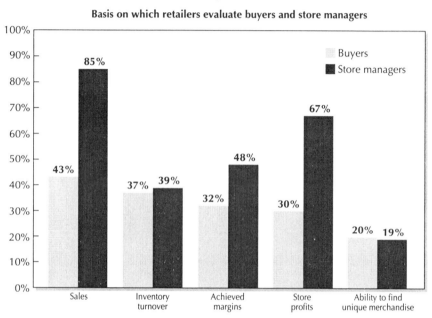

petitors and noncompetitors offer. Also, ask your employees what they want and need. Call a benefits broker for advice. Before establishing any new benefits, you need to look at two factors: the value of the benefit to the employee and the expense of the program for you. Decide what you can afford, accumulate the information, and adjust your compensation and benefits to be competitive. In general, the people with the most influence on results should receive a greater portion of their total compensation in the form of incentives.

In designing or modifying your incentive compensation program and your employee performance evaluation program, consider other issues in addition to sales goals, company profits, and achieved margin. Keep in mind that you have to adjust the mix to get the desired behavior and results from your employees. Following are some of the best practices you can use:

- Incorporate customer-satisfaction survey results and personnel feedback into the performance review of employees who interact with customers. This is important, since it completes the loop in customer satisfaction. Reward your employees accordingly.

Figure 6-14 Retailers say sales and store profits are the most important criteria for giving incentives to both buyers and store managers, but this is only partly true. Incentives are most effective when based on criteria that managers and buyers can directly affect.

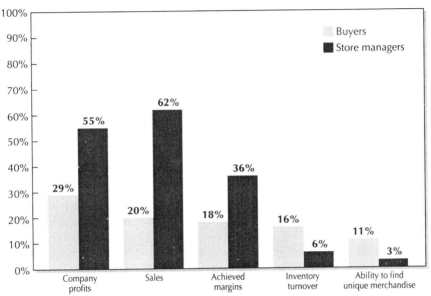

Basis on which retailers offer incentives to buyers and store managers

- Link appropriate individual performance measures (quantifiable and nonquantifiable) to your stated corporate goals and values. (If your goal is to be a sales-driven company, for example, an individual performance measure may be for a salesperson to generate $400 in sales per day.) This conveys to your employees that you value both their performance and the means by which they achieve that performance. It also allows your employees to compare their behavior with your established set of guidelines.
- Establish short-term rewards to motivate desired behavior in your employees. For example, you can reward employees for improved customer satisfaction based on comment cards, multiple-unit sales, or the number of credit applications processed. This will send a tangible message to motivate your employees. It will also provide immediate feedback on the types of employee behavior that you desire. Sending flowers or a brief note are examples of short-term rewards.
- Foster motivation and competition among employees by basing your incentive compensation program on individual or team goals. Consider posting scores for top performers in your store. If

you operate more than one store, consider holding incentive contests between your stores based on dollar sales goals, margin dollar goals, or number of units sold.

LESSONS LEARNED FROM CASE STUDIES

Empowered Employees Have the Drive to Succeed

As previously mentioned, one of the most effective ways to retain talented employees is to empower them. The Curtis brothers[6] do just that at their ten hardware stores.[7] They take pride in providing their associates the opportunity to make their own decisions and execute their own ideas. This runs the gamut from buying merchandise to resolving customer complaints. Such empowerment, the Curtises believe, reduces turnover and leads to a team of associates working toward the common goal of satisfied customers.

The brothers also encourage their employees to take advantage of continuing education, such as internal self-study courses and outside seminars, which increases customer-service skills and product knowledge of employees.

The Curtises' belief in empowerment and training creates a cohesive group of associates that wants to succeed.

Another effective way to retain top-notch associates is to offer incentives, as Greg Short[8] can attest.[9] Incentives help to reduce turnover, and they help Greg achieve his goal of increased sales. Together, Greg and his store managers determine individual monthly goals for increasing customer traffic and average transaction size. The incentive to achieve these goals is a cash reward, which the managers appreciate.

---

[6] Curtis is a pseudonym.
[7] See Chapter 8 for a complete case study.
[8] Greg Short is a pseudonym.
[9] See Chapter 8 for a complete case study.

7

FINANCE

Business Is a Gamble
without Sound Financial Strategy

With today's challenging economy and highly competitive retail environ-ment, the deck is stacked against those retailers who do not have adequate financing, timely and accurate records, and a basic understanding of financial analysis. These foundations of finance should support all strate-gic decision-making. Odds are that any business without such a founda-tion will crumble, so retailers need to integrate financial strategies throughout all areas of their businesses. Only then can small-store retail-ers spot problem areas and react accordingly before the problems become full-blown catastrophes (see Table 7-1 on the following page).

Although small-store retailers rated almost all areas as having roughly the same importance (see Figure 7-1), Arthur Andersen and retail-ers agree that cost reduction and budgeting are the most important areas of finance for small-store retailers. Cost reduction is analyzing cost elements of the business and determining ways to reduce them. Budgeting is deter-mining revenues, expenses, and cash-flow needs for the upcoming year.

But retailers clearly need to improve their performance in these areas. Most do not take advantage of the many internal and external resources available to them to help control costs across all areas of their businesses. They are not aggressive enough in their negotiations for goods and ser-vices, and many do not sufficiently challenge charges they are expected to pay. Why? Some believe that they have no leverage because of their small business size. Others lack understanding of the services or goods provided.

Table 7-1   Tier rankings

Arthur Andersen's First Tier	Retailers' First Tier
1. Cost reduction	1. Cost reduction
2. Budgeting	2. Budgeting
Second Tier	**Second Tier**
3. Capital resources	3. Information systems
4. Information systems	4. Capital resources
5. Key-factor and internal reporting	5. Key-factor and internal reporting
6. Taxation	6. Taxation

In addition, many small-store retailers are not using budgets to analyze and measure their performance. Most either do not understand the value of a budget or lack the knowledge necessary to develop one. Yet without such a tool, small-store retailers have no way to set financial goals or measure their ability to meet those goals.

This chapter provides some tools to help retailers better manage their business finances, most importantly by focusing on cost containment

Figure 7-1   Small-store retailers need to improve their performance in a variety of financial areas, especially in the categories of cost reduction, budgeting, and information systems. How do you compare? Ask yourself how important each business practice is to you and how well you perform it. Then fill in the chart in the section on operations assessment.

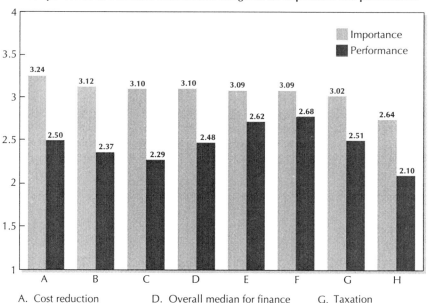

Comparison of how retailers rank finance categories for importance and performance

A. Cost reduction   D. Overall median for finance   G. Taxation
B. Budgeting   E. Capital resources   H. Key-factor reporting
C. Information systems   F. Internal reporting

and budgeting. Though these are the most critical areas of opportunity for small-store retailers, other areas of finance will also be addressed:

- *Capital resources.* Planning for and raising capital (equity or debt) to fund ongoing operations and expansion.
- *Information systems.* Using a computer to capture key financial information to aid decision-making.
- *Key-factor and internal reporting.* Reporting key area results (such as exception reporting based on predetermined criteria like mark-downs that exceed estimates) and communicating that information to other decision-makers.
- *Taxation.* Planning to minimize all tax liabilities.

COST REDUCTION

Ingenuity and Control Help Cut Costs

In today's economic environment, small-store retailers find it difficult to generate additional gross margin dollars. As a result, retailers have been forced to look more closely at methods of reducing costs as a way to survive. This is why respondents rank cost reduction as their top financial priority. Almost 90 percent say cost reduction is important or very important, but their performance lags: Only 40 percent rate it as fair; and 43 percent, as good (see Figure 7-2).

Figure 7-2 In today's environment, flat or declining gross margins are a fact of life for most retailers. To improve performance, retailers must become low-cost operators.

Retailers' breakdown of importance and performance for cost reduction

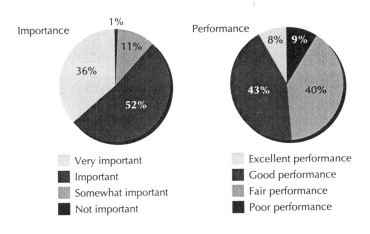

Retailers should call on a variety of resources for cost-reduction ideas and opportunities. But as Figure 7-3 shows, most small-store retailers do not take advantage of all of the resources available to obtain fresh ideas, probably because of lack of time and money. Trade and business publications are excellent sources, as are outside advisers, accountants, bankers, noncompeting retailers, and other business owners. Moreover, retailers can tap often overlooked internal resources: store managers and sales associates. These are the best ways to generate cost-reduction ideas specific to the store.

Best Practices You Can Use

Review and benchmark your costs. The most important element to cost reduction is to review all areas of your operation critically and continually. Is there a more efficient or less costly way to execute certain tasks within the operation? Does this activity add value to customer service or control?

Figure 7-3   Although retailers identify which methods of cost reduction are most important, they fail to use these methods enough. Store-manager meetings and team problem-solving are particularly important to generate creative new ideas. Both are key building blocks to quality management.

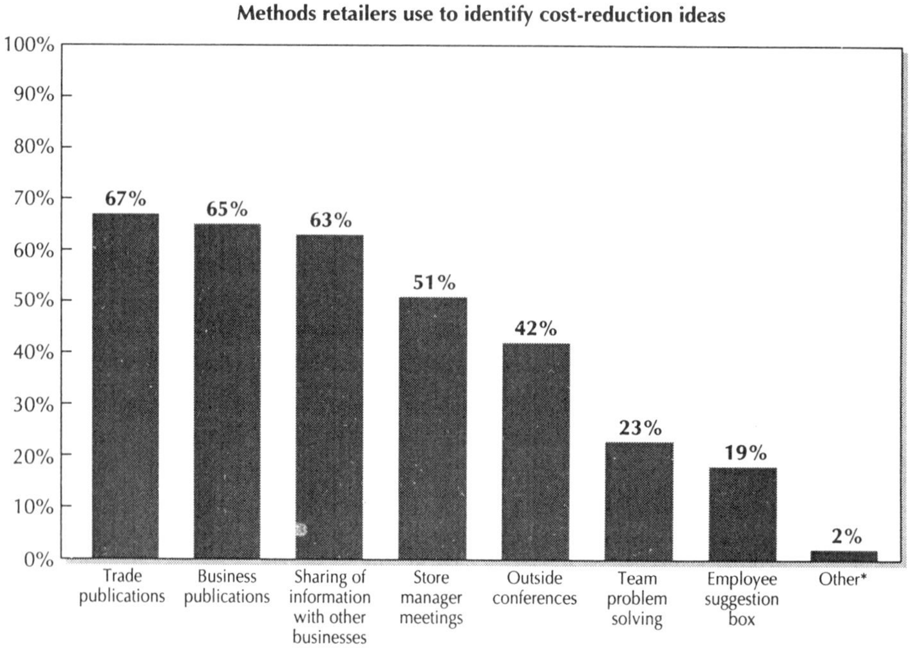

Methods retailers use to identify cost-reduction ideas

* Includes industry standards.

If not, consider eliminating the task as a way to cut costs. One method of determining which specific areas of costs offer the most opportunity for reduction is to record the costs and measure them against benchmarks. You can obtain benchmarks from industry surveys, trade associations, budgets, historical performance, and other retailers in your community. The most common method of measuring variable costs, such as store labor and utilities, is as a percentage of net sales or cost of sales. Refer to the benchmarks section for additional areas of your business to measure.

Once you have pinpointed where to reduce costs, you need to research effective cost-containment methods. Throughout this process, however, you need to evaluate your cost-reduction ideas and consider how the changes will affect customer service and satisfaction, both now and in the future. What may save you money in the near-term may ultimately cost you in the long-term because of lost customers and sales. Some ideas:

- Reevaluate all of your policies and procedures. Look for ways to reduce cost while maintaining or improving efficiency. Challenge your assumptions. For instance, it may be more cost-effective to outsource your payroll than to perform the task yourself. Consider automating inefficient processes, such as maintenance of mailing lists or charge-account customers. Remember that automating an inefficient process may help in the short term but will not by itself make the process efficient. Improve the process first; then automate.

- Consider POS scanning. The long-term benefits of the technology may outweigh the initial cost. The payoffs include accurate selling prices, reduced waiting time for customers, and improved customer satisfaction. See in Chapter 4 "Computers Necessary to Keep Up with the Joneses," and "Computer Revolution Changing the Way Retailing is Done" in this chapter.

- Develop an effective way to schedule store employees. Labor is a retailer's single largest operating cost, so effectively managing it can lead to big savings. See in Chapter 4 "Proper Labor Scheduling is the Key to Controlling Costs."

- Establish a loss-prevention program. Every piece of merchandise that "walks" out of the store is money lost. See in Chapter 4, "Reducing Theft and Shrinkage Adds to the Bottom Line."

- Negotiate the most cost-effective lease possible. There is substantial excess retail space in the marketplace, so you have leverage even though you are a small operator. But you must understand the negotiation process. All lease terms are important: number of years and base rent, option periods and corresponding base rents, percentage rents, real-estate taxes, and common-area maintenance. If you do not have the necessary skills in this area, hire an expert. It is well worth the cost. In addition to outside counsel, there are many third-party real-estate companies that specialize in lease negotiation. Contact your local chamber of commerce or talk with other retailers for a reference.

- Control utility costs. Although many small-store retailers take some steps to control utility costs, most hesitate to challenge charges and do not take advantage of consulting services that local utility companies offer. If you are in a strip center or mall, you should also challenge common-area maintenance costs. On average, you will recover $2 for every $1 you invest in auditing common-area charges, according to *Stores* magazine. See in Chapter 4, "Retailers May Miss Out on Opportunities to Control Costs."
- Control advertising costs. Often, simple changes in advertising can cut costs without reducing the effectiveness of the ads. You can experiment with smaller ads or less frequency. Try changing the paper or the number of colors you use in your flyers. Ask your printer about alternatives. And talk with other printers to see if they can offer you a better deal. For ideas to improve the effectiveness of your ads, see "Extra! Extra! Advertising and PR Let Customers Read All About It" in Chapter 2.

Control health-care costs. In a study by National Small Business United and Arthur Andersen, 85 percent of retailers experienced increased health-care costs in 1992, with an average increase of 22 percent. You will find it hard to survive if these rates continue, but there are ways to combat the problem:

- Consider changing insurance companies. At a minimum, solicit bids from at least three carriers. Even if you end up continuing with your current carrier, you are likely to have a better price as a result of putting your contract out for bid.
- Change to a policy with a higher deductible.
- Change to a policy with higher co-payments.
- Increase employees' contribution to insurance costs. One way to do this is to subsidize benefits with flat dollars instead of percents. This will likely help you save money, given the trend of rising health-care costs.
- Reduce the benefits you offer.
- Consider an HMO, a PPO, or a managed-care alternative. These are among the most popular choices of employers today for cost management, and many have plans for small employers. Obviously, the key issues and cost-control tactics in this area could change in the near future with the federal government's consideration of a health-care reform package.

Solicit multiple bids for all service arrangements and capital expenditures. Don't fall into the trap of using a vendor because he always has the goods or because it's easier than changing. You may be paying too much for the goods or services you are receiving. Require vendors such as insurance carriers, accountants, construction companies and contractors, maintenance companies and janitorial services to submit bids. Whenever possible, get three bids for every job. This will give you more information on which to base your decision and allow you to gain a better understanding of the various costs and service levels.

- Control investments in furniture, fixtures, and equipment. With continuing retail consolidation and corporate downsizing, there is an abundance of office furniture and used fixtures in the market, most of which can be purchased at a fraction of the new cost. There are many reputable vendors in the market. Find one that provides good value (quality for price).
- "Don't buy a Cadillac if you only need a Volkswagen." Generally there is a trade-off in cost versus quality. Determine what quality of goods or service you need and make your expenditures accordingly. For example, if you don't use a fax machine very often, consider purchasing a lower-end model, or help recover the cost by placing the machine in your store for customers to use for a fee. You might even share with another business.

BUDGETING

Measuring and Managing Go Hand-in-Hand

The fact is that retailers cannot manage what they do not measure. Respondents recognize this, with 81 percent rating budgeting as important or very important (see Figure 7-4 on the following page). Performance in this area, however, is not commensurate with level of importance: 42 percent of respondents rank their budgeting practices as fair and 34 percent as good.

Today's most successful retailers place considerable importance on the value of budgeting, from developing a sound annual budget to measuring actual results against the budget. The budgeting process not only allows retailers to take a critical look at all areas of their businesses but also enables them to anticipate their cash-flow needs and measure their business performance.

Despite the many benefits that retailers can accrue from having formal budgets, 51 percent do not have them (see Figure 7-5 on page 236). To be effective, retailers should prepare annual budgets for revenues, expenses, and cash flows, then update them periodically. Retailers need to measure actual performance against expected performance and then take necessary

Figure 7-4   Retailers recognize budgeting as very important, but they admit that their performance is lagging.

Retailers' breakdown of importance and performance for budgeting

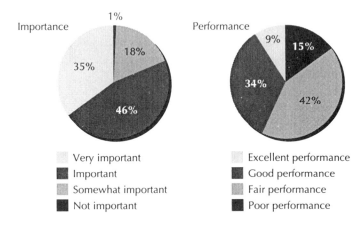

Importance
1%
18%
35%
46%

Performance
9%   15%
34%
42%

- Very important
- Important
- Somewhat important
- Not important

- Excellent performance
- Good performance
- Fair performance
- Poor performance

Figure 7-5   More than half of the retailers polled do not prepare a budget, though all should prepare one at least annually. Retailers can better manage cash flow by using exception reports, which analyze variances against actual results.

Characteristics of budgeting processes retailers use

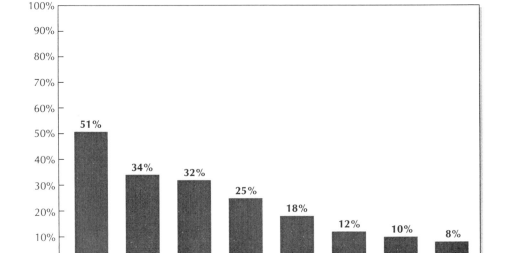

corrective action. Retailers should distribute budgets that include line-item figures to employees accountable for those items. Exception reporting is one way to help the owner or operator identify key items that fall outside acceptable levels.

Best Practices You Can Use

You can benefit from an annual budget that includes a month-by-month breakdown. While you may not have the resources available to undertake a rigorous formal budgeting process, you can obtain help and input from employees, other retailers, trade associations, and outside consultants.

Determine what areas can benefit most from a budget. While some retailers budget sales and margin only, others budget operating expenses only. The most effective budget incorporates all your revenue and expense items, including your cash-flow requirements. Here are some important items you should consider when you are preparing your budget, which you should do prior to the start of your fiscal year:

- Sales
- Markdowns
- Returns and allowances
- Cost of merchandise (including freight)
- Rent, if you lease your facility (including percentage rent, if applicable)
- Depreciation of fixtures and equipment (and building, if you are an owner)
- Common-area maintenance, if you are located in a mall
- Utilities
- Capital improvements
- Wages (including commissions and your salary)
- Benefits (including medical coverage, sick leave, profit sharing, and so on)
- Taxes (federal, state, local, property, payroll, and the like)
- Advertising
- Property, merchandise, and liability insurance
- Fees for proprietary or other credit cards, less finance charges for proprietary credit cards
- Outside advisers (legal, accounting, tax, and the like)
- Supplies and other operating expenses
- Interest expense and principal payments (if your loans are outstanding)

The easiest way to develop the budget is to start with last year's income statement results. Adjust for known current-year changes, and then compare your numbers to industry statistics and other similar retailers on a line-by-line basis. Also build in goals you want to achieve, and involve employees in the process. A budget should challenge the organization; if you make it too easy to attain, you will defeat the purpose. A cash-flow budget is similar, but it obviously focuses only on items that affect your cash—your ability to pay bills and reinvest in your business (see Table 7-2).

Solid budgets also include a return on equity (ROE) goal. To calculate this, divide net income by average shareholder's equity. A good after-tax goal is 10 percent to 25 percent, which approximates the return on a share of stock in S&P's 500. If you cannot achieve at least the low end of the range, investing in your business is not wise from strictly a financial perspective. However, if you're like some small-store retailers and you're not in the retailing business to get rich, decide on a goal that is more realistic for you.

The most effective budgets will involve employees in the development process and assign them accountability for the budget items they control. For example, your buyers should have accountability for gross margin and all its elements.

Once you have developed your budget, distribute it to employees who have accountability for specific budgeted items. Use your budget as a tool to measure performance, that of both your company and your employees who are responsible for specific budgeted items. Generate exception reports that identify variances from your plan, and use these reports to highlight areas for improvement. Take corrective measures as needed. To be effective, exception reports and reports that show planned vs. actual must be available on a timely basis. Monthly results should be available no more than two weeks after the end of the month as a general

Table 7-2   Sample cash-flow budget

	September		October		November	
	Planned	**Actual**	**Planned**	**Actual**	**Planned**	**Actual**
Cash on hand at beginning of month	$5,000	$3,000	$11,000	$3,500	$16,500	$10,000
Sales*	20,000	15,000	25,000	30,000	35,000	45,000
Disbursements:						
Merchandise payments	10,000	11,000	15,000	18,000	25,000	30,000
Fixed expenses	3,000	2,500	3,000	3,500	4,000	3,000
Variable operating expenses	1,000	1,000	1,500	2,000	2,000	2,500
Total disbursements	14,000	14,500	19,500	23,500	31,000	35,500
Monthly cash flow	6,000	500	5,500	6,500	4,000	9,500
Cash on hand at end of month	11,000	3,500	16,500	10,000	20,500	19,500

*Assumes all sales for cash as well as national credit cards and proprietary credit cards when receivables related to the credit cards are immediately sold.

guideline. It's likely that you will have to automate your ledger, however, to generate reports this quickly (see "The Computer Revolution Is Changing the Way Retailing Is Done" in this chapter).

CAPITAL RESOURCES

A Dollar a Day Keeps Business Booming

Obtaining and generating adequate capital is essential to start, acquire, or expand a retail business, which is probably why almost 80 percent of respondents feel capital resources are important or very important (see Figure 7-6).

Capital requirements vary widely across retail formats, so it is important for retailers to understand the requirements specific to their format. Almost all small-store retailers obtain capital funding from earnings of their existing business (see Figure 7-7). This is good management. Retailers should fund daily operations and capital expenditures with cash from operations. Assuming any debt beyond that required for short-term working capital needs is not prudent for small businesses. Long-term debt is appropriate only for property additions, although retailers can avoid this, too, by anticipating these needs and setting aside small amounts of cash from operations over a period of years.

In general, retailers should avoid jeopardizing their personal assets by personally guaranteeing loans and leases. Unfortunately, many retail-

Figure 7-6 Now more than ever, many retailers view capital resources as important or very important. These retailers often have limited capital to finance their businesses and do not know where to turn for additional financing.

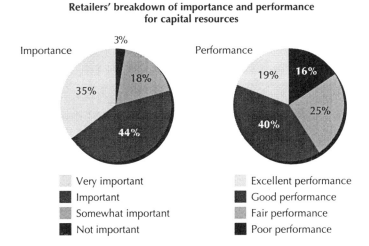

Retailers' breakdown of importance and performance for capital resources

Importance
3%
18%
35%
44%

Performance
19% 16%
25%
40%

- Very important
- Important
- Somewhat important
- Not important

- Excellent performance
- Good performance
- Fair performance
- Poor performance

Figure 7-7   Retailers' most common source for capital funding is earnings from their businesses. However, as business has declined over the years, more retailers have turned to banks and personal loans or mortgages.

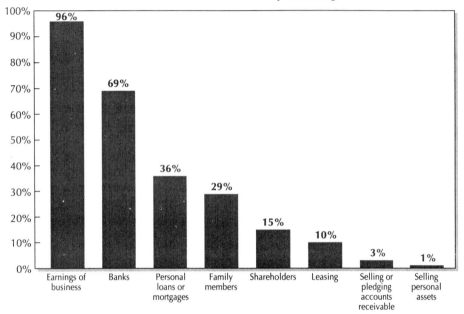

Sources retailers use for capital funding

ers used bank loans and personal loans or mortgages as the economy worsened in the late 1980s and early 1990s.

To aggravate the problem, obtaining capital from outside sources is difficult for small-store retailers. According to a study by National Small Business United and Arthur Andersen, 38 percent of retailers have capital needs that are not met. In addition, 11 percent of retailers who applied for bank loans in 1992 were turned down.[1]

Arthur Andersen research also indicates that many small-store retailers fail to correctly anticipate their capital requirements or adequately explore all possible avenues of funding.

Developing accurate capital-requirement plans and obtaining adequate sources of financing can eliminate potential business inefficiencies and interruptions, allowing retailers to devote their attention to running their businesses.

Through it all, retailers should take advantage of outside advisers and accountants who can help them identify capital resources. The most important trait of effective outside advisers is that they understand the

---

[1] Survey of Small- and Mid-Sized Businesses, Trends for 1993. Arthur Andersen LLP, and National Small Business United.

retail industry. Figure 7-8 shows that more than 50 percent of respondents feel their outside accountants and tax advisers understand the retail industry, but only 34 percent feel that way about their bankers and 17 percent about their outside counsel. This does not bode well for retailers. An outside attorney unfamiliar with the retailing industry may advise a retailer to sign a lease that is impracticably structured. For instance, a start-up retailer should probably not sign a 20-year lease, which would significantly limit his flexibility.

This shows that retailers need either to educate their advisers or choose ones who will give their business needs the appropriate level of attention and service. The relatively low percentages of retailers who feel that their advisers know their companies' goals and understand their problems indicate that retailers need to be more willing to spend time with their advisers and share cold, hard facts.

Best Practices You Can Use

Developing a cash-flow forecast, which is generally required to obtain bank financing, is a helpful tool for anticipating your cash needs, both for

Figure 7-8 Outside advisers have technical backgrounds that retailers need, but a common retailer complaint is, "They don't know my business!" Retailers need to consult with advisers who understand the industry and their businesses.

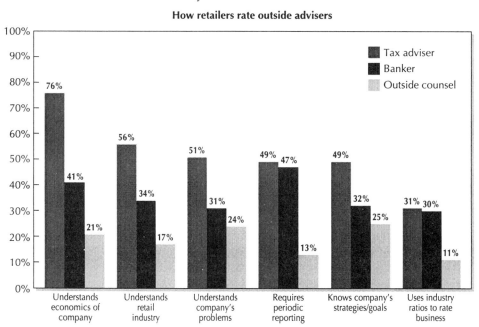

opening a new store and for funding ongoing operations. The primary purpose of a cash-flow forecast is to estimate your cash inflows and outflows for a given period. Cash flows vary by type of retailer, particularly those with seasonal sales. As a result, the period that a cash-flow forecast covers is just as important as the items that the forecast includes. For most small-store retailers, a cash-flow forecast by month for a 12-month period will suffice.

To develop a cash-flow forecast, start by estimating your cash inflows from sales and services after deducting markdowns, returns, and allowances. Then estimate all your applicable cash outflows, which include opening costs and ongoing operating costs. Opening costs include:

- Inventory
- Fixtures and equipment
- Exterior design
- Security system
- Cost of facility (if you are building or purchasing)
- Rent deposit (if you are leasing)
- Attorney and other outside adviser fees (for closing if you are building or purchasing or for lease negotiation if you are renting)
- License and permit fees
- Insurance
- Utility start-up fees
- Advertising

Ongoing costs include:

- Wages (including commissions and your salary)
- Costs of merchandise (including freight-in)
- Rent (including percentage rent, if applicable)
- Utilities
- Maintenance and repairs
- Capital improvements
- Common-area maintenance
- Benefits (including vacation, medical, dental, sick leave, profit sharing, and pension plans)
- Taxes (federal, state, local, property, payroll, and others)
- Advertising
- Insurance
- Proprietary or other credit-card fees less finance charges from proprietary credit cards
- Outside advisers (legal, accounting, and tax)
- Supplies

- License and permit fees
- Interest and principal payments (if you have outstanding loans)

Your net cash (inflows minus outflows) can result in a surplus or a deficiency. By conservatively estimating your cash flow, you can better anticipate deficiencies and obtain up-front funding. Use your business plan, budget, experience, and banker input to project your cash inflows and outflows.

You can obtain funding from various sources, depending on the duration and purpose of your needs. These sources include:

- Earnings of the business
- Banks
- Family members
- Shareholders
- Personal loans or mortgages
- Leasing of fixed assets versus purchasing (generally more expensive than bank debt but cheaper than many other means of financing)
- Venture capitalists
- Selling or pledging accounts receivable
- Selling portions of your business
- Selling personal assets
- Vendors (with longer cash terms)
- Government loans (Small Business Administration)
- Local small business development center loans

Retain competent outside advisers to assist in planning your resource requirements and raising capital. The retail division of the Illinois Certified Public Accountants Society can recommend advisers. Once you have obtained financing, keep the lender apprised of the business performance. This means keeping him updated beyond quarterly financial statements, which are often required. This practice not only educates the lender about the business and creates goodwill, but also helps you and the lender avoid unwanted surprises.

INFORMATION SYSTEMS

The Computer Revolution Is Changing the Way Retailing Is Done

Retailers who have trouble programming their VCRs may be leery of computerizing their stores. But thanks to the PC revolution, it's easier—and cheaper—than ever to apply technology to the retail-store environment.

Hardware is now available from many different manufacturers, software has been developed to run on almost any hardware platform, and independent companies have sprung up to service the equipment. All this is available to retailers at lower costs than ever before. There is only one problem. With so many choices, many retailers do not have the knowledge to sort through all the options. Retailers need to use outside resources to help them clarify their information-systems needs and identify solutions.

Perhaps that's why small-store retailers have difficulty in this area, even though they feel it is important. As Figure 7-9 shows, 58 percent of respondents rank their use of information systems as poor or fair, although 84 percent say information systems are important or very important.

Most small-store retailers do not use computer systems that capture key financial and merchandising information. The most common reasons: lack of knowledge, time, or money. As Figure 7-10 shows, few retailers have implemented some of the most basic technology, like POS systems. It would be one thing if retailers were evaluating the pros and cons of this technology, but few are even doing that. For example, the portion of retailers who have not considered installing POS registers is a surprising 36 percent. Retailers need to evaluate the benefits of computerizing their operations and then implement appropriate systems.

Many retailers can improve their ability to track critical financial, merchandising, and operating information by automating certain financial and merchandising functions. But they need to decide if the benefits

Figure 7-9   Retailers understand the importance of information systems. However, most have not taken action to assess their businesses' needs or to implement systems that will meet those needs.

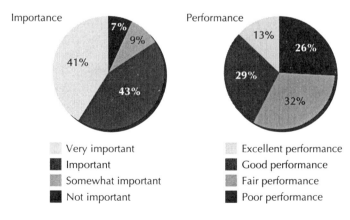

Retailers' breakdown of importance and performance for information systems

Figure 7-10   Retailers are slow to implement new information-system technology.

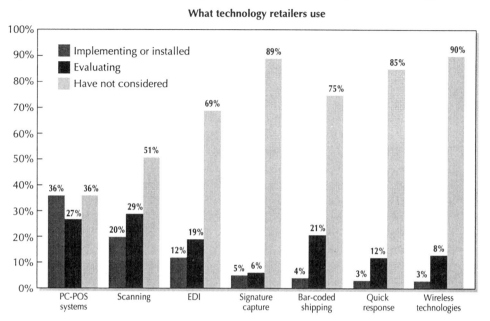

outweigh the costs. For instance, a POS system with scanning capability generally results in increased accuracy in sales price and shorter check-out lines. Arthur Andersen research indicates that small-store retailers reap the greatest benefits from automating point of sale, general ledger, accounts receivable, inventory management, accounts payable, payroll, and customer lists and purchase histories. Of course, the extent to which a retailer should automate depends on his individual situation.

Although many retailers shy away from computerized information systems because they lack the background and knowledge, another reason is cost. Although technology costs less than ever before, the costs still may seem prohibitive to some retailers. Small-store retailers should be aware that they do not have to purchase the equipment; leasing is a viable—but often overlooked—option (see Figure 7-11). Retailers can secure leasing from the original equipment manufacturer, a third-party distributor, or a software company. However, many retailers who leased equipment in the past have recently chosen to purchase new equipment because of lower costs. In addition, retailers often have several different kinds of equipment in their stores. Juggling five to ten equipment leases every month becomes an unwanted hassle.

Servicing the equipment also offers a variety of options. A number of independent third-party companies are authorized to service different manufacturers' equipment. Retailers with a number of different retail

Figure 7-11   Most retailers who use POS systems, as well as other computerized equipment, own them, though leasing is a good alternative.

Percentage of retailers who own, lease, or do not use equipment

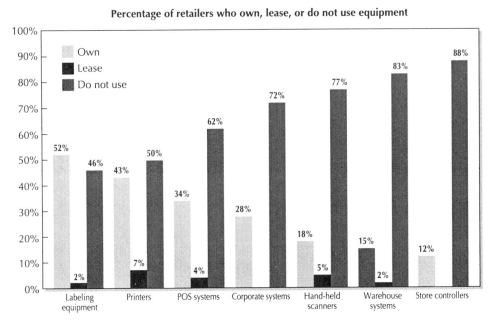

systems find this one-stop service concept very attractive. Only 39 percent of retailers take advantage of this opportunity, though. Instead, most retailers have in-house personnel service the equipment. These retailers must determine whether it is more cost-effective to pay their own employees to service the equipment or to outsource the service.

Best Practices You Can Use

Research the how-to's of implementing computerized information systems. Business publications and trade associations are good resources. Suggest to the associations that they sponsor a seminar.

Meet with your management team and other employees and ask them what they need to make their work more efficient. You need their input and support.

Research the availability, costs, and types of software. You can gather information on what software is best by reading software directories and talking with trade associations, vendors, and other retailers who have automated their businesses. Trade associations are usually aware of off-the-shelf software designed for small-store retailers. It's often less expensive to adapt this software to your own business than to develop your own software.

Once you identify what software is available, narrow down your choices by looking at capabilities, costs, flexibility, upgrades, and vendor and manufacturer support. Ask the manufacturer or vendor for a list of retailers who use the software; give them a call and ask how they like the product. Consider engaging an outside consultant to assist in the selection.

To determine the best method for financing and servicing your information systems, you should evaluate the following:

- What is the expected life span for these systems in your retail environment? Is an information system a short-term solution or a long-term strategy?
- What are the costs to buy and service the equipment vs. the costs to lease?
- How durable is the equipment? You may want to ask the manufacturer for several references or talk with a trade association. Ask if replacement parts are readily available.
- Do you have personnel in your stores who feel comfortable enough with the technology to learn basic maintenance—and actually use the equipment?

Develop a timeline for the implementation of the technology and software you have chosen. Include key dates and periodic performance assessments on your timeline and stick to them.

Involve employees in the decision and implementation process. Point out the positive aspects of using technology, like increased efficiency and additional marketable skills as you teach your employees how to use the new system.

KEY-FACTOR AND INTERNAL REPORTING

Reports Drive Sound Business Decisions

Key-factor reports summarize critical financial, operating, and business results. Internal reporting is the timely and accurate delivery of that information to company decision-makers and employees. Key-factor reports are critical for measuring performance, identifying opportunities for improvement, and taking corrective action. Internal reporting is vital for measuring improvement. Unfortunately, only 60 percent of respondents rate key-factor reporting as important or very important (see Figure 7-12 on the next page). And though 87 percent say internal reporting is important or very important (see Figure 7-13), only 59 percent rate their performance as good or excellent.

Figure 7-12   Respondents view key-factor reporting as the least important financial practice, primarily because retailers neither have the information to develop these measures nor know what factors are most important to report.

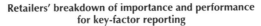

Retailers' breakdown of importance and performance for key-factor reporting

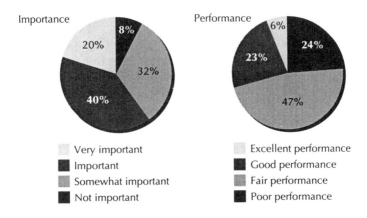

Arthur Andersen research finds that the best retailers report on results using industry benchmarks (many of which are included in this book) and performance goals determined during the budgeting process. They then relay this information to the employees responsible for the key business measures.

Figure 7-13   Retailers view internal reporting as important, but they indicate poor performance because they don't have time to deal with "the numbers."

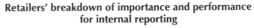

Retailers' breakdown of importance and performance for internal reporting

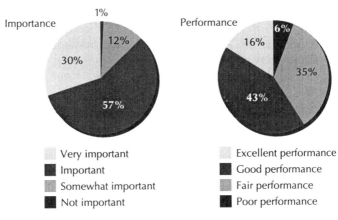

As Figure 7-14 shows, most small-store retailers use daily sales reports to make management decisions. Although this is a good practice, retailers need to follow up these daily reports with weekly and monthly reports on such items as inventory levels and aging, markdowns, payroll, and operating expenses. All of the items shown in the graph are critical to helping retailers manage their businesses and identify areas of weakness and opportunity.

Because of their size and sophistication level, many small-store retailers neither appreciate the value of key-factor reporting nor feel they have the resources and systems necessary to produce such reports. While retailing has always required—and will continue to require—a good instinct, the "gut feel" that many small-store retailers rely on is just not enough in today's competitive retail environment.

Those retailers who track performance commonly do not share detailed financial information with their employees, even those responsi-

Figure 7-14 A large percentage of retailers track daily sales, but many lack reporting in important areas such as weekly store payroll, monthly markdowns, monthly operating expenses, and monthly budgets to actual reports.

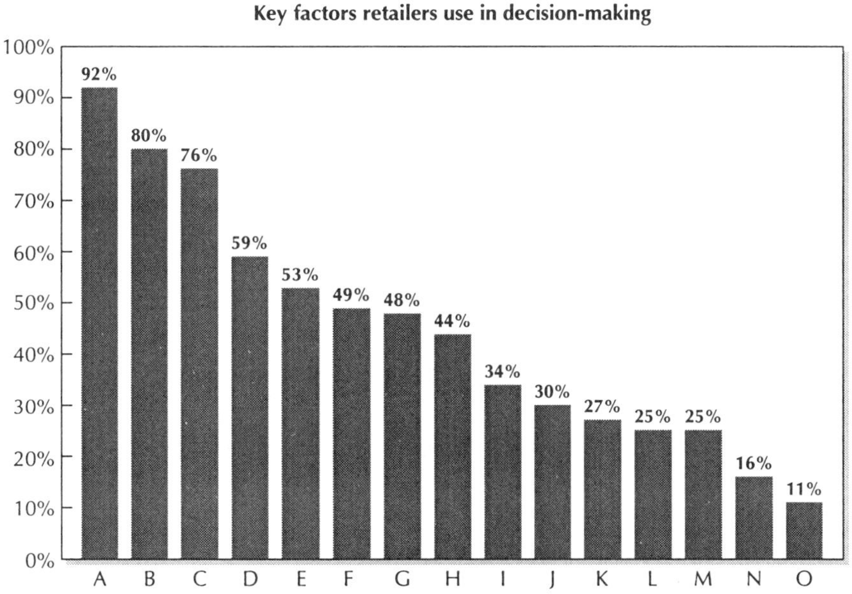

Key factors retailers use in decision-making

A. Daily sales
B. Annual income and balance sheet statements
C. Monthly income and balance sheet statements
D. Inventory levels
E. Inventory aging
F. Monthly operating expenses by line item
G. Weekly store payroll
H. Receivables aging

I. Item movement
J. Monthly open-to-buy
K. Stockouts
L. Monthly markdown
M. Daily gross margin
N. Monthly budget to actual reports
O. Other*

* Includes monthly payroll, cash flow, and turnover.

ble for given areas of operation, simply because they do not understand the potential benefits of sharing such information. To improve operational performance and profitability, retailers should at least share departmental sales and gross margin performance with their employees on a timely basis. Those who seize the opportunity to generate and use key information will have a significant competitive advantage over those who rely only on gut feel.

Best Practices You Can Use

Measuring key success factors is critical to evaluating your store's performance. You should determine what key reports will provide you with the most beneficial information and then generate those reports on a regular basis and compare them to established budgets, goals, and industry benchmarks. You should also distribute the reports to employees responsible for those measures and take timely corrective action. The following are examples of key-factor reports, performance measures, and key information, based on Arthur Andersen research:

Daily sales (in total and by department). These reports may be available from your cash register or POS system. They can help your store manager and buyer determine your fast- and slow-moving items and analyze department performance. You can also use these reports to help schedule labor. Use the information as an overall measure of your selling performance by store, department, class, and item.

Weekly customer returns (in total, by reason code, and by department). Use this information as a measure of merchandise quality (such as defective products) and effective selling (when the customer purchases the right product the first time due to a knowledgeable salesperson). This information is generally available from your cash register or POS system. If not, you can track it manually on a ledger card placed next to the register.

Monthly markdowns (in total and by department). These reports will help your buyer analyze department performance. Again, this information is generally available from your cash register or POS system. If not, you can track it manually on a ledger card placed next to the register.

Inventory levels and aging. These reports also will enable your buyer to determine your fast- and slow-moving items, which will help you make future purchasing decisions and determine when to take markdowns. In general, these reports will help you reduce investment in working capital and increase cash flow. If you do not have a perpetual inventory system, the only way to generate such a report is to mark the receipt date on the price tag. Additionally, the store manager should walk the store each week and note receipt dates to determine when to take markdowns.

Receivables aging. This report will help you manage the collections process and increase cash flow. Usually this report is generated by accounts-receivable software. If you record receivables manually, the office employee should indicate the date of sale and payment on your ledger cards. It is best to group your aging receivables in categories of 30 days from date of sale.

Monthly open-to-buy. This merchandising tactic, which determines the budgeted dollars to commit to purchases, is critical to managing inventory. See "Inventory Control Is the Best Way to Increase Profits," in Chapter 3.

Monthly operating expenses by line item. Use this information to measure performance of your cost-control efforts. You should highlight variations from budget to actual on a monthly basis.

Weekly and monthly payroll. Compute payroll as a percentage of sales, gathering the information from the payroll register and sales reports. Use this information to determine the effectiveness and productivity of your store labor. See "Proper Labor Scheduling Is the Key to Controlling Costs" in Chapter 3.

Weekly customer complaints (in total and by type). Use this information to gauge the performance of your salespeople and your merchandise selection. Pay close attention to comments on merchandise availability, helpfulness of sales staff, and speed of checkout.

Quarterly income statement and balance sheet. Use this information as an overall measure of your financial performance.

TAXATION

The Taxman Cometh All Too Soon

As everyone knows, the only sure things in life are death and taxes. Retailers cannot do much about the first, but they can—and should—do a lot about the second. Taxes are just like any other cost element of a retail business and must be managed accordingly.

If left unattended, taxes can hinder growth. Considering all the other financial practices demanding retailers' attention, they ascribe about the

Figure 7-15   Retailers recognize that understanding taxation is important. The combination of complex tax laws and retailer inexperience, however, results in a fair or poor performance by nearly half of them.

Retailers' breakdown of importance and performance for taxation

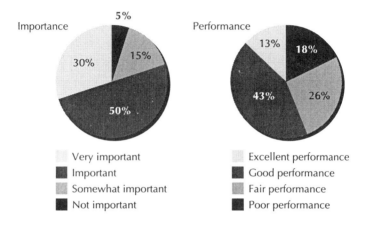

right importance to taxation. As Figure 7-15 shows, 50 percent of retailers feel taxation is important, and 30 percent feel it is very important.

Generally speaking, retailers do not consider taxes as a controllable cost since governmental bodies impose a complex, and always changing, set of tax regulations. Because it is so difficult to understand these tax laws, retailers, like most other people, view it as difficult—if not impossible—to effectively manage this cost element of their operations.

As Figure 7-16 shows, 46 percent of retailers feel that the complexity of tax laws contributes to the difficulties of filing income, sales, and payroll tax returns. But retailers should not concern themselves with the intricacies of understanding tax laws and forms if it is not their area of expertise. The most successful retailers concentrate on retailing and let expert tax advisers provide tax-planning services and complete tax returns.

The benefits of effective tax management are many. Most importantly, it minimizes cash outflow for taxes. Taxes on federal and state income, social security, Medicare, unemployment, sales, property, and franchise represent a major cash outflow. Overpayment of these taxes or penalties and interest attributed to underpayments can impair retailers' cash flow, causing inefficiencies in operating and building their businesses.

Some of the steps retailers take to manage tax costs are shown in Figure 7-17 on page 254. As explained before, engaging tax advisers is important. Additionally, more retailers should dispute tax assessments—these assessments are not always valid.

Figure 7-16   Complex tax laws and forms add to retailers' confusion over taxes.

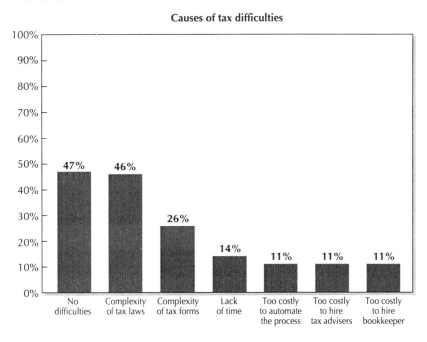

Causes of tax difficulties

In addition, Arthur Andersen was surprised to see a large number of companies structured for purposes of federal income tax as a C corporation versus an S corporation. Owners of operations structured as C corporations should contact their tax advisers to determine if converting to an S corporation could reduce federal income taxes.

Best Practices You Can Use

You should take steps to ensure that you and your outside advisers are analyzing and implementing tax strategies that will improve your cash flow. To avoid unexpected charges for interest and penalties, you should never take inappropriate tax positions. The following are some of the options available to control your tax costs and manage your tax risks:

- Consult with your tax adviser before making significant changes in your business (such as capital spending and compensation structure).
- Ask your tax adviser to inform you of changes in tax requirements (such as form or timing of filings and tax consequences of routine business transactions).

Figure 7-17   Retailers should use professional tax advisers so they can spend their time doing what they know: retailing. They also should not be afraid to dispute a tax assessment; it may not always be valid.

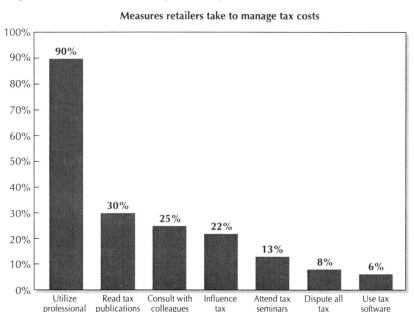

Measures retailers take to manage tax costs

- Share ideas with and solicit input from other retailers. Industry groups, trade associations, and direct conversations with other retailers are appropriate forums for this exchange of information.
- Educate yourself through periodicals, publications, and seminars.
- Challenge notices from tax authorities. Do not assume they are correct.
- Communicate directly with the various federal, state, and local tax authorities.
- Evaluate the technology available for reporting and administering your tax-compliance requirements.

LESSONS LEARNED FROM CASE STUDIES

POS and Computer Systems Help Harried Retailer

With six women's specialty clothing stores spread across rural Illinois, Bob Jones[2] has his hands full.[3] That's why he invested in new high-tech POS sys-

---

[2] Bob Jones is a pseudonym.
[3] See "Tough Competition for Shrinking Market Scares Profitable Women's Specialty Retailer" in Chapter 8 for a complete case study.

tems and computers at the corporate office. These systems provide timely and accurate sales information. They also help Bob track inventory movement, which aids in merchandise replenishment and reduces overstock.

In addition, the new systems possess capabilities that Bob has yet to exploit. The POS systems, for example, have the ability to track customer profiles and purchase histories. Bob can use this information to identify his best customers, which in turn would help him with target-marketing efforts.

8

CASE STUDIES

The Key to Success Is Never to Stop Learning[1]

CASE STUDY #1: EXCEEDING CUSTOMERS' EXPECTATIONS KEEPS AN APPLIANCE STORE ON TOP

When Bud Taylor started his bicycle and radio repair shop in 1930, he immediately realized the value of selling service contracts. More than 60 years later, the bikes and radios are gone, but the service contracts remain.

"Our company philosophy is to go beyond the customers' expectations. One way to do that is to offer extended service contracts on every item in the store," says Kevin Keller, president of what is now an appliance and electronics store. Kevin prominently displays the mission statement bearing the founder's philosophy for all the employees to see.

This attention to customer satisfaction pays off for the business: Despite the slow economy, the company is enjoying increasing net sales and gross margins. And first-, second- and third-generation customers keep coming back (see Table 8-2). So what else is Kevin doing to ensure the company's continued success?

Value-added services. Customers can have their new appliances delivered to their homes and assembled and their old appliances hauled away. Delivery people and service technicians carry cellular phones so they can call customers before they arrive. Kevin says customers realize the value

---

[1] The names of individuals appearing in this chapter are fictitious.

Table 8-1   Appliance store company profile

Format	Appliance and electronics store
Location	Rural Illinois city
Market size	70,000
Purchased	Early 1960s
Full-time employees	17
1992 net sales	$3 million

of these services and usually are willing to pay for them. The charges also help preserve profit margins. Other ways that Kevin and his crew of 17 ensure customer satisfaction include sending thank-you notes to customers with purchases greater than $250, offering a proprietary credit card with a 90-days-same-as-cash feature, and promptly following up with customer complaints.

Promotions. Tent sales, truckload sales, after-inventory sales, and six-months-same-as-cash deals keep customers coming back for more; while print, radio, and cable-television advertising let customers know about the company's value-added services. A computerized database, installed in 1989, keeps track of 12,000 customers for direct-mail purposes.

Satisfaction surveys. Kevin invites customers to fill out a comment card to determine their level of satisfaction with the merchandise and delivery service. He calls dissatisfied customers immediately. Salespeople respond in writing to other comments.

Employee empowerment. Kevin gives his employees the power to do whatever it takes to satisfy customers. If a customer is unwilling to pay the delivery charge, for example, the salesperson can remove the charge in order to make the sale.

Training classes. Every year, some employees attend sales-training classes sponsored by the National Association of Retail Dealers of America and the local Chamber of Commerce, where they learn motivational techniques, new business practices, and the latest industry news. Manufacturers also visit the store and offer product knowledge training.

Caring for employees. Kevin strives to make the store a fun place for his employees to work, which contributes to the low turnover rate. He

Table 8-2   Indicators of and reasons for financial success

- Increasing sales for past several years
- Recent sales up 7.1 percent
- Gross margin up 4 percent from previous year
- Focus on satisfying customers and exceeding their expectations helps maintain sales and increase customer traffic

encourages employees to discuss customer-service issues and opportunities at monthly meetings. And the company pays for 100 percent of employees' health benefits to foster the "we care" attitude.

Competitor shopping. Both Kevin and the current absentee owner, Bud's son Jake, get innovative ideas from their visits to other retailers and competitors in the community and across the nation.

Competitive response. To compete with major appliance retailers in surrounding communities, Kevin offers price-match guarantees. He carries higher quality products than the competitors and stocks brands that competitors cannot obtain. He also works closely with other local businesses, supplying washers and dryers to residential contractors, for example.

Vendor compliance. "If you don't ask, you won't get it," Kevin says. So he closely monitors vendors on delivery time, short shipments, and damaged goods. He uses the information to negotiate with vendors and quicken their response time. This also helps Kevin keep a firm grip on inventory levels, which he tracks daily and weekly.

More Action Is Needed for the Store to Remain the Market Leader

Both Kevin and Jake feel that every one of these actions helps the company. In fact, to determine whether to implement a particular business practice, they ask: "Why are we doing this, and should we eliminate the task or perform it differently?" This attitude enables them to adapt relatively quickly to change, which in turn helps them maintain their status as the market leader.

Kevin and Jake's future goals for the company include maintaining its role as the market leader and expanding store size and inventory to include computers and furniture. To meet these ambitious goals, they will have to take action.

Renew service contracts. Kevin does not follow up with customers who do not initially purchase service contracts. Nor does he contact customers with service contracts due to expire. Both of these actions would boost profits. Kevin could also consider automatic billing of renewed service contracts to customers' charge accounts; customers could cancel the option when they receive their statements.

Target market. Kevin does maintain an extensive database, but he doesn't utilize the information to its fullest extent. He could send focused mailings to specific customers, like dishwasher promotions to new homeowners.

Conduct focus groups. Kevin could recruit marketing students from the local university to conduct focus groups, which are effective ways to pinpoint customer wants and satisfaction. Or he could invite some of his top customers and their friends to a customer-appreciation lunch, where he could also find out more about what they want from his store.

Change store hours. Kevin should consider opening the store on Sundays to boost customer traffic. He could shorten hours on Tuesdays, which are historically slow days for traffic.

Consider alternative delivery channels. Students at the nearby university would probably frequent a kiosk of small electronic appliances. And the added exposure would benefit the main store.

Encourage credit-card applications. Offering employees incentives, such as a dollar per application, would motivate them to offer the opportunity to customers. Offering customer incentives, such as a 15 percent discount on the customer's next purchase, would encourage people to apply.

Measure advertising. Although the company advertises its promotions and services fairly extensively, it doesn't track the effectiveness of the ads. Asking customers to mention where and when they saw the ads or to bring in redeemable coupons would help with this.

Restructure management. As the company grows, Kevin will need to devote more time to long-term strategic planning. To have the time, he needs to groom people to handle more of the daily operations. Also, Kevin and Jake should talk to their tax adviser about restructuring the business from a C corporation to an S corporation in an effort to reduce federal income taxes.

The Bottom Line

Kevin is one of the leaders of the retailing pack. His innovative use of systems, budgeting, open-to-buy, and customer database combine with the company's emphasis on customer service and satisfaction to make the business thrive. Kevin and Jake's ability to adapt to change, evidenced by the changing merchandise mix, has seen the company through tough economic times. Their success will continue to depend on their innovative ideas and emphasis on customer service.

CASE STUDY #2: A CHANGING ENVIRONMENT CHALLENGES A DRUGSTORE TO MAINTAIN CUSTOMER TRAFFIC

A series of setbacks has battered this urban neighborhood drugstore, leaving it with tight cash flow and fewer customers. When Mike Sylvester and Andrew Kates purchased the strip-mall drugstore in 1989, their intent was

Table 8-3   Drugstore company profile

Format	Drugstore
Location	Urban Illinois community
Market size	50,000
Purchased	1989
Full-time employees	13
1992 net sales	$1.7 million

to expand the business quickly by purchasing or building additional stores. Changes in the retail environment and in both partners' business objectives have challenged the survival of the business.

The store is located in a neighborhood populated by a large number of senior citizens and welfare recipients. The store draws its customers from surrounding apartment complexes and two nearby hospitals.

A number of factors in addition to the slow economy have hit store sales hard in recent years.

One of the two nearby hospitals has a new HMO provider. The HMO has an exclusive arrangement with a national chain and requires participants to have prescriptions filled there, which reduces the store's pharmacy sales and traffic.

The other hospital reduced its staff by 60 percent, adding to the neighborhood's increasing unemployment.

Recent Medicaid payments are slow due to budget shortfalls, compounding the store's cash-flow problems.

The strip mall's anchor tenant, a grocery store, went out of business, further reducing mall traffic.

Mike is not active in store operations, and he is no longer interested in expanding the business. The store has a full-time manager whose morale is low because of her long daily commute. Andrew, however, is fairly committed to the business. He spends about 20 hours a week in the store overseeing the operation and working as a part-time pharmacist. To his credit, Andrew has implemented changes to help revive store traffic.

Value-added services. To attract more customers, the store offers other services for a fee, including money orders, notary public, UPS delivery, lottery tickets, and photocopying.

Customer counseling. Store pharmacists are required to give verbal information to Medicaid patients about their prescriptions. Reconfiguring the

Table 8-4   Indicators of and reasons for tight cash flow

- Decreasing sales for past 18 months
- Recent net sales down 8.1 percent
- Gross margin down to 30 percent from 34 percent
- Tight cash flow partially due to declining store traffic

store layout to enable pharmacists to work personally with customers has made the store more conducive to customer counseling. And Andrew has used the training he has received from trade organizations to improve the customer-counseling skills of the store's other pharmacists.

New products. The store now offers a limited selection of grocery items such as canned goods, bread, and milk to make up for the mall's loss of the grocery store.

New Markets Needed for Survival

To begin to solve cash-flow problems, Andrew and Mike need to implement more changes aggressively, particularly in the areas of marketing and merchandising.

Target market. Andrew distributes flyers to neighborhood apartment complexes. He needs to expand these efforts to include advertising in the two nearby hospitals. One of them is about to undergo a major remodeling, bringing jobs back into the area. Andrew needs to provide these potential new customers with information about the store's products and services before they choose to frequent other stores or pharmacies.

Develop strategic business alliances. The business the pharmacy receives from health-care providers instead of customers themselves (called third-party business) has increased as a total percentage of pharmacy sales. To offset the lower margins the store makes on this business, Andrew needs to consider alliances with local doctors and hospitals for more third-party and non-third-party business.

Survey customers. Instead of relying too much on instincts, Andrew needs to ask both customers and noncustomers what types of products and services they want and why they do or do not shop in his store.

Evaluate the product mix. The store has a broad mix of products, but Andrew's inventory of staple items such as toothpaste, shampoo, and other personal-care products is low. Inventory of other, mostly seasonal, categories like school supplies are very broad and deep. Andrew needs to focus inventory investment and merchandising on high-volume, high-margin items and make sure that the store has staple items in stock at all times. The store should consider expanding its line of grocery products to include dry goods, such as cereal and pasta, until a grocer takes over the vacant space in the mall. POS registers or scanning equipment would make it much easier to analyze product movement and sales performance in each department, and the store should consider this new technology if resources permit.

Make product displays more attractive. The store also needs remodeling, which likely won't be an option until cash flow improves significantly. In the meantime, however, Andrew needs to motivate his employees to keep the store and product displays clean and inviting. Employees should wipe down shelves and products and clean the floor regularly. They need to learn effective merchandising techniques by attending seminars or trade shows and asking suppliers how to build attractive product displays. And employees should visit other stores to see how competitors display and merchandise their products.

Improve employee morale and reduce turnover. Attracting and retaining qualified employees in the neighborhood is difficult. Though the store pays above minimum wage, Andrew should consider incentives to motivate employee performance and reduce turnover. He should base incentives on predetermined measurable goals, like store cleanliness, sales performance, or suggestions for improvements. Incentives could include cash, paid days off, or employee discounts, depending on employee response. In addition, employees need more training to improve their customer-service skills and make more decisions on their own.

Expand loss prevention efforts. Because employee morale is low, loss prevention is a significant concern. The store already has an employee awareness program, security guard, and secret shoppers. It also requires receipts for returns. Andrew should consider loss-prevention audits, security cameras, and background checks on employees.

Develop strategic plan. While all of these actions can help increase store traffic and improve the store's cash flow constraints at a relatively modest cost, Andrew and Mike need to agree on the strategic objectives of their joint venture. They need to sit down and develop a long-term strategic plan that includes:

- A vision that clearly identifies the objectives of the business venture
- A strategic marketing and merchandising plan
- Operating cash-flow needs and capital needs for expenses like store remodeling
- A list of potential sources of funds
- Renegotiation of the store's lease on more favorable terms, particularly reduced rent, and a plan for options, such as relocation, if negotiations fail
- A succession plan for each partner, both of whom are nearing retirement

The Bottom Line

Andrew and Mike did not anticipate the series of setbacks that has now left the business bruised and battered. Store traffic is down, employee morale is low, and cash flow is tight. Andrew and Mike need to assess the strategic objectives of the venture and decide if their goals can be met in the current environment and store location. They need to analyze their customer base and determine whether they can rebuild it in the short-term. They also must determine long-term capital needs and operating-cost structures, especially lease terms.

CASE STUDY #3: INDEPENDENT HARDWARE CHAIN MUST TAP NEW MARKETS TO FEND OFF NATIONALS

Dan Curtis opened the doors to his hardware store in the Depression-ridden 1930s. Sixty years later, that one store has grown into a 10-store chain, with annual sales of over $11 million. Dan's two sons opened or bought out a variety of hardware stores in industrial towns across northern Illinois.

Over the years, the family has witnessed enormous marketplace changes: Manufacturing declined and service-based businesses increased; farmland turned into offices, retail complexes, and housing developments. Ace and TrueValue were the only major national players, and now the influx of other national chains and category killers is threatening the family-owned business more than ever (see Table 8-6).

These chains serve the newly created housing developments in the suburban "power communities." They advertise on television and radio. They offer a large selection of products at the lowest prices. The Curtises have not been blind to these changes. Nor have they been idle. Case in point: Many of their newer stores are in more accessible strip malls instead of downtown business districts. Indeed, they have taken many steps to ensure their success.

Cost controls. High-tech computer systems at point-of-sale locations and the corporate office improve efficiency and provide more timely and accurate sales and inventory data. In addition, the family outsources noncore financial processes, such as payroll and accounts receivable, to trim corporate overhead costs.

Table 8-5   Hardware chain company profile

Format	10 hardware stores
Location	Suburban and rural Illinois cities
Market size	Average of 250,000
Purchased	1930
Full-time employees	90
1992 net sales	$11 million

Table 8-6   Indicators of and reasons for slow growth

- Recent sales down 3.2 percent
- Recent gross margin percentage up 2.4 percent
- Increased competition from national chains and category killers moving into the market

New ideas. Company managers look for new products and advertising ideas at trade shows and conferences. Store managers visit their competitors to garner new signage and promotion ideas.

Employee empowerment. The Curtises don't have corporate buyers. Instead, individual store managers are responsible for merchandise mix and reordering. New associates undergo an intensive training program; all associates can take advantage of continuing education. Employees appreciate their high levels of responsibility and variety of training, contributing to a low turnover rate.

Family Needs Stronger Customer Base to Survive

The Curtises have maintained their gross margins in the face of this new competition, but their declining sales require help. What else can the Curtises do to salvage their market share from the competition and ensure their continued prosperity?

Research target market. Many ways exist for the family to learn more about its target market and identify new marketing opportunities. Focus groups composed of existing and potential customers would help identify customer wants. The extensive communication between upper and lower management would help the company pinpoint opportunities for new customers or special promotions. And mailing lists of potential new customers purchased from an outside marketing group would aid in direct-mail efforts.

Formalize customer service. While individual store managers identify customer needs and attempt to meet them, the effort ends at the store level. The Curtises need to establish a formal means for store managers to communicate these needs to upper management so all the stores have uniform services.

Establish solution centers. End caps make effective places for solution centers, which focus on solving specific needs, such as how to weatherproof a house and what products customers need to complete the project. These centers provide the opportunity to showcase higher-margin merchandise to convenience-minded consumers.

Expand rental business. The company should offer more rental equipment, which would increase customer traffic and accessory sales. Store managers can help determine what rental equipment their local consumer and commercial markets need.

Offer incentives and profit sharing. As the Curtises develop and monitor more operating statistics, they should consider offering incentives or profit-sharing programs based on the performance of individual stores. Performance goals should be based mostly on quantitative measures, and they should be jointly developed by company, store, and department managers.

Control inventory. The Curtises' decision to keep ten stores fully stocked sometimes leaves excess inventory. Their new computer system should help keep a tighter rein on inventory while still enabling store managers to track their own inventory.

Manage power categories. As the Curtises remerchandise the stores to fully develop their power categories, such as plumbing and paint, a store or department manager needs to be given the responsibility of that power category for all stores. That person would communicate successful selling techniques and advertising methods for that category to all store managers.

Identify key performance indicators. As the company develops its operating systems, it will become more important to identify key performance indicators, both financial and nonfinancial, to measure goal achievement. Examples of such performance indicators include sales per employee, gross margins by department, and payroll as a percent of sales. One suggestion: Make a list of the year's top ten goals, develop key performance indicators, and communicate the information and progress to company and store managers every month.

The Bottom Line

While the Curtis family is doing many things right, the stores need to build their customer bases to survive the onslaught of national chains. Ways to do this include exploring new target customers and conducting focus groups and customer surveys to determine what the customers want. The family then must act on those wants. The stores also need to get a firmer grip on their inventories.

CASE STUDY #4: FATHER-SON TEAM STRESSES THE NEED TO RETURN TO THE "OLD WAY" OF DOING BUSINESS AT A PAINT AND WALLPAPER STORE

"The only way that small, independent retailers like me can survive is by returning to the old way of doing business: showing the customer that you care," says Richard Snow, who inherited the paint and wallpaper store from his father in 1980.

Table 8-7   Paint and wallpaper store company profile

Format	Paint and wallpaper store
Location	Suburban city
Market size	30,000
Founded	1912
Full-time employees	14
1992 net sales	$1.2 million

Richard, 65, has always been a hands-on owner, rolling up his sleeves and pitching in with his employees. He believes in leading his employees by example, especially when it comes to showing his younger employees the way retailing was done in the good ol' days.

"You need to welcome customers," he says. "You need to treat them like family, show them around the store, help them find what they're looking for. You need to give them advice on colors and textures. You need to sell the products, the store, and yourself, so that the customers come back to us when they want to redecorate again."

It's that attitude that helped Richard grow the one store that his father founded in 1912 into three by 1960. But by 1992, increased competition from chain stores and lack of a long-term business strategy forced him to bring the count back down to one (see Table 8-8). Richard also became ill and now spends less time on the day-to-day operations and management of the company. His son, Dave, manages purchasing, sales, and store operations, and will one day own and manage the entire store.

To help ease the management transition and to secure the future of the one remaining store, Richard is trying to return to the old way of doing business. Some steps he and his son are taking:

Customer education.   Richard writes how-to articles on subjects like refinishing furniture and exterior painting for local newspapers, which publish the articles at no charge to Richard. He and Dave also organize in-store seminars for customers in which decorating professionals teach them how to hang wallpaper or apply a faux finish.

Decorating consultants.   Most of Richard's employees have extensive interior-decorating experience. These consultants provide free in-store and in-home consultations to their personal customers, helping them decide which colors or techniques to use, for example. Consultants also decorate model homes to gain exposure.

Table 8-8   Indicators of and reasons for declining sales

- Recent net sales down 5.1 percent
- Recent gross margin down 2.4 percent
- Declining sales partially due to increased competition, lack of a long-term business strategy and management transition

Aggressive advertising. Richard uses aggressive advertising techniques to combat the competition from mass merchants and 800 numbers. In his ads, Richard challenges consumers to look beyond the percentage discounts and consider the quality of what they are buying.

Store layout. The open layout of the store and the detailed signage enable customers to scope out the merchandise as soon as they walk through the front door. In addition, large workstations in the wallpaper section encourage customers to spread out the sample books, which facilitates the consultative selling process.

Wide inventory. Over the years, Richard has added a variety of merchandise, such as window treatments, carpeting, and bathroom fixtures, all of which fits in well with paint and wallpaper. While these experiments have not always succeeded, their creativity does demonstrate Richard's true passion to satisfy customers.

Community involvement. Both Richard and Dave play key roles in local and national trade associations, which helps them stay on top of the industry. And Richard feels that his involvement in the local chamber of commerce is a way of contributing to his community.

Corporate Strategy Would Facilitate Management Transition

Richard and Dave are both doing a lot of the right things to ensure their store's survival. But to ensure its prosperity and ease the management transition, they need to take some stronger actions.

Review corporate strategy. Given Richard's age and illness, conducting a thorough strategic review would be a good idea. Richard and Dave need to work together to identify the problems that the store faces. The strategic review not only would allow Richard to formally share with Dave his views on all aspects of the business, but it also would help Dave focus his efforts. Richard especially needs to pass on his expertise in public relations and advertising, since he always held these responsibilities.

Develop succession plan. A thorough succession plan is also critical to keeping the company in operation. The plan should include distribution of assets and beneficiaries of life insurance.

Control inventory. Currently, Dave purchases about half of the inventory through a buying group, but a formal open-to-buy system would help control inventory and budgeting. (One bonus of the buying group: It provides an idea book for advertising to all of its members.) Dave also keeps a lot of back stock in storage. For example, he carries two brands of paint:

one private label and one national brand. Some product overlap exists, creating higher inventory levels. Dave needs to review the cost effectiveness of this strategy and consider thinning out some products.

Track sales. Dave does not track sales, margins, or inventory by department. This needs to be done to assess profitability, and it may lead to further improvements in product mix.

Delegate accounting. For years, Richard has kept detailed financial records by hand, which greatly contributed to the company's success. Now he needs to pass along that expertise to a clerical person or outside accountant. He also should consider automating the system.

Hold monthly meetings. Because of his illness, Richard discontinued the monthly management and employee meetings a few months ago, although they had a positive affect on everyone; now it's time to hold them again.

Evaluate employees. "You can't be tough and heartless with employees," Richard says. "But, on the other hand, you can't be full of emotions." Richard needs to take some of his own advice and evaluate the performance of all his employees based on their selling skills and customer-service ability. The recent reduction in store count may have left the company with too many employees.

Improve consulting process. Consultants should keep portfolios on the work they do for customers, which would help them overcome credibility concerns with new customers. Consultants should also keep detailed customer records—including family size, home size, income, and decorating notes—that would help them know when to follow up with customers and provide information for direct marketing. Giving consultants an incentive to bring in new accounts and increase transaction sizes would help improve the company's bottom line, as would sending consultants to trade shows and training seminars, where they could learn selling strategies and decorating techniques, for example.

Extend education. Richard needs to hold the in-store seminars for customers on a more regular basis. He also should consider extending the how-to customer education through handouts and product brochures.

Alter advertising. Richard's ads are good, but they and the storefront sign need to tell customers that the store carries more than paint and wallpaper. Richard should use ads to promote other competitive advantages, like attention to detail. For example, he should let consumers know that special wallpaper orders often come from different dye lots and thus don't match the rest of the customer's order. Unlike mass merchants, consultants at his store inspect each order before they deliver it to the customer.

The Bottom Line

Richard and Dave are certainly on the right track with their emphasis on customer service. They exceed customers' expectations through seminars and decorating consultants. But to improve their net sales and ease the management transition, they need to take some strong steps, like formulating a corporate strategy and developing a succession plan.

CASE STUDY #5: TOUGH COMPETITION FOR A SHRINKING MARKET SCARES A PROFITABLE WOMEN'S SPECIALTY RETAILER

"Success," says retailer Bob Jones, "is operating profitable businesses in quality communities."

By that definition, Bob Jones is indeed successful. His story of prosperity began in the late 1960s, when he opened his first women's apparel shop in the central business district of a small town. There, he began by specializing in young misses apparel. As the business thrived, Bob opened three other stores in the same town, each addressing a different segment of the women's apparel market.

About seven years ago, Bob decided to expand even more and opened his first free-standing store in an adjacent metropolitan area. Under one roof, this store offered the same apparel as the three other stores. The community quickly embraced this super store, so Bob opened a second such store in another medium-sized rural market.

To achieve his first requirement of success—operating profitable businesses—Bob strives to give his customers what they want: good service, fair prices, a variety of sizes, and a large inventory of sportswear and dresses. And to achieve his second goal of operating in quality communities, Bob actively contributes to a variety of social, cultural, and charitable causes.

Despite an impressive track record of strong gross margins and increasing net sales, Bob worries about prospects for continued growth. Over the years, Bob has clearly identified a demographic profile of his typ-

Table 8-9   Clothing store company profile

Format	Six women's specialty clothing stores
Location	Rural Illinois cities
Market size	Average of 140,000
Founded	Early 1960s
Full-time employees	75
1992 net sales	$4.4 million

Table 8-10   Indicators of and reasons for tough competition

- Recent net sales up 15 percent
- Recent gross margin up 4.7 percent
- Target market size is decreasing as overall communities decline in size
- Competition for target customers is increasing due to other retail stores and other formats, such as mail order and home shopping networks
- Increasing willingness of consumers to drive to shopping malls in other communities
---

ical customer: middle-income women over 18 years of age, housewives in the smaller markets, and career women in the metro market. But that customer base is in trouble: It's stable at best. And the number of competitors—including shopping malls, mail-order catalogs, and the Home Shopping Channel—is growing.

Bob is intent on beating the competition with up-to-date, high-quality merchandise and attractive, comfortable stores. Other steps he has taken to ensure the business's success include:

Marketing strategy. Bob has been using television advertising since 1978 in an effort to reach a broad base of customers. In addition, customers receive flyers announcing the latest promotions. Bob also uses direct mail and outdoor billboards in his marketing strategy.

Employee empowerment. Through monthly meetings and constant communication, general managers, buyers, and store managers are able to participate in the entire decision-making process, from advertising to merchandise selection. And Bob keeps his employees motivated through a variety of contests and rewards, such as financial bonuses for selling a package deal of a dress and accessories. To Bob's credit, his employees reward him by doing all they can to satisfy customers.

Inventory control. New high-tech systems at point-of-sale locations and the corporate office provide timely and accurate sales and inventory data. This also helps Bob manage inventory aging, despite his lack of a formal markdown plan or budget. (An example of a formal plan is a progressive markdown strategy; that is, as inventory ages, markdowns are taken at preestablished times.) And backroom stock of out-of-season goods is practically nonexistent.

Customer Marketing Is a Key Area for Future Growth

While these actions are obviously steps in the right direction—recent net sales jumped 15 percent—many other opportunities exist for reaching new customers, increasing sales, and keeping the competition at bay. Among them:

Research the target market. Many ways exist for Bob to learn more about his target market and identify new marketing opportunities. Focus groups composed of existing and potential customers would help him identify customer wants. The extensive communication between upper and lower management should help the company to pinpoint opportunities for new customers or special promotions. And mailing labels of potential new customers purchased from an outside marketing group would aid in direct-mail efforts.

Formalize customer satisfaction information. While individual store managers identify customer needs and attempt to meet them, they don't communicate their experiences to upper management. This results in disjointed customer satisfaction and services between stores. A formal means of communicating customer needs to upper management would improve this haphazard method.

Review advertising strategy. The current advertising campaign emphasizes the store itself, not merchandise or promotions. This makes it difficult for Bob to quantitatively measure the results. Rethinking the advertising strategy, building in measurement criteria and possibly hiring an advertising agency when finances allow would lead to a more effective campaign.

Formalize associate training. Bob needs to develop a formal sales-training manual and include such items as attire, register functions, job expectations, and performance standards. One idea is to develop selling productivity measures, such as sales per employee hour, as standards to review the performance of every sales associate.

Identify key performance indicators. As the company develops its operating systems, it will become more important to identify both financial and nonfinancial key performance indicators to measure goal achievement. Examples of such performance indicators include sales per employee and percent of total sales needed for payroll. One suggestion: Make a list of the year's top ten goals, develop key performance indicators, and communicate the information and progress to company and store managers every month.

Pinpoint expansion opportunities. Bob's decisions regarding existent and future store locations are driven as much by his real-estate investment as by the potential for retail business. Still, with the limited long-term prospects for real-estate appreciation, he shouldn't rule out other options, such as leasing.

Use POS system more effectively. Bob's new system is capable of detailed reporting, including customer profiles and purchase histories. Generating and forwarding this information to the sales associates would enable employees to call customers when their favorite style of merchandise arrives.

The Bottom Line

While Bob is doing many things right, he needs to attract new customers while retaining existing customers to succeed and prosper in an increasingly competitive marketplace. He needs to institute ways to measure the effectiveness of his advertisements. He also needs to develop goals for long-term growth and determine the steps he needs to take to reach those goals.

CASE STUDY #6: POOR FINANCIAL PERFORMANCE AND DECLINING STORE TRAFFIC HINDER LIFESTYLE GOALS FOR A MENSWEAR RETAILER

Many boutiques, including a men's clothing store, surround the town square in this rural Illinois city. Within this store, which is stocked with suits, formal wear, and sportswear, John and Mary Smith work for the success of the business that they bought in 1970.

John and Mary live by the maxim "The customer is king"—or queen, in this instance. The majority of the Smiths' customers are middle-income, white-collar workers age 25 to 55. Forty percent are women. The Smiths special-order merchandise for customers. They custom tailor. They offer in-home and in-business service. They give a free accessory with every suit. And, to reinforce the store's personal touch, John slips a preprinted thank-you card in the pocket of every suit he sells. "Customers like it when they put on their suit for the first time and find a thank-you card in one of the pockets," he says.

The Smiths also make certain that their store is comfortable for their customers. Customers can relax in overstuffed chairs, and their children can play with a variety of toys while their parents shop.

Table 8-11   Menswear retailer company profile

Format	Men's clothing store
Location	Rural Illinois city
Market size	15,000 to 20,000
Purchased	1970
Full-time employees	Two
1992 net sales	$275,000

John says his goal is not to be rich in a monetary sense. Rather, he wants to make enough money to support a comfortable life, rich instead in family and friends. This hasn't been an easy goal to attain these last few years. Three years ago, John and Mary invested heavily in remodeling their 3,100-square-foot store. Though it seemed important at the time, John says that in hindsight he should have invested in merchandise, a point-of-sale system, or less elaborate remodeling. Now, with the slow economy, decreased consumer demand, and competition from discount chains and another independent menswear retailer, the couple has to inject bank loans and personal finances to keep their business afloat (see Table 8-12).

John and his wife have taken other steps to ensure the success of their business, including:

Extensive advertising. Currently they rely on print ads and direct mail to increase customer traffic. They are considering using cable television and other media as part of a new advertising strategy.

Creative promotions. John and Mary use creative promotions to attract customers. They send Christmas cards to customers, inviting them to redeem the enclosed coupon the next time they visit the store. New customers who did not receive a card are given coupons if they register on the mailing list.

Customer survey. Five years ago, John conducted a customer survey to understand better his customers' needs and wants.

Database management. To keep close track of their customers, John and Mary maintain a database, which includes customers' names, addresses, telephone numbers, birth dates, and anniversary dates. With this information, they can send general and specific information, including sales promotions and birthday cards, to customers.

Reducing Costs and Increasing Sales Are Top Areas of Opportunity

These actions are steps in the right direction, but many other opportunities exist for John and Mary to overcome their key problem of poor financial performance by decreasing expenses and increasing sales, including:

Table 8-12   Indicators of and reasons for poor financial performance

- Declining sales for past several years
- Recent sales down 12 percent from a year ago
- Selling, general, and administrative expenses remain flat at 51 percent of net sales
- Inventory turnover up from 2.4 to 3.1 because of decreasing inventory to remain afloat financially and increasing markdowns to liquidate slow-moving merchandise
- Cash bind, partially due to poor cash management with vendors and recent remodeling costs

Reduce costs. This is the couple's number-one way of boosting profits. To this end, they recently renegotiated their rent, and they contacted public-utilities companies for help with reducing their utility costs. Other venues include paying vendors upon receipt of merchandise, unless a vendor requires prepayment. The Smiths could ask customers to pay a percentage up front for special-order merchandise. These latter steps should improve cash flow.

Analyze advertising. Before the Smiths turn their advertising focus to cable television, they need to analyze and compare the response rates between print and television to determine which medium is more effective. One way to do this is to track the coupons from print ads. Another way is to ask customers how they found out about the store and what attracted them to it.

Redesign advertising. A key advertising problem the Smiths face is designing creative ads. No local advertising agencies exist. They could recruit the marketing department at the local college to conduct a case study on their business and formulate advertising strategies and designs.

Announce promotions. John and Mary could place signage in store windows announcing their coupon offers and Christmas sales. They could also extend this idea of sending cards and coupons to couples celebrating an anniversary.

Promote services. John and Mary provide a high level of service, including custom tailoring and in-home service, but they need to promote these services more. They should use advertising and signs to this end.

Expand database. To increase the database, John could contact new people in the community, introducing them to the store and informing them of the store's variety of services. He could obtain newcomers' names from the local newspaper, which includes real-estate transactions. John could also use direct marketing to target other communities that match his customer profile.

Survey customers. Now it's time to do a survey again, incorporating both customers and noncustomers. Survey respondents should explain why they do or do not shop in John and Mary's store and what services customers would like to have. A general rule of thumb is that customer surveys should be done every six months to a year.

Improve store layout. Although John and Mary spent quite a bit of money in remodeling the store, it still looks sparse, primarily because of financial constraints on inventory as well as the sheer size of the store. Partitioning off part of the store would give the appearance of a more intimate space filled with more merchandise. Bringing in a leased department, such as shoes or women's apparel, would also fill the space.

Showcase suits and formalwear. Currently John and Mary sell suits, formalwear, and sportswear. But they want to phase out the sportswear and distinguish themselves for providing tailored clothing. One way to achieve this goal is to move the tailored clothing from the back of the store to the front, where it would be more noticeable. Another way is to utilize advertising, signage, and mannequins.

Update services. The Smiths need to rename their in-home and in-business tailoring service to reflect the service they offer. They should also consider calling customers after major purchases to determine their satisfaction with the merchandise and service. And they should consider instituting an annual frequent buyer program, which would enhance the store's database and increase the average sale.

Analyze buying. The Smiths do the buying "based on the seat of their pants," John jokes. In the past, they used an outside service, which provided them with an open-to-buy situation on a departmental basis. But now, due to the low number of SKUs and sparse merchandise offerings, John is able to determine inventory needs by walking through the store. They do try to stock the basics, but they don't have a formal open-to-buy system. One benefit of the small inventory is that it decreases the necessity of an electronic POS system, although John did consider purchasing such a system a few years ago. Financial resources could be better channeled to advertising and signage instead of a POS system.

Comparison shop. John spends most of his time at the store and doesn't take the time to visit other retailers outside his community. Analyzing what others in the industry are doing would give John new ideas for his own business. He could also have power breakfasts with local retailers, and he could visit outlying stores to garner fresh ideas.

The Bottom Line

To succeed and prosper, John and Mary need to attract new customers by enhancing their advertising and matching it with their desired image. They also need to talk with customers and noncustomers to determine what additional services they should offer.

CASE STUDY #7: EVEN AFTER 100 YEARS, A DEPARTMENT STORE CANNOT REST ON ITS LAURELS

Any retail establishment about to celebrate its 100th anniversary must be doing many things right, and this family-owned department store is no

Table 8-13   Department store company profile

Format	Department store
Location	Rural Illinois city
Market size	100,000
Founded	Late 1800s
Full-time employees	29
1992 net sales	Approximately $2 million to $3 million

exception. In the last few years, many changes have hit the surrounding area: Scores of small family farms have consolidated into a few major enterprises; a mall was erected about 30 miles away, and many Main Street stores have faltered.

But the Johnson family has retained a firm grip on its customer base. This is largely due to thrifty financial management, sharp merchandising practices, and a commitment to customer service that permeates the organization (see Table 8-14).

The family that owns this business is happy, to say the least. The players: Larry Johnson, former store manager, who purchased the business with the help of his brother in the 1950s; his son, Brent, who joined the company in the early 1960s and is now president; and his daughter, Nancy, who came on board in the mid-1980s.

The Johnsons' success is well-deserved, considering the variety of creative and innovative practices they employ. Perhaps the most innovative practice is that of hiring interns from marketing and fashion merchandising departments of the local university. These students provide fresh perspectives and knowledge on how to merchandise and market the store. Other innovative techniques include the following:

Niche marketing. The Johnsons have expanded the inventory to include higher-end and exclusive lines. They have also added private-label products, like gourmet coffee and candy.

Promotions. To keep customers interested, the Johnsons hold frequent tent sales and sidewalk specials. Employees change the eight window displays every month. And cost-effective cooperative advertising keeps customers up to date on the latest specials.

Mailing lists. The Johnsons maintain a mailing list of 7000 customers and prospects from information obtained at the point of sale and from proprietary credit-card applications. Nancy uses the lists to send flyers announcing in-store promotions and new merchandise; when the flyers incorporate

Table 8-14   Indicators of and reasons for financial success

- Constant net sales of $2 million to $3 million
- Constant gross margin of 33 percent
- Maintain sales with innovative marketing techniques and strong management
- Control costs with outsourcing and cooperative advertising

coupons, Nancy receives a response rate as high as 25 percent. She also recently started writing a quarterly newsletter that features trends, new merchandise, and fashion tips.

Key customers. Each salesperson works with 50 key personal customers, sending them flyers announcing new merchandise and offering their personal shopping services. Employees also send thank-you cards to customers who purchase more than $100 worth of merchandise.

Comment cards. Located at the point of sale, these cards solicit comments relating to service, merchandise, and store operations. Nancy sends thank-you notes and $5 gift certificates to customers filling out the cards.

Team playing. The Johnsons keep their employee turnover rate low by making everyone part of the management team and keeping the lines of communication open. The employees also feel empowered to do whatever it takes to get things done, be it responding to customer complaints or special-ordering merchandise. Brent and Nancy keep their employees up to date on industry trends and business practices by holding monthly employee meetings. They bring in outside business consultants to lead training seminars and motivate employees. And they bring in members of the police force to teach employees how to deter shoplifters.

Prompt ticketing. "If it's not on the sales floor, it can't be sold," Brent says. So employees inspect and ticket 100 percent of the merchandise as soon as it comes in the door and quickly move it onto the sales floor. Then, to keep that inventory fresh, the company has a policy of not carrying slow-moving merchandise into the next season. If goods aren't moving after 30 days on the floor, buyers start to mark them down and continue to do so until they are sold.

Buying structure. The Johnsons and their buyers read a variety of trade journals and attend buying shows to learn about the latest products. The company's four buyers talk frequently with customers and sales associates to find out what merchandise customers need and want. The buyers can also make all decisions regarding merchandise purchases.

Vendor relations. Once the owners and buyers know what products they're interested in, they invite the vendors to come and show their goods, letting them know up front what they expect in terms of performance. Keeping in line with their desire for fresh merchandise, the family places high value on the sell-through quality of merchandise. They stick with vendors with fast-selling goods; they quickly dismiss vendors with slow-moving merchandise. The Johnsons bring new merchandise in on a trial basis and restock based on its selling power.

Finances. To keep the focus on retailing, Brent outsources payroll and monthly accounting. He also developed a sound succession plan and shared it with the rest of his family.

Going Another Extra Mile Would Tighten Grip on Target Market

Nearly 100 years in business is proof positive that Brent and Nancy are doing a lot of the right things. But the market is changing yet again, and they expect another mall to enter the market sometime soon. But they can do more to make their good business even better.

Market specific departments. The Johnsons could market their specific departments to target markets. For example, they could send flyers to new mothers promoting infant and toddler clothing. Or they could display their luggage line at a local travel agency.

Conduct focus groups. With the help of their marketing interns, the Johnsons could conduct focus groups to determine customers' needs and satisfaction.

Prepay postage on comment cards. The comment cards currently at the point of sale are meant to be filled out in the store and so are not postage paid. But time-constrained consumers appreciate filling out the cards at home and dropping them in the mail. The Johnsons should then share the information from comment cards with their employees.

Push proprietary credit card. Offering employee incentives such as a dollar per application would encourage the employees to offer the opportunity to customers. Offering customer incentives such as a 15 percent discount on the next purchase would encourage them to apply.

Create a friendly atmosphere. To help achieve their goal of being friendly and helpful to customers, Brent and Nancy should have all employees wear name tags—they should also lead the trend by wearing name tags themselves. Employees should have their own business cards to enhance the personal shopping program.

Computerize mailings. Printing the names and addresses of customers from the computerized database instead of handwriting them would give salespeople more time to write personal notes on the flyers.

Promote easy access. One competitive advantage that the Johnsons do not promote is the user-friendliness of their store, especially for disabled people. They could work with local and regional handicapped associations to promote this.

Rethink advertising strategy. Brent and Nancy need to advertise their unique private-label merchandise (coffee and candy) to boost sales. They also need to encourage customers to redeem coupons or mention ads, which would help them track their advertisements more effectively and determine their return on investment. And they should place directories near the entrance and larger signs by the stairs and elevators to help customers find their way around the store.

Experiment with alternative delivery channels. The nearby university convenience store does not offer gourmet coffee, so the Johnsons could market their private-label gourmet coffee at a campus kiosk.

Develop image. Although Brent intuitively knows what image he wants for the store, he does not have a formal image statement or mission statement. A clear, concise statement incorporating employee's suggestions would help employees focus on their common goals.

Train employees. Although the Johnsons have intensive training programs, they need to focus on employee assertiveness. Their salespeople seem too reluctant to approach customers. They also need to encourage employees to sell package deals, like accessories with a dress.

Automate point of sale. Currently the Johnsons use a manual point-of-sale system. They may want to consider automating this system. Employees and other retailers could provide valuable input.

Focus on finances. A formal open-to-buy system would help control inventory and budgeting. Changing from a C corporation to an S corporation might reduce federal income taxes. And an outside board of directors would help provide valuable input on issues facing the business.

The Bottom Line

Brent and Nancy understand their customers, but they can do even more to enhance this understanding. They have a strong, solid, and capable management team. They have succeeded in empowering their employees so that salespeople and store managers feel comfortable in making decisions and taking action on those decisions. Brent and Nancy feel that someday soon a mall will enter their market area. They feel ready to meet that looming challenge, but they understand that they need to update their merchandise and services to keep their existing market share.

CASE STUDY #8: REGIONAL SHOPPING MALLS REDUCE DOWNTOWN TRAFFIC AND SALES AT A WOMEN'S APPAREL STORE

Over the years, Pete Gates has changed the selection in his grandfather's dry-goods store to reflect the changing needs of his customers and to find a profitable market niche. But Pete's store is suffering from a phenomenon occurring in small towns across America. Sales are declining in the down-

Table 8-15 Women's apparel store company profile

Format	Women's apparel
Location	Rural Illinois town
Market size	30,000
Founded	Early 1900s
Full-time employees	20
1992 net sales	$994,000

town area, where his store is located, as more customers patronize three regional shopping malls that offer greater variety (see Table 8-16).

Major employment in the area comes from petrochemical, nuclear energy, and manufacturing industries, as well as agriculture, and provides relatively high-income blue collar jobs. Most of Pete's customers are older women who wear large sizes, and more than half his customer base lives outside of town.

Pete's business philosophy includes more than a desire to run a profitable store. He actively works to preserve the integrity of small-town life by owning and operating other businesses in town, employing local companies to provide goods and services for his businesses, and staying involved in town government. He has done a number of things to stimulate traffic in his store and the downtown area.

Promotions. Pete's store has developed several creative in-store promotions, such as raffles and frequent shopper bonuses, that generate excitement and traffic.

Event marketing. Downtown merchants have gotten together to coordinate a series of special events to attract customers, including street fairs and sidewalk sales.

Niche marketing. Pete has identified a niche in women's apparel and services it well with good merchandise and a consistent pricing strategy. He offers his customers a proprietary credit card. He also offers birthday gifts and discounts to customers over 50.

Cooperative buying. The store purchases merchandise through a buying group to get more competitive prices. The buying group also periodically gives Pete flyers that have been personalized with the store name to distribute to customers.

Table 8-16 Indicators of and reasons for declining store traffic

- Decreasing sales for past several years
- Recent net sales down 3.5 percent
- Gross margins down 4.9 percent
- Consumer shopping patterns are shifting as more residents, particularly younger ones, frequent area shopping malls

Competitor shopping. Pete shops his competitors' stores and reads their advertisements. He also gets innovative ideas from his involvement in the community and from various retail trade organizations.

Employee retention. To keep employee turnover low, Pete offers them 401K and profit-sharing plans. He also provides them with an excellent employee handbook detailing key store operating procedures and what is expected of them. New hires are required to view a series of training films, and continuing training is offered periodically to all employees.

Store Must Focus on Customers to Generate Traffic

To regain some of the traffic the store is losing to the shopping malls, Pete has to find new ways to compete. He needs to focus his efforts on what his customers want in the way of merchandise and service to give them reasons to shop downtown.

Target market. The town's recorder of deeds maintains a list of new homeowners. Pete could offer potential new customers on this list certain incentives to shop in his store. He also could offer an incentive to his existing customers if they bring in first-time shoppers.

Measure advertising. Pete advertises the store and its promotions fairly extensively, but he does not track the effectiveness of different ads or promotions. Having sales employees ask customers where they learned of an event or saw an ad would help measure effectiveness. More formal methods include using coupons in ads, which would increase store traffic and provide a quantifiable medium. Measuring the response rates is done by dividing the total coupons redeemed by the total coupons issued.

Survey customers. Though he has used surveys, Pete has not conducted one in many years. Pete could invite customers to fill out comment cards to find out their level of satisfaction with merchandise, pricing, and service. He could also use the cards to track demographic information.

Improve store merchandising. If Pete moved high-volume niche departments to higher visibility areas of the store and moved slower moving items to less desirable locations, he could better maximize store profitability. T-stands and four-ways would do a better job of displaying upscale merchandise than the rounders the store now uses. And Pete should consider eliminating categories that do not meet minimum performance standards.

Change store hours. Pete should consider keeping the store open on Sundays and offering later hours on weeknights to compete with the malls.

Solicit employee suggestions. Pete's low turnover suggests his employees are both loyal and knowledgeable about the business. He could conduct regular employee meetings and implement a suggestion box to challenge employees to come up with innovative ideas for improving the business.

Improve store signage. Customers have a negative perception of the store's hand-lettered signs. The store could invest in a laser printer or use a local print shop to develop more attractive signage.

Focusing on what customers want may help Pete better compete with the shopping malls and regain some of his customer base. There are other actions he can take to tighten up the operation and prevent the continued erosion of his bottom line.

Develop a mission statement. Pete can verbally articulate the store's mission. He should commit it to paper, distribute it, and share it with his employees. He needs to use it as the cornerstone of a strategic plan for the business.

Improve merchandise planning. Current planning is month-to-month. Pete should consider yearly planning to keep merchandise consistent with the store's image and strategic plan. His industry trade contacts could help him find or develop staff training programs in use of open-to-buy and in merchandise planning for small businesses.

Tighten loss prevention programs. Loss prevention is not a major concern, but doorways hidden from view in some departments should be locked. Gift certificates, too, should be kept locked up. Pete also might consider working with other downtown merchants and local police to coordinate awareness seminars for employees.

Restructure management. As Pete and his wife near retirement age, Pete needs to identify and groom a successor to run the business. Also, Pete should consult his tax adviser to assess potential benefits of restructuring the business from a C corporation to an S corporation.

The Bottom Line

Despite his influence in town government and his prominence as a downtown business and real-estate owner, Pete's business continues to erode. He has shown a willingness to change with the times, adapting his merchandise lines to find a niche. He has also developed a number of innovative promotions and events to drive store traffic. His survival will depend on his ability to find ways to compete with the regional shopping malls. That means finding out what customers want, improving in-store merchandising, and enhancing assortment planning.

CASE STUDY #9: SHRINKING POPULATIONS AND WEAK LOCAL ECONOMIES ERODE MARGINS AT GIFT STORES

"We want to be the big fish in the small pond," says Greg Short, owner of seven gift stores sprinkled across western Illinois and eastern Iowa.

It's that philosophy that led Greg's father, a wholesale distributor of newspapers, magazines, and books, to open his first retail newsstand in the mid-1940s. And that same philosophy pushed Greg and his wife, Michelle, to expand that one newsstand into seven gift shops in a handful of rural communities.

Although Greg and Michelle owned 12 stores by the early 1970s, competitive pressure forced them to cut back to seven. Still, with net sales up 5 percent and gross margins for their merchandise category a low but constant 40 percent, the Shorts are barely breaking even. Weak local economies are pushing their customers to suburban and urban communities, leaving even weaker economies in their wake. Those remaining members of the target audience—women aged 25 to 40 with incomes less than $30,000—tend to shop at the new strip malls springing up across the rural midwest. These larger stores carry a greater assortment and depth of merchandise (see Table 8-18).

To attract the members of the diminishing target market and promote local businesses, Greg and Michelle take active roles in local chambers of commerce, especially in their hometown's revitalization committee. Committee members retained an economic developer to direct the process, and they asked local banks to subsidize the cost of low-interest loans to revitalize the downtown district. Other steps that the Shorts have taken to improve their business include:

Financial focus. Greg keeps a close eye on the finances of the business. He uses critical benchmarking data to compare his company with other gift retailers of similar size. This helps him focus on areas that he needs to improve. Currently he is focusing on improving gross margins by assessing gross profit by department. He also uses gross profit per selling square foot to determine the level of commitment to a product line, and he uses

Table 8-17 Gift store company profile

Format	Seven gift stores
Location	Downtown business districts of rural Illinois and Iowa towns
Market size	Average of 12,000
Founded	Mid-1940s
Full-time employees	39
1992 net sales	$2.5 million

Table 8-18   Indicators of and reasons for weak financial performance

---

- Recent net sales up 5 percent
- Gross margin percentage low but stable at 40 percent
- Slow inventory turnover of 2.29
- Reduced traffic in downtown locations due to new strip malls on outskirts of towns
- Declining market populations and weak local economies

---

monthly listings of purchases by department to help with ordering and assortment planning. He makes revisions to assortments based on historical sales.

Transaction tracking. Greg monitors monthly sales, customer traffic, average transaction size, and sales per labor hour at every store.

At the beginning of every month, he provides store managers with targets based on the prior month and year for each of these categories. Managers' goals, then, are to maintain customer traffic while increasing the average transaction size. Greg offers cash incentives to encourage managers to meet their goals.

Frequent buyer program. Armed with a vendor-supplied mailing list, the Shorts send frequent buyer cards to area residents, offering them a $5 discount after accumulating $100 worth of purchases. Greg and Michelle use the same list to send customers their Christmas catalog.

Comment cards. Located at the point of sale, these self-addressed, postage-paid comment cards encourage customers to let the Shorts know what they think. Greg receives about 10 cards each month and personally responds to all of them—positive and negative.

Strategic Plan a Must

Greg and Michelle must take some strong, innovative steps to ensure their business's success.

Develop strategic plans. As mentioned before, depressed margins and decreasing customer traffic are two of the Shorts' biggest problems. Greg should address these issues, which are relatively pervasive for small-store retailers, in a strategic meeting with store managers. He also needs to develop a strategic plan that includes employee training, value-added services, advertising, and marketing. A company brainstorming session would enable the store managers to provide creative, critical input that is particularly beneficial in multistore settings.

Implement POS system. One of Greg's vendors has offered him a computerized POS system at a relatively low cost, but he needs to research this high-tech tool more to determine if it meets his needs and those of his management team.

Formalize buying. A formal open-to-buy system would help control inventory and budgeting.

Make better use of space. Greg's office is housed in the basement of the flagship store. Moving it to the main floor would put him closer in touch with the employees and customers at that store. Greg should also consider alternative uses for the basement to help defray operating costs. Options include offering children's activities, establishing a leased department, or creating a corporate conference room for internal and external use.

Consider a kiosk. Greg and Michelle could link up with a florist, for example; they could then sell their goods at each others' stores.

Visit outlying stores. Current performance indicates that Greg should visit his outlying stores more often, perhaps every two to three weeks. This would send a positive signal to store managers that Greg is indeed interested in their performance. During his visits, Greg should make sure to take a look at merchandising, pricing, cleanliness, loss prevention, and record keeping.

Train employees. Most of the stores' employees work part-time, do not depend on the income, and thus lack assertiveness. Educating employees on suggestive selling techniques and product knowledge would help improve the bottom line. Greg and Michelle need to lead by example and show employees how to sell. They also need to invite vendors and store managers to share their product knowledge with the salespeople.

Advertise services. Although the Shorts' stores offer a variety of value-added services, such as gift wrapping, special orders, layaway plans, and gift certificates, they don't advertise these services. Once communicated to customers, these services can help justify higher but reasonable prices, which would help improve gross margins. The couple should also expand their services to include gift-wrap seminars, mailing service, and comfortable chairs in which customers can relax while browsing through books.

Expand direct marketing. With their comprehensive database of 12,000 customers, the Shorts can send flyers announcing new products and in-store promotions.

The Bottom Line

Greg and Michelle are on the right track. Their principal vendor fully supports the business, giving the Shorts a competitive advantage. Future success will depend greatly on developing a clear vision and strategy for all the stores as well as the revitalization of the downtown business districts.

CASE STUDY #10: UNINTERESTED HEIRS HINDER SHOE RETAILER'S RETIREMENT GOALS

Jay Robinson always thought that he would pass his shoe business on to his children.

Now that he is 65 years old, he's ready to do just that. Unfortunately, his children have absolutely no interest in the retail business.

Though he still hopes that one of his children will take a sudden interest in retailing, Jay is reevaluating his plans and trying to prepare his ten stores for sale to employees within the next five years. Part of Jay's new retirement strategy is to foster entrepreneurship among his managers. He hopes to groom future store owners from managers by giving them primary responsibility for their stores. Already three store managers oversee all operational functions at their stores, including purchasing, pricing, and human resources. Other locations also operate autonomously, though to a lesser degree.

Despite these efforts, Jay's dream of passing his business onto younger generations is in jeopardy. Already, declining sales and profits are threatening the closure of one store. If Jay doesn't rectify the situation fast, more will follow. Part of the problem is the lack of a corporate image. The ten stores do not operate under the same name, making it difficult for customers to recognize the chain. Jay is thinking about adding "Robinson" to the stores' names in an effort to unite them. And part of the problem is the high rent incurred at mall locations. In fact, if Jay could do it all over again, he says that he would have tried harder to acquire real estate in strip malls, where he would have lower overhead costs (see Table 8-20). Some of the steps Jay and his managers are taking to improve his company's financial position include:

In-store promotions. Since each store operates autonomously, individual store managers must develop and implement their own promotions, such as Senior Citizens Day or customer appreciation gifts. One manager gives good customers free shoes in order to receive their opinions. Another manager, whose store primarily sells women's shoes, tries to build business by working closely with hospitals and nurses' associations. He also holds style shows for his customers to show off new fashions.

Table 8-19   Shoe store company profile

Format	10 shoe stores
Location	Shopping malls in large rural Illinois and Iowa cities
Market size	Average of 300,000
Founded	1888; acquired by present owner in early 1950s
Full-time employees	20
1992 net sales	$3.3 million

Table 8-20   Indicators of and reasons for declining financial performance

- Recent net sales down 5.9 percent
- Recent gross margin percentage down 2 percent
- Declining profits partially due to high rent and lack of uniformity of stores

Customer interaction. Most store managers, who are actively involved in the daily operations of their stores, make a point of talking with customers to understand their wants and levels of satisfaction.

Customer service. Jay tries to instill the importance of customer service in all his managers. But each manager is still responsible for the service efforts and level at his own store. Also, each store manually keeps track of customers and their shoe sizes to speed customer service. And all managers try to get out-of-stock shoes for customers, but they differ in how they do so. Some special-order the merchandise, while others try to obtain the shoes from a different store.

Strategic Planning Necessary for Retailer's Retirement

Jay's emphasis on the autonomy of each store does encourage entrepreneurship, but his hands-off attitude does have disadvantages, especially since all managers have different levels of experience. To bolster his business, Jay could:

Formulate a strategic plan. If Jay is ever going to achieve his retirement goal, he needs to formulate a strategic plan for his entire company as well as each store. This plan should incorporate short-, medium- and long-term performance goals.

Formalize policies. Along with that strategic plan, Jay needs to devise a formal policy for certain store operations, like that on obtaining out-of-stock shoes for customers. Do managers special-order the goods, or do they see if another store has them? If Jay chooses to promote the latter, he needs to change the transfer policy, which currently discourages managers from transferring inventory by crediting the store that actually makes the sale, while the other store loses out on a sale. The right policy is the one that benefits the customers and is written with the customer in mind.

Name change. Adding "Robinson" to the name of all the stores would unite the chain. It would also strengthen the company's advertising, marketing opportunities, and store image if supported by strong ads and promotions. If Jay can't afford to hire an outside advertising agency, he could solicit help from marketing students at local colleges.

Hold companywide meetings. Jay needs to hold regular meetings with store managers and salespeople to encourage cooperation, solicit team help in solving problems, and provide a forum for sharing creative ideas, such as in-store promotions and selling techniques. Employee incentives would also help in these areas. Currently, Jay awards bonuses whenever he feels like it. But offering financial incentives to managers would encourage them to improve their performance, as would contests between stores.

Revamp purchasing. Currently each store is responsible for its own inventory and negotiates its own prices with vendors, which is very expensive. Significant savings in the forms of lower prices and higher co-op advertising could result from centralized group buying. Jay should also consider implementing a formal open-to-buy system, which would help control inventory and budgeting.

Change corporate status. Jay should talk with his tax adviser about changing from a C corporation to an S corporation to lower federal income taxes and other taxes that may be incurred upon distribution of the business.

Computerize stores. The lack of computers means that each store manager must spend at least an hour every day on paperwork. And the company accountant spends an enormous amount of time on each of her duties, many of them redundant. Computerizing the corporate office and all of the stores would save time and increase efficiency. Jay should also consider computerizing customer records to give salespeople quicker access. Inexpensive electronic Rolodexes are another option for this.

Determine customer wants. Formalizing the method of determining customer wants would enable managers to meet those wants better. Ways to do this include conducting surveys and focus groups, encouraging customers to fill out comment cards, and calling customers to ask about their recent purchase and the service they received.

Excite customers. Companywide promotions would attract customers, build the company's image, and encourage cohesiveness. One idea is an annual Customer Appreciation Week, when customers could bring in their shoes to be repaired, cleaned, and polished. Another idea is to implement value-added services, such as product trunk shows, free shoe polishing, and listings of local podiatrists, that would strengthen the company's position within the communities in which they operate.

The Bottom Line

Overall, Jay is a very enthusiastic entrepreneur. He is very happy with his lifetime achievements, both personal and with regard to his business. But his dream is in trouble. Admittedly, certain items require attention, especially strategic direction, succession planning, and inventory management. And it's attention to these items that will ensure the company's success.

9

MANAGEMENT TOOLS

Careful Study Needed to Put Small-Store Retailers on Top

OPERATIONS ASSESSMENT TOOLS

Tools of the Trade Include Store Assessments

The operations assessment tools are designed to prompt you, your management team, and your sales associates to reexamine your retail operations. They are designed in a questionnaire format, and you should use them to identify areas that need improvement. These tools are broken down into the six major areas of study:

- Customers and marketing
- Merchandising
- Store operations
- Management
- Human resources
- Finance

Each section contains several questions in either yes/no or checklist form. Options and techniques are listed in order of relative importance as suggested by Arthur Andersen.

After you complete each section, identify particular questions to which you have checked off very few responses or answered no. You should then review the relevant section of the study for recommendations to enhance the business practices you are currently using.

CUSTOMERS AND MARKETING

Customer Wants and Satisfaction

Determine what customers want and how satisfied they are when they visit the store.

1. Does your company have a standard means of identifying customer wants and expectations?

   _____ Yes   _____ No

   If you answered no, see "Marshall Field: 'Give the Lady What She Wants' " in Chapter 2.

2. If you answered yes, indicate which techniques you effectively use to identify your customers' wants and expectations:

   _____ Store interviews and conversations

   _____ Customer comment cards

   _____ Customer focus groups

   _____ Mail surveys

   _____ Phone interviews

   _____ Customer books (notes on individual customers)

   If you cannot check three or more techniques, see "Marshall Field: 'Give the Lady What She Wants' " in Chapter 2.

3. Indicate which practices you follow to ensure that your customers' wants are met or exceeded:

   _____ Share survey results with employees

   _____ Constantly communicate customer expectations to employees or at weekly meetings

   _____ Formally train employees

   _____ Consider giving special rewards to employees to encourage customer satisfaction

   _____ Consider customer satisfaction when awarding employee bonuses or raises

   If you cannot check three or more practices, see "Marshall Field: 'Give the Lady What She Wants' " in Chapter 2.

4. Indicate which techniques you effectively use to respond to verbal or written customer comments and suggestions:

Figure 9-1 How do you compare? Rate the importance of each business practice and how well you perform at each. Use the list below to rate yourself on a scale from one to four, with four being the highest. Have your management team and sales employees do the same, and calculate averages for your company. Then compare your results to the survey averages here and to Arthur Andersen's rankings and best practices in Chapter 2.

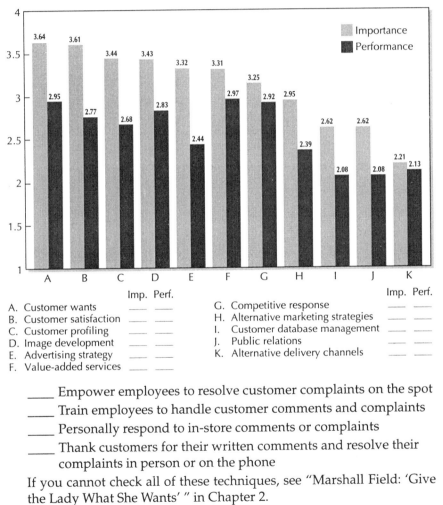

How retailers rank customers and marketing categories for importance and performance

	Imp. Perf.		Imp. Perf.
A. Customer wants	___ ___	G. Competitive response	___ ___
B. Customer satisfaction	___ ___	H. Alternative marketing strategies	___ ___
C. Customer profiling	___ ___	I. Customer database management	___ ___
D. Image development	___ ___	J. Public relations	___ ___
E. Advertising strategy	___ ___	K. Alternative delivery channels	___ ___
F. Value-added services	___ ___		

_____ Empower employees to resolve customer complaints on the spot

_____ Train employees to handle customer comments and complaints

_____ Personally respond to in-store comments or complaints

_____ Thank customers for their written comments and resolve their complaints in person or on the phone

If you cannot check all of these techniques, see "Marshall Field: 'Give the Lady What She Wants' " in Chapter 2.

Competitive Response

Investigate and shop your competition to understand and anticipate what competitors are doing.

1. Indicate which techniques you use to learn more about your competitors:

____ Analyze their advertisements

____ Shop their stores

____ Talk with other retailers within your community

____ Ask customers where else they shop

If you cannot check two or more techniques, see "Nothing Motivates Like Stiff Competition" in Chapter 2.

Advertising, Public Relations, and Direct Mail

This involves developing print, radio, and television advertising strategies to increase store traffic; effectively using the media to report positively on the business; and maintaining a database of customer information (such as age, address, family size, and shopping frequency) to be used for direct-mail advertising.

1. Does your company have a method of evaluating the effectiveness of its advertising?

____ Yes   ____ No

If you answered no, see "Extra! Extra! Advertising and PR Let Customers Read All About It" in Chapter 2.

2. If you answered yes, indicate which techniques you effectively use to evaluate the effectiveness of your advertising:

____ Retain advertising agency or internal marketing specialist

____ Track number of coupons redeemed

____ Match revenue increase with type of advertising for a specific time period

____ Track customer traffic with type of advertising

____ Ask customers if they saw the store's ads

____ Ask customers how they heard about the store

If you cannot check four or more techniques, see "Extra! Extra! Advertising and PR Let Customers Read All About It" in Chapter 2.

3. Indicate which public-relations techniques you effectively use to promote your business:

____ Retain a public-relations firm

____ Maintain personal relationships with local news media

____ Inform news media of upcoming in-store events or new merchandise

____ Sponsor charity or community events that receive media attention

____ Write news articles

If you cannot check three or more techniques, see "Extra! Extra! Advertising and PR Let Customers Read All About It" in Chapter 2.

4. Indicate for which activities you use database information to market products and services:

____ Merchandise planning (match make up of customers to merchandise assortment)

____ Direct mail (mail to frequent shoppers)

____ Advertising (focus on advertising to target customers)

____ Other marketing efforts (in-store events)

If you cannot check two or more activities, see "Extra! Extra! Advertising and PR Let Customers Read All About It" in Chapter 2.

Image Development

Present customers with a distinct impression of the store.

1. Indicate which items you consider when enhancing and communicating your company's image:

____ Visual merchandising

____ Depth and breadth of merchandise

____ Public relations

____ Advertising

____ Price

____ Store signage

____ Employee communications

____ Store ambiance

____ Service level

____ Employee attire

____ Store frontage

____ Civic or charitable activities

If you cannot check five or more items, see "Store Image Lets Customers Know What to Expect" in Chapter 2.

2. Indicate which techniques you use to enhance your relationship with your customers:

____ Approach customers before they approach you

____ Call most important customers

____ Send customer-appreciation letters

____ Seek customer input on desired services

____ Give gifts to the best customers

If you cannot check three or more techniques, see "Store Image Lets Customers Know What to Expect" in Chapter 2.

Value-Added Services

Provide services beyond customers' expectations.

1. Does your company provide value-added services, such as product consulting, gift wrapping, free mailing, or in-home service?

   ____ Yes   ____ No

   If you answered no, see "Customers Appreciate Those Little Extras" in Chapter 2.

2. If you answered yes, indicate which of the following techniques you effectively use to determine the types of value-added services to offer:

   ____ In-store interviews

   ____ Comment cards

   ____ Customer focus groups

   ____ Customer mail surveys

   ____ Customer phone surveys

   ____ Customer want slips or customer books

   If you cannot check four or more techniques, see "Customers Appreciate Those Little Extras" in Chapter 2.

3. Indicate which of the following value-added services you offer to your customers:

   ____ Product education and knowledge classes

   ____ Product consultants

   ____ House calls

   ____ Assembly assistance

   ____ Private showings

   ____ Gift registry

   ____ Storage

   ____ Personal shopping services

   If you cannot check any of the above services, see "Customers Appreciate Those Little Extras" in Chapter 2.

4. Do you advertise or promote these value-added services?

   ____ Yes   ____ No

If you answered no, see "Customers Appreciate Those Little Extras" in Chapter 2.

Alternative Marketing Strategies

Use target marketing and in-store promotions to increase traffic and sales.

1. Do you have quantifiable data to identify target markets of customers?
   ____ Yes   ____ No
   If you answered no, see "Product Demos and Fashion Shows Attract Customers" in Chapter 2.

2. If you answered yes, indicate which of the following techniques you use to determine your target market:
   ____ Retain a market research company
   ____ Review and analyze customer-profile information obtained from comment cards
   ____ From mail questionnaires
   ____ From focus groups
   If you cannot check any of these techniques, see "Product Demos and Fashion Shows Attract Customers" in Chapter 2.

3. Indicate which target-marketing techniques you effectively use to increase store traffic, build customer loyalty, and reach your target market:
   ____ Use proprietary credit-card files to develop targeting techniques
   ____ Advertise to target market
   ____ Issue handouts or flyers to target market
   ____ Call new community residents
   ____ Send direct mailings or flyers to new community residents
   ____ Support community organizations (sports teams, charities)
   If you cannot check four or more techniques, see "Product Demos and Fashion Shows Attract Customers" in Chapter 2.

4. Indicate which in-store promotions you effectively used during the last 12 months to increase store traffic:
   ____ Product demonstrations
   ____ Fashion shows
   ____ Special day promotions (St. Patrick's Day)
   ____ Drawings or raffle
   ____ Contests

____ Free samples
____ Charity events
____ Radio remotes
____ Guest appearances
____ Merchandise trade-ins
____ Gift with purchase

If you cannot check seven or more promotions, see "Product Demos and Fashion Shows Attract Customers" in Chapter 2.

Customer Profiling

Understand customers in terms of what they are buying.

1. Does your company have a method of recording all customer purchases by department, category, class, or SKU?

   ____ Yes   ____ No

   If you answered no, see "Profiling Gives Retailers a Picture of Their Customers" in Chapter 2.

2. If you answered yes, do you use this information in merchandise planning?

   ____ Yes   ____ No

   If you answered no, see "Profiling Gives Retailers a Picture of Their Customers" in Chapter 2.

3. Do you maintain information on customers' names, addresses, ages, and so on?

   ____ Yes   ____ No

   If you answered no, see "Profiling Gives Retailers a Picture of Their Customers" in Chapter 2.

4. Indicate what customer-profile information you maintain:

   ____ Customer name
   ____ Gender
   ____ Customer address
   ____ Buying preferences
   ____ Zip code
   ____ Store location visited
   ____ Phone number
   ____ Most recent purchase
   ____ Birthday

____ Average transaction size

____ Age

____ Size of family

If you cannot check four or more items, see "Profiling Gives Retailers a Picture of Their Customers" in Chapter 2.

Alternative Delivery Channels

Identify and execute nontraditional distribution methods to selling merchandise.

1. Indicate which alternative delivery channels you have considered using to sell your merchandise:

____ Direct mail or catalog

____ Home shopping

____ Leased department

____ Computer network

____ Charity functions

____ Flea market

____ Kiosk (sales display unit)

____ Door-to-door

____ At work

____ At school

If you cannot check any of these alternatives, see "Retailers Must Try to Go Where the Customers Are: Home, Work, Mall" in Chapter 2.

Action Plan

Now that you have completed the diagnostic exam, identified your weaknesses, and reviewed the corresponding information, you can formulate an action plan (see Table 9-1). Incorporating your short-, mid- and long-term goals will give you a plan of action that is achievable. Then give yourself a deadline. Reward yourself after you achieve each action step by its deadline.

MERCHANDISING

Niching

Successfully target a market segment or specific customer group with a unique mix of merchandise or services that customers see as important.

Table 9-1 Customers and marketing action plan

	Action	Responsibility	Deadline
Example:	*Conduct a customer focus group to determine what services my customers really want*	*Store manager*	*By the end of this month*
1.			
2.			
3.			
4.			
5.			
6.			
7.			
8.			
9.			
10.			

1. Do you feel niching is an important strategy to your business?
   ____ Yes   ____ No
   If you answered no, see "Unique Products and Services Carve Market Niches" in Chapter 3.

2. If you answered yes, indicate which of the following techniques you effectively use:
   ____ Offer unique categories or items
   ____ Offer expanded assortments of product
   ____ Carry deeper quantities of specific categories
   ____ Provide unique value-added services (like tailoring and delivery service)
   ____ Offer different or expanded store hours
   ____ Offer complimentary products that the competition does not offer
   ____ Offer upscale merchandise that the competition does not offer
   ____ Offer products in single quantities where competitors offer multipacks
   ____ Perform direct-marketing activities
   ____ Incorporate competitive advantages into all advertising
   If you cannot check five of these techniques, see "Unique Products and Services Carve Market Niches" in Chapter 3.

Figure 9-2 How do you compare? Rate the importance of each business practice and how well you perform at each. Use the list below to rate yourself on a scale from one to four, with four being the highest. Have your management team and sales employees do the same, and calculate averages for your company. Then compare your results to the survey averages and Arthur Andersen's rankings and best practices in Chapter 3.

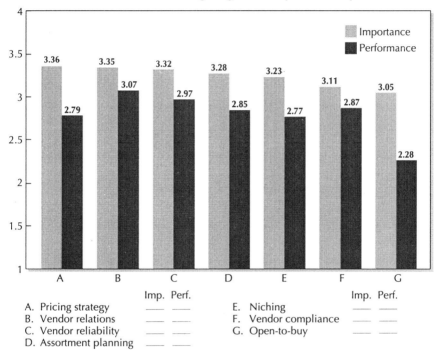

How retailers rank merchandising categories for importance and performance

	Imp.	Perf.			Imp.	Perf.
A. Pricing strategy	___	___	E. Niching		___	___
B. Vendor relations	___	___	F. Vendor compliance		___	___
C. Vendor reliability	___	___	G. Open-to-buy		___	___
D. Assortment planning	___	___				

Pricing Strategy

Establish a set of pricing parameters that meets customer wants and company profit objectives.

1. Indicate which factors you consider to establish your prices:

___ Customers' perceptions of value

___ Company image

___ Fashion vs. seasonal vs. basic

___ Expected margin

___ Landed costs (including freight and duty)

___ Manufacturer's suggested retail price

___ Competitors' prices

____ Perceived demand

____ In-stock position

If you cannot check four or more techniques, see "Consumers Look for Value, Not Always Price" in Chapter 3.

2. Indicate which techniques your buyers use to determine the timing of markdowns:

____ Inventory aging information

____ Sales movement

____ Predetermined markdown formula

____ Rule-of-thumb markdowns

____ Across-the-board markdowns

____ Walking the store

____ End of season

If you cannot check three or more techniques, see "Consumers Look for Value, Not Always Price" in Chapter 3.

Vendors

Develop a trusting relationship in which vendors meet retailers' needs, comply with their terms in delivering merchandise, and work with retailers to meet mutual goals.

1. Does your company have a standardized means of selecting vendors and managing relationships with them?

____ Yes   ____ No

If you answered no, see "Good Relationships Lead to Good Buys" in Chapter 3.

2. If you answered yes, indicate which factors you effectively use to select vendors and manage relationships:

____ Price for value

____ Product quality

____ Brand-name reputation

____ Honesty and integrity

____ Reputation of vendor

____ Product support (cooperative advertising, in-store promotions, couponing, and so on)

____ Other value-added services (preticketing, pack-by-store, direct-store delivery, and the like)

____ Product availability

____ On-time delivery

____ Return privileges

____ Lead times

____ Breadth of product line

____ Delivery accuracy (completeness, accuracy, and the like)

____ Sales representative skills and expertise (product knowledge, training)

____ Credit terms (days, discounts, total credit line, and the like)

____ Hot item

If you cannot check eight or more factors, see "Good Relationships Lead to Good Buys" in Chapter 3.

3. Do you share financial and merchandising information (such as gross margin, sales, and SKU movement) with your vendors?

____ Yes   ____ No

If you answered no, see "Good Relationships Lead to Good Buys" in Chapter 3.

4. Have you established and communicated minimum expectations to your vendors in such areas as acceptable level of substitutions, adherence to delivery dates, and so on?

____ Yes   ____ No

If you answered no, see "Good Relationships Lead to Good Buys" in Chapter 3.

5. If you answered yes, do you monitor the vendors' performances in meeting your expectations?

____ Yes   ____ No

If you answered no, see "Good Relationships Lead to Good Buys" in Chapter 3.

Open-to-Buy

Use budgets to control buying activities and merchandise levels.

1. Do you use open-to-buy planning in your buying activities?

____ Yes   ____ No

If you answered no, see "Inventory Control Is the Best Way to Increase Profits" in Chapter 3.

2. Indicate which strategies you use for planning your orders:

____ Model stocks

____ Minimum and maximum parameters

____ Safety stocks (reorder when depleted)

____ Automatic replenishment

____ Item testing (bringing in small quantities at the front of the buying season to test consumer response)

____ Identifying and developing "never out" lists (basic merchandise that must be in stock all of the time)

____ Customer books or want lists (lists of goods requested in the store that were not in stock all of the time)

If you cannot check three or more of these strategies, see "Inventory Control Is the Best Way to Increase Profits" in Chapter 3.

Assortment Planning

Determine classes, styles, colors, and sizes to carry in each category or department.

1. Indicate which techniques you effectively use to determine the appropriate merchandising assortments:

   ____ Historical customer feedback

   ____ Historical sales patterns

   ____ Historical purchases

   ____ Buyer input

   ____ Vendor-supplied assortment profiles

   ____ Input from the store manager

   ____ Suggestions from the sales representative

   ____ Owner instincts

   If you cannot check five or more of these techniques, see "Facts Must Back Owners' Instincts" in Chapter 3.

2. Indicate which items you use in the planning process for merchandising:

   ____ Current demographic and psychographic trends

   ____ Prior year's sales, inventory, and markdown reports

   ____ Current local economic trends

   ____ Competitor actions (store openings, advertising)

   ____ Overall financial goals and strategies of the company

   ____ Buyer instincts

   ____ Current inventory levels

   ____ Prior year's promotion and advertising calendars

   ____ Market research

   ____ Merchandise samples

   ____ Vendor performance records

Table 9-2 Merchandising action plan

	Action	Responsibility	Deadline
Example:	*Shop in competitor's store to find the best areas to carve a niche*	*Owner, manager, buyer, and full-time employees*	*During the first of every month*
1.			
2.			
3.			
4.			
5.			
6.			
7.			
8.			
9.			
10.			

If you cannot check six or more techniques, see "Facts Must Back Owners' Instincts" in Chapter 3.

STORE OPERATIONS

Customer Service

Assist customers in a timely and courteous fashion, making them feel welcome and exceeding their expectations.

1. Indicate which of the following customer-service techniques you emphasize:

____ Employees who smile

____ Employee name tags

____ Answer phone within four rings

____ Employees that offer assistance outside assigned department

____ Opening the store during non-store hours to accommodate customers

____ Employees that offer assistance

____ Greeters

____ Carry-out assistance

If you cannot check five or more techniques, see "Smiles Are Not Enough When It Comes to Serving Customers" in Chapter 4.

Figure 9-3 How do you compare? Rate the importance of each business practice and how well you perform at each. Use the list below to rate yourself on a scale from one to four, with four being the highest. Have your management team and sales employees do the same, and calculate averages for your company. Then compare your results to the survey averages and Arthur Andersen's rankings and best practices in Chapter 4.

How retailers rank store operations categories for importance and performance

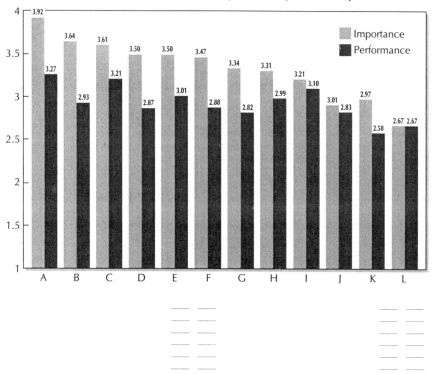

Store Staffing and Labor Productivity

Match the quantity and quality of store staffing with customer traffic and needs.

1. Do you have a formal program in place to schedule your sales staff?
   ____ Yes   ____ No
   If you answered no, see "Proper Labor Scheduling Is the Key to Controlling Costs" in Chapter 4.

2. If you answered yes, indicate how the store manager, sales employees, and owner spend time (approximate percentages):

	Manager	Employee	Owner
Selling merchandise	%	%	%
Customer relations (returns, telephones, and the like)	%	%	%
Receiving	%	%	%
Ticketing and tagging	%	%	%
Stocking displays	%	%	%
Pricing	%	%	%
Training	%	%	%
Planning (like sales and merchandise plans)	%	%	%
Buying	%	%	%
Analyzing operations	%	%	%
Administrating	%	%	%
Supervising	%	%	%
Shopping competitors	%	%	%
Total	100%	100%	100%

Benchmark your results with the results of this study. See "Proper Labor Scheduling Is the Key to Controlling Costs" in Chapter 4 to determine areas where you may need to refocus your employees.

3. Indicate how your buyers spend their time (approximate percentages):

In the stores communicating with and selling merchandise to customers	%
In the stores communicating with store employees	%
In the stores reviewing product availability, merchandise presentation, and so on	%
Buying	%
Identifying new vendors/merchandise	%
Reordering	%
At the manufacturers' facilities	%
Plan preparation	%
Review	%
Attending buying markets	%
Advertising	%
Total	100%

Benchmark your results with the results of this study. See "Proper Labor Scheduling Is the Key to Controlling Costs" in Chapter 4 to determine areas where you may need to refocus your buyers' time.

Store Layout

Maintain proper flow of traffic and merchandise location throughout the store.

1. Indicate which of the following are considered when establishing your store layout:

    _____ Space is allocated based on productivity ratios such as net sales per square foot

_____ Space is allocated based on a model stock plan (such as having what customers want, when they want it, at a price they are willing to pay)

_____ Space is allocated based on vendor-recommended plan-o-gram

_____ Space is allocated based on a trade-association plan-o-gram

If you cannot check at least one of these options, see "Audience Plays a Key Role in Aisle Style" in Chapter 4.

Customer Accommodations

Provide conveniences customers desire, such as chairs, changing tables, and validated parking.

1. Do you match the accommodations you provide your customers with their wants and expectations?

_____ Yes   _____ No

If you answered no, see "Accommodations Can Distinguish Stores from Competitors" in Chapter 4.

2. How do you determine your customers' wants and expectations in the area of accommodations?

_____ Mail survey

_____ Focus groups

_____ Store interviews

_____ Phone interviews

_____ Customer comment cards

_____ Employee comments

If you could not check two or more of these options, see "Accommodations Can Distinguish Stores from Competitors" in Chapter 4.

3. Indicate which of the following customer accommodations you provide:

_____ Ample parking

_____ Free parking

_____ Handicap access

_____ Store seating

_____ Public washroom

_____ Changing table

_____ Free use of telephone

_____ Refreshments

_____ Phone order

____ Mail order

____ House calls

____ Personal shopper

____ Gift registry

____ Free trial

____ Rain checks

____ Free delivery and assembly

____ Delivery and assembly with charge

____ Sales follow-up by mail

____ Sales follow-up by telephone

____ Liberal return policy at point of sale

____ Liberal return policy at central location

____ Proprietary credit cards

____ Check cashing

____ Major credit cards accepted

____ Personal charge accounts

____ Instant credit approval

____ Layaway

____ Deferred billing

Not all of these accommodations are necessary for any one store. Generally, customer wants and expectations will vary across formats. The key is for you to determine what accommodations your customers want and then provide them. See "Accommodations Can Distinguish Stores From Competitors" in Chapter 4.

4. Do you analyze and track why merchandise is returned?

____ Yes   ____ No

If you answered no, see "Accommodations Can Distinguish Stores from Competitors" in Chapter 4.

Store Location

Locate stores in the best places and know when to move.

1. Indicate the factors you use to determine where to locate a store:

____ Square footage

____ Demographics

____ Location to other major retailers

____ Proximity of competition

____ Freestanding vs. mall location vs. strip-mall location

____ Parking accessibility

____ Convenience

____ Owning vs. leasing

____ Zoning regulations

If you cannot check five or more factors, see "Real-Estate Rules Apply: Location, Location, Location" in Chapter 4.

Shelf and Display Management

Display merchandise effectively.

1. Indicate what you do to ensure the shelf display management strategy is consistent with other marketing techniques:

____ Buyers coordinate with store managers to ensure consistency

____ Match advertised items with displays in store

____ Use plan-o-grams or photos

____ Delegate responsibility to vendors

If you cannot check two or more techniques, see "Dynamic Displays Generate Traffic and Sales" in Chapter 4.

Store Hours

Adjust store hours to meet customer demands.

1. Indicate which of the following you use to determine store hours:

____ Customer feedback

____ Traffic pattern

____ Other retailers in your store's proximity

____ Competition

____ Employee feedback

____ Local laws

If you cannot check three or more of these factors, see "Time-Constrained Customers Want to Shop Around the Clock" in Chapter 4.

Loss Prevention

Control shoplifting, employee theft, and employee/customer team theft.

1. Indicate which of the following loss-prevention techniques you use:

____ Employee awareness program

____ Periodic loss-prevention "audits"

____ Secret shoppers

____ Background checks on job applicants

____ Reliance on store manager

____ Receipts required for returns

____ Two-way glass

____ Sensormatic or equivalent tagging

____ In-house security guard

____ Merchandise chains

____ Working cameras

____ TV monitoring screens

If you cannot check five or more techniques, see "Reducing Theft and Shrinkage Adds to the Bottom Line" in Chapter 4.

Utility Management

Control costs of heat, light, and common areas.

1. Indicate which of the following factors you use to control utility costs:

____ Employee education on effective usage

____ Programmed thermostats

____ Utility auditors

____ Common-area maintenance audits

____ Capital improvements and investment in new equipment

____ Negotiations with landlord

____ Energy consultants

____ Timers

____ Modified store hours

If you cannot check five or more of these alternatives, see "Retailers May Miss Out on Opportunities to Control Costs" in Chapter 4.

Cleanliness

Maintain a clean store and surrounding area and keep merchandise neatly organized.

1. Other than normal repairs and maintenance, indicate the average number of years between store remodels or significant improvements:

____ years

Benchmark your results with the study participant results in "Stores Must Clean Up Their Acts" in Chapter 4.

2. Indicate which cleaning programs you use:

____ Bathrooms cleaned daily

____ Floor dry-mopped daily

____ Windows washed weekly

____ Floors waxed monthly

If you could not check all of these cleaning tasks, see "Stores Must Clean Up Their Acts" in Chapter 4.

Register Functionality

Effectively use the cash register for sales reports, inventory, management, and so on.

1. Does your company have a computerized point-of-sale system?

____ Yes   ____ No

If you answered no, see "Computers Are Necessary to Keep Up with the Joneses" in Chapter 4.

2. If you answered yes, indicate the system's functions:

____ Scanning

____ Automated generation of sales reports

____ Credit card authorization

____ Check authorization

____ Customer address

____ Customer purchases

____ Centralized price changes

____ Perpetual inventory

If you cannot check four or more items, see "Computers Are Necessary to Keep Up with the Joneses" in Chapter 4.

Receiving, Stocking, and Distribution

Manage the flow of merchandise from the vendor through the store to the customer in a quick and cost-efficient way.

1. Indicate the average time it takes for delivered merchandise to reach the sales floor:

____ Less than 3 hours

____ 3 hours to 6 hours

____ 6 hours to 12 hours

_____ 12 hours to 24 hours

_____ More than 24 hours

If you did not check the first or second option, see "Profitability Depends on Moving Goods to the Floor Quickly" in Chapter 4.

MANAGEMENT

Vision and Culture

Communicate to the organization what the company should be and encourage employees to embody that vision.

1. Have you articulated a vision?

   _____ Yes   _____ No

   If you answered no, see "Retailers Need a Clear Sense of Who They Are and Where They Are Headed" in Chapter 5.

2. If you answered yes, indicate the techniques you use to articulate your vision:

   _____ The owner or operator champions this initiative

   _____ The owner-operator continuously incorporates the vision in all modes of communication (such as meetings, conversation, and correspondence)

   _____ The vision is communicated to all employees

   _____ The management team communicates the vision

Table 9-3   Store operations action plan

	Action	Responsibility	Deadline
Example:	*Investigate options for a POS system*	*Store manager and sales associate*	*By the end of this month*
1.			
2.			
3.			
4.			
5.			
6.			
7.			
8.			
9.			
10.			

Figure 9-4   How do you compare? Rate the importance of each business practice and how well you perform at each. Use the list below to rate yourself on a scale from one to four, with four being the highest. Have your management team and sales employees do the same, and calculate averages for your company. Then compare your results to the survey averages and Arthur Andersen's rankings and best practices in Chapter 5.

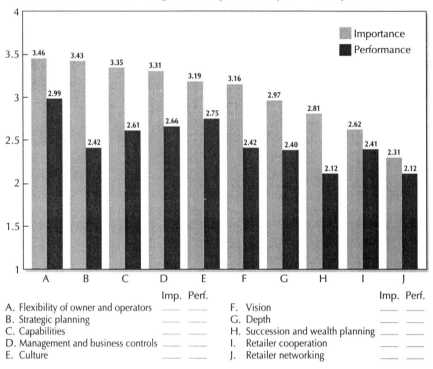

How retailers rank management categories for importance and performance

	Imp.	Perf.		Imp.	Perf.
A. Flexibility of owner and operators	___	___	F. Vision	___	___
B. Strategic planning	___	___	G. Depth	___	___
C. Capabilities	___	___	H. Succession and wealth planning	___	___
D. Management and business controls	___	___	I. Retailer cooperation	___	___
E. Culture	___	___	J. Retailer networking	___	___

If you cannot check all these techniques, see "Retailers Need a Clear Sense of Who They Are and Where They Are Headed" in Chapter 5.

3. Indicate which methods you use to create consistent values, protocols, and behaviors throughout the organization:

_____ The owner or operator and top managers serve as role models to the employees

_____ Expectations regarding behavior and demeanor are discussed during employee training

_____ Protocols are established through an employee handbook

_____ Conduct performance reviews on a periodic basis and build values, protocols, and behavior into that process

_____ Employees are reprimanded for unacceptable behavior

If you cannot check four or more techniques, see "Retailers Need a Clear Sense of Who They Are and Where They Are Headed" in Chapter 5.

4. Indicate which of the following techniques you use to empower your employees:

___ Incentives to employees who use creativity in serving customers and/or improve the business

___ Formal training (internal or external)

___ Learning by example on the job

If you cannot check all these techniques, see "Retailers Need a Clear Sense of Who They Are and Where They Are Headed" in Chapter 5.

Strategic Planning

Establish strategies for achieving goals and objectives by understanding the company's strengths, weaknesses, opportunities, and threats.

1. Do you have a documented strategic plan?

___ Yes   ___ No

If you answered no, see "Reaching Your Destiny Is Easier with a Road Map for the Future" in Chapter 5.

2. Indicate whether you use any of the following techniques to develop an understanding of your strengths, weaknesses, opportunities, and threats:

___ Competitor benchmarking

___ Management brainstorming

___ Industry seminars/outside publications

___ Ask outside advisers

___ Ask suppliers

___ Ask other retailers in the industry

___ Market research

___ Ask trusted friends/family members

If you cannot check five or more of these techniques, see "Reaching Your Destiny Is Easier with a Road Map for the Future" in Chapter 5.

Capabilities

Develop the skills and knowledge of the management team.

1. Indicate which of the following methods you use to develop the skills and knowledge of your management team:

____ Outside seminars

____ Formal internal training

____ Including needs assessment in periodic performance evaluations

____ Periodically interviewing or surveying managers to identify their management development needs

____ Owner or operator personally understanding the needs of his managers and responding accordingly

____ On-the-job training

____ Periodicals

If you cannot check four or more items, see "Skills Signify Success for Small Stores" in Chapter 5.

Flexibility of Owner or Operator

Show the willingness and ability to change.

1. Indicate which of the following activities you perform when making strategic or tactical changes to your business:

   ____ Involve employee teams in decision-making

   ____ Maintain communications

   ____ Identify training requirements

   ____ Monitor performance

   ____ Obtain leadership from owner and operator

   ____ Establish a work plan and timetable

   ____ Delegate responsibilities to others

   If you could not check four or more strategies, see "Owners Must Always Be Willing To Change" in Chapter 5.

Depth

Create an organization that can assume some of the owner's daily responsibilities.

1. Do you try to develop management depth within your company?

   ____ Yes   ____ No

   If you answered no, see "Grooming Promotable People Makes the Business Stronger" in Chapter 5.

2. If you answered yes, indicate which of the following strategies you use to build management depth within your company:

   ____ Rotate people in and out of positions

   ____ Offer a compensation and benefit structure that encourages long-term commitment

____ Promote from within

____ Hire outsiders who have worked in a retail environment

____ Establish a contingency plan in the event that a key employee were to leave the company

If you cannot check three or more techniques, see "Grooming Promotable People Makes the Business Stronger" in Chapter 5.

Wealth and Succession Planning

Prepare for the owner's retirement and the succession of ownership.

1. Indicate whether you have taken any of the following steps to preserve your wealth now and in the future:

____ Consult with professional advisers

____ Execute a will or living trust

____ Maintain life insurance

____ Maintain business liability insurance

____ Maintain personal liability insurance

____ Diversify investment

____ Appoint trustees and an estate executor

____ Appoint a guardian for your children

____ Consider a family gifting program

If you cannot check four or more of these steps, see "Retailers Need to Plan for the Next Generation" in Chapter 5.

Management and Business Controls

Safeguard assets and operations with people, policies, and practices.

1. Indicate which of the following techniques you use to effectively control assets and operations:

____ Culture and environment that encourage self-control among employees

____ Personal involvement in all areas of the business

____ Training and educating employees

____ Daily cash balancing

____ Budget controls

____ Vaults or safes

____ Annual outside audit or review

____ Segregation of duties

____ Computer passwords and user IDs

____ Periodic consultation with outside legal counsel

____ Use of security service during nonbusiness hours

If you cannot check six or more techniques, see "Keeping Your Investment in Top Condition" in Chapter 5.

Retailer Cooperation and Networking

Collaborate with local retailers on specific activities, and join co-ops or buying groups to achieve mutual goals.

1. Do you coordinate events with other retailers?

    ____ Yes   ____ No

    If you answered no, see "Working with Other Retailers Makes Cents" in Chapter 5.

2. If you answered yes, indicate whether you participate in any of the following activities that local area retailers perform:

    ____ Creating consistent shopping hours and shopping days throughout the year

    ____ Revitalizing downtown shopping areas

    ____ Group advertising (print, radio, and so on)

    ____ Organizing or joining frequent buyer programs with several local retailers

    ____ Joint sponsorship of community social events (festivals, carnivals, and so on)

    ____ Sidewalk sales

    ____ Coupon books focusing on local owners or operators

    ____ Developing consistent themes in promotion and advertising

    If you cannot check four or more activities, see "Working with Other Retailers Makes Cents" in Chapter 5.

3. Are you a member of any of the following?

    ____ A buying group (principal activity is merchandise procurement)

    ____ A cooperative (activities include merchandise procurement, physical distribution, coordinated advertising and promotion calendars, and other value-added services)

    ____ An advertising cooperative (principal activity is consolidating advertising)

    If you cannot check any of these groups, see "Working with Other Retailers Makes Cents" in Chapter 5.

4. Indicate which networking activities you use:

____ Working with other retailers to develop catalogs and other direct-mail pieces

____ Offering reciprocal discounts with other merchants

____ Developing market demographics in collaboration with other local retailers

____ Working together to identify and develop training

____ Meeting with other retailers to discuss business issues

____ Working together to evaluate each other's stores

____ Consolidating purchase orders (including merchandise and non-merchandise items independent of a co-op or formal buying group)

____ Working together to price-shop competition

____ Working with other retailers to combine store deliveries

____ Working with other retailers to negotiate inbound transportation

____ Sharing of corporate office space

____ Sharing distribution center/warehouse space with other local retailers

____ Bartering transactions

____ Sharing corporate clerical staff

If you cannot check six or more of these activities, see "Working with Other Retailers Makes Cents" in Chapter 5.

Table 9-4 Management action plan

	Action	Responsibility	Deadline
Example:	*Seek information on advertising from vendors*	*Buyer*	*Before next promotion*
1.			
2.			
3.			
4.			
5.			
6.			
7.			
8.			
9.			
10.			

HUMAN RESOURCES

Hiring and Retention

Carefully select competent employees and keep them satisfied to reduce turnover.

1. Does your company identify a personality profile for screening applicants?

_____ Yes   _____ No

Figure 9-5   How do you compare? Rate the importance of each business practice and how well you perform at each. Use the list below to rate yourself on a scale from one to four, with four being the highest. Have your management team and sales employees do the same and calculate averages for your company. Then compare your results to the survey averages and Arthur Andersen's rankings and best practices in Chapter 6.

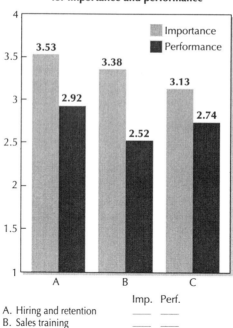

How retailers rank human resources categories for importance and performance

	Imp.	Perf.
A. Hiring and retention	____	____
B. Sales training	____	____
C. Compensation and benefits	____	____

If you answered no, see "Motivation Keeps Employees on the Team" in Chapter 6.

2. Indicate which techniques you use to reduce turnover:

____ Empower employees

____ Increase training

____ Improve hours

____ Increase base pay

____ Increase incentive pay

____ Increase health benefits

____ Improve working conditions

If you cannot check three or more of these techniques, see "Motivation Keeps Employees on the Team" in Chapter 6.

3. Indicate which of the following employee recognition programs you use to enhance employee satisfaction:

____ Customer-service awards

____ Employee suggestions.

____ Special project beyond regular job duties

____ Community-service achievement

____ Peer recognition

____ Length of service

____ Perfect attendance

If you cannot check four or more techniques, see "Motivation Keeps Employees on the Team" in Chapter 6.

4. If you have an employee recognition program, do you offer incentives (like days off and free lunches) to your employees?

____ Yes   ____ No

If you answered no, see "Motivation Keeps Employees on the Team" in Chapter 6.

Sales Training

Educate employees by providing appropriate instruction.

1. Do you have a training program for sales employees?

____ Yes   ____ No

If you answered no, see "Star Sellers Keep Customers Coming Back for More" in Chapter 6.

2. If you answered yes, indicate which techniques you implement as training tools for your sales employees:

____ Formalized training (internal or external)

____ Training is provided to all employees

____ On-the-job training

____ Seasonal and temporary employees are trained

____ Self-study courses

If you cannot check three or more techniques, see "Star Sellers Keep Customers Coming Back for More" in Chapter 6.

Compensation and Benefits

Provide competitive incentives, health insurance, vacation, retirement, and other benefits to employees.

1. Indicate which incentives or benefits you provide to your employees:

	Store manager	Buyer	FT sales employees	PT sales employees
Base salary	_____	_____	_____	_____
Bonus	_____	_____	_____	_____
Commission	_____	_____	_____	_____
Profit sharing	_____	_____	_____	_____
Pension	_____	_____	_____	_____
Merchandise discounts	_____	_____	_____	_____
Dental insurance	_____	_____	_____	_____
Life insurance	_____	_____	_____	_____
Long-term disability	_____	_____	_____	_____
Insurance for accidental death and dismemberment	_____	_____	_____	_____
Paid sick leave	_____	_____	_____	_____
Flex hours	_____	_____	_____	_____
Child-care reimbursement	_____	_____	_____	_____
Paid vacation	_____	_____	_____	_____
Tuition reimbursement	_____	_____	_____	_____

If you cannot check four or more of these techniques for each position, see "Employee Retention Hinges on Healthy Packages" in Chapter 6.

2. Indicate on what basis buyers and store managers are evaluated:

	Store manager	Buyer
Achieved margins	_____	_____
Sales	_____	_____
Company profits	_____	_____
Inventory turnover	_____	_____
Ability to find new or unique merchandise	_____	_____

If you cannot check three of these points for each position, see "Employee Retention Hinges on Healthy Packages" in Chapter 6.

3. Indicate on what basis you give buyers and store managers incentive compensation in addition to base pay:

	Store manager	Buyer
Sales	————	———
Achieved margins	————	———
Company profits	————	———
Inventory turnover	————	———
Ability to find new or unique merchandise	————	———

If you cannot check three of the above incentive measurements, or if you do not offer incentive compensation to your store manager or buyer, see "Employee Retention Hinges on Healthy Packages" in Chapter 6.

FINANCE

Cost Reduction

Analyze cost elements of the business and determining ways to reduce them.

1. Indicate which of the following you use to identify cost-reduction ideas or opportunities:
   ____ Outside conferences
   ____ Trade publications
   ____ Business publications
   ____ Share information with other business owners
   ____ Team problem solving
   ____ Store manager meetings
   ____ Employee suggestion box

   If you cannot check all of these techniques, see "Ingenuity and Control Help Cut Costs" in Chapter 7.

Budgeting

Determine revenues, expenses, and cash-flow needs for the upcoming year.

1. Do you have a budget?
   ____ Yes   ____ No

Table 9-5   Human resources action plan

	Action	Responsibility	Deadline
Example:	*Contact my accountant to discuss profit-sharing opportunities as incentives to employees*	*Owner*	*By the end of the fiscal year*
1.			
2.			
3.			
4.			
5.			
6.			
7.			
8.			
9.			
10.			

If you answered no, see "Measuring and Managing Go Hand-in-Hand" in Chapter 7.

2. If you answered yes, indicate which of these items are characteristics of your budgeting process:

_____ Prepared annually and updated periodically

_____ Designed for accountability by line item

_____ Operating outflows and capital spending budgeted

_____ Expenses budgeted

_____ Exception reports generated for variances from plan

_____ Cash management on a daily, weekly, or monthly basis included

_____ Sales and margin budgeted

If you cannot check four or more of these items, see "Measuring and Managing Go Hand in Hand" in Chapter 7.

Capital Resources

Plan for and raise capital (equity or debt) to fund ongoing operations and expansion.

1. Indicate which of the following resources you use for capital funding:

_____ Earnings of the business

_____ Bank(s)

Figure 9-6 How do you compare? Rate the importance of each business practice and how well you perform at each. Use the list below to rate yourself on a scale from one to four, with four being the highest. Have your management team and sales employees do the same, and calculate averages for your company. Then compare your results to the survey averages and Arthur Andersen's rankings and best practices in Chapter 7.

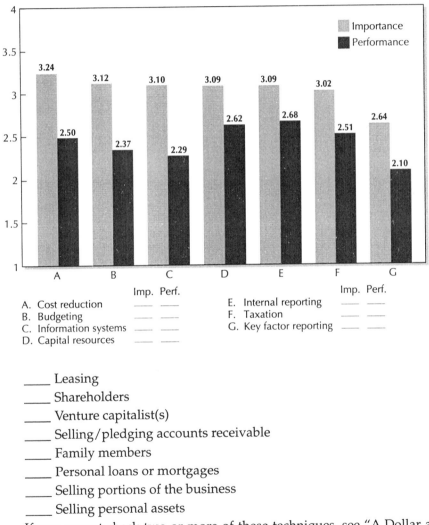

How retailers rank finance categories for importance and performance

	Imp. Perf.			Imp. Perf.
A. Cost reduction	___ ___		E. Internal reporting	___ ___
B. Budgeting	___ ___		F. Taxation	___ ___
C. Information systems	___ ___		G. Key factor reporting	___ ___
D. Capital resources	___ ___			

_____ Leasing

_____ Shareholders

_____ Venture capitalist(s)

_____ Selling/pledging accounts receivable

_____ Family members

_____ Personal loans or mortgages

_____ Selling portions of the business

_____ Selling personal assets

If you cannot check two or more of these techniques, see "A Dollar a Day Keeps Business Booming" in Chapter 7.

2. Indicate which of the following techniques you use to improve return on investment:

_____ Increase sales

_____ Increase gross margins

_____ Decrease operating costs

_____ Reduce investment in inventory

_____ Reduce working capital

_____ Change capital structure

If you cannot check three or more of these techniques, see "A Dollar a Day Keeps Business Booming" in Chapter 7.

3. Indicate which of the following characteristics applies to your outside advisers:

	Banker	Accountant/ tax adviser	Outside legal counsel
Understands my problems	_____	_____	_____
Understands retail industry	_____	_____	_____
Knows my company's goals and strategies	_____	_____	_____
Understands the economics of my company	_____	_____	_____
Requires a reasonable level of periodic reporting from my company	_____	_____	_____
Uses standard sources for industry ratios to compare my company to others in the retailing industry	_____	_____	_____

If you cannot check four or more of these characteristics for each outside adviser, see "A Dollar a Day Keeps Business Booming" in Chapter 7.

Information Systems

Use a computer to capture key financial information to aid decision-making.

1. Indicate whether you have implemented or considered implementing the following techniques:

_____ Electronic POS registers

_____ Scanning

_____ EDI

_____ Quick response

_____ Bar-coded shipping

If you cannot check two or more techniques, see "The Computer Revolution Is Changing the Way Retailing Is Done" in Chapter 7.

Key-Factor and Internal Reporting

Report key area results (such as exception reporting based on predetermined criteria like markdowns that exceed estimates). Communicate that information to other decision-makers.

1. Indicate which of the following key reports you use for management decision-making:
   ____ Daily sales
   ____ Weekly store payroll
   ____ Stockouts
   ____ Monthly markdowns
   ____ Inventory aging
   ____ Receivables aging
   ____ Monthly open-to-buy
   ____ Monthly operating expenses by line item
   ____ Monthly budget to actual results
   ____ Daily gross margins
   If you cannot check seven or more items, see "Reports Drive Sound Business Decisions" in Chapter 7.

2. Indicate which of the following internal reports are available:
   ____ Daily sales reports
   ____ Monthly income statement and balance sheet
   ____ Inventory levels (weekly or monthly)
   ____ Quarterly income statement and balance sheet
   ____ Annual income statement and balance sheet
   If you cannot check four or more reports, see "Reports Drive Sound Business Decisions" in Chapter 7.

Taxation

Plan to minimize all tax liabilities.

1. Indicate which measures you take to manage tax costs:
   ____ Using professional tax advisers
   ____ Disputing all tax assessments
   ____ Consulting with colleagues
   ____ Influencing tax legislation through lobbying groups or other organizations
   ____ Reading tax publications

____ Attending tax seminars

____ Using tax software technologies

If you cannot check three or more measures, see "The Taxman Cometh All Too Soon" in Chapter 7.

CALENDAR

Success Depends on Effective Time Management

One of the commonly cited concerns for many small-store retailers is having more to do than time permits. To make effective use of your time, you need to plan your time, prioritize your objectives, focus your activities, and delegate certain responsibilities. Otherwise, you may quickly become overwhelmed. This, in turn, leads to a poor attitude, poor decision-making, and poor performance.

To avoid these pitfalls, small-store retailers need to continuously improve their time-management skills. Self-discipline is critical.

This book presents many ideas for improvement. Some are short-term tactical ideas that you can easily implement; others are strategic in nature and require more time and effort.

The following exercise will help guide you through the process of planning your time.

Table 9-6   Finance action plan

	Action	**Responsibility**	**Deadline**
Example:	*Talk with tax adviser about changing from C corporation status to S corporation status*	*Owner*	*Within 60 days*
1.			
2.			
3.			
4.			
5.			
6.			
7.			
8.			
9.			
10.			

Once you know your general objectives and specific activities, you should budget your time accordingly. See Figure 9-7 for ideas on where to start.

Suggested Weekly Practices

You should perform some of the following actions weekly. Of course, you should spread them throughout the week and base your performance on the relative importance of each practice to your organization.[1] In the tables

[1] Adapt the frequency of these activities to your unique situation.

Figure 9-7   Sample schedule for June

Sunday	Monday	Tuesday	Wednesday	Thursday	Friday	Saturday
			1 Inspect new merchandise receipts. Meet with retailers to plan street fair.	**2** Hold sales meeting; discuss operational issues. Review space allocation.	**3** Hold training meeting.	**4** Distribute Human Resources assessment tool to management team.
5 Shop the competition.	**6** Plan advertising. Send news releases to local media.	**7** Interview new associates. Review new merchandise.	**8** Respond to customer comment cards and complaints.	**9** Hold store manager meeting.	**10** Review performance measures.	**11** Read *Small Store Survival.*
12 Shop the competition.	**13** Conduct focus groups. Meet with utility company representative.	**14** Generate key reports. Track progress against strategic plan.	**15** Plan store maintenance needs. Research new security system.	**16** Review cash flow. Plan July's open-to-buy.	**17** Evaluate advertising response rates.	**18** Read *Small Store Survival.*
19 Shop the competition.	**20** Spend time on the sales floor.	**21** Generate key reports. Compare actual performance to budgeted performance.	**22** Plan store labor. Start implementing mentor system.	**23** Review payroll.	**24** Analyze assortments. Look for new products.	**25** Read *Small Store Survival.*
26 Shop the competition.	**27** Recognize outstanding employees.	**28** Review space allocation.	**29** Change prices. Ask vendors about product-training seminars.	**30** Hold sales meetings; have role-playing session.		

that follow, the column on the left provides generalized practices; you should fill in the column on the right with your specific weekly activities. Some ideas to get you started are included.

General customers and marketing objectives	Example
Plan and evaluate advertising and promotions	*Evaluate the response rates from current advertising to help refine media to buy*
Review competitor ads and shop their stores	
Respond to customer comment cards and complaints	
Spend time on the sales floor	
Other	

General merchandising objectives	Example
Inspect new merchandise receipts	*Review new merchandise before it's put on sales floor*
Walk the store and consider the need for markdowns	
Analyze assortments	
Adjust prices	
Review on-hand inventory levels; assess reorder and cancellation needs	
Other	

General store operations objectives	Example
Hold sales meetings to discuss operational and customer-service issues	*Have role-playing session at regular weekly meeting to help employees brush up on service skills.*
Determine store labor requirements	
Adjust shelves and displays for advertised merchandise	
Visit your other stores	
Meet with store managers	
Plan store maintenance needs	
Change signage	
Other	

General management objectives	Example
Read a section of *Small Store Survival.*	*Distribute the human resources operations assessment tool to everyone; ask for feedback at next week's meeting*
Think about strategic plan	
Anticipate next week's problems and opportunities	
Read trade and business publications	
Other	

General human resources objectives	Example
Provide on-the-job training	*Start implementing mentor system; pair new associates with department managers*
Interview new associates	
Recognize outstanding employees	
Other	

General finance objectives	Example
Identify areas to reduce cost	*Meet with utility-company representative*
Review cash-flow needs	
Review bills and approve expenditures	
Analyze key reports	
Review investments	
Review payroll checks	
Other	

Suggested Monthly Practices

These suggested practices are more project-oriented, and you should concentrate on them every month. Your specific situation will determine whether you need to work on these items at the beginning of the month or toward the end of the month.[2]

---

[2] Adapt the frequency of these activities to your unique situation.

General customers and marketing objectives	Example
Meet with local media	*Send news release on upcoming fashion show to local newspaper editors*
Plan and evaluate advertising and promotions	
Conduct focus groups	
Correspond with customers	
Other	

General merchandising objectives	Example
Review and update open-to-buy and sales forecast	*Start planning next month's open-to-buy*
Review key reports	
Look for new products	
Evaluate and correspond with vendors	
Attend trade shows	
Analyze margins	
Other	

General store operations objectives	Example
Evaluate inventory losses	*Research costs of new security system*
Plan store maintenance needs	
Review space allocation	
Analyze returns	
Review key performance measures	
Other	

General management objectives	Example
Meet with local retailers to discuss collaborative opportunities	*Meet with other retailers to start planning this year's street fair*
Attend chamber of commerce meetings	
Consult with outside advisers	
Conduct town-hall meetings	
Meet with key employees	
Track progress against strategic plan	
Read the latest trade magazines	
Other	

General human resources objectives	Example
Hold training meeting	*Ask vendors about product-training seminars they offer*
Evaluate effectiveness of store managers, sales associates, and buyers	
Analyze performance measures (such as absenteeism and incentive achievement)	
Plan next month's activities	
Take employees to lunch	
Other	

General finance objectives	Example
Review actual performance against budget	*Identify reasons why actual performance did not meet budgeted performance*
Review financial reports with key employees	
Review operating expenses	
Review quarterly tax deposits	
Meet with banker or accountant	
Other	

BENCHMARKS

Key Performance Measures Show How Retailers Stack Up

Benchmarking is the process of continually comparing and measuring your business processes against those of industry leaders.

The following operational ratios represent imperative data that you should use to analyze your company's performance. They are critical to market positioning and sound financial planning and execution. However, you should know about the companies to which you compare your store so that the results will not be misleading.

Arthur Andersen suggests that community and area retailers band together to develop their own benchmark statistics.

The formula, implications, industry median, and range of respondents' performances are provided for each ratio. The industry median represents the midpoint for small-store retailers; you can use the median to benchmark your company's performance. Significant variance from the industry median could indicate an opportunity for improvement. See the applicable recommendations sections for suggestions. Keep in mind, however, that different retail formats have different optimal financial and operational structures; variance from the industry median does not necessarily indicate stronger or weaker performance. Many trade associations sponsor studies that accumulate similar information of a more specific nature. Contact your trade association for further information.

The following benchmark information is based on data provided by survey respondents.

Net sales per selling square foot, excluding leased departments

$$\frac{\text{Net Sales (excluding leased departments)}}{\text{Selling Square Feet (excluding leased departments)}}$$

This ratio measures the sales productivity of each square foot of selling space. A low ratio indicates excess selling space exists to support current sales. The results may identify additional profitable opportunities. The results may also indicate, on a department-by-department basis, a reallocation of space. If you feel that you cannot obtain additional profitable volume or a shift in mix, you and your management team should consider alternative uses for the space (subleasing, selling, leasing departments, and the like). See "Store Layout" in Chapter 4 and "Pricing Strategy" in Chapter 3.

Range	Industry median	Your company
$30–$722	$206	

Average transaction size

$$\frac{\text{Gross Sales}}{\text{Number of Sales Transactions}}$$

A low dollar value indicates that you are selling goods with low price points in greater quantity than goods with high price points. You can compare this ratio to the average price point in each merchandise category. There should be a close relationship between the average sale and average price point offered after allowing for markdowns. The ratio is also a function of the number of SKUs sold per transaction. See "Store Layout" in Chapter 4 and "Pricing Strategy" in Chapter 3.

Range	Industry median	Your company
$5–$865	$40	

Net sales per store employee (store manager, assistant manager, and sell-ing employees only)

$$\frac{\text{Net Sales}}{\text{Average Number of Store Employees}}$$

Although you should strive for a high sales per employee, high ratios may indicate that there are not enough employees to meet customer demands. You may lose sales if customers have to wait an excessive length of time for service. Low ratios indicate overstaffing, ineffective sales incentives, poor sales training, declining sales, or poor labor scheduling. See Chapter 6 and "Store Staffing and Layout Productivity" in Chapter 4.

Range	Industry median	Your company
$11,900–$579,000	$100,100	

Sales returns as a percentage of net sales, excluding leased departments

$$\frac{\text{Returns (excluding leased departments)}}{\text{Net Sales (excluding leased departments)}}$$

A low ratio indicates customer satisfaction and/or good quality of mer-chandise purchased. A high ratio indicates customer dissatisfaction with the goods or services purchased, ineffective selling personnel, or poor merchandise quality. See "Customer Satisfaction" in Chapter 2, "Niching" in Chapter 3, and "Customer Accommodations" in Chapter 4.

Range	Industry median	Your company
0%–12%	1.0%	

Markdowns as a percent of sales

$$\frac{\text{Markdowns}}{\text{Net Sales}}$$

A high ratio may indicate initial overpricing of merchandise, and you may need to give significant and/or constant sales or discounts to generate sales. In addition, a high markdown ratio may encourage a perception of low quality. A low number, while generally desirable, may indicate lost sales due to limited sales incentives. See "Niching" and "Pricing Strategy" in Chapter 3.

Range	Industry median	Your company
1%–35%	10.0%	

Gross margin return on inventory at cost (GMROI)

$$\frac{\text{Gross Margin}}{\text{Average Inventory (at cost)}}$$

This ratio measures the margin-generating power of your investment in inventory. A declining GMROI can indicate a reduction in gross margins and/or a reduction in inventory turnover. A declining GMROI may also indicate low inventory levels, which could lead to lost sales. You should calculate this ratio by department to identify departments that the company should consider discontinuing. High GMROI departments should be considered for high-traffic areas of the store.

Many retailers use GMROI as a basis for reallocating space among departments. An effective way to present and analyze this information is to graph GMROI against the number of square feet devoted to each department. This graph presents space allocation in a simple manner. For instance, departments with low sales per square foot likely have been allocated too much space. Such a graph often shows that you can decrease the size (in terms of space and inventory) of certain departments. See "Assortment Planning" and "Pricing Strategy" in Chapter 3 and "Store Layout" and "Shelf and Display Management" in Chapter 4.

Range	Industry median	Your company
$1.50–$3.65	$2.30	

Shrink as a percentage of sales, excluding leased departments

$$\frac{\text{Inventory Shrink (excluding leased departments)}}{\text{Net Sales (excluding leased departments)}}$$

High shrinkage is generally due to customer theft, employee theft, or paperwork errors. Paperwork errors that affect shrinkage include poor inventory cutoff, unrecorded markdowns, improperly priced merchandise, and improperly recorded purchases (errors in dollars, quantities, or departments). See "Loss Prevention" in Chapter 4.

Range	Industry median	Your company
0.2%–5.9%	2.8%	

Vendor rebates as a percent of purchases

$$\frac{\text{Vendor Rebates}}{\text{Purchases}}$$

A low ratio may indicate that you overpay for inventory or do not take advantage of available vendor rebates. A high percentage is desirable, but it may indicate that you limit purchases to discounted merchandise. See "Vendors" in Chapter 3.

Range	Industry median	Your company
0.1%–5%	1.5%	

Net advertising expense (after co-op) as a percent of net sales, excluding leased departments

$$\frac{\text{Net Advertising Expense (after co-op)}}{\text{Net Sales (excluding leased departments)}}$$

A ratio significantly below the industry median could indicate that you take advantage of the benefits of effective advertising (like increased consumer awareness and increased store traffic). If your ratio exceeds the industry median, this could indicate that you should cut advertising expenses by reviewing which advertising vehicles generate the greatest return. A ratio that exceeds the industry median could also indicate that you are not obtaining enough co-op advertising dollars or allowances from your vendors (also see the ratio for co-op advertising allowances as a percentage of purchases). See "Advertising Strategy" and "Alternative Marketing Strategies" in Chapter 2.

Range	Industry median	Your company
0.03%–7.0%	2.2%	

Co-op advertising allowances as a percentage of purchases

$$\frac{\text{Co-op Advertising Allowances}}{\text{Net Purchases}}$$

The purpose of this ratio is to provide a more specific measure of your ability to obtain co-op advertising allowances from your vendors. Generally, your ability to obtain allowances is driven by vendor programs (sometimes part of nationwide advertising campaigns) and your volume of purchases. Many small-store retailers are unable to generate their own allowances. Those retailers should consider joining a buying group. See "Advertising Strategy" in Chapter 2 and "Vendors" in Chapter 3.

Range	Industry median	Your company
0.03%–3%	0.9%	

Store payroll as a percentage of net sales, excluding leased departments

Payroll Expense
$$\frac{\text{(base, bonus, and commission, excluding benefits and taxes)}}{\text{Net Sales (excluding leased departments)}}$$

This measures selling productivity of store labor dollars. Whereas the ratio of net sales per employee measures selling productivity of employees, this ratio addresses the cost of those employees. Low ratios may indicate inadequate staffing to meet customer-service expectations. High ratios may indicate overstaffing of employees, poor mix of employees, labor scheduling opportunities, and inefficient operations. Pay scale is obviously a major factor in this benchmark measure. Compare your average base salaries or wage rates to the industry median, as follows:

	Range	Industry median	Your company
Store Managers (annual)	$10,000–$65,000	$30,000	
Assistant Store Managers (annual)	$12,800–$59,000	$24,000	
Buyers (annual)	$15,000–$45,000	$22,500	
Full-Time Sales Associates (per hour)	$4.50–$12.00	$6.90	
Part-Time Sales Associates (per hour)	$4.25–$14.85	$5.00	

For more information, see "Store Staffing and Labor Productivity" in Chapter 4, "Sales Training" and "Compensation and Benefits" in Chapter 6, and "Customer Wants and Satisfaction" in Chapter 2.

Range	Industry median	Your company
7%–32%	16%	

Employee benefits (health, pension, profit sharing, and so on) as a percentage of net sales, excluding leased departments

$$\frac{\text{Total Employee Benefits Expense}}{\text{Net Sales (excluding leased departments)}}$$

A low ratio may result in difficulty retaining quality employees due to poor benefits provided. A high number may indicate a need to redesign your benefits package or consider changing insurance carriers. See "Compensation and Benefits" in Chapter 6.

Range	Industry median	Your company
0.44%–12%	2.0%	

Store employee training cost per year per employee (store manager, assistant manager, and selling employees only)

$$\frac{\text{Store Employee Training Costs}}{\text{Average Number of Store Employees}}$$

An amount significantly below the industry median may indicate a lack of employee training, which is necessary to provide sales associates with enough information to meet customer expectations. This may result in lost sales due to errors or poor customer service. An amount significantly above the industry median may indicate high turnover, excessive training, or ineffective training that you need to redesign or enhance. See "Sales Training" in Chapter 6.

Range	Industry median	Your company
$100–$11,000	$250	

Common-area maintenance and utilities expense as a percent of net sales

$$\frac{\text{Common Area Maintenance and Utilities Expense}}{\text{Net Sales}}$$

A low ratio, although generally desirable, may indicate lack of cleanliness or poor preventive maintenance. This may lead to breakdown of equipment. An excessively high ratio may indicate obsolete property and equipment, which may cost more to maintain than replace; lack of cost-control measures; or lack of aggressive rate negotiations. See "Utility Management" and "Cleanliness" in Chapter 4 and "Cost Reduction" in Chapter 7.

Range	Industry median	Your company
0.66%–6%	2.0%	

Loss prevention expense, excluding shrink, as a percent of net sales

$$\frac{\text{Loss Prevention Expense (excluding shrink)}}{\text{Net Sales}}$$

This ratio may be used as a general benchmark to compare your investment in controlling loss prevention with others in the industry. Ratios significantly above or below the industry median indicate opportunities to improve loss prevention efforts. See "Loss Prevention" in Chapter 4 and "Cost Reduction" in Chapter 7.

Range	Industry median	Your company
0.01%–2%	0.2%	

MIS expense as a percent of net sales, excluding leased departments

$$\frac{\text{MIS Expense}}{\text{Net Sales (excluding leased departments)}}$$

You can use this ratio as a general guideline for controlling MIS costs. While a result significantly below the industry median could indicate strong performance, it could also indicate that you underuse MIS technology. A ratio significantly higher than the industry median could indicate old or obsolete equipment or unfavorably negotiated MIS purchase price, processing contract, or service arrangements. See "Information Systems" and "Cost Reduction" in Chapter 7.

Range	Industry median	Your company
0.09%–5%	0.8%	

Inventory leverage

$$\frac{\text{Trade Accounts Payable}}{\text{Inventory at Cost}}$$

This ratio is a measure of your ability to finance your inventory purchases through favorable payment terms from your vendors and optimal inventory levels. Generally, a high ratio is favorable, although it can indicate lost discount terms on accounts payable or low inventory levels (such as potential out-of-stocks). A low ratio could indicate unfavorably negotiated terms from vendors or excessive inventory levels, which reduces cash flow as funds are tied up in inventory. See "Vendors" and "Open-to-Buy" in Chapter 3.

Range	Industry median	Your company
4.5%–86%	35%	

Inventory turnover at cost

$$\frac{\text{Cost of Sales}}{\text{Average Inventory at Cost}}$$

A low turnover rate may indicate overstocking, obsolescence, or poor merchandise mix. In certain cases, a ratio that is too high could indicate lost opportunity due to not enough inventory (for example, out-of-stocks). See "Open-to-Buy," "Assortment Planning," "Niching," and "Pricing Strategy" in Chapter 3.

Range	Industry median	Your company
1–8 times	3 times	

RMA Annual Statement Studies

An alternative source of benchmark information is *RMA Annual Statement Studies*. The following is a sample.[3]

	Hard goods (% of sales)	Soft goods (% of sales)
Gross margin	34.2%	37.5%
Operating expenses	32.8%	34.9%
Profit before taxes	1.1%	1.2%
Inventory turnover	2.7 times	2.3 times

[3] Robert Morris Associates. *RMA Annual Statement Studies*. Philadelphia, PA. 1993. This information is sorted by standard industrial classification (SIC). The retailing industry SIC codes are 5200 through 5999. You can obtain this book from your local library.

APPENDIXES

Resources Give Retailers the Edge

Appendix A

Trade Associations

Trade associations are an exceptional resource for small-store retailers. Typically, trade associations conduct industry and technical studies, publish newsletters and other periodicals, sponsor training seminars, and share information among members. The following is a select alphabetical list of trade associations. Contact the local library for a complete list.

Retail trade associations	Address	Phone
American Booksellers Association	828 S. Broadway Tarrytown, NY 10591	(914) 591-2665
American Society of Travel Agents	1101 King St. Alexandria, VA 22314	(703) 739-2782
American Wholesale Marketers Association	1128 16th St. Washington, DC 20036	(202) 463-2124
Association of Retail Marketing Services	3 Caro Court Red Bank, NJ 07701	(908) 842-5070
Chain Drug Marketing Association	104 Wilmot Rd. Suite 550 Deerfield, IL 60015	(708) 267-8800
Christian Booksellers Association	P.O. Box 200 Colorado Springs, CO 80901	(719) 576-7880
Direct Marketing Association	1120 Avenue of the Americas New York, NY 10036	(212) 768-7277
Employers Mutual Association	150 N. Michigan Ave. Chicago, IL 60601	(312) 565-2311
Food Marketing Institute	800 Connecticut NW Suite 500 Washington, DC 20006	(202) 452-8444

Footwear Distributors and Retailers of America	1319 F St. NW Suite 700 Washington, DC 20004	(202) 737-5660
Illinois Retail Merchants Association	19 South La Salle Chicago, IL 60603	(312) 726-4600
Institution of Store Planners	25 N. Broadway Tarrytown, NY 10591	(914) 332-1806
International Council of Shopping Centers	655 Fifth Ave. New York, NY 10022	(212) 421-8181
International Credit Association	243 N. Lindbergh Blvd. St. Louis, MO 63141	(314) 991-3030
International Wholesale Furniture Association	P.O. Box 2482 164 S. Main St. High Point, NC 27261	(910) 884-1566
Mail Order Association of America	1877 Bourne Court Wantagh, NY 11793	(516) 221-8257
Museum Store Association	1 Cherry Center 501 S. Cherry St. No. 460 Denver, CO 80222	(303) 329-6968
National Association of Beverage Retailers	5101 River Road Suite 108 Bethesda, MD 20816	(301) 656-1494
National Association of Chain Drug Stores	413 North Lee St. P.O. Box 1417-D49 Alexandria, VA 22313	(703) 549-3001
National Association of College Stores	528 E. Lorain St. P.O. Box 58 Oberlin, OH 44074	(216) 775-7777
National Association of Retail Dealers of America	10 E. 22nd St. Lombard, IL 60148	(708) 953-8950
National Association of Retail Druggists	205 Daingerfield Road Alexandria, VA 22314	(703) 683-8200
National Association of Theatre Owners	4605 Lankershim Blvd. Suite 340 North Hollywood, CA 91602	(818) 506-1778
National Cosmetology Association	3510 Olive St. St. Louis, MO 63103	(314) 534-7980
National Decorating Products Association	1050 N. Lindbergh Blvd. St. Louis, MO 63132	(314) 991-3470
National Electronics Sales and Service Dealers Association	2708 W. Berry St. Suite 3 Ft. Worth, TX 76109	(817) 921-9061

National Home Furnishings Association	P.O. Box 2396 High Point, NC 27261	(919) 883-1650
National Ice Cream and Yogurt Retailers Association	1429 King Ave. Suite 210 Columbus, OH 43212	(614) 486-1444
National Lumber and Building Material Dealers Association	40 Ivy St. SE Washington, DC 20003	(202) 547-2230
National Restaurant Association	1200 17th St. NW Washington, DC 20036	(202) 331-5900
National Retail Dry Goods Association	100 W. 31st St. New York, NY 10001	(212) 631-7400
National Retail Federation	325 Seventh St. NW Washington, DC 20004	(202) 783-7971
National Retail Hardware Association	5822 W. 74th St. Indianapolis, IN 46278	(317) 290-0338
National School Supply and Equipment Association	8300 Colesville Rd. Suite 250 Silver Spring, MD 20910	(301) 495-0240
National Shoe Retailers Association	9861 Broken Land Pkwy. Suite 255 Columbia, MD 21046	(401) 381-8282
National Sporting Goods Association	Lake Center Plaza Bldg. 1699 Wall St. Mount Prospect, IL 60056	(708) 439-4000
North American Building Material Distribution Association	401 N. Michigan Ave. Chicago, IL 60611	(312) 321-6845
North American Equipment Dealers Association	10877 Watson Rd. St. Louis, MO 63127	(314) 821-7220
North American Wholesale Lumber Association	3601 Algonquin Rd. Suite 400 Rolling Meadows, IL 60008	(708) 870-7470
Retail Confectioners International	1807 Glenview Rd. Suite 204 Glenview, IL 60025	(708) 724-6120
Retail Loss Prevention Association	222 Middle Country Rd. Suite 209 Smithtown, NY 11787	(516) 366-4290
Retail Tobacco Dealers of America	107 E. Baltimore St. Baltimore, MD 21202	(410) 547-6996
The Retailer's Bakery Association	14239 Bark Center Drive Laurel, MD 20707	(301) 725-2149

Society of American Florists	1601 Duke St. Alexandria, VA 22314	(703) 836-0770
Video Software Dealers Association	303 Harper Drive Moorestown, NJ 08057	(609) 231-7800

Wholesale distribution trade associations	**Address**	**Phone**
General Merchandise Distributors Council	1275 Lake Plaza Drive Colorado Springs, CO 80906	(719) 576-4260
Hobby Industry Association of America	319 E. 54th St. Elmwood Park, NJ 07407	(201) 794-1133
Jewelry Industry Distribution Association	720 Light St. Baltimore, MD 21230	(410) 752-3318
Music Distributors Association	38–44 W. 21st St. 5th Floor New York, NY 10010	(212) 924-9175
National American Wholesale Grocers Association	201 Park Washington Ct. Falls Church, VA 22046	(703) 532-9400
National Association of Sporting Goods Wholesalers	P.O. Box 11344 Chicago, IL 60611	(312) 565-0233
National Association of Wholesaler Distributors	1725 K St. NW Suite 710 Washington, DC 20006	(202) 872-0885
National Kitchen and Bath Association	687 Willow Grove St. Hackettstown, NJ 07840	(908) 852-0033
National Lawn and Garden Distributors Association	1900 Arch St. Philadelphia, PA 19103	(215) 564-3484
National School Supply and Equipment Association	2020 N. 14th St. Suite 400 Arlington, VA 22201	(703) 524-8819
National Wholesale Druggists' Association	105 Oronoco St. Alexandria, VA 22314	(703) 684-6400
National Wholesale Furniture Association	164 S. Main St. Suite 404 High Point, NC 27261	(919) 884-1566
National Wholesale Hardware Association	401 N. Michigan Ave. Chicago, IL 60611	(312) 644-6610
North American Building Material Distribution Association	401 N. Michigan Ave. Chicago, IL 60611	(312) 321-6845
North American Horticultural Supply Association	1900 Arch St. Philadelphia, PA 19103	(215) 564-3484

North American Wholesale Lumber Association	2340 S. Arlington Heights Road Suite 680 Arlington Heights, IL 60005	(708) 870-7474
Pet Industry Distributors Association	5024-R Campbell Blvd. Baltimore, MD 21236	(410) 931-8100
Shoe Service Institute of America	5024-R Campbell Blvd. Baltimore, MD 21236	(410) 931-8100
Video Software Dealers Association	16530 Ventura Blvd. Suite 400 Encino, CA 91436	(818) 385-1500
Wholesale Florists & Florist Suppliers	410 Pine St. Vienna, VA 22180	(703) 242-7000

Appendix B

Publications

Reading industry books and magazines is an effective way to stay current on developments in retailing. Appendices B and C are select alphabetical lists of books, periodicals, and other publications organized by major business function. Publishers of magazines and newsletters frequently develop lists of past articles that readers can quickly scan to identify articles relevant to their needs.

Titles of Books and Directories	Author
Customers and Marketing	
Marketing Without Money	Nicholas Bade
How to Promote, Publicize, and Advertise Your Growing Business	Kim Baker
Mail Order & Direct Response	Tonya Bolden
Know Your Customer: A Guide to Finding Information Sources	Sarah A. Burke (ed.)
Marketing Myths That Can Kill Your Business	Kevin J. Clancy
Marketing Revolution: A Radical Manifesto for Dominating the Marketplace	Kevin J. Clancy
Direct Response Marketing: An Entrepreneurial Approach	William A. Cohen
Retail Marketing	Patrick M. Dunne, et al.
Marketing Small Shopping Centers: How to Increase Retail Traffic and Sales	Kim A. Fraser
Keeping Customers for Life	Richard F. Gerson
Field Guide to Marketing	Tim Hindle
Power Marketing for Small Business	Jody Horner
Marketing Without Megabucks	Shel Horowitz
The Customer is Key	Melind M. Lele
Guerrilla Marketing Weapons: 100 Affordable Marketing Methods for Maximizing Profits from Your Small Business	Jay C. Levinson

Achieving Customer Satisfaction	Joseph Malecki, et al.
Quality Customer Service	William Martin
Retail Marketing: For Employees, Managers, & Entrepreneurs	Warren G. Meyer, et al.
The Best of Retail Advertising Design	National Retail Federation
Successful Catalogs	National Retail Federation
Visual Selling and Design	National Retail Federation
Retail Marketing Channels	Luca Pellegrini, et al. (eds.)
Retail Marketing Strategy: Planning, Implementation and Control	A. Coskun Samli
Customers for Life	Carl Sewell
Seeking Customers: A Harvard Business Review Paperback	Benson P. Shapiro
Keeping Customers: A Harvard Business Review Paperback	John J. Sviokla
Managing & Marketing Services in the 1990s	Richard Teare
Fifty Ways to Win the New Customer	Paul R. Timm
High Probability Selling	Jacques Werth
Fifty Ways to Keep the Customer	Shelley Wolson

Merchandising

Management of Retail Buying	Joseph Friedlander and John Wingate
The Buyer's Manual	National Retail Federation
China and Glassware Merchandiser	National Retail Federation
Complete Dictionary of Buying and Merchandising	National Retail Federation
NRF Standard Merchandise Classifications (rev. ed.)	National Retail Federation
Practical Merchandising Math for Everyday Use	National Retail Federation
Standard Color & Size Code Handbook	National Retail Federation
Student's Workbook for Buyer's Manual	National Retail Federation
Successful Retailing: Your Step-by-Step Guide to Avoiding Pitfalls and Finding Profit as an Independent	Paula Wardell

Store Operations

Run Your Own Store: Proven Strategies for Profit in Every Type of Retail Business	Irving Burstinger
Think Green: A Retailer's Environmental Idea Book	Illinois Retail Merchants Association
Your Own Shop: How to Open & Operate a Successful Retail Business	Ruth Jacobson
Minding the Store	Stanley Marcus
The Manager's Guide: Basic Guidelines for the New Store Manager	Museum Store Association Staff

The Best of Store Designs	National Retail Federation
Retail Store Planning & Design Manual	National Retail Federation
Store Design for the '90s	National Retail Federation
Store Windows That Sell	National Retail Federation
Storefronts and Facades	National Retail Federation

Management

The Only Thing That Matters	Karl Albrecht
Specialty Retailing: Markets & Strategies for the 1990s	Peter Allen (ed.)
Contemporary Retailing: Cases from Today's Marketplace	John S. Berens
Applying Retail Management: A Strategic Approach	Barry Berman and Joel R. Evans
Retail Management: A Strategic Approach	Barry Berman and Joel R. Evans
The Entrepreneur and Small Business Problem Solver	William A. Cohen
Peebles: A Retail Tradition Begins its Second Century	Howard E. Covington, Jr.
Beyond Survival	Leon Danco
Inside the Family Business	Leon Danco
Outside Directors in the Family Owned Business	Leon Danco, et al.
Managing Corporate Culture	Stanley M. Davis
Small Business Source Book (2d ed.) vol. 1	Robert J. Elster
Retail Business Management	Karen Gillespie, et al.
Planning for Profits: The Retailers Guide to Success	Anita Goldwasser
Competitive Positioning	Graham Hooley
Corporate Transformation: Revitalizing Organizations for a Competitive World	Ralph H. Kilmann, et al.
Breakpoint and Beyond	George Land and Beth Jarman
Creating Strategic Leverage	Milind M. Lele
Retailing Management	Michael Levy and Barton A. Weitz
Retailing	J. Barry Mason, et al.
Modern Retailing: Theory and Practice	Joseph B. Mason and Morris L. Mayer
The Small Town Survival Guide: Help For Changing the Economic Future of Your Town	Jack McCall
Modern Retailing: Management Principles & Practices	Melvin Morgenstein and Harriet Strongin
Directory of Associate Members	National Retail Federation
Improving Apparel Shop Profits	National Retail Federation
A Selected Bibliography of Retailing	National Retail Federation
Strategic Planning	Joseph W. Norris, et al.

Downtown Retail Revitalization: Strategies to Maximize Your Market	Carol Patrylick and Jenny Murphy (eds.)
The Small Business Bible	Paul Resnik
Retail Marketing	Carl Sewell
Made in America: My Story	Sam Walton and John Huey
Creating Effective Boards for Private Enterprise	John Ward
Successful Retailing	Paula Wardell
Retail Merchandise Management	John W. Wingate and Elmer O. Schaller

Human Resources

The Salesperson's Success Book from A to Z	Brian Field
Finding, Hiring, and Keeping the Best Employees	Robert Half
Selling is Our Business	Illinois Retail Merchants Association
Selling is Your Job	Illinois Retail Merchants Association
Hiring & Firing: Employing & Managing People	Karen Lanz
Boosting Employee Performance Through Better Motivation	National Retail Federation
Effective Interviewing	National Retail Federation
Mid-Management Compensation Survey	National Retail Federation
Selling by Telephone	National Retail Federation
Selling Styles	National Retail Federation
Specialty Store Chain Executive Compensation Survey	National Retail Federation
Value-Added Sales Management: A Guide for Salespeople and Their Managers	Tom Reilly
Secrets of Successful Selling	Charles R. Whitlock

Finance

AICPA Software Catalog	AICPA
Family Wealth Planning (Arthur Andersen publication)	Arthur Andersen, Brian S. Halminiak
Preserving Family Wealth (Arthur Andersen publication)	Arthur Andersen, Brian S. Halminiak
Creative Fund Raising	Mary A. Burke
Benchmarking	Robert Camp
Commerce Clearing House (CCH) 1993 Guide to Illinois Taxes	Commerce Clearing House
RIS–Retail Info System News 1993/1994 Directory	Edgell Enterprises, Inc.
How to Manage Cash Flow in Your Retail Business	Kenneth F. Hatfield
Tax Guide For Small Business (IRS Publication 334)	Internal Revenue Service

1994 Tax Calendar (IRS Publication 509)	Internal Revenue Service
Federal Estate and Gift Taxes (IRS Publication 448)	Internal Revenue Service
Internal Audit Manual	National Retail Federation
Retail Accounting Manual book two	National Retail Federation
Retail Inventory Method Made Practical	National Retail Federation
Retail Technology Review '92	National Retail Federation
The Software Directory for Retailers (4th ed.)	National Retail Federation
How to Computerize Your Small Business	Patrick O'Hara
LIFO for Retailers: A Business, Financial, & Tax Guide	Paul W. Wilson and Kenneth E. Christensen
Retail Accounting & Financial Control	Robert Zimmerman

Appendix C

Magazines, Journals, Newsletters, and Other Periodicals

Titles of newsletters and periodicals	Address	Phone
Accent on Living	P.O. Box 700 Bloomington, IL 61702	(309) 378-2961
Accessories Magazine	50 Day St. Norwalk, CT 06584	(203) 853-6015
Accessory Merchandising	400 Knights Bridge Pkwy Lincolnshire, IL 60069	(847) 634-2600
Action Sports Retailer	310 Broadway Laguna Beach, CA 92651	(714) 376-8144
American Baby	249 W. 17th St. New York, NY 10011	(212) 462-3500
American Bookseller	828 S. Broadway Tarrytown, NY 10591	(914) 591-2665
American Demographics	P.O. Box 68 Ithaca, NY 14851	(607) 273-6343
American Druggist	60 E. 42nd St. New York, NY 10165	(212) 686-8584
American Health	28 W. 23rd St. New York, NY 10010	(212) 366-8900
American Shoemaking	P.O. Box 198 Cambridge, MA 02140	(617) 648-8160
American Turf Quarterly	306 Broadway Lynbrook, NY 11563	(516) 599-2121

Antique Monthly	2100 Powers Ferry Road Atlanta, GA 30339	(770) 955-5656
Apparel News South	110 E. 9th St. #A-777 Los Angeles, CA 90079	(213) 627-3737
Appliance Manufacturer	5900 Harper Road #105 Solon, OH 44139	(216) 349-3060
Archery Business	601 Lake Shore Pkwy. #600 Minnetonka, MN 55305	(612) 476-2200
Army-Navy Store & Outdoor Merchandise	567 Morris Ave. Elizabeth, NJ 07208	(908) 353-7373
Art Direction	456 Glennbrook Rd. Glennbrook, CT 06906	(203) 353-1441
Automotive Marketing	1 Chilton Way Radnor, PA 19089	(610) 964-4396
Automotive News	1400 Woodbridge Ave. Detroit, MI 48207	(313) 446-6030
Baby Talk	25 W. 43rd St. New York, NY 10036	(212) 840-4200
Barnard's Retail Marketing	1181 Raitin Rd. Scotts Plain, NJ 07076	(908) 561-2300
Book Dealers World	P.O. Box 606 Cottage Grove, OR 97424	(514) 942-7455
Casual Living	3301 Como Ave. S.E. Minneapolis, MN 55414	(800) 999-6311
Catalog Age	P.O. Box 0949 Stamford, CT 06907	(203) 358-9900
Centre	1450 Don Mills Road Don Mills, Ontario Canada M3B 2X7	(416) 445-6641
Chain Drug Review	220 Fifth Ave. New York, NY 10001	(212) 213-6000
Chain Store Age Executive	425 Park Ave. New York, NY 10022	(212) 756-5252
Chicago Apparel News	110 E. 9th St. #A-777 Los Angeles, CA 90079	(213) 627-3737
Children's Business	7 W. 34th St., 3rd Floor New York, NY 10001	(212) 630-4500
Christian Retailing	600 Rinehart Road Lake Mary, FL 32748	(407) 333-0600
Collector's Mart	700 E. State St. Iola, WI 54990-0001	(800) 258-0929
Convenience Store News	233 Park Ave. So. 6th Floor New York, NY 10003	(212) 979-4800

Craft & Needlework Age	225 Gordons Corner Road Manalapan, NJ 07226	(908) 446-4900
Crain's Small Business	740 N. Rush St. Chicago, IL 60611	(312) 649-5411
Dealerscope Merchandising	401 N. Broad St. Philadelphia, PA 19108	(215) 238-5300
The Dean Report	116 New Montgomery St. San Francisco, CA 94105	(415) 512-7305
Decor	330 N. Fourth St. St. Louis, MO 63102	(314) 421-5445
Decorating Retailer	403 Axminister Dr. St. Louis, MO 63026	(314) 326-2636
Discount Merchandiser	233 Park Ave. S. New York, NY 10003	(212) 979-4860
Discount Store News	425 Park Ave. New York, NY 10022	(212) 756-5100
Do-It-Yourself Retailing	5822 W. 74th St. Indianapolis, IN 46278	(317) 297-1190
Drug Store News	425 Park Ave. New York, NY 10022	(212) 756-5100
Drug Topics	Five Paragon Drive Montvale, NJ 07645	(201) 358-7200
Electronics	611 Route 46 West Hasbrouck, NJ 07604	(201) 393-6060
Entrepreneur Magazine	2932 Morse Ave. Irvine, CA 92614	(714) 261-2325
Esquire Gentlemen	250 W. 55th St. New York, NY 10019	(212) 649-2000
Fabricnews	80 Park Ave. #6K New York, NY 10016	(212) 697-5780
Floral and Nursery Times	P.O. Box 8470 Northfield, IL 60093	(847) 441-0300
Floral Mass Marketing	120 S. Riverside Plaza Chicago, IL 60606	(312) 258-8500
Flower News	120 S. Riverside Plaza Chicago, IL 60606	(312) 258-8500
Footwear News	7 West 34th St. New York, NY 10001	(212) 630-3800
Gifts and Decorative Accessories	51 Madison Ave. New York, NY 10010	(212) 689-4411
Giftware News	P.O. Box 5398 Deptford, NJ 08096	(609) 227-0798
Grocery Marketing	625 N. Michigan Ave. Chicago, IL 60611	(312) 654-2300

HFD—Retailing Home Furnishing	7 West 34th St. New York, NY 10001	(212) 630-4230
Hardware Age	One Chilton Way Radnor, PA 19089	(610) 964-4272
Hardware Merchandising	777 Bay St. 5th Floor Toronto, Ontario Canada M5W 1A7	(416) 596-5259
Herbalgram	P.O. Box 201660 Austin, TX 78720	(512) 331-8868
Home Accents Today	7025 Albert Pick Road Greensboro, NC 27409	(910) 605-0121
Home Furnishings Executive	305 West High Ave. High Point, NC 27260	(800) 888-9590
Horizons	P.O. Box 8 Orrville, OH 44667	(330) 682-2055
Housewares Executive	45 W. 21st St. New York, NY 10010	(212) 989-4933
Inc. Magazine	38 Commercial Wharf Boston, MA 02110	(617) 248-8000
International Trends in Retailing	Arthur Andersen Attn: Stanley N. Logan 33 W. Monroe St. Chicago, IL 60603	(312) 580-0033
Jewelers' Circular—Keystone	One Chilton Way Radnor, PA 19089	(610) 964-4464
Jewelry Newsletter International	2600 S. Gessner Rd. Houston, TX 77063	(713) 783-0100
Journal of Retailing	44 W. 44th St. Room 8-176 New York, NY 10012	(212) 998-0550
Kids Fashion Magazine	485 Seventh Ave. #1400 New York, NY 10018	(212) 594-0880
LDB/Interior Textiles	342 Madison Ave. Suite 1901 New York, NY 10017	(212) 661-1516
Loeb's Retail Report	P.O. Box 1155 New York, NY 10018	(212) 596-4034
Medical Advertising News	820 Bear Tavern Road West Trenton, NJ 08628	(609) 530-0044
Medical Marketing & Media	7200 W. Camino Real, #215 Boca Raton, FL 33433	(407) 368-9301
Modern Bride	249 W. 17th 2nd Floor New York, NY 10011	(212) 462-3400

Modern Jeweler	7619 Johnson Dr. Overland Park, KS 66202	(913) 432-9678
The Music and Sound Retailer	25 Willowdale Ave. Port Washington, NY 11050	(516) 767-2500
NARDA News	10 E. 22 St. Lombard, IL 60148	(708) 953-8950
National Home Center News	425 Park Ave. New York, NY 10022	(516) 756-5151
New England Bride	215 Newbury St. #207B Peabody, MA 01960	(508) 535-4186
Nursery News	120 S. Riverside Plaza Chicago, IL 60606	(312) 258-8500
Party & Paper Retailer	70 New Canaan Ave. Norwalk, CT 06850	(203) 845-8020
Pet Age	20 E. Jackson Blvd. Chicago, IL 60604	(312) 663-4040
Pet Business	7-L Dundas Circle Greensboro, NC 27407	(910) 292-4047
Pharmacy Times	1065 Old Country Road Suite 215 Westbury, NY 11590	(516) 997-0377
Photo Marketing	3000 Picture Place Jackson, MI 49201	(517) 788-8100
Progressive Grocer	263 Tresser Blvd. Stamford, CT 06901	(203) 325-3500
Publishers Weekly	249 West 17th St. New York, NY 10011	(212) 463-6758
Purdue Retailer	1262 Matthews Hale Purdue University W. LaFayette, IN 47907	(317) 494-8292
Retail Performance Monitor	Ralph H. Sullivan 205 Regency Exec. Pk. Dr. Suite 105 Charlotte, NC 28217-3989	(704) 523-8511
The Retail and Marketing News	P.O. Box 191125 Dallas, TX 75219	(214) 871-2930
Retailing Issues Newsletter	Arthur Andersen and Texas A&M University Center for Retailing Studies Department of Marketing College Station, TX 77843	(409) 845-0325
Retailing Today	Robert Kahn & Associates Box 249 Lafayette, CA 94549	(510) 254-4434

RIS—Retail Info Systems News	One West Hanover Ave. Suite 107 Randolph, NJ 07869	(201) 895-3300
Salon News	7 West 34th St. New York, NY 10001	(212) 630-3547
The Shooting Industry	591 Camino De La Reina #200 San Diego, CA 92108	(619) 297-5352
Shopping Center World	6151 Powers Ferry Road NW Atlanta, GA 30339	(770) 955-2500
Sporting Goods Business	1 Penn Plaza 10th Floor New York, NY 10119	(212) 714-1300
The Sporting Goods Dealer	445 Broad Hollow Road Melville, NY 11747	(516) 845-2700
Stores Magazine	325 Seventh St. NW Washington, D.C. 20004	(202) 783-7971
Supermarket News	7 W. 34th St. New York, NY 10001	(212) 630-4230
Tennis Industry	230 W. 13th St. New York, NY 10011	(212) 242-3687
Tire Business	1725 Merriman Road #300 Akron, OH 44313	(330) 836-9180
Tire Review	11 S. Forge St. Akron, OH 44304	(330) 535-6117
Value Retail News	15950 Bay Vista Dr. Suite 250 Clearwater, FL 34620	(813) 536-4047
Women's Wear Daily	7 W. 34th St. New York, NY 10001	(212) 630-4230

Titles of Articles	Periodical	Issue
Customers and Marketing		
"Providing Incentives with Programs"	*Chain Store Age Executive* 425 Park Ave. New York, NY 10022 (212) 697-2165	October 1993
"Hills Instills Employee Incentives, Work Ethic to Lure Repeat Business"	*Discount Store News* 425 Park Ave. New York, NY 10022 (212) 697-2165	May 3, 1993
"The Little Extras Keep Customers Coming Back"	*Discount Store News*	May 3, 1993

"Menswear Stores Tailor Service to Fit the Customers"	*Discount Store News*	May 3, 1993
"Retailers Adapt Home Depot Service to Their Business"	*Discount Store News*	May 3, 1993
"Stuarts Learns the Importance of Nurturing a Service Culture"	*Discount Store News*	May 3, 1993
"Target Empowers Employees to Be Fast, Fun and Friendly"	*Discount Store News*	May 3, 1993
"Technology Fills Multitude of Roles in Improving Customer Service"	*Discount Store News*	May 3, 1993
"Who Satisfies CE Shoppers Most: Commissioned or Noncommissioned Help?"	*Discount Store News*	May 3, 1993
"The Tough New Consumer; Demanding More—and Getting It"	*Fortune* (special edition) Time & Life Building Rockefeller Center New York, NY 10020 (800) 621-8000	Autumn/ Winter 1993
"How to Get Better Service While Cutting Costs"	*Inside Retailing* 425 Park Ave. New York, NY 10022 (212) 697-2165	September 6, 1993
"The Winners Will Know Their Customers"	*Inside Retailing*	January 6, 1992
"Our Mission is to Create Happy Customers"	*International Trends in Retailing* Arthur Andersen	Vol. 8 No. 2 1991
"On the Subject of Image"	*International Trends in Retailing* Arthur Andersen Attn. Nadine F. Habousha 1345 Ave. of the Americas New York, NY 10105 (212) 708-4689	Vol. 8 No. 2 1991
"Access to Information, or What Customers Really Consider Service"	*International Trends in Retailing* Arthur Andersen	Vol. 10 No. 2 1993
"Mall of America: Can a Big-Time Entertainment Destination Win by Fighting Customers?"	*International Trends in Retailing* Arthur Andersen	Vol. 11 No. 2 1994
"The Pharmacy America Trusts"	*International Trends in Retailing* Arthur Andersen	Vol. 11 No. 2 1994

"Benetton: After Internationalization We Work for Diversification"	*International Trends in Retailing* Arthur Andersen	Tenth Anniversary Edition, 1994
"Crate & Barrel: Success Develops from Unique Idea"	*International Trends in Retailing* Arthur Andersen	Tenth Anniversary Edition, 1994
"Warehouse Home Centers and Wholesalers: The Battle for the Business Customer"	*International Trends in Retailing* Arthur Andersen	Vol. 12 No. 1 1995
"The Profitable Incentive of Loyalty"	*International Trends in Retailing* Arthur Andersen	Vol. 13 No. 1 1996
"Relationship Selling in Retailing"	*Retailing Issues Newsletter* Arthur Andersen Texas A&M University Center for Retailing Studies Department of Marketing College Station, TX 77843 (409) 845-0325	November 1993
"Taking Responsibility for Service"	*Retailing Issues Newsletter* Texas A&M University	November 1991

Merchandising

"Retailers Rely on Manufacturers to Help Deliver Better Service"	*Discount Store News* 425 Park Ave. New York, NY 10022 (212) 697-2165	May 3, 1993
"Tornado Watch"	*Forbes* 60 5th Ave. New York, NY 10011 (212) 620-2200	June 22, 1992
"Fire a Buyer and Hire a Seller"	*International Trends in Retailing* Arthur Andersen Attn: Nadine F. Habousha 1345 Ave. of the Americas New York, NY 10105 (212) 708-4689	Tenth Anniversary Edition, 1994
"Marks & Spencer: A Manufacturer Without Factories"	*International Trends in Retailing* Arthur Andersen	Tenth Anniversary Edition, 1994
"Price Club: One of California's Best Retailing Ideas"	*International Trends in Retailing* Arthur Andersen	Tenth Anniversary Edition, 1994

"Merchandising for the 1990s"	*Retailing Issues Newsletter* Arthur Andersen Texas A&M University Center for Retailing Studies Department of Marketing College Station, TX 77843 (409) 845-0325	Vol. 2 No. 7 July 1990
"Mass Market Report: Jousting with Wal-Mart; Better Clothes, Better Trappings"	*Women's Wear Daily* 7 W. 34th St. New York, NY 10001 (212) 630-4230	October 6, 1993

Store Operations

"Disney 'Cast Members' Put 'Guests' in the Spotlight"	*Discount Store News* 425 Park Ave. New York, NY 10022 (212) 697-2165	May 3, 1993
"Can System That Brought Revolutionary Change in Car Factory Work in a Retail Store"	*International Trends in Retailing* Arthur Andersen Attn: Nadine F. Habousha 1345 Ave. of the Americas New York, NY 10105 (212) 708-4689	Vol. 11 No. 2 1994
"Please Hold for Service"	*International Trends in Retailing* Arthur Andersen	Vol. 13 No. 1 1996
"How to Prevent Slips and Falls"	*Stores Magazine* 325 Seventh St. NW Washington, D.C. 20004 (202) 783-7971	June 1993
"Taking Responsibility for Service"	*Retailing Issues Newsletter* Arthur Andersen Texas A&M University Center for Retailing Studies Department of Marketing College Station, TX 77843 (409) 845-0325	Vol. 3 No. 6 November 1991

Management

"BSHC's Resource Guide— Category Management"	Building Supply Home Centers circular 44 Cook St. Denver, CO 80206 (303) 388-4511	November 1993

"Retailing: Who Will Survive?"	*Business Week* 1221 Ave. of the Americas New York, NY 10020 (212) 512-2000	November 26, 1990
"Big Service For the Small Retailer"	*Chain Store Age Executive* 425 Park Ave. New York, NY 10001 (212) 697-2165	October 1993
"Town Takes on Wal-Mart and Coexists"	*Chicago Tribune* 435 N. Michigan Ave. Chicago, IL 60611 (312) 222-3232	June 14, 1993
"25 Ideas for Achieving Competitive Advantage"	*Inside Retailing* (special report) 425 Park Ave. New York, NY 10022 (212) 697-2165	November 1993
"What is Strategic Retail Management?"	*International Trends in Retailing* Arthur Andersen	No. 7
"Almost Anyone Can Buy A Crowd, But Few Can Be 'Reason Why' Retailers"	*International Trends in Retailing* Arthur Andersen	Vol. 10 No. 1
"EST Retailing: A Message From the Black Hole"	*International Trends in Retailing* Arthur Andersen	Vol. 10 No. 2
"Managing Store Employees— The Biggest Challenge to Retail Management"	*International Trends in Retailing* Arthur Andersen Attn: Nadine F. Habousha 1345 Ave. of the Americas New York, NY 10105 (212) 708-4689	Vol. 3 No. 2 1986
"Authority"	*International Trends in Retailing* Arthur Andersen	Vol. 10 No. 2 1993
"Strategy for Success: J. Sainsbury"	*International Trends in Retailing* Arthur Andersen	Tenth Anniver- sary Edition, 1994
"The History of Ahold"	*International Trends in Retailing* Arthur Andersen	Tenth Anniver- sary Edition, 1994
"The Wal-Mart Partnership"	*International Trends in Retailing* Arthur Andersen	Tenth Anniver- sary Edition, 1994

"Why Do Some Organizations Do Better and Last Longer than Others"	*International Trends in Retailing* Arthur Andersen	Tenth Anniversary Edition, 1994
"Price, Employees or Customers"	*International Trends in Retailing* Arthur Andersen	Vol. 12 No. 1 1995
"Are Your Priorities in Order?"	*International Trends in Retailing* Arthur Andersen	Vol. 12 No. 2 1995
"IKEA: Create a Better Everyday Life for the Majority of People"	*International Trends in Retailing* Arthur Andersen	Vol. 12 No. 2 1995
"Tomorrow is Here at Sears"	*International Trends in Retailing* Arthur Andersen	Vol. 12 No. 2 1995
"Survival Tactics For Retailers"	*Nation's Business* 1615 H St. NW Washington, DC 20062 (202) 463-5600	June 1993
"The Internalization of American Retailers"	*Retailing Current Analysis* 25 Broadway New York, NY 10004	Vol. 161 No. 37 September 16, 1993
"Competing with the Mass Merchandisers"	*Small Business Forum* Kenneth E. Stone, Ph.D. Iowa State University of Science and Technology Department of Economics 460 Heady Hall Ames, IA 50011 (515) 294-6269	Spring 1991
"An Independent Point of View: For and about the Independent Retailer—Sale-ing in the '90s . . . or is it swimming against the tide?"	*Stores Magazine* 325 Seventh St. NW Washington, D.C. 20004 (202) 783-7971	October 1993
"An Independent Point of View: For and about the Independent Retailer—Re-inventing your store. . . taking a hard look in the mirror"	*Stores Magazine*	December 1993
"Kudos to Jim Baum; Pride of Morris, Ill., Wins 1993 Retailer Honors"	*Stores Magazine*	January 1993

"M&A's, New Technologies, Priorities Add Up to Changing Cultures"	*Stores Magazine*	February 1989
"Pathways to Corporate Excellence"	*Retailing Issues Newsletter* Arthur Andersen Texas A&M University Center for Retailing Studies Department of Marketing College Station, TX 77843 (409) 845-0325	Vol. 2 No. 1 February 1989
"Playing Fair in Retailing"	*Retailing Issues Newsletter* Arthur Andersen	Vol. 5 No. 2 March 1993
"Qualities of Leadership"	*Retailing Issues Newsletter* Arthur Andersen	Vol. 4 No. 1 January 1992
"Retail Census Findings and Strategic Implications"	*Retailing Issues Newsletter* Arthur Andersen	Vol. 1 No. 3 February 1988
"Retail Control Systems for the 1990s"	*Retailing Issues Newsletter* Arthur Andersen	Vol. 2 No. 5 January 1990
"Retailing's Five Most Important Trends"	*Retailing Issues Newsletter* Arthur Andersen	Vol. 3 No. 2 March 1991

Human Resources

"Profit Sharing and the Associate Dealer"	*International Trends in Retailing* Arthur Andersen Attn: Nadine F. Habousha 1345 Ave. of the Americas New York, NY 10105 (212) 708-4689	Tenth Anniversary Edition, 1994
"The Franklin Story—A Unique History of a Discount Retailer in Australia"	*International Trends in Retailing* Arthur Andersen	Tenth Anniversary Edition, 1994
"The Hy-Vee Story"	*International Trends in Retailing* Arthur Andersen	Tenth Anniversary Edition, 1994
"Planning Priorities for Empowered Teams"	*Journal of Business Strategy* 1 Penn Plaza New York, NY 10119 (212) 971-5026	Sept./Oct. 1992
"The Planned Evolution of a Team Culture"	*Journal for Quality and Participation* 801B W. 8th St. Cincinnati, OH 45203 (513) 381-1959	Jan./Feb. 1992

"Empowering a Team to Revamp the Suggestion System"	*Quality and Productivity* Management Association Tapping the Network Journal 300 N. Martingale Road Schaumburg, IL 60173 (708) 619-2909	Spring 1993
"Is Salesmanship the Dinosaur of the 90's?"	*Retailing Issues Newsletter* Arthur Andersen	Vol. 3 No. 3 May 1991

Finance

"Retail and Information Industries: Partnering for Tomorrow"	*Inside Retailing* (special report) 425 Park Ave. New York, NY 10022 (212) 697-2165	October 1993
"Using Store Performance Research to Maximize Sales and Profits"	*International Trends in Retailing* Arthur Andersen Attn: Nadine F. Habousha 1345 Ave. of the Americas New York, NY 10105 (212) 708-4689	Vol. 12 No. 1 1995

Reinvention of Retailing

"Change"	*International Trends in Retailing* Arthur Andersen Attn: Nadine F. Habousha 1345 Ave. of the Americas New York, NY 10105 (212) 708-4689	Vol. 11 No. 1 1994
"Virtual Retailing"	*International Trends in Retailing* Arthur Andersen	Vol. 11 No. 1 1994
"The Less Decade: Dream or Nightmare?"	*International Trends in Retailing* Arthur Andersen	Vol. 12 No. 1 1995
"Retailing on the Internet"	*International Trends in Retailing* Arthur Andersen	Vol. 12 No. 2 1995
"Retailing at the Millennium: How Changes in Consumer Buying Behavior are Driving Concentration"	*International Trends in Retailing* Arthur Andersen	Vol. 13 No. 1 1996

Appendix D

Studies and Surveys on Retailing

Titles of studies and surveys	Publisher	Phone
Retail Store Management Compensation Survey: Summary of Results	Arthur Andersen Attn. Nick Bubnovich 33 W. Monroe St. Chicago, IL 60603	(312) 507-6915
Chicago's Competitive Apparel Arena	Chicago Tribune and Research Services 435 N. Michigan Ave. Chicago, IL 60611	(312) 222-3232
1992 Retailing Industry: The Statistical Review for Fiscal Years 1992, 1991, & 1990	First Chicago One First National Plaza Chicago, IL 60670	(312) 732-5379
Annual Harris Bank Retail Study	Harris Trust and Savings Bank P.O. Box 755 111 W. Monroe St. Chicago, IL 60690	(312) 461-2121
Strategies for Co-Existing in a Mass Merchandising Environment	Iowa State University Department of Economics Kenneth E. Stone, Ph. D. 460 Heady Hall Ames, IA 50011	(515) 294-6269
Financial & Operating Results of Retail Stores in 1992	National Retail Federation 325 Seventh St. NW Washington, D.C. 20004	(202) 783-7971
Merchandising & Operating Results of Retail Stores in 1992	National Retail Federation 325 Seventh St. NW Washington, D.C. 20004	(202) 783-7971

366

1993 Small Business Issues Priorities	National Small Business United, National Association of Women Business Owners, and Arthur Andersen's Enterprise Group 1156 15th St. NW Suite 1100 Washington, DC 20005	(202) 293-8830
User's Guide to the Survey of Buying Power	Sales and Marketing Management 355 Park Ave. South New York, NY 10010	(212) 592-6300
U.S. Industrial Outlook 1993	U.S. Department of Commerce International Trade Administration 55 W. Monroe St. Suite 2440 Chicago, IL 60603	(312) 353-8040

Appendix E

Retail Trade Shows

Investigating the thousands of trade shows that market consumer products and services is often a daunting task. In addition to major national shows, regional expositions are often closer to home, more affordable, and more focused.

The NRF Annual Convention is held every January in New York City. It is the largest retail show in the country.

The Retail Information Systems Conference (RisCon) is held every October in various cities.

The In-Store Systems Conference is held every April in various cities.

For more information on these conferences, contact:

National Retail Federation
Conference Registration
325 Seventh St. N.W.
Washington, D.C. 20004
(202) 783-7971

For trade shows applicable to your merchandise category, contact the trade associations listed in Appendix A.

The following directories, which list shows by name, category, and region and pinpoint tightly focused niches, are also excellent sources for trade shows:

Tradeshow Week Data Book
121 Chanlon Rd.
New Providence, NJ 07974
(800) 521-8110
Fax (908) 665-6688

This book is found in library reference sections. Cost: $315.

Appendix F

Advisers and Consultants

Often owner-operated companies avoid consultants because of the predominant perception that they are too costly. On the other hand, many consultants to the small-business community are themselves owner-operated. Consequently, they frequently provide tailored services and will work with you in establishing reasonable fees. The following is a selected list of associations you can contact to obtain additional information regarding consultants. For a complete listing of advisers and consultants, contact your local library.

An exceptional resource is *Dunn's Consultants Directory,* published annually by Dunn's Marketing Services. This directory is sorted by state and by city, making it easy to identify a consultant in close proximity to your business.

Association	Address	Phone
Accounting and Tax Assistance		
American Institute of Certified Public Accountants (AICPA)	1211 Avenue of the Americas New York, NY 10036	(212) 596-6200
Financial Executives Institute	P.O. Box 1938 Morristown, NJ 07962	(201) 898-4600
National Society of Public Accountants	1010 N. Fairfax St. Montvale, NJ 07645	(201) 573-9000
Legal Assistance		
American Bar Association (ABA)	750 N. Lake Shore Dr. Chicago, IL 60611	(312) 988-5000
Financial Institutions		
American Bankers Association	1120 Connecticut Ave. NW Washington, DC 20036	(800) 872-7747

Public Relations		
Public Relations Society of America	33 Irving Place 3rd Floor New York, NY 10003	(212) 995-2230
Other Consultants		
American Management Association	1601 Broadway New York, NY 10019	(212) 586-8100

Appendix G

Survey Methodology

THE GENESIS OF THIS STUDY

In the course of this six-month, three-phase study, Arthur Andersen sent surveys to more than 1500 Illinois retailers; approximately 150 completed all three surveys. Arthur Andersen, working with a Steering Committee composed of representatives from the Illinois Retail Merchants Association and seven small-store retailers, determined the methodology used to perform the study. Together these people identified six major areas of study:

- Customers and marketing
- Merchandising
- Store operations
- Management
- Human resources
- Finance

They also determined detailed areas of study within these major areas. The chapter on merchandising, for example, includes details on vendors, assortment planning, open-to-buy, niching, and pricing strategy. Each of the other major areas contains a similar level of detail.

The Steering Committee obtained consensus on every decision relating to overall methodology of performing the study as well as to each major step involved in completing it.

In Phase I of the three-phase study, a questionnaire was mailed to 1500 retailers, half IRMA members and half non-IRMA members, in a variety of hard-goods and soft-goods categories throughout the state of Illinois. This survey asked for baseline company information, such as number of stores, sales, sales per square foot, retail format, store location, competition, and use of technology. The survey also asked retailers how they define success, what business issues they face, and what actions they have taken recently to improve their competitive positions. This information formed the basis for the profile of the Illinois small-store retailer.

The same retailers were surveyed in Phase II of the study. During this phase, they were asked to gauge their attitudes toward those areas of business that are most critical to their success. This survey also asked retailers to rank their performance in those areas. The information provided a clear consensus on the activities these retailers felt were important and how well they are performing. To validate the findings, 13 retailers from across the state were invited to a half-day brainstorm session that probed their attitudes about their business activities, the importance of each activity to the success of their businesses, the resources they devote to these activities, and the critical issues they face today.

Phase III consisted of a final questionnaire that was sent to retailers who had completed surveys in Phase I and/or Phase II. This final survey asked retailers for an in-depth assessment of their business practices and the means they use to measure their performance. To validate survey findings, day-long site visits were conducted with 10 retailers throughout Illinois. During these visits, interviewers focused on the challenges these retailers face, their current business practices, and areas in which they perform well in addition to those areas requiring improvement. The results of these site visits were developed into case studies, which appear in Chapter 8.

In addition to the surveys and site visits, information was obtained from industry research contained in Arthur Andersen's knowledge base of retailing best practices and Arthur Andersen's experience serving clients in the retail industry. From this information, specific recommendations on how small stores can adapt retailing best practices were developed for each area of business.

A PICTURE OF THE RESPONDENTS

Of the 1500 small-store retailers surveyed, approximately 150 responded to all three surveys, providing a good understanding of what is happening in small-store retailing. Sixty-two percent of respondents operate in hard-goods formats, including hardware, furniture, appliances and electronics, drugs, gifts and cards, books, and sporting goods. The remaining 38 percent represent soft-goods formats such as department stores, specialty apparel, footwear, bridal, and jewelry. Respondents were located throughout the state with a slightly higher number coming from the northern half of the state. Excluding the Chicago metro area, populations of retailers' market areas range from 1400 to 420,000. Illinois retail customers resemble customers everywhere. Respondents reported that hard-goods customers are predominantly male, ages 20—55, with annual incomes greater than $25,000. Soft-goods customers are predominantly female, ages 20—55, also with annual incomes greater than $25,000 (see Table A-1).

When statistics for all respondents were combined and averaged, a profile of the small-store retailer emerged. Except for gross margin and sales per square foot, no major differences existed between hard-goods and soft-goods retailers surveyed.

After asking about these basic statistics, the survey asked retailers for details about their business practices and what actions were helping them succeed (see Table A-2). When retailers were asked what they saw as their competitive advantages, the three answers cited most often were high levels of service, high-quality merchandise, and many years in business. Competitive

Table A-1   Profile of the typical respondent

Net sales:	$1.8 million (50% have net sales of less than $950,000)
Gross margin	40%*
Pretax income	$39,000
Sales per square foot	$206[†]
Number of stores	2 (68% have only one store)
Years company in business	43 (range from 1 to 150)
Full-time store employees	11 (46% have five or less)
Use of non-POS cash register	61%
Legal status	
Subchapter C	51%
Subchapter S	27%
Sole proprietorship	19%
Partnership	3%
Principal's years with company	24

* Hard-goods retailers typically have a gross margin of 36 percent, and soft-goods retailers typically have of a gross margin of 42 percent. (Source: Dun & Bradstreet Information Services.)
[†] Hard-goods retailers typically have sales per square foot of $350, and soft-goods retailers typically have sales per square foot of $150.

disadvantages retailers cited most often were limited number of locations, higher prices than those of competitors, and lack of greater depth in inventory. Given these competitive advantages and disadvantages, retailers indicated that the key business issues they face today, in order of the frequency of their responses, are:

- Local competition and large discounters
- Eroding margins
- Lack of qualified employees, training, and difficulty in retaining qualified personnel
- Cost containment
- Rising health-care costs
- Compliance with government regulatory controls
- Need for computerization
- Deterioration of downtown business districts
- Advertising effectiveness
- General economy

When asked what actions retailers were taking to address these issues, the responses came back, in order of frequency, as follows:

Table A-2 Factors determining competitive advantages
and disadvantages

Percent of respondents who identified factor as an . . .	Advantage	Disadvantage
High service level	100	0
High quality	97	3
Years in business	93	7
Large selection	82	18
Fashion leader	73	27
Convenient store location	73	27
Great depth	66	34
Low price	34	66
Number of locations	31	69

- Change merchandise mix and assortment
- Increase training and incentives to sales employees
- Increase promotional activity and modify advertising to include radio and television
- Adjust prices to be more competitive
- Increase awareness and attention to customer service
- Expand service levels (special orders, in-home sales, and so on)
- Remodel
- Join a buying group
- Computerize

Business areas that still need improvement, according to retailers' frequency of responses, are:

- Employee training and empowerment
- Merchandising
- Computerization
- Store cleanliness and appearance
- Inventory control
- Customer service
- Advertising
- Image development
- Margins (better buying practices)
- Cost control
- Long-range planning

Although retailers feel they need to improve their performance in many areas, they generally feel successful with what they have accomplished. Most defined their success in terms of profitability, ability to survive, and capability of paying the bills. But other telling responses cropped up as well, as related in the Executive Summary. Regardless of the definitions used, respondents indicated that certain business practices within the six major areas of study are more critical than others to their success. Using a scale of excellent (E), good (G), fair (F), and poor (P) performance, respondents ranked themselves in each area. The most critical are sum-marized hereafter.

It is interesting to note that in all areas ranked, while most respondents as a group rated their performances as good, there were a few "fairs" but no "poors" or "excellents" (see Table A-3).

Retailers were also asked to list the major areas of study in order of critical importance to business. When the responses were combined, the order, from most to least critical, was:

- Customers and marketing
- Merchandising
- Store operations
- Management
- Human resources
- Finance

The business practices that survey respondents use and the percentage of retail-ers who apply each practice are noted throughout this report. Survey results were validated during a half-day discussion with 13 retailers who had responded to the first two surveys. During the discussion, this group was asked to rank by level of importance each business practice in each major area of study. The rankings validated earlier responses. These retailers also learned that they were spending too much time on areas of less importance and not enough on areas of more importance.

Table A-3   Performance ranking of respondents

Area	Critical Process	Performance			
		E	G	F	P
Customers and marketing	Customer wants		✓		
	Customer satisfaction		✓		
	Customer profiling		✓		
Merchandising	Pricing strategy		✓		
	Vendor relations		✓		
	Vendor reliability		✓		
Store operations	Customer service		✓		
	Store staffing and productivity			✓	
	Cleanliness		✓		
Management	Flexibility and adaptability		✓		
	Strategic planning		✓		
	Capabilities		✓		
Human resources	Hiring and retention		✓		
	Sales training		✓		
	Compensation and benefits		✓		
Finance	Cost reduction		✓		
	Budgeting			✓	
	Information systems		✓		

BIBLIOGRAPHY

Best Practices, Putting Insight into Practice, Global Knowledge Base. Arthur Andersen & Co.

"Big Service for the Small Retailer." *Chain Store Age Executive,* October 1993.

"BSHC's Resource Guide: Category Management." *Building Supply Home Centers News,* November 1993.

The Buyer's Manual. National Retail Federation.

Chicago's Competitive Apparel Arena. Chicago Tribune Marketing and Research Services.

"Competing with the Mass Merchandisers." *Small Business Forum,* Spring 1991.

Davidson, William R., et al. *Retailing Management,* 6th ed.

"Disney 'Cast Members' Put 'Guests' in the Spotlight." *Discount Store News,* May 3, 1993.

Family Wealth Planning. Arthur Andersen & Co.

Financial & Operating Results of Retail Stores in 1992. National Retail Federation.

"Hills Instills Employee Incentives, Work Ethic to Lure Repeat Business." *Discount Store News,* May 3, 1993.

"How to Prevent Slips and Falls." *Stores Magazine,* June 1993.

"An Independent Point of View: For and about the Independent Retailer. 'Playing hard-ball with your orders . . . it's the follow-through that counts.' " *Stores Magazine,* November 1993.

"An Independent Point of View: For and about the Independent Retailer. 'Reinventing your store . . . taking a hard look in the mirror.' " *Stores Magazine,* December 1993.

"An Independent Point of View: For and about the Independent Retailer. 'Sale-ing in the '90s . . . or is it swimming against the tide?' " *Stores Magazine,* October 1993.

International Trends in Retailing. Arthur Andersen & Co.

Kilmann, Ralph H., et al. *Corporate Transformation: Revitalizing Organizations for a Competitive World.*

"Kudos to Jim Baum; Pride of Morris, Ill., Wins 1993 Retailer Honors." *Stores Magazine,* January 1993.

"The Little Extras Keep Customers Coming Back." *Discount Store News,* May 3, 1993.

"M&A's, New Technologies, Priorities Add Up to Changing Cultures." *Stores Magazine*, February 1989.

Mason, J. Barry, et al. *Retailing*, 4th ed.

"Mass Market Report: Jousting with Wal-Mart—Better Clothes, Better Trappings." *Women's Wear Daily*, October 6, 1993.

McCall, Jack. *The Small Town Survival Guide: Help for Changing the Economic Future of Your Town.*

"Men's Wear Stores Tailor Service to Fit the Customers." *Discount Store News*, May 3, 1993.

1992 Retailing Industry: The Statistical Review for Fiscal Years 1992, 1991, & 1990, First Chicago.

1993 Small Business Issue Priorities. National Small Business United, National Association of Women Business Owners, and Arthur Andersen's Enterprise Group.

Practical Merchandising Math for Everyday Use. National Retail Federation.

Preserving Family Wealth. Arthur Andersen & Co.

"Providing Incentives with Frequency Programs." *Chain Store Age Executive*, October 1993.

"Retailers Adapt Home Depot Service to their Business." *Discount Store News*, May 3, 1993.

"Retailers Rely on Manufacturers to Help Deliver Better Service." *Discount Store News*, May 3, 1993.

Retailing Issues Newsletters. Arthur Andersen & Co.

"Retailing: Who Will Survive?" *Business Week*, November 16, 1990.

Retail Store Management Compensation Survey: Summary of Results. Arthur Andersen & Co.

Sewell, Carl. *Customers for Life.*

Strategies for Co-existing in a Mass Merchandising Environment. Iowa State University of Science and Technology.

"Stuarts Learns the Importance of Nurturing a Service Culture." *Discount Store News*, May 3, 1993.

Survey of the Greater State Street Market. Rosalind Redd Enterprises.

"Survival Tactics for Retailers." *Nation's Business*, June 1993.

"Target Empowers Employees to Be Fast, Fun and Friendly." *Discount Store News*, May 3, 1993.

"Technology Fills Multitude of Roles in Improving Customer Service." *Discount Store News*, May 3, 1993.

37th Annual Harris Bank Retail Study. Harris Trust and Savings Bank.

"Tornado Watch." *Forbes*, June 22, 1992.

"The Tough New Consumer; Demanding More—and Getting It." *Fortune* (special ed.), Autumn/Winter 1993.

"Town Takes on Wal-Mart and Coexists." *Chicago Tribune,* June 14, 1993.

"U.S. Industrial Outlook 1993." U.S. Department of Commerce, International Trade Administration.

Walton, Sam, and John Huey. *Sam Walton: Made in America—My Story.*

Wardell, Paula. Successful Retailing: *Your Step-by-Step Guide to Avoiding Pitfalls and Finding Profit as an Independent Retailer.*

"Who Satisfies CE Shoppers Most: Commissioned or Noncommissioned Help?" *Discount Store News,* May 3, 1993.

INDEX